The Tank in Action

Crossing the Steenbeek for the attack beyond St Julien (The Cockcroft), August 19, 1917.

The Tank in Action

BY

CAPTAIN D. G. BROWNE, M.C.

WITH ILLUSTRATIONS

The Naval & Military Press Ltd

Published by

The Naval & Military Press Ltd
Unit 5 Riverside, Brambleside
Bellbrook Industrial Estate
Uckfield, East Sussex
TN22 1QQ England

Tel: +44 (0)1825 749494

www.naval-military-press.com
www.nmarchive.com

In reprinting in facsimile from the original, any imperfections are inevitably reproduced and the quality may fall short of modern type and cartographic standards.

TO THE
*OFFICERS, NON-COMMISSIONED OFFICERS,
AND MEN*
OF THE
7TH & 12TH (G. & L.) TANK BATTALIONS.

CONTENTS.

PART I.

THE FIRST PHASE: FROM THE SOMME TO YPRES.

CHAP.		PAGE
I.	INTRODUCTORY: THE GENESIS OF THE LANDSHIP . .	3
II.	THE MARK I. AND MARK IV. TANKS: THE FIRST COMPANIES	15
III.	THE SOMME BATTLES	28
IV.	EXPANSION: THE BATTLES IN FRONT OF ARRAS . .	47
V.	THE PALESTINE DETACHMENT	71
VI.	MESSINES	89
VII.	YPRES: THE PRELIMINARIES	98
VIII.	YPRES: THE 31ST JULY	125
IX.	YPRES: THE 31ST JULY (*continued*)	153
X.	THE "HUSH" OPERATION AND THE COCKCROFT . .	181
XI.	THE COCKCROFT (*continued*)	204
XII.	FROM THE COCKCROFT TO CAMBRAI	231

PART II.

THE SECOND PHASE: CAMBRAI AND AFTER.

XIII.	CAMBRAI	257
XIV.	MISCELLANEOUS. THE GERMANS AND THE TANK: THE FRENCH ARTILLERIE D'ASSAUT	285
XV.	THE GERMAN OFFENSIVE. MEAULTE, BOUVIGNY, AND BÉTHUNE	306

CONTENTS

XVI. THE GERMAN OFFENSIVE (*continued*). ANNEQUIN: AND THE TANK CORPS IN RETREAT 328
XVII. HAMEL, MOREUIL, AND THE THIRD BATTLE OF THE SOMME 347
XVIII. THE GREAT ADVANCE: FROM BUCQUOY TO BAPAUME . 368
XIX. THE FIGHTING FOR BEUGNY, AND THE ADVANCE TO THE CANAL DU NORD 400
XX. THE CANAL DU NORD AND BOURLON . . . 431
XXI. THE FIGHTING ROUND CAMBRAI: SANCOURT . . 459
XXII. FROM NIERGNIES TO THE ARMISTICE: CONCLUSION . 486

INDEX 511

ILLUSTRATIONS.

CROSSING THE STEENBEEK FOR THE ATTACK BEYOND ST
JULIEN (THE COCKCROFT), AUGUST 19, 1917 . . *Frontispiece*
THE MARK V. TANK . . . . . . *Facing p.* 16
DISABLED MARK II. TANK, ARRAS, 1917 . . . " 16
TANK ON OUTPOST HILL, GAZA . . . . " 78
KITCHENER'S WOOD AND GERMAN SECOND LINE. PHOTO
TAKEN JULY 3, 1917. SHOWING POSITION OF TANKS
G 45 AND 46 . . . . " 132
TANK G 46 AS I LEFT HER (EXCEPT FOR HIT ON TRACK),
AUGUST I, 1917 . . . . . . " 162
D BATTALION TANK DITCHED ON REMAINS OF POEL-
CAPELLE CHURCH, OCTOBER 4, 1917 . . . " 240
POELCAPELLE CHURCH BEFORE THE ADVANCE IN AUGUST,
SEPTEMBER, ETC., 1917. (GERMAN PHOTO) . . " 240
BATTLE OF CAMBRAI. BOURLON WOOD AND VILLAGE, WITH
BAPAUME-CAMBRAI ROAD IN FRONT . . . " 276
DISABLED TANK IN FONTAINE-NOTRE-DAME, NOVEMBER
1917. (GERMAN PHOTO) . . . . " 282
G BATTALION TANKS AT THE SHOOTING-BOX, BOURLON
WOOD, NOVEMBER 1917. (GERMAN PHOTO) . . " 282
GERMAN TANK, "ADALBERT." (GERMAN PHOTO) . . " 288
FRENCH HEAVY SCHNEIDER TANK, CARRYING .75 FIELD-
GUN. (GERMAN PHOTO) . . . . . " 288

ILLUSTRATIONS

ABLAINZEVELLE, LOGEAST WOOD, AND ACHIET-LE-GRAND	*Facing p.*	376
BUCQUOY AND ACHIET-LE-PETIT	"	382
BAPAUME BURNING. END OF AUGUST 1918	"	404
CANAL DU NORD AT LOCK 4	"	438
TANKS OF "A" COMPANY, 7TH BATTALION, PARKED IN CANAL DU NORD AFTER CAPTURING BOURLON VILLAGE, SEPTEMBER 27, 1918. (OFFICIAL PHOTO)	"	452
SANCOURT, WITH CAMBRAI-DOUAI ROAD AND RAILWAY	"	476
CAPTURED ENGLISH TANKS BEING USED DURING THE REVOLUTION IN BERLIN	"	500
MARK V. TANKS OF THE 12TH BATTALION AT COLOGNE	"	500

PART I.

THE FIRST PHASE: FROM THE SOMME TO YPRES

CHAPTER I.

INTRODUCTORY: THE GENESIS OF THE LANDSHIP.

I.

This book is not, in a formal sense, a history of the Tank Corps. Such a history must necessarily be impersonal in tone, and probably would aim at being judicial in manner—this last an almost impossible feat in our present state of knowledge. A more elastic form of narrative, based to some degree on my own experiences as a subaltern in the corps, appears to me to be preferable, as it will allow greater freedom of method and opinion and a large scope for the merely interesting and picturesque. Moreover, there already is in preparation (and likely to be in print before this appears) more than one semi-official history. It is my aim, therefore, to avoid giving a monotonous tale of battles which (to the lay mind) seem very familiar in type, and to describe instead in general terms the actual work of the tank in action at various stages of its career as an arm of the service, with its problems, its tactics, and its influence upon the war as a whole.

At the same time, it is necessary to use chronological facts as a scaffolding. The operations of the Tank Corps in the field, up to the date of the Armistice, fall naturally into two phases, marked very happily by a change in nomenclature. During the first phase, as the Heavy Section of the Machine Gun Corps, the new organisation was definitely on trial, finding its feet, learning its job, conquering obstruction, indifference, and other impediments: during the second phase, as a separate arm with a name and establishment of its own, the corps moved onward from success to success, became indispensable and ubiquitous, grew to an astounding size, suffered (from friend and enemy) the sincerest form of flattery, and effected a complete revolution in the tactics of battle. The turning-point in its fortunes is marked approximately by two actions, of widely different scope, fought in the autumn of 1917—the little affair known as the Cockcroft, on August 19th, and the first battle of Cambrai ten weeks later. Such milestones as these, and certain of the final operations in which the corps played a conspicuous part and with which I am personally familiar, I shall treat at considerable length; but for the rest a mere skeleton of history will amply serve.

II.

Introductions, if so labelled, are often left unread; and for this reason I have introduced already into this chapter matter belonging more properly to a preface. There remain certain other points which should be borne continually in mind by all who read this (or any other) account of the birth, growth, and achievement of the corps. I am enumerating them here, out of their real order in the narrative, because, in the present general ignorance of the subject, it is only by the help of some such basis for judgment that an adequate estimate of performance can be attempted.

The points are these :—

(1) The tank, even when the war ended, was still in an experimental stage.

(2) The Tank Corps was the only arm of the service equipped with an entirely novel weapon which was formed while the war actually was in progress. Every one had to learn everything from

INTRODUCTORY : GENESIS OF THE LANDSHIP

the beginning. There were no traditions, nor any experience of any kind to draw on until the first battle had been fought.

(3) The corps suffered at the outset from a surfeit of parents. For months it was governed in turn or together by a number of departments; and often the right hand did not know what the left hand was about.

(4) Perhaps at that time it was taken seriously by only two classes of persons—firstly, the actual projectors, a few naval and military officers and civil engineers, who worked tirelessly, without reward or even recognition, and to whom most of the credit for the eventual triumph is due; and, secondly, that commercial element which, in our country, profits by every national crisis and sees in every new and struggling enterprise for the public benefit only another opportunity of making money.

(5) Until the first battle of Cambrai the corps was still on probation. It had enemies among the conservatives at the War Office and at G.H.Q. in France; and its early fights, which in effect were practical experiments on an ever-increasing scale, abounding in lessons for those who cared to learn, were taken as proof of its permanently limited value. At Cambrai, for the first time, it was given a chance under favourable conditions; and after that, all was changed. No one could have too many tanks. Infantry commanders clamoured for them in and out of season.

(6) The functions and limitations of the tank as a weapon were very imperfectly apprehended in the beginning by the other arms of the service. Again it was Cambrai, that greatest of all military experiments, which, by its magnitude and success, drove home once for all the lesson that notwith-

standing wire, entrenchments, and machine-guns, surprise frontal attacks on a large scale were become practicable once more.

(7) The tank was now taken up in earnest. Co-operation with infantry, unheard of as a feature of training until just before that battle, was practised regularly behind certain army fronts, and was not suspended even during the German offensives in the following spring. It was realised at last that when we regained the initiative we should be in possession of a weapon which had revolutionised the principles of attack. The evil of the long preliminary bombardment, warning the enemy days and weeks before an assault, and destroying one set of obstacles only to set up another of its own making, had reached excessive proportions at Ypres in the past autumn. It was now laid for ever. The sound of it, at least from the British lines, was hardly heard again during the remainder of the war. The tank was to lead the infantry over instead.

(8) If any one invention hastened the end, it was the tank. The German Higher Command, who ought to know, repeatedly coupled the new weapon with the blockade as one of the ultimate causes of their defeat. Captured German orders during the final year were filled with warnings and instructions concerning tanks. Telephonic messages referring to them were to have priority over all others. Troops were to be trained or cajoled into learning to face them. Special officers, to deal with anti-tank defence, were attached to divisional headquarters. Traps were to be dug. Minefields were to be laid. Anti-tank stockades, in village streets or defiles, were a common feature of the later battlefields. If it sounds extravagant to claim that tanks won

the war, it is indisputable that they hastened its end by six months or a year. The final advance would have been an impossibility without them.
(9) The corps was consistently disregarded in official despatches. It was hampered at every turn by the conservative outlook of senior officers. Out of six army commanders, only three fought offensive actions over ground where tanks could properly be used, and they, at least, understood their value. But for a just appreciation one must turn to the official reports and grateful personal acknowledgments of infantry brigade and battalion commanders, and to the infantry rank and file themselves.
(10) As some proof of the vital part which tanks played in the final advance, it may be pointed out that, from the 8th August 1918 to the 7th November—approximately ninety days—the corps led the infantry of two armies in seventy engagements, ranging from full-dress battle, where two or three hundred tanks were employed, to the daily local attacks in which only half a dozen took part. Simultaneously, the French were using their light Renaults in scores: the Americans took Renaults in at St Mihiel and our Mark V.'s beyond Le Cateau; and one of the few German counter-attacks which gained a temporary success was led by tanks captured from us in the March retreat. On this occasion a serious reverse was only stayed by the arrival of some of our own machines, which drove the Germans off when our infantry was breaking.

Enough has been said at this stage. It will be necessary, at the risk of becoming tedious, to reiterate and amplify these points from time to time as the narrative grows; but it is well to get them tabulated here. We can proceed now to a brief consideration of the modern tank, its genesis, its growth, and its early days of experiment and training.

III.

The curious might spend a profitable week or so at the British Museum investigating the origins of the landship. These are indeed obvious enough, for although there is a school (in the halfpenny press) which traces them no further back than to a story by Mr H. G. Wells, the tank is, in fact, the lineal descendant of the knight in armour, the "war carts" of the Scots, the Roman testudo, the elephants of Hannibal, and the chariots of Boadicea. Among the innumerable activities of Leonardo da Vinci was a scheme for "secure and covered chariots," carrying guns; and as recently as 1888 (but still forestalling Mr Wells) a steam-driven vehicle on the caterpillar principle was projected. All of these manifestations were but varieties of shock troops, calculated to overcome the defensive tactics of their period. Perhaps the elephant was the least reliable, as he showed a tendency to turn about in the heat of battle and forthwith trample down his own friends. Within the last twenty years the caterpillar tractor, the immediate ancestor of the tank, was pulling 60-pounder guns over ditches on Salisbury Plain; and this form of locomotive was still in use for such haulage purposes when war broke out in 1914.

It occurred to no one in the first stages of this conflict that a continent would prove too small for the manœuvres of modern armies. But the open fighting in the early autumn of 1914 came to an end with the race for the coast; and the opposing forces found themselves entrenched along the whole of the immense front, their flanks resting on Switzerland and the Channel, and therefore perfectly secure, and with no apparent way out of this *impasse* but the costly method of frontal assaults. Here, in fact, was that German bugbear, the "parallel battle." The enemy proceeded to launch his series of attacks in Flanders, in an endeavour to create a flank, and learnt again that a stubborn and disciplined infantry, given time to dig itself in, even "if only with a spoon," could beat off greatly superior numbers. The assailant had everything in his favour, for on top of our numerical weakness we were lamentably short of machine-guns, howitzers, and, in particular, field artillery H.E. ammunition. (Batteries about this time were limited — except during an enemy attack — to five rounds per gun per day; and it is said that on one occasion two of these precious rounds having been expended in answer to some call from our infantry, the gunners rang up the latter to ask if they really needed the remaining three!) It was manifest, therefore, that if opportunity for a serious counter-attack had arisen, even supposing we had the men available, we had no means of preparing the way for their advance. And if and when we had both men and guns, what were the chances of success against the precision of modern weapons? The Germans, tackling the same problem from their side, tried again with poison gas; but to this, after its initial triumph, the chemists speedily found an antidote, and it fell to be a mere adjunct of the ordinary harassing tactics of artillery. The Flammen-werfer, a far more futile invention, went the same road. And when, after several months, our new divisions had been trained, and guns and ammunition manufactured in what then was thought to be sufficient quantity, we found out in our turn at Neuve Chapelle and Loos that the resources of the defence were still too manifold and powerful: that concrete, barbed-wire, and machine-guns, if sown lavishly and backed by well-trained infantry and artillery, could fend the assailants off from any but the most limited objectives. It is astonishing and rather pitiful to recall now the optimism of those days. Before the morning of Loos there was much confident talk of our being in Douai the next evening. The cavalry—the phrase was not then as stale as it afterwards became—the cavalry was moving up, ready (in the ingenuous euphemism of operation orders) to be "passed through" the gap which the bombardment and infantry assault would create. Every one, in fact, was anticipating a big advance and a resumption of open warfare. And this in 1915! There was to be no "passing through" for any arm until the tanks broke the Hindenburg Line at Cambrai; and even then we had not the courage of our convictions, and the cavalry was four hours late.

All this, of course, is the obvious wisdom after the event; but there were many who had misgivings at the time. Certainly there was then at work in England a small committee, consisting of naval and military officers and technical advisers, who, realising that no expenditure of blood and shells, as then employed, would carry an attack far enough against modern prepared positions, were seeking for a means by which to overcome the difficulty. Trench warfare, indeed, was hardly begun before they were ready with a suggestion. As early as November 1914, the Committee of Imperial Defence was approached by Colonel Swinton with a proposal for the construction of so-called landships for use on the Western Front.

It will be fitting here to set down the names of these innovators. They were, Colonel E. D. Swinton; Admiral Sir R. H. S. Bacon; Captain T. J. Tulloch, manager of the Chilworth Powder Factory; Mr Diplock, who had designed an improved gun-tractor earlier in the year; and Major Hetherington, of the R.N.A.S.

The problem they were attempting to solve has been indicated already, and, with its developments, will be considered more fully later on; but it may be repeated that in essentials it was this: How to break down the triple obstruction of trenches, wire, and machine-guns to such an extent as would allow the infantry to reach an objective with sufficient numbers and spirit left to ensure its capture and retention. This, roughly, was the limited aim of the first landship. It was known or suspected that artillery alone could not be counted on to do the work thoroughly. After the most intense bombardment, patches of wire would remain uncut, strongly emplaced machine-guns undestroyed, if not in the first hostile line, then in the second or the third; and, in any case, we had not then enough guns or ammunition to make even the effort worth the while. But if in addition to gun-fire some secondary means of crushing wire and neutralising machine-guns could be devised, much might be effected later on. The answer to this problem, in the opinion of Colonel Swinton and his colleagues, was a combination of two existing machines, the tractor and the armoured car—in other words, the tank.

Perhaps this idea smelt too much of Mr Wells and Jules Verne for the Committee of Imperial Defence. Perhaps it really was not their business after all. In any case, they displayed no marked enthusiasm for it, but seem to have forwarded it a little later, not, as might have been expected, to the War Department, but to Mr Winston Churchill, then First Lord of the Admiralty. They may have thought that so chimerical a project, introduced, moreover, by an officer who had been guilty of writing fiction, was something peculiarly in Mr Churchill's line. If they did reason in this manner, they wrought better than they knew. They rendered excellent service to the budding enterprise, which secured in the First Lord a powerful and pertinacious advocate. A man so restless and intelligent could not fail to score a hit with some of his shots; and amid the long catalogue of his disastrous experiments it should at least be laid to his credit that he saw at once some of the possibilities of this new weapon of offence. Whether he foresaw all the developments of warfare which it entailed may be doubted; but the thing itself was novel and startling: it appealed instantly to his imagination; and he wrote forthwith a long letter to the military authorities recommending its immediate adoption, and incidentally rebuking them for having failed to think of something of the sort themselves. He pointed out that, modern battles being fought at short range, assaulting troops were exposed to a storm of bullets from the moment they left their cover, and that some kind of steel shelter, running on caterpillar tracks and carrying guns, would be invaluable for convoying them through wire and machine-gun fire. Such an experiment would cost little : if it failed, no harm was done; and if it was moderately successful, its moral effect alone would be great. Going somewhat beyond his brief, the First Lord then proposed the manufacture of steel shields of various types—to be carried, to be worn as body armour, and to be pushed on wheels. He recommended also the use of smoke-screens in the attack, and ended by remarking that if we did not take the lead at once in this department of warfare we might find that the enemy had forestalled us.

This letter was written in January 1915. It produced no immediate effect. Probably any suggestions from this source were suspect at the War Office, and stood little chance of consideration on their merits; and it is true that Mr Churchill's letter was not conciliatory in tone. About this time Colonel Swinton endeavoured to obtain a hearing on his own account, but with no better result. Shortly after, he returned to his duties in France. Here, during the next six months, he made repeated unofficial attempts to get the landship idea considered, and these may have paved the way; for when, on 4th June, he tried official channels again and forwarded a memorandum on the subject to G.H.Q., he received some encouragement at last. Sir John French, with practical experience of the difficulties before him in the field, thought well enough of the idea to submit it to the War Office.[1]

In the meantime, however, things had been moving in England, although in a manner impossible, one would imagine, in any other country. While the War Office had long forgotten all about this pestilent and unpractical proposal, the Admiralty had been defraying the cost of various experiments carried out with a Foster tractor by Admiral Bacon and Major Hetherington, and with an adapted Holt tractor by Captain Tulloch. The trials of the Holt machine at Shoeburyness were highly successful. Immense cutters, like lobster claws, had been fitted for shearing wire entangle-

---

[1] The first reply to this memorandum from the Engineer-in-Chief was characteristic. After a few preliminary objections, General Fowke concluded as follows: "I therefore think that before considering this proposal we should descend from the realms of imagination to solid facts."

ments, but it was found that the tractor flattened out the wire so effectually that these implements were not needed. And now, while Colonel Swinton was drafting his memorandum in France, a Landship Committee came into being at the instance of Mr Churchill. The President was Mr (now Sir Eustace) D'Eyncourt. The Consulting Engineer was Lieutenant (now Major) W. G. Wilson; and Mr (now Sir William) Tritton not only lent his great authority and technical experience, but produced at once designs for an armoured tractor, to be run either on wheels or caterpillar tracks. The first two genuine landships evolved from these and earlier designs, known respectively as "Mother" and "Little Willie," were discarded; but "Big Willie," their successor, the joint product of Mr Tritton and Lieutenant Wilson, was to embody all the main features of the Mark I. Tank.

The situation, as regards the War Office, was now rather ludicrous. For when that Department, stirred at length into activity by Sir John French's advocacy of Colonel Swinton's scheme, began to look around and make inquiries, it discovered with astonishment that the Admiralty had taken up the idea months before, and had been experimenting quietly ever since. It was impossible, however, that the work could be continued under a dual control; and accordingly, toward the end of June a joint committee was formed to manage the whole enterprise. Henceforth, in effect, the tank became a child of the Army; but it is doubtful if the public ever knew that it was adopted more or less under compulsion, and to the Admiralty is due the credit of having realised its possibilities long before the War Office took a step in the matter. The work now proceeded steadily toward fulfilment. Colonel Swinton, returning in July to assume the post of Assistant-Secretary to the Committee of Imperial Defence, was able to watch over his scheme and help it on its way. "Little Willie," already on the stocks under the ægis of the original committee, was tested at Lincoln and found wanting; but in the meantime the new joint-control had ordered the building of "Big Willie" on the lines laid down by Tritton and Wilson. This experimental machine was tried at Wembley and accepted as a basis for future construction; and Messrs Foster of Lincoln, Agricultural Implement Makers, embarked at once on the slightly modified copy which became the Mark I. tank. This was indeed (to quote from Mr Williams-Ellis's book)[1] a case of beating our ploughshares into swords. At the close of the year Mr Churchill, still true to his old love, sent to G.H.Q. in France a memorandum on "Variants of the Offensive," in which he recapitulated his earlier suggestions for an attack by armour. As a direct result of this, Lieut.-Colonel H. J. Elles, R.E., was ordered to England in January 1916, to report on the progress made; and on February 2nd the improved Wembley machine carried out trials at Hatfield before representatives of the Army Council and G.H.Q. in France. The demonstration was successful. Within a week application was made officially for the construction by Messrs Foster of 150 similar machines in six months. By this time the joint-control had ceased to exist, at least in name; for the new Ministry of Munitions, seeking what it might devour, had descended upon the Landships Committee, swallowed it entire, defined its powers by charter, and then reindued it with life as the Tank Committee. But it was soon felt that here a great chance had been let slip: no Government institution could thrive beneath so simple and banal a designation; and in August, by yet one more feat of legerdemain, the much-harassed control became the Mechanical Warfare Supply Department. All was now well; and under this euphonious title it continued to supply the British Army with tanks until the end of the war.

Hand in hand with these events, a military unit was formed to fight the new machines. The Heavy Section of the Machine-Gun Corps came into being in March, with Colonel Swinton in command.

[1] 'The Tank Corps.' C. A. Williams-Ellis.

CHAPTER II.

THE MARK I. AND MARK IV. TANKS: THE FIRST COMPANIES.

I.

THE tank was only just emerging from the primitive stage when the war ended. The Mark V., which entered the field in 1918 (in excellent time for the Amiens retreat), was in the opinion of many people the first tank worthy of the name. But the heat and burden of the day had been borne by the earlier types, whose carcases littered a dozen battlefields all down the line, from the Salient to Cambrai, and whose successes and misfortunes provided the foundation for the final triumph. It will be convenient to deal here with those early types, Marks I. and IV., together, for they differed only in comparatively minor features. Marks II. and III. had no genuine existence. The Mark II. was simply the Mark I. in a slightly advanced stage of evolution without its tail, and the Mark III. was experimental.

Half a chapter on the idiosyncrasies of these machines will not be exciting. It will be difficult even to make it interesting. But such details have to be faced sooner or later, and are better done with for good and all early in the book.

"Big Willie" and its one hundred and fifty Mark I. successors were designed to cope with the conditions encountered on what was then considered to be a typical modern battlefield — namely, that of Loos. On account of its very limited success and disproportionate casualties, this battle won many converts to the theory of the "attack by armour"; but it misled to some extent those who were responsible for specifying the capabilities required of the new weapon. It was not fully realised that by the date when the tanks would be ready for the field, the conditions on most battle-fronts must certainly have changed materially for the worse. Owing to the enormous projected increase in our artillery, the autumn of 1916 was likely to find the terrain immediately behind the enemy's front line pounded to atoms. But no one foresaw the appallingly destructive effect of such gun-fire as was to blast the Somme and Ypres battlefields during the two ensuing years. It is commonly supposed that the original tank was constructed expressly to meet this difficulty. It was not: it was designed to fight over the moderately shelled areas (as they seem to us now) with which we were familiar at the end of 1915. Actually it made its entry upon ground which, for miles ahead, was convulsed as if by an earthquake, or water-logged like a quagmire; and not until Cambrai did tanks operate under anything approaching favourable conditions.

It was desired to have a machine which, in the first place, would cross a trench nine feet wide. The engineers' earliest solution embodied huge wheels with caterpillar tracks. But as these wheels, to fulfil the specification, must have had a diameter of fifteen feet, they were ruled out as offering too big a target; and after several intermediate stages, in which varieties of the ordinary tractor model (such as "Mother" and "Little Willie") were tried and discarded, an ingenious compromise was discovered. In the Mark I. tank (and all later types conformed to this shape) the tracks passed completely round the body of the machine. The underside of this body was in effect a segment of a wheel, as will be apparent to any one who looks at the outline; and the tracks, instead of continuing round the whole periphery, turned back virtually at right

The Mark V. Tank.

Disabled Mark II. Tank, Arras, 1917.

angles over the nose and so along the top of the body. The width of trench which could be crossed by machines of this design depended only on their length, or, in other words, on the circumference of the wheel. The Mark I., 26 feet long, could in fact cross an 11-foot gap, climb a vertical obstacle 5 feet high, and crawl up any slope of 1 in 2. Craters, however big, presented no difficulty provided the ground was firm.

On the level the tank was resting on no more than 4 or 5 feet of its length (the wheel again), which gave it when moving a slight fore-and-aft rocking motion. The point of gravity was almost in the centre, and with this admirable balance a skilful driver could lower his machine quite gently down over any drop that was not absolutely sheer. In the Mark I. this operation was facilitated by a cumbersome atrocity known as the hydraulic stabiliser, or, more simply, the tail,—a pivoted structure at the stern carrying two large wheels which was controlled (in theory) by an hydraulic ram. This tail was designed also to assist steering, but when the tank was swung (of which more later) the whole affair had to be raised. It was an abomination from the start; it took anything from five minutes to half an hour to lift; and in action it was the first thing to be disabled or shot away. It was discarded after the Somme battles, where it was found that its loss made little or no difference to the efficiency of the machine, and was, from every other point of view, a godsend.

The tank mounted its main armament in sponsons—a form of projecting gun-casemate borrowed from naval architecture.[1] The male tank carried two Hotchkiss 6-pounder Q.F. naval guns on recoil mountings, protected

---

[1] Although the Navy has specialised in the science of mechanical warfare, and although the very idea of the "landship" involves the application on land of some of the principles of war at sea, the Army, as soon as it assumed control of the tanks, refused to profit by the expert knowledge at its disposal. Had it been possible, no doubt every trace of the tanks' original parentage would have been sedulously erased. As it was, the sponson and the 6-pounder gun, for which no feasible military equivalents could be proposed, necessarily were retained; but on

by close-fitting revolving shields, which gave an arc of fire of about 120 degrees. These are extremely handy little weapons, especially when shortened as in the Mark IV., and could be loaded and fired if necessary by one man. With a calibre of $2\frac{1}{4}$ inches, they fired percussion common shell and case-shot; and although sighted up to 2600 yards, were used normally at quite short ranges, when their enormous flash and detonation, out of all proportion to their size, had a great moral effect. In addition, there was a port in each sponson for a Hotchkiss machine-gun or automatic rifle. The tank commander also was provided with one of these weapons, to be fired (with extreme difficulty) through a port in the cab.

The Mark I. female carried Vickers' machine-guns, two to a sponson, or four in all, behind revolving shields. The water-jackets were protected by a kind of armoured sleeve, and the gunners sat on bicycle-seats which moved with the shields. The tank commander was again given a Hotchkiss. The Vickers, a beautiful gun, was perfectly satisfactory in a tank; but in the Mark IV., either on account of a shortage of Vickers' or of some commercial influence, the Lewis gun was introduced as the light weapon throughout both male and female types. As no armoured casing was provided for the barrel, it was disabled very easily by bullets alone, a defect which the Germans did not fail to discover; and in the Mark V. and later types the Hotchkiss (which is all but indestructible) reappeared.

The sponsons of the Mark I. tank were heavy affairs bolted to the side of the machine. The latter then being too wide over-all for carriage by rail, it was necessary before entrainment to unbolt the sponsons and hoist them by a laborious process with a girder and tackle on to

such technical questions as ventilation, the use of telegraphs, and the various mechanical contrivances in respect of which the tank, in its small way, resembles the engine-room of a ship, all the suggestions put forward by experienced nautical engineers were contemptuously rejected.

THE MARK I. AND MARK IV. TANKS

specially constructed trolleys, which were towed by the tank. In the Mark IV. an infinitely superior system was substituted. The male sponson, reduced in size and weight, could be pushed inwards, gun and all, after unbolting. On the female tanks a double door, flush with the body, replaced the lower half of the old sponson; the remaining upper half, also more compact than in the Mark I., was bolted down the middle and hinged to the main structure at each end. It was necessary only to unscrew these few bolts and swing the two portions back on their hinges. Although not so simple as they sound, these operations were child's play in comparison with the earlier abomination of girder and tackle. Moreover, this new arrangement on the female tank had the great advantage of facilitating the entrance or escape of the crew. The manhole in the roof and a dreadful little aperture beside the radiator in the stern were common to both types; but for ordinary use the Mark I. female possessed only a small door, some two feet high, in either sponson; and if the tank were hit and set on fire, some of her men were almost certain to be trapped. With the improved sponson all could escape in a few seconds. Male sponsons, it may be noted, always allow for quite reasonable doors.

So much for the shell and armament of the landship. The motive power was a more difficult problem. There was no time to design and construct special plant: some petrol-driven engine already in use had to be selected. The choice fell eventually on the Daimler 105 H.P. six-cylinder sleeve-valve tractor unit. It must be left to the mechanically-minded to decide whether a more suitable engine could have been discovered. The greatest merit of the Daimler was its comparative simplicity. It was very nearly fool-proof. It took up an immense amount of space, however, for in the Mark I. the differential gear, radiator, and petrol-supply were all enclosed in the body of the tank. There was left just sufficient room for a narrow gangway on either side between the engine and the sponson, for the two seats for the officer and driver in the cab in front, and for further seats on the casing above the crank-shaft and gear-box. Over this casing was the crank-handle for starting up the engine—a process which required normally the efforts of three or four men.

A serious fault existed in the method of transmitting the motive power from the engine to the tracks. Working off the differential, and manipulated by levers, a primitive and infuriating system of secondary gears, pinions, and Coventry chains connected with the sprocket wheels which performed the actual labour of propulsion. Two men were required to work these gears; and no member of any tank crew who took a Mark I. or Mark IV. into action is ever likely to forget the sweat and tears and blasphemy expended over this atrocious system. Apart from the labour and waste of time (and consequent danger) which it involved, it has been asserted by pessimists that 75 per cent of power was lost in the secondary gears and transmission. In addition to changes of speed, these gears played a prominent part in the more frequent act of "swinging." To alter direction to any appreciable degree the tank had to be swung. The differential was locked, the track on the side toward which the turn was intended was disconnected by putting the secondary gears on that side into neutral, and the other track, with the whole drive behind it, then pulled the tank round—if the soil was firm, virtually on its axis. Handbrakes, working from the officer's seat to the extension shafts on the differential, assisted in the process, and could be used alone for small changes of direction. Swinging with this transmission was unsatisfactory in the extreme. It required the work of four men, and often was very slow. In the Mark V., epicyclic gears and a one-man control were introduced.

In the Mark I. the petrol-supply was carried in two tanks, one on either side of the cab in front. With this arrangement, whoever else might escape when the machine was set

THE MARK I. AND MARK IV. TANKS

on fire, the officer and driver stood an excellent chance of being burnt alive; and in the Mark IV. an armoured tank holding sixty gallons, placed outside in rear, was substituted. In all types, every available inch of space within was utilised for ammunition racks. The male tank was designed to carry 160 rounds of 6-pounder shell, and 1500 rounds of S.A.A.; the female to carry 7800 rounds of the latter; but, in fact, these numbers were often exceeded, and as much as 27,000 rounds of S.A.A. have been taken into action in a tank. Spare supplies of water, oil, and grease, together with two days' rations and the crew's equipment, were tucked away wherever room could be found. It will be apparent, therefore, that there was little scope for movement and no possibility of comfort in a fully-loaded tank. Although ventilation was assisted by a rotary-fan, placed in the stern and worked off the half-time shaft, the heat was terrific: no one could stand upright; and the uproar of the engine was so loud that orders had to be transmitted by signs. Visibility was limited in the extreme. The officer and driver had flaps which, when fully open, gave a fair range of vision immediately in front; but when it was necessary to close these there remained only a number of double glass prisms[1] let into the armour, and some inadequate periscopes thrust up through the roof. After a while naval compasses on gimbals were provided, but in such a mass of steel and iron they proved of very small value.

A few words must be said as to a tank's method of progression. The two caterpillar tracks, passing completely round the body of the machine, consisted each of ninety hard steel plates with lips for gripping the surface. These tracks did not actually move over the ground; the tank in effect laid its own track, clawed its way along it by means of the two sprocket wheels in the rear, and then picked it up behind and passed it over its head, as it were, before laying it down in front again. During this process the whole weight of the machine rested on a number of flanged

[1] Steel plates, with pinhole perforations, replaced the prisms in the Mark IV.

rollers, which wore out very rapidly, as did the early sprocket wheels. Tracks and rollers required continual lubrication—the latter by injections from grease-guns. The less said of this ghastly operation the better.

It will be fitting to include in so tedious a section a few statistics. The length of the Mark I. tank was 26 feet 6 inches; its width (including sponsons) 12 feet 9 inches in the male, 10 feet 5 inches in the female; and its height was 8 feet 1 inch. It weighed approximately 26 tons. The armour throughout the body was 12 mm. thick, but on the sponsons, for some obscure reason, only 10 mm. It was proof against shrapnel and ordinary S.A.A., but failed to keep out the "K" armour-piercing bullet which the Germans, apparently on the strength of vague warnings received, had just introduced.

Combinations of the primary and secondary gears gave four different speeds forward and one reverse, the highest reaching something over four miles an hour on level ground. Not more than 30 to 40 yards a minute was expected of a tank across trench systems and heavily-shelled areas. The estimated radius of action without a refill was ten hours; and it was not believed that a crew could endure for longer the exhausting conditions amid which they must work and fight. Finally, it was thought that the track-rollers and the sprockets and pinions of the secondary gears would require to be replaced after about fifty hours' running. As a matter of fact, most of these estimates were conservative. Tanks ran for fifteen hours and more without a refill; their crews withstood the heat and gases for even longer periods; and with improved steel in the sprockets and pinions these were found to survive such journeys as were not dreamed of in the early days.

The Mark IV. was virtually identical with the Mark I. in shape, dimensions, and method of propulsion. Owing to its modified sponsons it was of less width. Its armour was slightly thicker and harder, and kept out the "K" bullets, although the impact of the latter drove splinters from the inside wall.[1] The exhaust, instead of opening direct on to the roof, where its flames often betrayed the position of the tank at night, was led down over the stern. A number of Daimlers of 125 H.P. were mounted in this class, and, with a better type of radiator, raised the speed to about five miles an hour on the level.

In conclusion, we will describe briefly the method of conveying tanks by rail. A 50-ton truck of great length, known officially as a "K.T.," was designed especially for the purpose; and after a few preliminary rites the tank was driven direct on to this over a ramp. The normal train used in France carried twelve tanks, so that the leader had to drive over eleven trucks before it arrived at its own, the second ten, and so on. The trucks were only four inches wider than the span of the caterpillar tracks: the act of entraining or detraining took place almost invariably at night: occasionally, owing to the faults or exigencies of the railway service, the tanks had to be driven off stern first; and if the line up to the ramp was curved, as often it was, a very nice judgment in driving and guidance was demanded. It often happened that some machine suffering from mechanical trouble required to be towed off by one of its fellows. Finally, at times of great urgency (as for the big concentration before Cambrai), it became necessary to make use of French 30-ton trucks, which were never intended to carry such a load, and were, moreover, actually narrower than a tank. Yet all ranks became so expert in this work that it was not uncommon for an entire company to be entrained in the dark in less than thirty minutes, and detrained in little more. The whole process, with its harrowing contingencies, will fall to be described at a later period in the book; but I may add here that, speaking from memory, I can recall only one serious accident during a move by rail. This happened just before Cambrai, when a tank fell

---

[1] For protection against these splinters, and against the "splash" from ordinary bullets hitting crevices round the gun shields, crews were provided with small vizors of steel and chain mail.

from a French truck as the train was taking a sharp curve. And for that battle some 470 were detrained in a few days in the same area.

II.

In Easter week, 1916, two new companies of the M.G.C., known as the Heavy Section, and lettered "K" and "L," were formed at Bisley under Lieut.-Colonel Bradley. Colonel Swinton remained at Headquarters in London. The personnel was recruited principally from the A.S.C. (M.T.) and from the classes attested under the Derby scheme. For officers, volunteers for what was described as a new armoured-car unit were gathered in from the ranks of the 18th, 19th, and 21st Royal Fusiliers—the so-called public-school battalions, then in France—and from the Motor Machine-Gun Corps. There being as yet no tanks available for training purposes, the programme of work at Bisley was limited virtually to drill and courses in the Hotchkiss guns. It would be absurd to pretend that any of this was taken very seriously. The other established arms of the service, now expanding beyond belief, absorbed all the best regular soldiers left in England; and the new formation suffered inevitably from a lack of competent and energetic senior officers. Many of us must be familiar with the casual methods and discipline which obtained in such embryo organisations in those days, and it is unnecessary to fill in the details. Of the subaltern officers, probably 75 per cent represented as good material as could be found anywhere—a high proportion, in view of the extraordinary and haphazard processes by which the commissioned ranks of the New Army were filled, and one which compared very favourably with that of most infantry units. From the outbreak of war, while the uneducated and unintelligent were obtaining commissions for the asking, there were fighting and dying as private soldiers or N.C.O.'s thousands of men accustomed to responsibility and leadership; and amid this criminal wastage the new corps was lucky to obtain so good a nucleus. As for the original rank and file, they were admirable. A large number, of course, were skilled mechanics; and the fighting qualities of all, under conditions entirely novel and trying in the extreme to nerve and body, were beyond praise.

The prelude at Bisley did not continue long. Arrangements had been made to take over Lord Iveagh's estate at Thetford, in Norfolk, for training purposes; and the Heavy Section was translated thither in June to make the acquaintance of its new machines. Within the estate the R.E.'s had constructed a model battlefield, with trenches, craters, and other obstacles. Since the enterprise, theoretically, was shrouded in mystery, the whole area was swept clear of inhabitants. Farms and cottages were evacuated. Fences, barbed wire, and sentries kept the East Coast labourer intrigued and amused. Aeroplanes which came too near were fired at. These methods seem, on the whole, to have been successful. It was impossible to conceal the fact that something was doing: beautiful female spies and their less attractive colleagues of the other sex are said to have transmitted vague warnings to the enemy; but until the Mark I.'s appeared on the Somme front the Germans had no definite information to work on. Messrs Foster, building the first 150 at Lincoln, preferred simpler, yet perhaps more subtle, deceptions. There was no secrecy in their yards. Any one could see what they were doing. They were building mobile water-tanks for the Russians, those useful people, Russia being notoriously a waterless country and badly served with roads. There are still to be seen a few old training machines which bear inscribed on their sides a legend in large white Russian characters, setting forth their alleged purpose and destination. This last was Petrograd. In such a manner the word "tank" came into use as a convenient code expression, and remained to stay. And as the completed tanks arrived by rail at the training area after dark, it is probable that few persons outside the corps were aware of any connection between the simple Russian water-carriers at Lincoln and the mysterious armoured cars which manœuvred behind the walls of the huge enclosure at Thetford.

On its arrival in the new area the Heavy Section began work in earnest on the machines available. At first, unfortunately, there were not many: there was some delay in delivery, and already there were upwards of a thousand officers and men to be trained. It had been decided to form six fighting companies, of which four were to be ready by the beginning of August. These companies were now lettered from " A " to " F," and were each to be composed of four sections of six tanks (three male and three female), with one reserve tank, making twenty-five in all. Each section was divided again into three sub-sections of two tanks. A tank crew consisted of a subaltern, three drivers, and four gunners, including an N.C.O. The company was commanded by a major, the sections by captains. The total strength was thirty-one officers and about 200 other ranks. To every two companies there was a quartermaster's establishment and a workshop's section of three officers and thirty men. By the 14th August the first four companies—A, B, C, and D—were complete as regards personnel; and the right half of C, with thirteen tanks, had already left for France.

We can prepare to follow. There is no need to enlarge upon the training at Thetford. With the arrival of the actual machines, decorated with Russian characters, interest and zeal revived. It was difficult to remain enthusiastic about the Hotchkiss gun for weeks on end; but to drive a tank across trenches and in and out of craters, even in July, was a novel and piquant form of work. It was felt that things were moving at last: the atmosphere of secrecy was attractive, and there were many indications of the importance already attaching to the new arm. Generals and staff officers came down to witness demonstrations, and the necessary element of humour was provided when a tank-load of them was upset in a trench. The men were both clever and keen, and the most serious trouble was the insufficient supply of machines in which to train them. Many drivers had spent no more than an hour or two in a tank when they left for France. It may well seem, indeed, that the first companies were rushed out too soon; but there were good arguments for the move. The difficulties encountered in the Somme offensive led to a request for the early departure of tanks; and although the training of both officers and men was lamentably incomplete, it was thought that a month or two of actual battle experience would outweigh all the manifest disadvantages of a premature entry. The winter could then be spent in profiting by the lessons learnt. A startling success in the beginning was not anticipated by any one who realised the difficulties to be overcome. The danger rather was of a complete failure, and consequent discouragement; and this possibility had to be faced. It was hoped, however, that the new arm would at least play so good a part as to justify its present claims and its demands for future development.

As we have seen, the right half of C Company left England on the 13th August. The left half followed on the 22nd. D was the next to go, and then A and B. There remained the two later companies, E and F, but these never left the country as units. The other four did all that was asked of them: the experiment was justified; and E and F stayed to form the nucleus of the battalions raised at home when the great expansion of the corps was authorised later in the year.

CHAPTER III.

THE SOMME BATTLES.

I.

As the companies of the Heavy Section arrived in France, they were assembled with their tanks at Yvrench, near Abbeville. This was before the days of the Channel Ferry. The heavy machines had to be shipped like any other form of ordnance; and they were but a part of the load which required to be carried overseas. Several complete workshops, dozens of sponson trolleys, light cars, lorries, and motor-bicycles, together with tons upon tons of spare parts, furnished the first instalments of that vast collection of material which the Tank Corps came to accumulate in France.

A training centre was established at Yvrench, at first under Lieut.-Colonel Brough, but early in September Colonel Bradley came out to take over the command. It was known that the unit would soon be called upon, and there still was an immense amount of work to be done. Drivers and gunners had to receive further training. The tanks required to be overhauled and tuned up. Workshops and depots must be established. Above all, a host of novel problems concerning administration, supply, tactics—in short, the whole method and manner of tank-work in the field—fell to be solved without delay, and, what was more, without assistance. The tank companies in France were nobody's children. Their nominal parent, the M.G.C.

(itself a mushroom growth of doubtful antecedents and
future), had in fact no actual connection with them whatever; and it would seem that a new technical unit, in so
experimental a stage, should more properly have been made
a branch of an established technical corps, such as the
Royal Engineers. As it was, the companies were self-
contained and unattached. The infantry, whom they had
come to help, knew nothing of them except by rumour.
The Generals and staff officers who came to see them perform regarded them as a curious and rather dangerous
innovation, unlikely to be of much practical value. In so
far as this isolation was intentional, it is very doubtful
whether the measure of secrecy obtained by it outweighed
its disadvantages. The first battle was near at hand; and
a few minutes after zero the secret would be exploded for
ever. In the meantime, a fuller comprehension by other
arms, a more liberal interchange of views, in especial some
tuition of the infantry who were to co-operate in action,
might have saved much disappointment and many lives.
Nothing of the kind was attempted; and the companies
had to think out and master other people's problems in
addition to their own, in the field and with small aid from
outside. Some contingencies inevitably were overlooked.
Not only was experience of this new warfare yet to seek,
but many of the officers and a larger proportion of the
men actually were in France for the first time, and knew
nothing of normal battle conditions. It is surprising how
much was foreseen and provided for in spite of these disadvantages. The matter of supply, for example, seems to
have been dealt with adequately from the beginning, for
the tanks were seldom hampered for want of petrol or
ammunition, wherever they might be. As regards general
tactics, the new unit was fortunate in possessing a basis
to work on in a valuable memorandum issued by Colonel
Swinton early in the year. In this he outlined the probable
scope of tank warfare, dealt with infantry co-operation and
artillery support, and laid down a definite system of attack

which in essentials is in use to-day.[1] On the other hand, less thought was given to a Department that proved to be of vital importance. This was Intelligence, or (as the branch of that service in the Tank Corps is more accurately styled) Reconnaissance. Circumstances peculiar to tank operations call for the training of special officers in this duty alone, as well as an unusually high standard of proficiency in all tank commanders; but these needs were not recognised fully at the outset, and one Intelligence officer, Captain Hotblack, was responsible for the welfare of all four companies. A little later, and there were seven Reconnaissance Officers to each battalion; and the corps soon won so high a reputation for thoroughness in this work that every formation in the Army, from Headquarters downward, came to it for assistance.

II.

In the beginning of September the situation along the Somme Front was as follows:—

After two months' very sanguinary fighting two stages of

[1] The tactical recommendations set out in this document were disregarded completely by the general staff until the compulsion of events enforced their adoption. Colonel Swinton insisted on the necessity of tanks leading the attack in masses, and pointed out that, to ensure the rapid exploitation of any opening they should make, a very large force of infantry must be launched at once behind them. "Not only," he says, "does it seem that the tanks will confer the power to force successive complete and unbattered defence lines, but, as has been explained, the more speedy and uninterrupted their advance, the greater the chance of their surviving sufficiently long to do this. *It is possible, therefore, that an effort to break right through the enemy's defensive zone in one day may now be contemplated as a feasible proposition.*" Cambrai, notwithstanding the half-hearted support afforded, proved absolutely the justice of these contentions; and in 1918 they were accepted as a matter of course—without, however, any acknowledgment of their origin. Colonel Swinton also pointed out that field artillery was the tank's chief danger, and one which could be countered only by the help of other arms. Numerous minor recommendations, such as the use of case shot, smoke, and wireless, the necessity of intelligent co-operation by infantry and artillery, and questions of administration, supply, and transport in the field, were either turned down at once by the general staff or were disregarded; yet every one of them subsequently had to be adopted.

the battle had been completed, more or less satisfactorily.
In the British sector, which alone concerns us, the enemy's
first and second positions had been captured from a point
just west of Combles (where we touched the French
6th Army) to Pozières on the Albert-Bapaume road.
Farther northward, from Pozières to Gommecourt, we
had failed badly, and were still in our old front line. The
casualties had been extremely heavy. Before Beaumont
Hamel and Thiepval, whole brigades were destroyed on
the first day without gaining a yard of ground; and along
this moiety of our front the battle came virtually to a standstill for months. In the southern portion our advance,
although slow and costly, had progressed fairly methodically, side by side with that of the French. The result
was a flattish salient biting into the enemy's old position
from the Albert-Bapaume road, southward across the
Somme, to the road from Amiens to Brie. Correspond-
ing to the curve of the salient was the German third line
of defence, completed since the battle began. On the
British front it ran along the reverse slope of the Pozières
Morval ridge (most of which was in our possession), some
five miles west of Bapaume. It was now intended to resume
our advance in an easterly and north-easterly direction toward that town. The tunnelled positions of Thiepval and
Beaumont Hamel were to be left, for the present, still un-
assailed, except for a few minor enterprises required to
improve the existing line.

The main attack was fixed for the 15th of September. Both
the British armies now engaged in the general offensive were
taking part: the 4th, under General Rawlinson, whose front
extended from the point of junction with the French to west
of Martinpuich, and a part of Gough's 5th or Reserve Army,
which continued the line northward. From right to left the
4th Army was to carry the villages of Morval, Les Bœufs,
Gueudecourt, and Flers; while Gough, after a preliminary
operation south-west of Thiepval on the 14th, had in hand
the capture of Martinpuich and Courcelette. The usual

orders were issued for a vigorous exploitation of any opening—a poor hope on the Somme—and once more the Cavalry Corps, with all its impedimenta, clattered noisily up toward the battlefield to be at hand if needed.

The tanks were to make their entry in this attack. C and D Companies, commanded respectively by Major Holford Walker and Major Summers, D.S.C., were allotted to the two armies, and on the 10th moved up to the railway centre called the Loop, near Bray. From there the tanks trekked to their lying-up positions for the battle—C to the Briquetterie near Trônes Wood, and D to the Green Dump behind Delville Wood. The companies' headquarters followed on the 14th. For the actual attack the tanks were to be distributed as follows:—

Three sections of each company (17 tanks apiece) worked on the right and right-centre with the 14th and 15th Corps. One section of 8 tanks of D Company was attached to the 3rd Corps in the centre, while the remaining section of C (7 tanks) came under the orders of the Reserve Army on the left. This made a total of 49. It was intended for the machines to be used in sub-sections of two or three against specified strong points. There was some discussion as to whether they should precede or follow the infantry at zero. If they led, it was feared that the noise of their approach to the front line would bring down the enemy's barrage upon our assembly trenches; and eventually it was decided that their arrival should be so timed that they could reach the first objectives—roughly the line of villages—five minutes before the infantry. For this purpose lanes were to be left in our own barrage.

I shall not attempt a detailed account of this or any other early tank action. In the first place, it would be difficult to do so, for the records of those days are meagre and inaccurate. Again, the *rôle* of the tanks on the Somme was so largely experimental and subsidiary that infantry operation orders, even after the secret was blown, were framed to be carried out irrespective of the action of what was then regarded in most quarters as an unreliable innovation of doubtful future. As regards the tactical methods employed, an organisation in its infancy, with everything to learn, had to take what chances it was offered, and had little say in the direction of events. No attempt was or could be made at this stage, or for long after, to introduce those revolutionary tactics (already discussed and advocated by Colonel Swinton and others) in which the tank was to be the vital instrument, and wherein lies the chief interest of its history. Finally, since all tank battles as such bear very similar features, I prefer to concentrate on later ones of which I have personal knowledge.

The attack on the 15th September was highly successful on the left and centre, but failed on the right, where the strong point known as the Quadrilateral held up our advance against Morval and Les Bœufs. On the whole, it may be said that the work of the tanks fully justified expectations. No startling triumph could be recorded, but under the circumstances none was anticipated. Enough was done to demonstrate the inherent soundness of the design, the correctness of the tactical axioms laid down, and the enormous potential value of the machine when faults had been rectified and the personnel more highly trained. The test to which the Heavy Section had been put was a severe one. The ground everywhere was so pulverised by the ferocious shelling of the past two months, that out of 49 tanks which left the Briquetterie and Green Dump that night, 17 failed to reach their starting-points. These broke down or were ditched on the way, the absence of any unditching gear, such as was supplied later, proving a serious handicap. Half an hour before zero, which fell at dawn, the other 32 began to crawl forward to the front line. The three sections of C Company, on the right, had been particularly unfortunate during the approach march, and the few tanks remaining were able to effect little or nothing against the Quadrilateral and Les Bœufs. In most cases they were ditched or knocked out by shell-fire soon after they crossed the German front line. D Company's three sections, working with the 15th Corps farther north, were far more successful. Every one who read the newspapers at the time knows how one tank preceded the New Zealanders up the main street of Flers, driving the terrified Germans down into the cellars, where the infantry rounded them up. The tank then moved on to a trench strongly held by the enemy, enfiladed it, moved along behind it, and took 300 prisoners. Farther north, the two sections assisting the 3rd Corps and the Reserve Army reached Gueudecourt and the famous sugar factory at Courcelette. In almost every case where a tank succeeded in arriving at its objective, the mere sight of it was enough. Save for some picked machine-gunners and a few other desperate men, the enemy fled or surrendered on the spot.

The moral effect, all proverbs about familiarity to the contrary, is still and will always remain the chief asset of the tank as a weapon. No body of infantry, unless very closely supported by guns, will stand for long in the open before a properly concerted attack led by tanks. They cannot: accidents apart, they are entirely helpless, and they know it. The fire from the machine may be erratic, as usually it is, for the gunners can see very little, and their platform is continually in motion; but this does not abate in any degree the moral effect of its onset. In the last five months of the war, when the proper use of tanks had come at last to be understood, it was only by the bold use and sacrifice of field artillery, pushed far forward, that the German armies were able to protract for as long as they did the final struggle. And this moral influence works both ways: it helps the attacker as much as it demoralises the attacked. The tank is terrifying, or inspiring and rather ludicrous, according to whether it is against you or for you. It is not only a known antidote to the dreadful trinity of trench, wire, and machine-gun. Its very appearance is a comfort. Its shape, unlike that of any other example of man's handiwork, its deliberate but at times curiously active and disconcerting movements, its obvious weight and power, even the two ports, like lidded eyes, which ornament the front of the cab, combine irresistibly (as all journalists will testify) to suggest some huge prehistoric animal—some giant sloth or toad. Indeed, to visit a training-ground in the evening when some dozens of these creatures are rolling home to their stalls or hangars is, for all the world, like being at a Zoo during the Pleistocene Age. The striking pattern of colours with which the machines were painted in the early days only aided the illusion. The British soldier, whose great merit it is to see the comic side of everything, could not fail to be exhilarated by these gorgeous monsters. It was long before he came to rely on them as he could rely, let us say, on an old-established and perfected arm like the artillery; but this is not remarkable. Rather is it something of a miracle, and an abiding testimony to the efforts of the new corps, that a similar confidence between infantry and tanks actually was created during the war's lifetime. And from the very first their mere appearance in the field was a great moral factor in our favour.

In this, their first battle, their casualties in personnel were insignificant. One tank, after attacking a field battery in Gueudecourt and destroying one gun, was itself hit and burnt out, only two of the crew escaping. Most of the others got off lightly. Altogether ten were disabled by shell-fire, and seven more were hit, but returned to the rallying-point.

Reserving remarks and criticism for the end of the chapter, we will run through the remaining actions fought by the Heavy Section that autumn and winter. A comparative lull of rather more than a week (marked by a successful minor operation which gave us the Quadrilateral) followed on the battle of the 15th; but during this period the tank companies were feverishly busy. At first no fewer than 50 tanks were asked for to assist in the next attack. So large a demand at that stage meant an immense amount of work; and in the end nothing like this number was required, the co-operation of the Heavy Section being limited to the northern assault on Gueudecourt, Thiepval, and the height overlooking the Ancre from the south. Work on the tanks was hampered by the multitude of visitors who came to see these novelties now that the secret was disclosed. There was much uncertainty as to the method of attack, the supply of maps was insufficient, and operation orders, when they did arrive, were meagre and ambiguous.

The ground along the Thiepval ridge was in an appalling condition. It had been shelled more or less continuously for upwards of three months by guns of every calibre. On top of this came two or three days of heavy rain just before the attack. "The plan," to quote Colonel Buchan, "was for an attack by the 4th Army on Monday, the 25th, with— on its left wing—small objectives; but, on the right and centre, aiming at completing the captures which had been the ultimate objectives of the advance of the 15th. The following day the right wing of the 5th Army would come into action, and it was hoped that from Thiepval to Combles the enemy would be driven back to his fourth line of defence, and our own front pushed up well within assaulting distance." The enemy's fourth line of defence ran just in front of Bapaume. Five tanks only were detailed eventually to work with the 4th Army on the 25th, and they were able to effect little or nothing. Unable to leave their starting-point until zero, for the attack was made at midday, they seem to have become ditched very early. They were hardly needed, except at one point. The assault was entirely successful everywhere but at Gueudecourt, where uncut wire held up the 21st Division. It had been a bitterly disappointing day for the tanks, but the fault was hardly theirs. It was an error in the first place to employ them at all in an operation starting in broad daylight, for it was impossible to conceal them near enough to the front line to enable them to go over with

THE SOMME BATTLES   37

the infantry. Corps and divisional commanders had not
yet learnt the elements of tank warfare. Secondly, the
ground was so riven and pulverised, so absolutely rotten
with shelling and rain, that without any unditching gear
or spuds (iron shoes afterwards provided to grip sodden
or crumbling soil) the odds were all against their getting
far.

As it happened, an opportunity was soon offered of re-
deeming these mishaps, and was seized in a very brilliant
manner. The 21st Division, we have seen, was brought to
a standstill in front of Gueudecourt. Here was a formidable
obstacle known as Gird Trench, and as a preliminary to a
further assault on the village it was essential that this
should be cleared. Orders were issued that night for an
attack at dawn, and the help of a tank was asked for.
With immense toil one was brought up in the dark across
the frightful waste of half-obliterated trenches and shell-
holes and water. For the ensuing action I will quote the
report of the 15th Corps.

"On the 25th September, the 64th Brigade, 21st
Division's attack on Gird Trench was hung up and
unable to make any progress. A footing had been
obtained in Gird Trench at N. 32 d 91, and our troops
held the trench from N. 26 c 45 northwards. Between
these two points there remained approximately 1500
yards of trench very strongly held by the Germans and
well wired, the wire not having been cut. Arrangements were made for a tank (female) to move up for
an attack next morning. The tank arrived at 6.30,
followed by bombers. It started moving south-east-
ward along the Gird Trench, firing its machine-guns.
As the trench gradually fell into our hands, strong
points were made in it by two companies of infantry
which were following in rear for that purpose. No
difficulty was experienced. The enemy surrendered
freely as the tank moved down the trench. They
were unable to escape, owing to our holding the trench

at the southern end at N. 32 d 91. By 8.30 A.M. the whole length of the trench had been cleared, and the 15th D.L.I. moved over the open and took over the captured trench. The infantry then advanced to their final objective (Gueudecourt), where the tank rendered very valuable assistance. The tank finally ran short of petrol south-east of Gueudecourt. In the capture of Gird Trench 8 officers and 362 other ranks were made prisoners, and a great many Germans were killed. Our casualties only amounted to 5. Nearly 1500 yards of trench were captured in less than an hour. What would have proved a very difficult operation, involving probably heavy losses, was taken with the greatest ease entirely owing to the assistance rendered by the tank."

It should be added that an aeroplane also lent a hand, flying low over the trench and machine-gunning the defenders.

This admirable little demonstration of what a tank could do came at a most opportune moment. The months of slaughter on the Somme were in fact having their inevitable effect on the armies in France. Already the best of the volunteers who enlisted in the first year of the war were gone, and the new recruits were of a very different type. Again and again battalions, brigades, whole divisions even, came out of the line decimated and shaken from what was trumpeted at home as a cheap and glorious success. A mile or two of trenches, a wood or a village, had indeed been won, and with much glory. But at what a cost! Whether or no these Pyrrhic victories were worth the sacrifice—and presumably they were—the men on the spot, seeing only their small corner, remembered nothing but the horror of it all. The Somme, together with Gallipoli, and the third battle of Ypres, stand apart in the minds of those who lived through them as long-drawn nightmares; and it was the peculiar abomination of the first-named that it seemed but the foretaste of an endless future. The war

might go on for ever in this fashion. There can be no
doubt that the Higher Command itself viewed with apprehension a prolonged continuance of these conditions, and
was prepared at last to welcome any suggestion or innovation which promised to alleviate them. Hence the demand
for the services of the Heavy Section before, in fact, it was
prepared to take the field. The tanks came; and the little
action just described, together with other similar if less
spectacular performances, went far to convert doubters to
the possibilities of the attack by armour. Gird Trench,
however insignificant in itself, was a singularly perfect
example of how the new weapon could help toward economy
of life and effort. At a conservative estimate the enemy
had lost not only a strong position, but also some 600
officers and men killed, wounded, or taken. Our infantry
casualties totalled five, and the tank crew who were
directly responsible for the success numbered only eight.
Such figures in themselves were convincing.

On the same morning eight tanks went over on the left
with the right wing of the 5th Army against Thiepval.
The ground was all but impossible, and most of them were
ditched on or about the German front line; but two got
into Thiepval and gave valuable help to the infantry at a
time when the artillery support for once had failed.

III.

The Heavy Section had no more fighting for nearly two
months. With October the bad weather set in: the rain
fell in torrents: when it did not rain a heavy mist gave
the sodden ground no chance of recovery; and the over-
burdened roads went from bad to worse. While the armies
struggled in the mud and water on the slopes of the final
ridge before Bapaume, the tank companies were withdrawn
to Acheux to refit.

By the end of October it was plain that a condition of

stalemate had been reached on the main battlefield. To relieve this it was decided to make a flank attack along and north of the Ancre, where we had been repulsed in July. The capture of the Thiepval height had improved the prospect of a fresh attempt in this quarter. The northern edge of the salient we had created now ran east and west along high ground south of the river; and it was possible for our artillery to enfilade and even take in reverse the immensely strong positions of Beaucourt and Beaumont Hamel.

The attack was fixed for the 13th November. Originally, twenty tanks were to have been used, but the weather was so bad that this number was reduced to five—three to assist at St Pierre Divion, south of the Ancre, while the other two endeavoured to reach Beaumont Hamel. By this time the absolute necessity of good reconnaissance had been recognised; and before the action, tank commanders were taken to observation-points from which they could see something of the ground beyond the front line. Landmarks were indicated to them, aeroplane photographs were studied, and, on zero night, the tank routes were taped as far as possible. But no foresight could avail against the weather. Gales blew, the rain fell, and, on the night of the 12th-13th, came snow. The three southern tanks were bogged in the mud as they moved up. The northern pair found the tapes obliterated by the snow, but Captain Hotblack, the Intelligence Officer, led one forward under heavy fire, and then going back, brought up the second to a point where the infantry was hung up. Both these tanks did good work before getting ditched, and Hotblack received the D.S.O. Meanwhile the attack had succeeded beyond expectation. St Pierre Divion and Beaumont Hamel were taken, although once more an assault on Serre was repulsed. One battalion of the Naval Division, led by Lieut.-Colonel Freyburg, actually pushed right up the river valley to the outskirts of Beaucourt. Here it hung on all day, far ahead of our main advance. The failure to capture a powerful redoubt between Beaucourt and Beaumont Hamel prevented any adequate support reaching the battalion, but Freyburg, who was wounded in all four times, refused to withdraw. A Territorial unit contrived to get in touch with him, and communication of a sort was maintained with the rear along the river bank. But his position was as precarious as it was valuable; and that night three tanks were brought up for another attack on the redoubt. One was hit by a shell and disabled. The others got within close range of the strong point before getting ditched. They were able to bring their guns to bear, and in a short time the place surrendered, no fewer than 400 prisoners falling to the two tanks alone. The subsequent infantry advance closed up the line and enabled Freyburg to crown his exploit by capturing Beaucourt at the head of his men.

A few days later the battles of the Somme came definitely to an end. If the autumn advance had come up to expectations there was an intention of continuing the offensive throughout the winter, but the powers which modern weapons give to the defence, combined with the October rains, had limited our successes and brought the army to a pitch of exhaustion; and now a complete break-up of the weather put any idea of further operations out of the question. The troops set about making themselves as comfortable as possible in their new positions. Shattered roads were remade and light railways laid down across the waste behind the front line. Preparations began for a renewed onslaught in the spring. With the rest, the companies of the Heavy Section were to be very busy that winter. The increasing difficulties of the attack, and their own demonstration of how those difficulties might be overcome, had established their position as a valuable, if not yet an indispensable, auxiliary. But they had fought their last battle as individual units. The corps was growing; and they withdrew from the line only to form the nucleus of the four battalions which were to be raised in France.

IV.

An immense amount of nonsense was talked and written about the first appearance of the tanks in the field. The newspapers, as perhaps was to be expected, excelled themselves in absurdity. Any lie was good enough for them. The war correspondents, in their safe and comfortable château in the valley of the Ternoise, ransacked Scripture and zoology for suitable similes. There is a story of those halfpenny strategists, Messrs Gibbs and Beach Thomas,[1] tossing up a coin (no doubt a halfpenny) to decide who should use the word Behemoth. All this ignorant flapdoodle did an ill service to the new unit. Its exploits in battle had been witnessed by few; but tens of thousands had seen tanks lying derelict in the Somme mud or holding up traffic through mechanical breakdowns on important thoroughfares; and exaggerated encomiums in ill-informed newspaper articles only brought ridicule upon men who had done wonders in circumstances inconceivable to the writers. The Heavy Section, in its early days, is said to have been the victim of more chaff (and not always good-natured) than any unit except the London Scottish. People at home, who believe anything they read in print and have the Press they deserve, naturally expected miracles of machines which pushed down houses on battlefields, where, in fact, no house had been standing for months.

No one disliked this sort of thing more than the men concerned. They knew well enough where they had succeeded and where they had failed. The necessary experience had been bought; and there were many lessons to be learnt from it and carried into practice, so far as was possible, before the next battle. It was proved that the Mark I. was designed on sound lines, and needed only a few structural alterations to make it equal to all reasonable demands until such time as it could be superseded by an altogether

[1] Now, I believe, Sir Philip Gibbs and Sir Beach Thomas.

superior type. The "Hydraulic Stabiliser" or tail, for
example, must be got rid of. Its essential worthlessness
was discovered quite early, when a tank came under shell-
fire while waiting for zero behind our front line. The
whole crew being inside for shelter, with the engine just
ticking over, a projectile burst under the stern and blew the
tail away without doing any other damage: amid the general
uproar no one was aware of what had happened; and the
tank moved forward and was in action for some time before
the loss of this absurd appendage was discovered. Other
faults to be remedied were the position of the petrol-tanks,
the overhead exhaust-outlet, emitting conspicuous flame and
sparks, the needlessly broad sponsons (accessories in many
cases of ditching), and the lack of any gear by which a
ditched tank could free itself under its own power.
"Ditching," an unpleasant commonplace of tank warfare,
can happen in many ways; but in essentials this misfortune means one of two things. Either the machine has
got itself into such a position (*e.g.*, tail down in a wide and
very deep trench) that although the tracks will grip the
surface the engine-power is insufficient to pull it out; or
the belly, with a dead weight of nearly 30 tons on top
of it, is resting on comparatively hard ground, while the
tracks, happening on soft patches, cut through without
gripping at all. The tank, for example, is moving parallel
and close to the forward edge of a trench. The edge gives
way under the weight of the near track, which slides down
until the sponson on that side hits the rear wall of the
trench. The fallen track is now revolving uselessly in air
or crumbling earth, the belly of the tank is resting heavily
on the parapet, and the efforts of the outer track, still on
firm ground, to overcome the consequent friction, only
succeed in embedding the sponson in the parados until the
engine can no longer force the machine forward. What
was needed was something which would give one or both
tracks a more secure grip or leverage in such cases. After
the experiences on the Somme, two separate devices were

adopted. For permanent use over soft ground iron shoes or "spuds" were clamped at intervals along the tracks; while in addition each tank carried a pair of what were known as torpedo-booms. These were cigar-shaped objects of wood and iron, about six feet long, to be clamped to each track by chains when the tank became ditched. As the tracks revolved, these booms in theory were pulled round underneath the tank until they became jammed in the ground, when, the tracks being thus brought to a standstill, the machine was able to climb out over them in the normal way. In practice, although of great use on many occasions, these booms were found to be too small and weak. In soft ground they often were dragged under the whole length of the tank and up to the surface again behind: in hard ground, the chains were apt to part under the strain. A greatly superior development of this idea (to be described in its turn) was tested and adopted after the battle of Messines.

I offer no apology for this digression on unditching. Throughout the battles of the Somme, Arras, Messines, and Ypres, by day and by night, during approach marches and under fire in action, this unsavoury process might fall at any moment to the lot of any crew. On at least one occasion at Ypres a whole company of twelve tanks was ditched hopelessly before it even reached the front line, and a few days before, in the same dismal area, out of two companies of the same battalion (my own) which went over at zero, only one tank returned before the end of the day. One other had been blown to pieces, the remaining twenty-one were ditched, temporarily or for ever, here and there about our little sector of that water-logged battlefield. Most of them had struggled somehow into action, and some were extricated from bogs or shell-holes half a dozen times before their exhausted crews gave up the struggle. At least another fifty from other battalions were in similar case that evening. Ypres, of course, was exceptional, and tanks should never have been used there; but until their proper function was discovered at Cambrai, he was a fortunate commander who could take his machine in and out of action anywhere without a case of ditching on the way.

Reverting finally to the lessons of the Somme, it was felt by most officers and men of the new unit that, well as they had done on many occasions, more might have been accomplished. They suffered none of the delusions which the Press was fostering at home. The lack of foresight in some directions was obvious enough now. At the same time it was realised that the tanks had been put to an unreasonable test. They were constructed for fair ground and fair weather; they had been granted neither. There had been insufficient time to train the crews. On account of the secrecy maintained at the start, it was impossible for infantry commanders and their men to become acquainted with tank tactics; but this want of co-operation was not remedied, as it should have been, before the later actions. Springing from the same source of ignorance was the mischievous tendency to use tanks in driblets instead of in masses—a tendency which the Tank Corps had to fight throughout its existence.

It was proved that the preparations for a battle required an infinite amount of work and forethought. There were contingencies to be considered such as affected no other arm. Especially was this the case with reconnaissance; for success or failure hung upon the tank commanders' familiarity, from thorough coaching beforehand, with the ground they had to cover. Once in action, they could see very little, while maps were almost useless in a devastated country, and each officer instead had to carry in his mind the look of almost every tree-stump and every mound of rubble.

If tanks lost their way, apart from other consequences, the infantry were very apt to follow them and lose their own direction. Another difficulty, springing in part from the small size of the unit and in part from the bad practice of employing tanks in driblets, was that subaltern tank officers often found themselves working alone or in pairs with divisions or even with corps, and conferring on tactical points with G.S.O.I.'s and Generals. They had not the experience or authority needed to combat ill-advised demands, and as a result were often set to perform impossible tasks.

If the Heavy Section was to remain, still more if it was to be expanded, everything went to show the urgent need of reforming it as a fully equipped and independent organisation like the Flying Corps, whose requirements in many ways resembled its own. It must have its responsible staff to decide finally all questions dealing purely with tank warfare, its intelligence branch run on individual lines, its technical officers, its signal service, its workshops and depots, its transport and supply. Such a proposal was put forward after the first Somme battles, and as a proof that the mistakes and disappointments of that period were outweighted greatly on the credit side, the suggestion was adopted at once. Before the end of September the expansion and new establishment were authorised. Lieut.-Colonel Elles was given the command in France; and the building of a thousand improved tanks was put in hand without delay.

CHAPTER IV.

EXPANSION: THE BATTLES IN FRONT OF ARRAS.

I.

A BIG step forward had been taken; but its initial symptoms were very modest in character. The headquarters of the Tank Corps (as the companies had now become in fact if not in name) began life in a single hut in the village of Beauquesne. The provisional establishment allowed only for a Colonel Commanding (Colonel Elles), a Brigade Major, a Staff Captain, a D.A.A. and Q.M.G., and an Intelligence Officer. The corps was still known officially as the Heavy Section or Heavy Branch, M.G.C., and continued to be so styled for another nine months; but actually, the moment it became a self-contained organisation, with its staff, its brigades and battalions, and its administrative powers, it severed for good and all the paper ties which had connected it with its foster-parent.

Unhappily, the official attitude toward this expansion was marked throughout by that grudging spirit which the pedants in every Government Department manifest when they have to adopt an innovation against their will. There seemed to be a tacit understanding in Whitehall that the budding enterprise must be kept in its place and reminded continually of its youth and insecure status. It was not until May 1917 that the commanding officer was given the rank of Brigadier, although by that time he was command-

ing two tank brigades in the field, and the headquarters of
a third formed to receive the new battalions from England.
He had ten battalions under him when he became a Major-
General. Until he received that step his brigade commanders were only colonels, so that, although in action
they worked directly with Army Corps, any infantry
Brigadier was senior to them. Apart from the slur on
the corps and its officers, this deliberate omission caused
serious inconvenience. In its early days the Tank Corps
needed every ounce of authority it could get to help it
through its inevitable difficulties. Notwithstanding these,
at the end of 1918 it had eighteen battalions in France and
seven more in England: it had created immense workshops,
schools, and depots in both countries: it had sent detachments to Ireland and Egypt; and in the final months it
had not only led the infantry of three armies in almost every
attack, but had dictated in the most important respects how
those attacks should be conducted. Yet the officer directing
this enormous force in the field had the rank only of a
divisional commander. This plainly was wrong in principle. Had the Royal Air Force (let us say), whose position
was in many ways comparable, found itself in a similar
predicament: had it been cast brand-new during the war
instead of developing from a pre-war regular establishment
with its machinery complete, it would have advertised its
disabilities in Parliament and in the Press, and would have
forced a terrified officialdom to invest its chief with some
fantastic title and costume invented by the 'Daily Mail.'[1]
The Tank Corps, however, for all its youth and inexperi-
ence, has assimilated at least one of the better traditions of
the regular service: it does not advertise. I do not suppose
there are a thousand people outside the Army who know
anything about its work. As the tank itself has no money-
making future in peace time, it can have no permanent
interest for newspaper proprietors. And for this relief, at

[1] The spirit of prophecy must have inspired this remark, as it was written some months before the creation of Air Marshals and other heavenly bodies.

EXPANSION: THE BATTLES IN FRONT OF ARRAS

least, much thanks. The corps has done the better work because of it.

The antagonistic spirit to which I have adverted discovered another fertile field for its intrigues in England. Expansion was in progress there as well. There can be no difference of opinion as to the unexpected common-sense which placed Colonel Elles, an experienced soldier from a technical corps, in command in France; nor, unhappily, can there be any as to the injustice (to put it on the lowest grounds) of shelving Colonel Swinton at home. He also was an engineer, and therefore peculiarly suitable for the command; but apart from that, if any one man was responsible for the official adoption of the tank — the solitary triumphant experiment which the war produced—it was he. There was no so-called public pressure, engendered by the agitation of cheap newspapers; for neither Press nor public knew anything worth disclosing until the first machines were already at Thetford. It was Colonel Swinton's fertility of thought, the inspiration of his belief, his influence and persistent advocacy, which did more than all else to wear down the maddening barrier of departmental indifference. He won at last some measure of support for his ideas: he organised the new unit, and saw his hopes of it justified in the field; and then, just as the embryo was expanding into full life and vigour, the old influences made themselves felt once more. Somebody said (or so it will be most charitable to suppose), "Hullo, here's another of these infernal sappers! This won't do! The whole war is being run by R.E.'s and gunners, as it is. We must get rid of him!" He was got rid of. It was found (most opportunely) that the Committee of Imperial Defence could do without his services no longer, and he returned to his duties as Assistant-Secretary. An infantry Brigadier, who had performed a very notable feat of arms in the first months of the war, but who knew nothing about tanks, came down to Thetford to take over the command, and gave an encouraging tone to the proceedings by declaring quite openly, the moment he arrived, that he was come to put some discipline into the corps, that he took no interest whatever in the tanks, and that he did not want to see them.

In view of these and other examples of our methods and manners, the rapid and enormous growth of the corps may seem surprising. To a great degree it wrought its own salvation. But in fact the opposition came mostly from those quarters at home where every reasonable being would expect to find it, and could to that extent be disregarded as merely symptomatic and inevitable; and the supporters of the enterprise were far more influential. In France also there was an ever-increasing body of opinion in its favour. And once it was taken up in earnest, those qualities of energy and thoroughness which our race seems always to reserve for times of crisis came fully into play. It is indeed refreshing to turn from these petty irritations to the really astonishing work which now was carried through in both countries. At home, the camp at Thetford was abandoned. E and F Companies, or what was left of them, with all their tanks and stores and baggage, were transferred bodily to the other end of England. At Bovington, near Wool in Dorsetshire, a hutted camp capable of holding as it stood half a dozen infantry battalions had been taken over toward the end of 1916. By the first weeks of the new year five tank battalions and a reinforcement depot were in process of formation there. On the great moors which stretched away to the north there was ample room for training; and once more rows of hangars and repair-shops were springing up, trenches were being dug and craters blown, while the inhabitants of Wool were annoyed rather than mystified by the melodramatic precautions attending the arrival of every trainload of tanks. Instructors appeared like mushrooms: there were courses in tank-driving, maintenance, gunnery, signalling, reconnaissance, bombing, and the care of pigeons. Near Lulworth Cove, where trippers used to make pilgrimage before the war, a battle-practice range came into being. A little later, while

EXPANSION: THE BATTLES IN FRONT OF ARRAS 51

Bovington itself was growing week by week, other camps were taken over at Wareham and Swanage, until most of the military accommodation in the Isle of Purbeck housed what once had been the Heavy Section. And in the meantime, developments even more striking had been taking place in France. From four rather forlorn little companies, living as it were from hand to mouth, the corps sprang at a bound into a huge and complicated organisation, with its own territory, works, and depots, and every apparatus for carrying on its lethal industry. A large area, lying between the river Ternoise and the direct Hesdin-St Pol road, was allotted to it. To Bermicourt, a village almost in the centre of this country, Colonel Elles removed his headquarters from Beauquesne early in October '16. Twenty-four acres near the river were taken for central workshops and stores. In a few weeks, as well as the ubiquitous hangars, immense steel and iron sheds had arisen, and continued to grow in numbers and size until they covered six acres. Stalls for tanks, like the old elephant stables of Carthage, lined one side of the testing-ground. There were huts for a staff which grew to 1200 officers and men, cinema-theatres, a rest-camp and hospital, a compound holding 500 Chinese labourers, and, for a time, a reinforcement depot. From Erin Station, eleven lines of rail, with 10,500 feet of sidings, led into the main enclosure. A few hundred yards away was a driving and mechanical school, with its own training-ground. And long before the end of 1917 the original twenty-four acres of stores and workshops were getting overcrowded. In addition to the vast accumulation of equipment, ranging from engines and armour-plate down to split-pins and motor-bicycle parts, there were always there two or three hundred tanks in every stage of dismemberment or reconstruction. Every machine sent out from England (perhaps 3000 in all) came from Le Havre to Erin to be tested, equipped, and issued to units; and every machine salved on the battlefield was returned there for repair. More ground, therefore, was taken over in the area itself; a great driving-school was formed on the old front line at Wailly, near Arras; the whole reinforcement depot moved out to Le Treport; and a school of gunnery, capable before long of taking three battalions at a time, came into being among the sand-dunes and gimcrack villas of Merlimont, on the coast near Etaples. In the Bermicourt area there was not a village now which did not house some detail of the corps—M.T. Workshops, Salvage, Supply, and Signal Companies, &c.—or was not reserved for billeting battalions as they arrived from England or returned from the line to refit. It should be needless to add that the headquarters in Bermicourt Château kept pace with this expansion. In the beginning the staff was palpably inadequate; before the end it was comparable in size to that of an army.

Taking it all in all, I doubt if there can be anything, even in the exceptional records of this war, to equal for extent and variety the growth of the technical, instructional, and supply branches of the Tank Corps during the last two years. It was the natural habit of the combatant units to complain loudly of all three; but to visit Erin at any time, to see there the scores of tanks, the acres of vast workshops and store-sheds, the miles of sidings, and the tons upon tons of gear and equipment, and to reflect that every pound of this material had come from England since the winter of '16, was enough to make one pause and wonder; and looking back now at the whole industry, raised in so short a time from nothing at all, it appears, with all its obvious shortcomings, a highly remarkable achievement of forethought and energy.

I have gone a little far ahead. The growth was rapid, but it was not all accomplished at a blow; and it was the least known and advertised aspect of the expansion. Side by side with the rise of Erin as a base, the combatant branch was growing also. The old companies in France had become battalions, and the latter were multiplying at a rate of one a month.

EXPANSION: THE BATTLES IN FRONT OF ARRAS

About the time when E and F Companies were leaving Thetford for Bovington, A, B, C, and D were withdrawn from Acheux to Bermicourt. They were raised at once to their new status, under the same alphabetical designations, and volunteers were called for from other arms of the service. Originally each of these new battalions was to have had 72 tanks; but partly on account of the difficulties of production, partly for simplicity of tactical handling, this number was by degrees whittled down to one-half. The eventual establishment for a battalion was fixed at three companies of 12 tanks each, and a Workshops Company; making a total of 36 tanks, and some 800 officers and men, commanded by a Lieutenant-Colonel. Each combatant company consisted of three fighting sections of 4 tanks, and one spare or supply section. The Workshops Company, like the others, was commanded by a Major, and was responsible for the upkeep of the tanks and for all repairs which could be executed in the field. At a later date these battalion workshops were abolished and merged into brigade organisations, Engineer Officers, with a small staff, remaining with the units. The latter, in theory (and to a large extent in fact), were now capable of effecting their own minor repairs and maintenance.

There was an Equipment Officer to each battalion, and subsequently three assistants for the companies. No less important was the Reconnaissance branch. In addition to the Battalion R.O. (a Captain), there were three company R.O.'s and three assistants, with a staff of draughtsmen. In most of the battalions the standard of this essential work, both in the office and in the field, was very high. The Tank Corps was responsible for many innovations in this branch of Intelligence, such as the more general use of layered maps, and of the study of aeroplane photographs. The Germans, whose map-making, oddly enough, was usually poor, were led to adopt the device of layering by examples which they found in captured tanks.

Finally, each battalion started life with an imposing array of every type of motor transport—light cars, box-cars, lorries, mobile repair shops, motor-bicycles, &c. But this Utopian equipment was too good to last. In France the transport was pooled; and over this fatal step, and the appeals and recriminations evoked by it ever since, it is better to be silent. General Grant has said that military history should be truthful; but no good purpose can be served by dwelling on such tragedies. They are common to the human race—or at any rate to the human army.

With the nine battalions now in process of formation, four in France and five at home, it was proposed to make up three brigades. Two came at once into being: the 1st, consisting of C and D Battalions, under Colonel C. D. A. Baker-Carr, D.S.O.; and the 2nd, of A and B Battalions, under Colonel A. Courage, M.C. The 3rd Brigade H.Q., Colonel J. Hardress Lloyd, D.S.O., commanding, was formed soon after to await the new arrivals. As the latter assembled in France the units would be redistributed until there were three battalions in each brigade.

Before finishing with the subject of expansion, certain auxiliary services fall to be mentioned. The Tank Corps had its own signal branch, including wireless and pigeons. The former was tried in tanks especially fitted for the purpose, but was not strikingly successful. Cable-laying machines were also used in the Ypres salient. Pigeons, until the final advance, when the lofts could not keep up, proved by far the most rapid and reliable means of communication during an action. Two birds, when available, were carried in each tank; and their behaviour in the most trying circumstances imaginable was truly exemplary. I shall never forget the placid and almost *blasé* air with which a couple in my own tank continued to sip their water, and take apparently an intelligent interest in the proceedings while, in a sweating atmosphere of petrol fumes, high explosive, and decomposing humanity, we were crashing over fallen tree-trunks along the Poelcapelle road.

EXPANSION: THE BATTLES IN FRONT OF ARRAS 55

Supply-tanks were first used at the battle of Messines. These were old Mark II.'s with their guns removed, and special sponsons substituted — the equivalents, in fact, of the eighteenth-century warships armed *en flûte* and filled with stores. Each tank carried 300 gallons of petrol and 80 of water; track and engine-oil and grease in proportion; and upwards of 10,000 rounds of S.A.A. and 6-pdr. shell. This improvisation was found so invaluable, especially in devastated areas where roads were few, that a little later regular supply companies were formed, each of three sections, and attached to brigades, the sections working with battalions. A further development ensued when the infantry, profiting indirectly by this service, asked for supply tanks of their own. A number of gun-carriers, as well as Mark II.'s, were used for this purpose in the autumn of 1918.

The gun-carriers deserve a word of notice. They were tanks built on the tractor principle and designed to carry 60-pounder guns across country. The gun was lifted up bodily, carriage and all, by long arms projecting from the front of the machine, between the tracks; it was then carried like a baby to its destination and there lowered to earth again. These G.C. tanks, although driven by Tank Corps mechanics, came under the orders of the Garrison Artillery. They were used for the first time at Ypres on 31st July 1917. But that half-drowned battlefield, which all but ruined the Tank Corps itself, was the beginning and the end of the gun-carriers' legitimate career. On fair ground they might have proved valuable, but they were never tried again; and after a period of desuetude they were consigned to the hack-work of supply.

The salvage companies formed yet another branch of the corps, and a most hard-working and ill-requited one. It was their tedious, and often perilous, duty to salve all tanks left completely derelict, from whatever cause, behind our front line. More than once the personnel were working for days on end under shell-fire, and they suffered a high percentage of casualties. This was especially the case in the Ypres salient in the dreadful winter of 1917-18, when there were close on 190 tanks lying rusting in the mud. Some had disappeared almost completely, and round others coffer-dams had to be built to raise them from the lagoons in which they lay half-submerged. Yet ninety were salved here in ten months; and from the battalions, fresh from the fighting in this God-forsaken area, came volunteers to help in the work! No words can do justice to the difficulties which the salvers had to overcome in that morass, or to the labour and ingenuity which overcame them. I can speak with some authority on these amphibious conditions, for I left my own tank there with two feet of water already above the floor, and all the King's coffer-dams and all the King's men failed to get her out. I have no figures to quote as to the numbers salved on later and less inhuman battlefields, but the total must have run into hundreds. And this devoted work, unrecognised as it was, had its unexpected reward. When strikes at home were delaying production, it was the old rescued tanks lying in scores at Erin that were furbished up and put into commission again to bring battalions up to strength for Cambrai and the big battles of August 1918.

II.

While expansion was in progress the lessons of the Somme with regard to the capabilities of the tanks themselves were considered and put to good purpose. In November '16, at a conference of the Mechanical Warfare Supply Department, Lieut.-Colonel Stern, the chief engineer, dealt with the programme of future construction. There were then in France seventy Mark I. tanks. Fifty Mark II.'s were to arrive by January, and a similar number of Mark III.'s by the following month. (These last, of course, never materialised.) From February to

EXPANSION: THE BATTLES IN FRONT OF ARRAS 57

May Mark IV.'s were to be produced at the rate of twenty a week; Mark V.'s would be available in August; and a new light tank, the Medium A or "Whippet," by Christmas. We have already dealt with the Mark IV., and the Mark V. and Whippets can be considered when eventually they did make an appearance. For this programme was too optimistic: no Mark IV.'s arrived until after the battle of Arras, and the Mark V. was not ready in any numbers for another year.

In the spring of 1917, therefore, when the Tank Corps went into battle for the first time in its new form, the situation was as follows: At Bovington, Brigadier-General Gore Anley, D.S.O., with Colonel M. B. Matthew Lannowe as G.S.O.I., superintended the training of the five new battalions, until in March he went to the Administrative Headquarters of the Heavy Branch in London, where two months later he was succeeded by Major-General Sir John Capper, K.C.B., R.E. Brigadier-General W. Glasgow, C.M.G., took over the command at Bovington. In February or March the first Mark IV.'s arrived there for training purposes, followed in April by an experimental Whippet. Meanwhile in France Colonel Elles and his brigade commanders were organising and training the new establishment, and the great shops at Erin were growing appreciably every day. A highly interesting development, launched the previous autumn from Thetford—namely, the Palestine detachment—was nearing the day of trial in that inhospitable region, and will be dealt with in the next chapter.

The general situation in France and Flanders was altered greatly by the German withdrawal in March. During the winter minor operations had cleared the enemy out of the positions north of the Ancre which he had held so tenaciously and so long, and by the beginning of March we were within 2000 yards of Bapaume on the Albert road. Between Bapaume and Arras the Germans now occupied a very pronounced salient. A proposal to drive in its northern flank with the help of two battalions of tanks was cancelled because it was found impossible to provide the latter at the time. Before anything further could be done the enemy forestalled this and other plans of attack by an extensive and very skilful retreat, reaching at one point a depth of twenty miles. The pursuing armies, following up from Arras to Soissons, found themselves confronted by the Hindenburg Line, whose existence was well known but whose character had been hitherto a matter of conjecture. It is the custom to depreciate this much-advertised defence system. Colonel Buchan, allowing his natural hankering after prophecy to outrun his usual discretion, observed rather rashly (in the beginning of 1918) that "the marvellous new Siegfried line was not a fortress from which he (the enemy) could sally, but a prison." In view of the "sallies" which followed hard upon this assertion, it would appear, with others of its kind, to be susceptible of modification. In point of fact, the Hindenburg Line was neither a fortress nor a prison: it simply was what it professed to be, an extremely strong entrenched system designed for an especial purpose which, on the whole, it adequately fulfilled.

Sir Douglas Haig, writing of the intended stroke which was frustrated in part by the withdrawal of the enemy, says, "My object was to deal him a blow which would force him to use up reserves." South of the Ancre such a blow was now out of the question: the pursuing armies found themselves faced by this new defensive system, while behind them there lay the whole devastated area of the Somme to complicate their lines of supply. Much had to be done before an advance was possible here. But the northern half of the plan, to drive the enemy farther back from Arras and from off the Vimy Ridge, remained unaffected; and it was decided to carry it through. Its main object was still to divert the mass of German reserves away from the Soissons region, where the French were to make the principal attack on the southern pivot of the Hindenburg Line.

EXPANSION: THE BATTLES IN FRONT OF ARRAS

The battle of Arras, as it is called, was timed to open at dawn on the 9th April. Three armies were taking part, and Colonel Baker-Carr's 1st Tank Brigade was to co-operate with all three. Only 60 tanks, Marks I. and II., were available, of which 8 were allotted to the 1st Army in the attack on the Vimy Ridge, 40 to the 3rd Army astride the Scarpe, and 12 to the 5th Army (which did not come into the battle until the 11th) on the right. As this operation had been long foreseen, the reconnaissance officers of the 1st Brigade had begun their survey of the area as early as January. Dumps were formed at Neuville St Vaast, Roclincourt, Achicourt, and Beaurains. The three groups of tanks were detrained respectively at Acq, Montenescourt, and Achiet-le-Grand. These preliminary movements were as trying as they always are: the trains were forty-eight hours late, the sponson trolleys gave endless trouble by breaking away or overturning, and much extra work and anxiety resulted from the loss of 20,000 gallons of petrol in a railway accident. Some days before the battle, however, all the machines were lying up in positions close to the front line, some of C Battalion being concealed in the ditch of the citadel of Arras.

For tank operations the ground north of the Scarpe possessed every possible disadvantage. No one who has seen the region of the old front line about Ecurie and Neuville St Vaast in early spring can wonder that Mark II. tanks, provided only with torpedo-booms for unditching, failed to get far. The soil is heavy loam above chalk, inclined to be wet in any season; and as it had been fought over since 1914, it was one great maze of half-obliterated trenches and craters whose walls crumbled at a touch. South of Arras conditions were slightly better. The ground was hardly less cut up, but the surface was firmer. Much depended, however, upon the weather. The early days of April were fine and clear, and the soil, except in the marshy valley of the Scarpe, dried rapidly. But on zero night, with that fatality which seemed to pursue our efforts for so long, the wind shifted, the sky clouded over, and rain began to fall. Before long it was snowing.

Zero was at 5.30 A.M. With every big offensive our artillery fire had increased in intensity; and on this morning, after seven days' preliminary bombardment, the opening barrage was more tremendous than anything which had been seen on the Somme. Under its protection the Canadians and the 12th Corps reached the crest of the Vimy with little trouble. But the tanks were unable to follow. While the real struggle was beginning in the rain and sleet around La Folie Farm and Hill 145, the eight tank crews were toiling with their ineffective gear to extricate their machines from the hopeless ground on the slope below. Not one of them got into action. To the right, however, in the Scarpe Valley, the section working with the 6th Corps had done good work; and south of the river, C Battalion had given another convincing example, to those who had eyes to see, of the new methods which were subverting the ancient principles of attack. The night had begun with a serious disaster. The tanks started from the village of Achicourt. The little river Crinchon, flowing into the Scarpe, had created patches of bog which in places had become covered with a crust of what appeared to be hard soil. The reconnaissance of the route had been perfunctory: it led straight over one of these concealed traps; and the officer responsible had not even tested the ground with his stick. The night was intensely dark, the wind was gusty, and the rain falling heavily; while in Achicourt, close by, a dump had been blown up, and was still burning and drawing the enemy's fire. Amid this uproar and confusion six tanks drove one after the other into the bog, and were engulfed beyond all immediate repair. This inexcusable calamity would have entailed more serious consequences than it did but for the admirable work of other tanks engaged in the same region. The German position here was one of great strength. South of the elaborate system of trenches around Tilloy-les-Mofflaines extended a formidable work, upwards of half a mile long, known from its shape as the Harp. It marked the junction of the northern end of the Hindenburg Line with the old front system, and it rested partly on the height called Telegraph Hill, also heavily fortified. "The Harp," to quote Colonel Buchan, "was such a place as in the early days of the Somme would have baffled us for a month or more. It was stronger than Contalmaison or Pozières or Guillemont. It was rushed by a batch of tanks, some of which stuck fast in its entanglements, while others forced their way through to the plain beyond. In a very short time there was no Harp, and the garrison were on their way westward to the cages." No one acquainted with the deliberate progress of the Mark II. over bad ground would speak of it as "rushing" anything; but, fast or slow, these old machines on this occasion achieved a really notable success on a large scale. While some had been dealing faithfully with the Harp, others to north and south had cleared Tilloy and crawled up and over Telegraph Hill; and their exertions were largely responsible for the capture by the 3rd Army of the whole German second position south of the Scarpe, including two miles of the Hindenburg Line, within four hours after zero.

The 5th Army attack was not due to begin until the 11th. But an attempt, arranged at the last moment, was made the same morning to break the line opposite Bullecourt with a company of tanks of D Battalion. It suffered the fate of most enterprises so hastily planned. A regular blizzard broke soon after dark: the tanks, although they never lost their way, could not arrive in time; and the Australians, who had been lying out all night on the railway embankment south of Bullecourt, were withdrawn before daybreak. Had the attack materialised, it would have possessed especial interest, for it was designed on the principles advocated throughout by the Tank Corps itself and now universally accepted. The tanks, massed on a narrow front, were to have preceded the infantry with no artillery preparation and no barrage until they actually reached the German front line. In other words, a genuine surprise was aimed at. But the fiasco caused by the snowstorm discouraged the 5th Army Staff. When the attempt was repeated on the original date, April 11th, they reverted to the usual methods — with lamentable results. The enemy, already on the alert by reason of the battle farther north, was warned of the attack by the barrage coming down at zero before the tanks had crossed No Man's Land. Field-guns, pushed far forward for anti-tank defence, were ready to get on to their mark at once; while the tanks showed up clearly on the snow the moment the dawn broke. The sections of the company were scattered on a wide front, and one, in the centre, was detailed to push through the Hindenburg Line without any infantry support at all. There were eleven tanks in all, most of which, handled with extreme gallantry, crossed the dreaded Hindenburg trenches and got well into the fight. One, with all on board wounded and every round spent, was hit and disabled on its way back. Another reached the edge of Bullecourt village, came to a standstill there through gear trouble which could not be remedied, and after holding out for some time without seeing any of the infantry who should have been in support, was only evacuated when the Germans brought a field-gun into the houses and opened fire. A third, less fortunate, received a shell in the petrol-tanks on the edge of the enemy's wire, and went up instantly in flames, only three of the crew escaping. A fourth was hit twice within a minute, the first shell coming in through the cab, decapitating the driver and then bursting inside. In all, nine tanks were known to have been disabled by shell-fire, although one of them returned later with a hole in its roof. Of the fate of the remaining two nothing was ever known with certainty. They disappeared into the blue. Major W. H. L. Watson, D.C.M., who commanded the company, gives the following account of their loss: "Our aeroplanes had seen

EXPANSION: THE BATTLES IN FRONT OF ARRAS

two tanks crawling over the open country beyond the Hindenburg trenches to Riencourt, followed by four or five hundred cheering Australians. Through Riencourt they swept, and on to the large village of Hendecourt, five miles beyond the trenches. They entered the village, still followed by the Australians...."[1] No further definite news of them was ever received. Tanks and infantry alike were swallowed up and lost in the smoke of the battle. At the end of the day the Germans still held Riencourt; and Hendecourt, far behind, with all its gallant but unsupported assailants, was retaken at once. But the feat was a startling one, and by itself it makes the Australians' complaint, that they were "let down" by the tanks, seem, to say the least of it, ungenerous. This charge, which Colonial troops are but too ready to fling at every one except themselves, was further confuted by the whole record and losses of D Battalion in the attack. Almost the whole company got into action: every one of the eleven tanks was disabled or lost; and 50 per cent of the personnel were killed, wounded, or missing. The attack was a costly failure, for while hardly a yard of ground was won, the infantry casualties totalled several thousand, and an entire company of tanks was destroyed; but the responsibility rested, not with the latter, but with whosoever insisted on their employment in a manner continually condemned by every officer in the Tank Corps itself. No one outside that corps understood the proper functions of the machines, or had even taken to heart the lessons of the Somme. The German position at Bullecourt, protecting as it did the vital junction at Queant of the main Hindenburg Line with the Drocourt Switch, was immensely strong. It had an outer belt of wire 25 feet broad, machine-gun emplacements of ferroconcrete 125 yards apart along both the main and support lines, a continuous tunnel, stretching for miles, beneath the latter, and numerous semi-independent strong points. The

[1] 'A Company of Tanks,' by Major W. H. L. Watson, D.C.M., chapter iv., 'Blackwood's Magazine' for June 1919.

tanks had proved that even this was no obstacle to them; but if they were used at all, they should have been used in greater numbers and in mass, with infantry trained beforehand, and supported by a barrage designed not to warn, but to aid in surprising, the enemy. Far more just than the Australians' complaints was Colonel Elles's remark after the battle: "This is the best thing tanks have done yet."[1]

On the same morning, C Battalion was in action again in front of Arras. Here the Germans still held the villages of Fampoux and Monchy, with the Hindenburg trenches south of Telegraph Hill. In the centre of this position, south east of Arras, between the Scarpe and the Cambrai road, there rises a very conspicuous height known to fame as Orange Hill. It commands a view behind the whole length of the Vimy Ridge, and, in consequence, overlooked our new battery positions and lines of approach on that side. On the eastern end of the hill, beyond a slight dip in the crest, stood the village of Monchy-le-Preux, once a pleasant cluster of trees and red-tiled roofs, but now, since our heavy howitzers had been at work on it, no more than a mass of rubble and splintered stumps. It is a famous village, not only for the fighting which has centred about it, but also for the remarkable myth which it perpetuates. The attack launched on the 3rd Army front on April 11th had Monchy for its main objective; and before telling the true story of its capture, it is interesting to note how the latter is usually represented. In Sir Douglas Haig's despatch the event is described as follows: "Two English infantry brigades, acting in cooperation with cavalry, attacked Monchy-le-Preux at 5 A.M., and after hard fighting, *in which tanks arrived at an opportune moment*, carried the position." The italics, of course, are my own. Colonel Buchan, always too faithful to his brief, goes one better. He does not mention tanks at all. He does, however, mention the cavalry. "Next day, the 11th," he says, "Monchy was carried, with the assistance of a

[1] 'A Company of Tanks,' by Major Watson.

detachment of cavalry, but not without heavy losses."
Now, in the first place, as thousands of people know what
really happened at Monchy, these repeated references to
the mounted arm almost compel one to paraphrase the
plaintiff in Whistler v. Ruskin, and ask, "Why drag in the
cavalry?" The skeletons of General Bulkeley-Johnson's
men and horses still litter Orange Hill[1] to testify that the
tactics of Balaclava, Salisbury Plain, and Amiens are in
no sense suitable to modern warfare. Secondly, this distortion of the facts has done a grave injustice to a newer
and less socially popular corps. There is a still more pertinent question which might be asked: "Why leave out the
tanks?" For what actually happened at Monchy-le-Preux,
put very briefly, was this.

On the evening of 10th April there were in the neighbourhood of Feuchy Chapel, on the Cambrai road at the
foot of Orange Hill, the headquarters of one of the infantry
brigades due to attack Monchy next morning, a brigade of
cavalry, and six tanks of C Battalion, who were to lead
the assault. Our line then ran beyond the crest of the
hill, within five hundred yards of Monchy itself. Zero had
been fixed for 5 A.M. After dark four tanks (the other two
having developed mechanical trouble) moved forward. One
soon became badly ditched; but the remaining three
climbed the slope during the black early hours of the 11th,
and at the advertised time of zero passed through the line
of half-frozen outposts lying in shell-holes across the hill.
But no barrage came down, nor was there any sign of the
supporting infantry. Although no notification whatever
had reached the tank commanders or even their company headquarters, which was close to that of the infantry
brigade at Feuchy Chapel, zero, after being altered twice,
had been postponed finally for two hours! In the meantime dawn was breaking; and for the tanks to loiter about
the snow-covered ground of No Man's Land, on the summit

[1] This was written in the spring of 1919, when the bones of horses and a great
accumulation of rotting cavalry equipment still lay thick in front of Monchy.

E

of the hill, would have been to invite destruction. After waiting a short time, the tank commanders therefore decided to go on alone, trusting to the infantry to overtake them. As day came, the trio, still entirely unsupported, entered Monchy. They proceeded methodically to clear the whole village, cruising about the ruins and driving out before them, after some stiff fighting, all of the garrison who had not gone to earth in dug-outs or cellars. Following up the fugitives, the tanks presently emerged through the last demolished houses on the far side. They were now on the reverse slope of the hill; and their triumphant crews could see, on the falling ground along the Scarpe Valley, the enemy's supports hurrying forward, and even the smoke of the light trains bringing up his supplies.

In the meantime, however, the dispossessed garrison of Monchy, having been cursed, exhorted, and reinforced, and realising that no infantry was following the tanks, began to work back round the outskirts of the village to north and south. It reoccupied the western edge, collected odd parties who were cowering in dug-outs, and re-manned its abandoned machine-guns. This manœuvre, besides interposing a considerable force between the tanks and our still silent lines, helped also to bring about the great cavalry fiasco. Bulkeley-Johnson's brigade, which had lost its commander the day before, was standing by its horses near Feuchy Chapel, when it was discovered by one of the German aeroplanes which usually came over about daybreak. The aeroplane dropped a few coloured lights and departed. Shortly after, shells began to fall among the horsemen; whereupon, instead of withdrawing to the rear or flank, they mounted and rode forward up the hill. The returned German machine-gunners in the enclosures west of Monchy were astonished and delighted, a little later, to perceive the whole brigade appear on the summit[1] and trot down upon them in a formation impossible

---

[1] Orange Hill, strictly speaking, is only a spur of the height on which Monchy stands, and is separated from the latter by a slight depression.

EXPANSION: THE BATTLES IN FRONT OF ARRAS 67

to miss. The result was a mere massacre. Hundreds of men and horses dropped in a few minutes; and the remainder, turning about, fled for shelter again behind the crest.[1]

All this time the three tanks were still isolated in the village. Discovering that the Germans had got round behind them, they started back through the ruins to clear the way once more and to look for their own infantry. It was nearly seven o'clock; *for an hour and a half*, in broad daylight, they had maintained their lone battle actually within Monchy-le-Preux, needing only a couple of platoons to take over what they had won. And now it was too late. At seven, as they reached the near side of the village again and began to disperse the enemy gathering there for the second time, our delayed attack opened: the barrage came down with a crash upon Monchy; and, one after the other, all three tanks were hit and disabled by our own shells!

It is difficult to write patiently about the manner in which this affair was wilfully misrepresented. It may literally be true to say that our infantry carried Monchy "after hard fighting"; for when at length they advanced, the Germans had reoccupied the place in force, and the tanks, through our own negligence, were disabled. Yet even this statement is a mere juggling with words. And as for the operation reports which misled the compilers of the official despatch at G.H.Q. into describing the single-handed victory of the tanks as an "arrival" at "an opportune moment," and which presumably burked all reference to the blunders of the staffs concerned, no adequate comment seems possible. The distortion of the facts may be left to speak for itself.

Circumstances rather similar, although not attended by such unhappy results, marked a second operation undertaken by C Battalion that morning. Four tanks started with the infantry at the proper time from Neuville Vitasse

[1] The cavalry also ran into the hostile barrage which fell on our front line as soon as the tanks advanced.

to attack that portion of the Hindenburg Line which the enemy still held from below Telegraph Hill to the village of Heninel, on the Cojeul river. Working down the trenches, followed by bombing parties, the tanks killed many of the enemy, drove the remainder underground, and helped to secure the front system at a very moderate cost. Having reached the lateral limit of their objective at Heninel itself, the four, still together, turned north-east through the village, and, moving up the north bank of the Cojeul, reached Wancourt, a larger place about a mile in rear. But the infantry was unable to follow. The tanks entered Wancourt alone, and carried on there for a long time, amid intermittent falls of snow, just such a rambling fight as their fellows had waged a few hours before in Monchy. They signalled repeatedly to the infantry to come on, but in vain; and by themselves they could secure no permanent hold on the village. At length, as their supplies of petrol were running low, they effected a successful withdrawal. This was in the afternoon, for they were in action altogether for eight or nine hours. In such execrable weather the whole performance was most creditable, and deserved better support than it received.

So far as the British armies were concerned, the battle of Arras might now have been allowed to die a natural death. With the capture of the Vimy Ridge, Orange Hill, and the Siegfried Line to the south, our immediate limited objectives had been secured, and it was plain that the larger success hoped for was beyond our powers. It had been laid down, as a condition antecedent to any serious attempt at breaking through, that not only the Hindenburg or Siegfried Line, but also the Drocourt-Queant Switch beyond, should be carried within forty-eight hours. That period had elapsed, and we had not touched the Switch except at Bullecourt, which was only an outwork to the junction at Queant. The enemy was getting up his reserves and beginning to counter-attack. But it was necessary to hold these reserves on our front, to aid the French offensive in Champagne; and in consequence the battle was continued far beyond the limits necessary to round off our initial victory. It was continued, in fact, for another month, and produced some of the most sanguinary fighting of the whole war. The tanks took part in several actions, notably at the Roeux Chemical Works on the 23rd, when they received the thanks of the corps and divisional commanders with whose units they were working. Finally, they went in again at Bullecourt on 8th May, when the infantry failed to support them, and they suffered heavy losses to no purpose.

The two battalions were now completely crippled. They had fought in nearly a dozen separate actions in a month. The losses in experienced personnel had been severe, and could not easily be replaced. As for tanks, which mattered less, since Mark II.'s would never again be used as fighting machines, C Battalion had none left at all, and D only two or three. The shattered brigade, therefore, was withdrawn to the Bermicourt area in the middle of May. There it rested and trained, received reinforcements, drew Mark IV.'s from Erin, and underwent that reshuffling of battalions which preceded its next appearance in the field in the Ypres Salient.

III.

The Arras battles marked a great step forward in the history of the Tanks Corps. Not only had it placed a brigade of two battalions in the field, but its own tactical ideas had begun insensibly to leaven the old-established theories of attack. The capture of the Harp, the wasted heroism at Hendecourt and Monchy, even the first Bullecourt fiasco on 10th April—all pointed the same way. It had been shown, more by local accidents than by design, that the classical methods of artillery preparation could be replaced by a more effective substitute; and, conversely, that the long preliminary bombardment was highly prejudicial to the use of tanks. It was proved once more that trenches, unless of exceptional width, were no obstacle at all. Another lesson to be drawn was the necessity of devising a more effective unditching gear for use in badly broken or boggy ground. The old moral of co-operation with other arms was rubbed in again and again. The senseless complaint that the tanks " let down " the infantry would never have been uttered if the latter had taken the obvious course of trying to learn something about the former's difficulties and methods, and had grasped the fact that they never were intended for use in such conditions as the guns and weather between them had produced on the Arras front as well as on the Somme. This point was the the more important because a gratifying feature of the operations had been the small percentage of mechanical breakdowns—a proof that officers and men were profiting rapidly by experience.

By the loss of the two tanks at Hendecourt—the first which the enemy had captured—a great fault in the Marks I. and II. was disclosed to him. This was the penetration of the armour by his " K " bullets. Many casualties had been incurred in this way: in the attack on the Roeux Chemical Works on 23rd May, five tanks out of eleven had the majority of their crews disabled by armour-piercing bullet wounds. The Germans now ordered every infantryman to carry a clip of this ammunition, while several hundreds of rounds were issued to each machine-gun team. But happily this discovery came too late to do any harm. The next tank action was fought by Mark IV.'s, whose improved armour was proof against the " K " bullets, which at very short range only splintered its inner facings.

CHAPTER V.

THE PALESTINE DETACHMENT.

I.

WHILE the tanks of the 1st Brigade were fighting in mud and snow at Arras, climatic problems of a very different type confronted a little detachment of the Heavy Section nearer the Equator. After the Somme it was decided to send a company of twelve tanks to Egypt to assist in the advance on Syria.[1] Major Nutt, of E Company, who had been in Egypt before with the armoured cars, was given the command. E Company also supplied most of the personnel. The total combatant strength was 22 officers and 226 other ranks; while there was a workshop section provided with two 120-h.p. Holt tractors, a number of sponson trolleys and workshop trailers, two lorries, and the necessary complement of spare parts. The detachment, in spite of its diminutive size, would have to be self-supporting. It left Thetford in December 1916, the personnel sailing from Devonport, and the tanks and workshops from Avonmouth a week later. An extraordinary and inexcusable error signalised the embarkation. Instead of twelve Mark

[1] The idea of employing tanks in Egypt and Syria originated with Colonel Swinton, who proposed that they should be used in the advance on El Arish, early in the campaign. The authorities laughed at the idea of tanks operating over sand; and it was only after the fall of El Arish that the suggestion was grudgingly adopted. In this connection I would like to point out that in the "Report on the Advance of the Egyptian Expeditionary Force," an official publication edited by Lieut.-Colonel Pirie Gordon, which professes to give the name and details of every unit connected, however remotely, with the Third Battle of Gaza, and which actually includes in the list A.S.C. depots at Alexandria, the Tank Department is not so much as mentioned!

II.'s, fresh from the makers, eight old training machines, which had been in use for months and were due to proceed to the new camp in Dorset, were shipped at Avonmouth, while the Egyptian detachment's tanks were on their way to Bovington! Before the Admiralty could be informed of the mistake, tons of cargo, including heavy guns, had been lowered on top of the changelings in the ship, and then permission to unload the latter was refused. The company, therefore, on its arrival in Egypt in January, found itself with only two-thirds of its establishment of tanks, and those not even new. Some of them, indeed, were nearly worn out, and all were dirty; and the Thetford mud, baked hard by a month in a ship's hold close to the engine-room, had to be chipped out of the tracks with chisels. It was a week or more before some of the machines could be moved at all.

The secrecy which, in theory, shrouded their coming was so fallacious that within six weeks photographs of them were found on a captured Bedouin. This in itself was a small matter; but it was a pity that the demonstrations carried out on the desert at Gilban, which advertised to all and sundry the fact of the tanks' arrival, were not devoted to a better purpose than the satisfaction of the natural curiosity of General officers and their staffs. No infantry took part in these displays. Only after the second battle of Gaza were combined rehearsels by the two arms instituted as a regular feature of training. Nevertheless, the army in Egypt seems to have realised far sooner than the army in France that without co-operation founded on mutual familiarity with each others' tactics and limitations, tanks and infantry would never work together to the best advantage. In Egypt also there was from the start less of the jealousy and obstruction which hampered the heavy branch nearer home. The isolation of the detachment put it to some extent out of reach of meddling interference, and enabled it to solve its peculiar problems in its own way.

When the detachment arrived Sir Archibald Murray was already across the Sinai desert and had reached the Egyptian frontier. While the railway was being pushed up behind him along the coast to El Arish and Rafa, the Turkish Army commanded by the German General von Kressenstein withdrew to a prepared position in front of Gaza. This position we attacked on 26th March, but a dense sea-fog at dawn upset the time-table, and after suffering 4000 casualties, such ground as we had gained was abandoned under pressure of heavy counter-attacks and a threat against our flank by reinforcements from Beersheba. The tank detachment, rushed up at a few hours' notice on Egyptian 30-ton trucks to take part in these operations, was delayed at El Arish, and it detrained at Khan Yunus, fifteen miles south-west of Gaza, only to find the battle over. At Khan Yunus it remained for ten days. On 6th April the tanks trekked for eight miles across soft sand to Deir-el-Belah, nearer to the line, preparatory to the second assault on the Gaza position.

Gaza, a city of great age, acquainted with numerous battles and sieges, stands amid vast fig-groves about two miles from the sea-shore, on the old coast-road from Egypt to Syria. The Turkish position, defended now by five infantry divisions, one cavalry division, and numerous batteries—in all, perhaps 30,000 men—was one of great natural strength, as we had discovered in March. Since our first attack miles of new trenches had been dug and the whole front was very heavily wired. It stretched from Sheikh Hassan, among the sand-dunes on the coast, by El Arish Redoubt and Samson's Ridge, to the Cairo road two miles south of Gaza, and thence south-east along a series of hills to the Atawineh Ridge. Within this line was the strongly fortified Ali Muntar Ridge, immediately in front of Gaza. Detachments of cavalry and infantry at Hereira, sixteen miles from the coast, protected the left flank. The hills, seamed with gullies and old water-courses, where infantry and machine-guns found perfect cover, were admirably adapted to defence, and the trenches, under German supervision, had been skilfully sited.

Sir Archibald Murray had four Territorial infantry divisions, the 52nd, 53rd, 54th, and 74th (dismounted

Yeomanry), two mounted divisions, and the Camel Corps. His line of communications was a single railway track running for 150 miles across the Sinai Desert. Everything the army needed, even water, came by this line out of Egypt.

The plan of the second attack on Gaza fell into two phases, divided by an interval of forty-eight hours. In the first phase, while a desert column attended to the Turkish left at Hereira, three infantry divisions and the tank detachment were to carry the Sheikh Abbas and Mansura Ridges, east of the Cairo road. The attack was fixed for dawn on April 17th. After dusk on the 15th, the eight tanks trekked northward again from Deir-el-Belah, and before daybreak had reached their final lying-up positions along a dry water-course called the Wadi Ghuzze, which ran parallel to our front line. By this time, after three months' experience in Egypt and Syria, all steps possible under the circumstances had been taken to cope with the novel conditions attending tank operations over sand. It was found, for example, that the ordinary process of soaking the track links and rollers in oil produced in the desert a perfect grinding mixture which wore out very rapidly the driving sprockets. All such lubrication, therefore, was abandoned. The tracks were run absolutely dry, and with satisfactory results; for although the sprocket wheels were of the early soft-steel type, they seem to have endured longer under these arid conditions than in the mud of European battlefields. While the mud stuck everywhere, and brought with it grit and stones which induced friction, sand merely ran out of the tracks like water. From every point of view, indeed, once this and a few other modifications of treatment and mechanism had been introduced, the tanks showed a surprising aptitude for desert warfare. Ditching was almost unknown: the sand ran away from under the belly of the machine, while the tracks, with their broad bearing surface, compressed it and got a grip; and for similar reasons the steepest sand-dunes and hills were climbed with ease and at any angle. The chief troubles were the heat and the difficulty of obtaining water, and these were felt by every other arm, although, at least as regards the former, not so severely. On account of the heat no movement of tanks, save in battle or some other exceptional circumstance, took place after eight o'clock in the morning.

Six tanks were detailed for the first phase of the battle. Four, if required, were to assist the 52nd Division in the capture of the Mansura Ridge. These advanced behind the assaulting infantry up the Wadi-el-Nukhabir, a gully with high banks affording perfect cover which ran, like a huge communication trench, downward from the ridge to the Wadi Ghuzze. The tanks were not needed, however, for the enemy, taken by surprise owing to the absence of any artillery preparation beyond the ordinary counter-battery work, fled in confusion from the ridge, which was in possession of the 157th Brigade soon after six o'clock. Meanwhile, on the right, the other two tanks had led the troops of the 54th Division toward Sheikh Abbas Ridge. Here also the Turks were surprised, but they put up a stouter resistance than their fellows on Mansura. The tanks, lacking such a covered approach as the big gully on the left provided, came under observation soon after dawn, before they had reached the enemy's trenches, and one soon received a direct hit. Two of the crew were killed, and the officer lost an eye from a splinter. The hostile guns now concentrated on the derelict machine, which, after it had been abandoned, was hit again and again, set on fire and destroyed. The second tank, however, was able to carry out its task of clearing the trenches to the north and northwest of the ridge, giving the infantry valuable help. When the position was consolidated the tank returned and rallied in the Wadi-el-Nukhabir, having covered in all some 15,000 yards from the time it crossed the Wadi Ghuzze to its return. The crew, who had been in the tank for fourteen hours, were completely exhausted. In such conditions of heat as they suffered, their gallantry and endurance were remarkable.

The second phase of the battle, which opened at 5.30 A.M.

on the 19th, was designed to capture the final positions covering Gaza—namely, El Arish Redoubt and Samson's Ridge, between the sea and the Cairo road, and the Ali Muntar Ridge with its foot-hills to the south and south-east of the city. From left to right the divisions and tanks employed were as follows: 53rd Division (two tanks), 52nd (four tanks), 54th (one tank). To the right of the 54th, mounted divisions were to carry out subsidiary operations as before against the Turkish left. The French battleship *Réquin* and two British monitors assisted from the sea.

The forty-eight hours' interval between our attacks, however unavoidable, was unfortunate. The Turks, to some extent demoralised on the 17th, had time to recover themselves again, and their main position on Ali Muntar was one of exceptional strength. This ridge, ten or more miles in length, is an attenuated spine of sandy hills, covered with cactus scrub, which runs parallel to the coast just east of Gaza. It forms roughly a right-angle with the Mansura heights farther to the east. Its loftiest crest, 265 feet above the sea, looks down on the city from south of the Beersheba road. From this point the spine falls away southward, by successive narrow hillocks known to us as Outpost Hill, Lees Hill, Queen's Hill, Kurd Hill, and so on, to the valley of the Wadi Ghuzze. Two thousand yards west of the ridge, and also parallel to it, is the Cairo road, beyond which Samson's Ridge rises fairly steeply to a height of 200 feet before descending to the low sea-cliffs at Sheikh Ajlin. From Samson's Ridge the Turkish trenches ran north-east by El Arish Redoubt up the coast to Sheikh Hassan. These seaward trenches were the objectives of the 53rd Division on the left, with whose operations we will deal first.

For the whole of this battle I will paraphrase or quote textually the official report on operations drawn up by Major O. A. Forsyth-Major, second in command of the tank detachment, who writes as follows of the events on the 53rd Division's front. (Italics and interpolations in brackets are my own.)

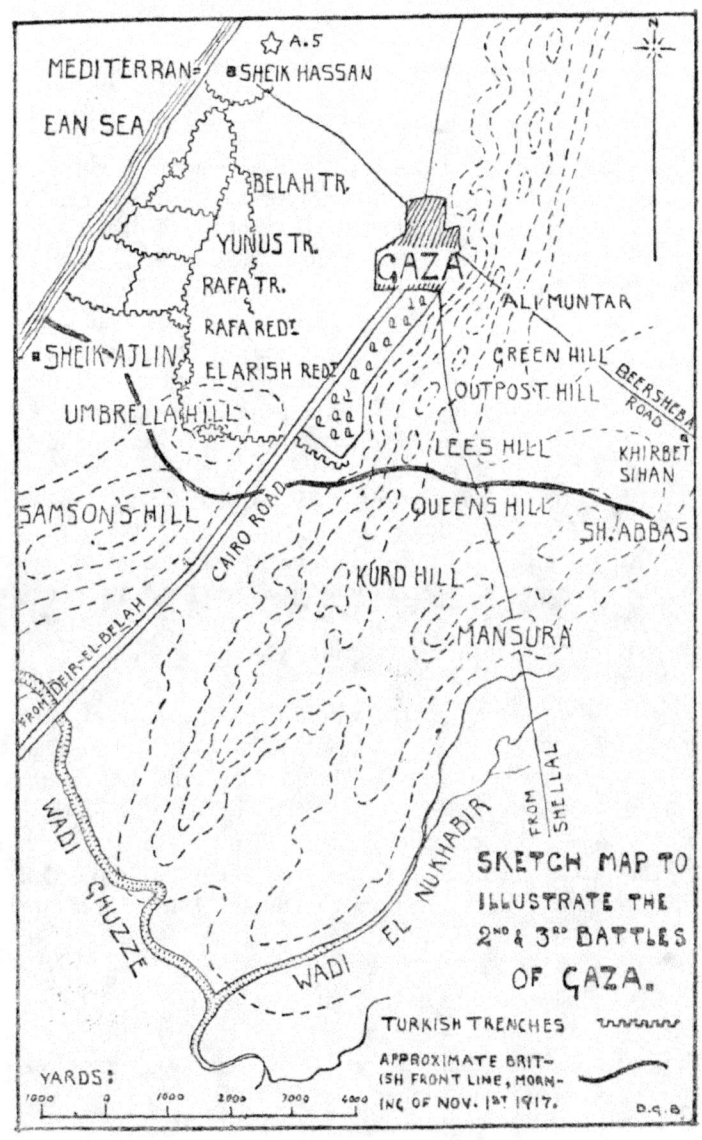

"Of the two tanks allotted to this division, one broke a track soon after going into action and remained *hors de combat* for the ensuing operations. The other tank, the 'Tiger,' therefore undertook the advance alone, and proceeded (in front of the infantry) across the sand-dunes to Samson Ridge, where it captured the redoubts, awaited the infantry's arrival, and thence advanced to attack El Arish Redoubt, being all this time under concentrated enemy machine-gun fire. Having reached this second objective, the tank was unable to swing, and the officer in command, receiving no support whatsoever from the infantry, which advanced no farther, owing to the changed tactical situation occurring in the centre of the general attack, returned over the sand-dunes *in reverse* under shell and machine-gun fire till it reached a point near Regent's Park (upwards of 5000 yards S.W. of El Arish), having fired *27,000 rounds* of ammunition during this action. All the crew, including the officer, were wounded, and all, except the officer, who took the driver's place, were in a state of complete collapse as a result of six hours' continuous strain under heavy fire."

Further advance on this flank had been postponed owing to the failure in the centre, where the 52nd Division, with four tanks, was to advance from Mansura Ridge against Outpost Hill, the strong point known as the Labyrinth, and Ali Muntar itself. The tanks were ready, and their routes taped to avoid the gullies which abounded, when, at the last moment, the G.O.C. 52nd Division cancelled their orders. They were now told to move from Mansura Ridge to the foot of Kurd Hill, 3000 yards to the westward, and there await further orders. "It was pointed out to the G.S.O.I.," says the report, "that such a move in complete darkness over unknown country might result in the tanks disappearing into the deep gullies which intersected the suggested route, and that even if the tanks reached Kurd Hill, it was highly impracticable to attack positions which had never been observed in daylight and over ground which had not been reconnoitred by the tank personnel."

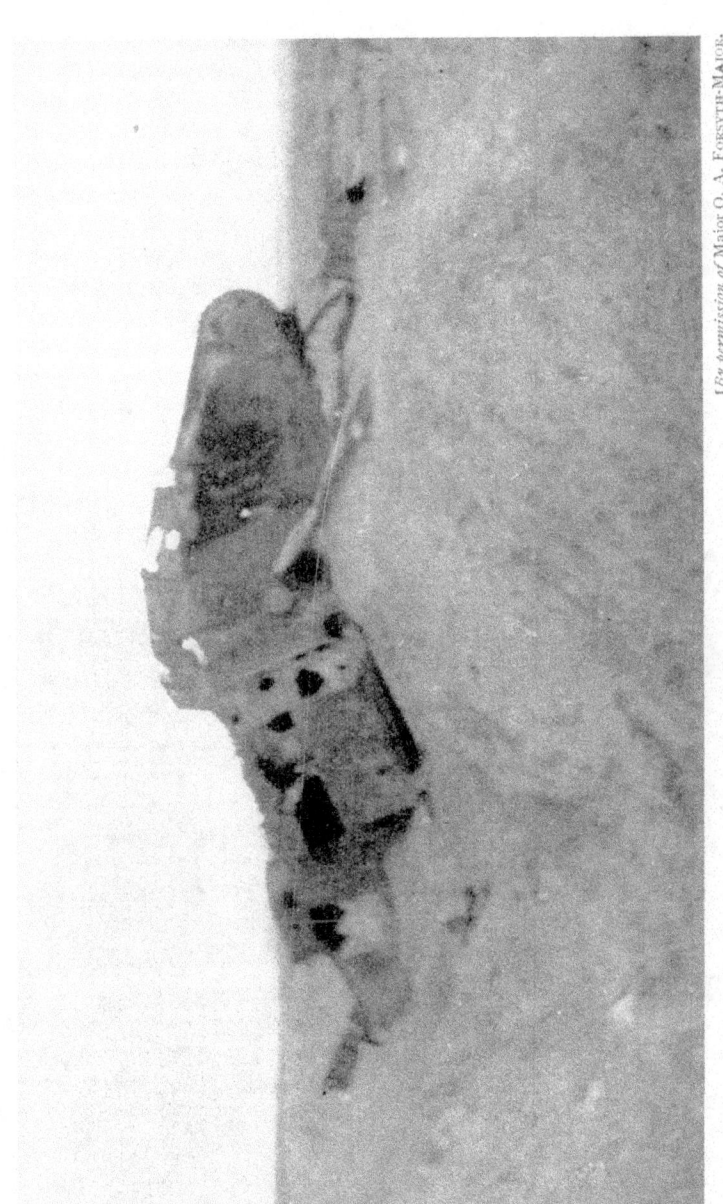

Tank on Outpost Hill, Gaza.

[*By permission of* Major O. A. Forsyth-Major.

The G.S.O.I. was obdurate, however, and at 9 P.M. the four
tanks started. In the pitchy darkness which prevailed the
cross-country route was considered too risky, and accordingly they moved by the Wadi Nukhabir and the Wadi
Ghuzze — in other words, round three sides of a square.
They did not reach Kurd Hill until 2 A.M., zero being at
6.30. As the officers were entirely ignorant as to what
they were expected to do four hours later, they had the
temerity to arouse the G.O.C. 155th Brigade from his sleep,
but as he felt disinclined to discuss matters at that early
hour, they were told that all necessary instructions would
be issued at 5.30 A.M. At six o'clock no instructions had
been received: a subaltern came from the brigade, however,
to point out the route to the infantry starting-point. Without waiting any longer, the tanks moved forward to this
line, reaching it just as the barrage fell at zero and the
enemy began to reply. No further orders of any kind had
arrived, and the second in command of the detachment
spent the next hour galloping about under fire, collecting
information from the infantry, and by these haphazard
means determining what the tanks were expected to do.
Two of them, it appeared, were to remain in reserve at
Kurd Hill. Of the other pair, one was to help in the
assault on Lees and Outpost Hills. This tank, however,
fell into a gully whose sides collapsed, and did not get into
action. The remaining machine, having been assigned an
objective on Ali Muntar, was recalled to Outpost Hill
owing to the breakdown of the tank on its left. It climbed
the hill, killed a number of Turks in the trenches there,
and was still waiting for the infantry when it was disabled
by a direct hit. The infantry being unable to advance, one
of the reserve tanks was summoned; but although, after
repeated attempts and murderous losses, the crest at length
was gained, it could not be held; and our line eventually
fell back to its original position on Queen's Hill. The first
tank, lying derelict in the Turkish trenches, had already
been abandoned by its crew. The second returned in safety
to its companion in reserve.

The report gives the following account of the loss of the remaining tank, in action with the 54th Division on the right :—

"To the tank operating on this front had been assigned the capture of the large redoubt north-west of Khirbet Sihan (north of the Sheikh Abbas Ridge on the Beersheba road). As instructions to this effect had only reached the tank commander during the previous night, he was likewise confronted with the task of attacking an unfamiliar objective over unfamiliar ground. However, this tank finally reached the redoubt in question and captured its Turkish garrison. Our infantry then arrived and consolidated the new position. The tank had no sooner swung round to return to its rallying-point at Abbas, when a shell struck one of its tracks, whereupon it was subjected to a systematic bombardment. The enemy then counter-attacked and captured the British infantry and tank. The commander and several members of the crew had meanwhile been severely wounded. The officer and one other rank subsequently died of wounds in a Turkish hospital."

Except for a modified success on the left, the attack, although pressed with extreme gallantry, had definitely failed. Sir Archibald Murray wished to renew it the following morning, but was dissuaded from making the attempt. With no superiority of numbers in the beginning, we had lost 12,000 men : every one was exhausted : we were short of water; and the Ali Muntar position, notwithstanding a bombardment by heavy guns of every calibre, including those of the *Réquin* and the 11-inch pieces on the monitors, seemed little damaged, and plainly was impregnable to a frontal assault with the means at our disposal. The army, therefore, settled down on the ground it occupied at the close of the fighting. For the next six months no further attempt was made to capture Gaza.

The tank detachment, after withdrawing across the Wadi Ghuzze to some fig-groves west of Sheikh Nebhan, returned eventually to its old quarters near Deir-el-Belah railhead. Its proportionate losses had been heavy. Twenty-eight officers and men were killed, wounded, or missing—40 per cent of the total engaged. Three tanks out of eight were permanently disabled or lost. The report which I have used so freely already concludes with some general observations on the work of tanks in the battle. This work was fully appreciated by the infantry, who "generously attributed their own success to the opportunities created by the tanks." The three divisional commanders also expressed their admiration. That some of the fleeting openings made by the tanks were not promptly seized "was less due to lack of initiative on the part of infantry leaders than to the wholly unexpected intensity of the enemy's well-directed fire." At the same time, further co-operative training was shown to be very necessary. Reference, of course, is made to the faulty staff work through which, on 19th April, the centre section was left without any instructions after its original orders had been cancelled at the eleventh hour. It is pointed out also (although this perhaps was unavoidable) that the task allotted to the tanks was far too ambitious for their numbers. The eight operated on a five-mile front, where thirty or forty would not have been too many. The successful assembly prior to zero was held to prove that "tanks which are properly looked after by competent crews need not necessarily be placed in forward positions," as they can be trusted (accidents apart) to accomplish up to time final approach-marches of considerable length. And this brings us to what were, perhaps, the most notable features of the operations—the actual distances covered by these obsolete and worn-out machines and the absence of any mechanical breakdowns. In both respects the work of the little detachment compares very favourably indeed with that performed by the larger units in France. Some of the tanks travelled forty miles and fought two actions between the time they left Deir-el-Belah on the 15th and their final withdrawal behind the Wadi Ghuzze five days later; and every machine which left

England got into action, or was ready to do so, on zero morning. Such efficiency is a high testimonial to the labours of the commanding officer and his combatant and engineering personnel.

II.

It will be convenient, at the expense of strict chronological sequence, to carry the story of the Palestine detachment to its conclusion in one chapter. Six months supervened between the second and third battles of Gaza. During this period our dispositions were readjusted, reinforcements arrived (including French, Italian, Indian, and West Indian details), and Sir Archibald Murray having returned home, Sir Edmund Allenby came from the 3rd Army in France to take over the command. The surviving tanks, meanwhile, were overhauled and provided with some especial roller-sprockets, constructed in the workshops of the Egyptian State Railways. Requests for more and newer tanks had been sent to England; but the only reinforcement received consisted of three Mark IV.'s. One or more others of this type, together with a supply of much-needed spare parts for the original Mark I.'s, were lost in a torpedoed transport.

Towards the end of the autumn preparations for a renewed attempt on Gaza had reached completion. Our line in front of the city still ran where the second battle had left it —from Sheikh Ajlin, on the coast, by Samson's Ridge and the Mansura and Abbas Ridges, down to the Wadi Ghuzze, and thence to the new railhead at Shellal on the right. The Turkish defences on Ali Muntar had been strengthened still further; and now that our increased forces permitted us to choose, it was decided to avoid the hazards of another frontal assault. Instead, while the enemy's centre was kept employed with demonstrations, the main attacks were to develop between Hereira and Beersheba and on the western flank, from Gaza to the sea. The whole area of operations extended over forty miles. " The Australian Corps and desert column were responsible for the operations from Beersheba north-westwards to Hereira. Numerous mounted and dismounted divisions were entrusted with the frontage from and around Hereira towards Gaza, while a composite force of French, Italian, and West Indian troops were assigned the task of executing minor raids near Outpost Hill. The operations around Gaza were entrusted to the 21st Army Corps, which began to make the necessary preparations for a general assault on the defences between Umbrella Hill (north of Samson's Ridge) and the sea."[1] This was to be the main attack, with its left resting on the coast and its right on the Cairo road. In the second phase of the last battle our only permanent success had been won on this flank; and our extreme left at Sheikh Ajlin was due west of Gaza. The general line of the assault therefore was north-eastward, with the idea of so far enveloping the city as to threaten its communications from the north. The distance from the Cairo road to the sea was less than 5000 yards; and the initial penetration aimed at was moderate— two miles up the coast on the extreme left, and elsewhere an average of a mile. For this narrow frontage and depth of attack four infantry brigades were available (the whole 54th Division and one brigade of the 52nd), assisted by an Indian cavalry division, the 54th Divisional Artillery, a machine-gun company, and the tank detachment of eight machines. (The presence of a number of anti-tank guns of $1\frac{1}{2}$-inch calibre about Green and Outpost Hills led to the tank operations being confined to the left sector.) The Navy again was to co-operate from the sea. The whole area over which this advance was to take place was a wilderness of sand-dunes, covered here and there with coarse grass and cactus, and rising in places to a height of 150 feet.

There had been ample time on this occasion for reconnaissance and other preliminaries. All tank commanders and N.C.O.'s surveyed the enemy's position both from the land and from a drifter off the coast. In addition to

[1] Report on Tank Operations in Egypt and Palestine, &c.

combined rehearsals by tanks and infantry already carried out during the summer, "officers and other ranks of the tank detachment and the various infantry brigades with whom they were to work were attached to each other for ten days in order personally to get to know each other and study the characteristics of the other's particular arm." *O si sic omnes!* An adequate supply of large-scale maps and aeroplane photographs was provided by the 21st Corps "I," together with a barrage-table and map for every tank commander. Each tank was to carry two pigeons, to be released at pre-arranged points; and also a ton of R.E. supplies and ammunition for the infantry. The whole question of supply was a serious one, as the only roads behind our line in this coastal area were constructed by the simple process of laying down wire-netting on the sand, which provided a surface suitable for marching infantry or even light cars, but of no use for heavy vehicles. The detachment workshops rendered a signal service by improvising a number of tractor trucks out of old track-plates, driving sprockets, and iron girders. The necessary dumps of oil and ammunition were then formed near Sheikh Ajlin, lorries and tractors conveying the material thither after dark by way of the beach. Finally, as the attack itself was due to start in the night-time, the tanks were variously camouflaged to suit the conditions amid which they might expect to find themselves at dawn. Two were daubed with different colours, and another pair were painted white and splashed with sand, while the remaining four were disguised with imitation cactus.

As little as possible had been left to chance; and I have enumerated the main features of this preparatory work both on account of its thoroughness and forethought, and because it is a characteristic example of the preliminaries to a tank action. Before such an action there are always a hundred odd things of this kind to be seen to; and in this case, unlike some others nearer home, they were seen to. The labour expended over them was fully justified in the results.

The coming attack was divided into four phases, known

on the map as the Blue, Red, Green, and Yellow—a polychromatic scale which was to proceed in succession from the south. The first or Blue phase was concerned with the capture of Umbrella Hill, and was to start an hour before midnight on 1st November. This was a distinct operation, to be accomplished by the 156th Brigade without the help of tanks. At 3 o'clock in the morning a second zero would launch the second and subsequent phases, constituting the main attack, the final or Yellow phase pushing our left flank two miles up the coast to Sheikh Hassan, north-west of Gaza. The tanks were allotted as follows: one with the 156th Brigade on the right, one with the 163rd in the centre, and four with the 161st and 162nd on the left. Two in reserve were to follow up 1000 yards in rear and replace any disabled machines.

The detachment trekked from Deir-el-Belah to Sheikh Ajlin on the night of 22nd October. On the last day of the month routes were taped to the assembly positions selected for the battle. The following evening, as the roar of the first zero broke out on the right, the tanks moved forward under a full moon and reached these positions at 1.30 A.M. At 2.15 the six detailed to lead crept away again, and, passing through the infantry starting line, drew up a couple of hundred yards ahead in No-man's-land. All were in position half an hour before the second zero. In the meantime, under cover of a heavy barrage, Umbrella Hill had been carried and the Blue phase was over. The enemy, anticipating a general attack, at first retaliated by shelling violently the whole of our front line; and the tanks experienced an unpleasant half-hour while moving toward their assembly posts. None, fortunately, were hit. As we made no further movement, the Turkish gunners presently concentrated their fire on the captured hill, and about 2 o'clock, misled by the continued quiet, ceased altogether. An hour later they were disillusioned when our main barrage crashed down upon their whole line, and tanks and infantry went forward under its cover.

A thick mist had risen, which, with the smoke of the barrage, completely obscured the moon, upon whose light we had been counting. The tanks, however, advancing on compass-bearings, successfully reached their first objectives within three minutes, well ahead of the infantry. In the prevailing gloom some of the latter lost direction almost at once; and a tank officer, observing from a point called Windy Post, on our front line, collected some hundreds of men of one battalion and directed them to their objective. The first Turkish line, nevertheless, was carried without difficulty, the attack coming as a complete surprise. Behind the creeping barrage the tanks and infantry pressed on; and although the two brigades in the centre met with stiff opposition on the second line, and lost ground before a succession of counter-attacks, on both flanks, and especially on the all-important left, everything went more or less according to programme. By 6 o'clock the 162nd Brigade had consolidated its final objective at Sheikh Hassan. On the right El Arish Redoubt had at last been captured, and our troops were on the edge of the fig-groves which shelter Gaza to the south-west.

The tanks had done all, and more than all, that was expected of them. On the right two had helped in the taking of El Arish. It was still dark when they pushed on into the maze of trenches beyond, and both became ditched, one eventually being disabled by a shell. The crews took out their machine-guns and joined the infantry. Numbers 3 and 4, next on the left, working with the 161st Brigade, attacked and carried with the latter the Rafa Redoubt and the trenches to the north-west. Owing to the mist they had great difficulty in reaching their further objectives, and finding that the infantry had been unable to advance beyond the redoubt, they returned to the rallying-point, having deposited their spare ammunition and R.E. stores. Number 5 broke a track at Beach Post, its first objective, and was unable to assist in the next phase. On the extreme left Number 6 had a varied and exciting career. To quote from the report, it "captured Sea Post (close to the beach), moved along the enemy's trench line, crushing the wire as far as Beach Post, turned north and attacked Cricket Redoubt, then proceeded to Gun Hill and Tortoise Hill, both of which positions it subjected to 6-pounder and machine-gun fire, and finally reached Sheikh Hassan, where it deposited its load of R.E. stores. Thence it descended to the beach and endeavoured to attack A5 (a Turkish strong-point on the coast beyond our farthest objective), but in scaling the cliff broke a track. The crew removed all machine-guns, rendered the engine useless, removed the 6-pounder wedges, and retired to Sheikh Hassan, where they reported to the infantry commander." As the abandoned tank was several hundred yards in advance of our front, the enemy was able during the ensuing night to creep up and place a charge beneath it, the explosion of which, in addition to effecting other damage, bent the crank-shaft. When, after the retreat of the Turkish Army a few days later, it was possible to move the machine, it was found necessary to remove the engine and tow the hull back to Deir-el-Belah.

In the meantime the reserve tanks, Numbers 7 and 8, had come into action. At 4 A.M. they received orders to support the infantry on the right, beyond El Arish redoubt. Both tanks were loaded with R.E. material, and, unfortunately, were carrying empty sandbags on the roof. Number 7 was set on fire from this cause as it reached its first objective, east of the captured redoubt. While it was attempting to return to shelter, the tracks jumped and broke the switches, and the tank was left ablaze between the lines. Number 8 also caught fire. It was now broad daylight, and the tank was in view of the enemy, who proceeded to shell it; but being screened to some extent by vegetation, with which its own camouflage blended, it was never hit.

By 8 o'clock, three tanks had rallied at Sheikh Ajlin, and a fourth returned three hours later. During the battle some machines had been in action for five hours, and had covered upwards of 10,000 yards; but the casualties in personnel were extraordinarily light, only one man being killed and two wounded. At this trifling cost the tank detachment had helped materially to place our left flank in such a position that the Turkish Army around Gaza was seriously endangered. On the right, progress had been made also, and the double threat was enough. Within a few days the enemy evacuated the city and the position he had held so long, and retreated toward Jaffa and Jerusalem.

With the third battle of Gaza the work of the tanks in Palestine came to a fitting end. Although most of the machines were soon prepared for action again, all were manifestly worn out, and it was felt that they would be of little use in the limestone hills of Judah, amid which the army was now advancing. On the other hand, the need was felt for some light and swift machine to help the mounted columns in the desert area; and to this end Major Nutt and the second in command were sent to France early in 1918 to ask for a detachment of the new Medium A's, or Whippets, which were then lying idle. The arrival of this mission at Bermicourt, however, coincided with the great German offensive on 21st March. In the strain consequent upon that blow, and the others which followed it, not a Whippet could be spared. The two officers returned to Syria, and after further consideration it was decided to disband the detachment. The tanks were handed in to the ordnance depot at Alexandria, where probably they still remain, while the personnel returned to England.

I have gone at some length into these oriental adventures for various reasons. One of the chief, perhaps, was the pleasure to be gained in working from a narrative so lucid and well arranged as the official "Report on Operations," &c., which I have used with such freedom. This may not be a good reason for discursiveness, but after exhausting struggles with the loose jumble of irrelevancies and misstatements which constitute the normal unit history, much may be forgiven. And, indeed, the Palestine detachment has other and far better claims to a resurrection from the obscurity in which its accomplishments have lain hidden. There is no need to labour those claims again here. They speak for themselves in the energy and courage, the foresight, adaptability, and fertility of invention which overcame all the obstacles that a strange country and climate could add to an initial poverty of means.

CHAPTER VI.

MESSINES.

During the second half of May there was much coming and going of units in the Bermicourt area. The remnants of C and D Battalions returned there to refit. A and B, forming the 2nd Brigade, drew 76 Mark IV. tanks, and left for the Belgian frontier and the forthcoming attack on the Messines Ridge. Two new battalions, F and G, arrived from England. The 3rd Brigade was now formed of C and F, G replacing the former in the 1st Brigade. Preparatory to this increase in the corp's fighting strength, Colonel Elles was raised to the exalted rank of Brigadier-General.

The battle of Messines, and the part taken in it by the 2nd Brigade, can be dealt with very cursorily. It was the opening stage of our attack in Flanders, which followed on the collapse of the French effort in Champagne and our own failure to break the Drocourt-Queant line. The new offensive, long premeditated, was planned on a large scale and inspired by very sanguine ideas. It was hoped to drive the enemy off the whole coast-line as far as the Dutch frontier, and then, by forcing the evacuation of Lille, to open the way for an advance on Brussels and Antwerp. The preliminary operations fell into three stages. The monotonous Flemish plain is diversified, between St Omer and Menin, by a line of hills shaped like a note of interrogation lying on its back. Starting at Cassel, a very conspicuous isolated height, these hills run due eastward to Kemmel, over the Belgian border, and thence curve round Ypres to the north. The enemy held the whole of this curve, which, from the village of Wytschaete, 250 feet above the sea, falls gradually away to nothing beyond the forest of Houthoulst. Our first object was to dispossess him of the Wytschaete or Messines Ridge, which overlooks the whole Ypres salient. The second stage would be the capture after an interval of the rest of the curve, known as the Passchendaele Ridge. This, it was estimated, would be effected in three or four days. The moment the ridge was ours, the third stage was to open with the landing of a force of all arms, including even tanks, at Middelkerke, between Nieuport and Ostend, to get behind the enemy's forces along the Yser, and so facilitate an advance on that water-logged front. No one can say how far this ambitious scheme would have prospered if the weather had remained fair. As it fell out, the first stage alone was carried through successfully. Wytschaete and Messines were taken in a few hours, but owing to the rain it took us three months instead of three days to reach Passchendaele; and long before that the amphibious enterprise at Middelkerke, the most interesting and hazardous feature of the whole plan, had perforce been cancelled. I shall give some account of its elaborate machinery later on.

Sir Herbert Plumer and the 2nd Army had been facing the Messines Ridge for two years, and plans for its capture had been developed at leisure. The surface soil in the neighbourhood lay upon a substratum of clay, very suitable for tunnelling; and for upwards of twelve months we had been driving mine-shafts beneath the German trenches. The ridge was enclosed in a small salient, with the chord of the arc, about six miles long, represented by the enemy's third defence system, known as the Oostaverne Line. This was to be our final objective. The battle was to be finished in one day. Considering the lengthy and precise preparations for it, the moral effect of the explosion of twenty huge mines, and the powerful artillery fire which was to be concentrated on the small area within the salient, it will be apparent that there was no very urgent need for tanks. The state of the ground, moreover, already bad, would not be improved by the seven days' preliminary bombardment; and if rain fell it would soon become impassable. Messines, in fact, was not a tank battle at all. It was one of those rare occasions when a section or two, to deal with obstinate strong-points, would have been as useful as the entire brigade which ultimately went into action.

Warning of possible operations in the Ypres salient had been received at Bermicourt early in the year. The Intelligence branch of the corps began a survey of the whole area in March; and the following month, when the 2nd Brigade was detailed to assist in the attack at Messines, the R.O.'s of A and B Battalions went forward to reconnoitre the southern sector. Ample information was available, for the 2nd Army knew all that there was to be known about the German position. It had also constructed one of the familiar large-scale models of the ridge and the country beyond; but although such representations are always worth a visit, it is doubtful if they are of much value from a tank commander's standpoint. They bear no real resemblance to the actual ground to be traversed, and the view from a tank is so limited that the larger details of a landscape are of small use in getting bearings.

Between the 23rd and 27th May the tanks of the two battalions were detrained at Ouderdom and Clapham Junction (near Dranoutre). They lay up before the battle in the neighbourhood of the railheads—B Battalion's machines in a wood, and those of A in timber and canvas shelters built to represent huts. These assembly positions were within four miles of the line. The usual precautions were taken to conceal the fact of the tanks' arrival, the tracks left by their movements (which show up very clearly in aeroplane photographs) being obliterated by harrows. This was the first appearance of Mark IV.'s in the field;

and another novelty was the use of old Mark II.'s for supply purposes. Twelve were attached to the brigade, carrying between them one complete fill of petrol, oil, grease, and ammunition for all the 76 fighting tanks.

The attack was to take place at dawn on 7th June. Three corps were taking part—from left to right, the 10th, 9th, and 2nd. Eventually 64 tanks were allotted to them—40 to attack the first objective, the German second line beyond the crest of the ridge, and 24 more to help in the final rush for the Oostaverne trenches. On 24th May the preliminary bombardment opened. The weather was hot and dry: there had been no rain for a fortnight; and now, day after day, the ridge was smothered in dust-clouds thrown up by the bursting shells. The gun-fire slackened on the last day, 6th May; but the enemy became nervous after dark and began to shell the back areas. He used a large amount of gas, which caused much discomfort to the tank crews on the final approach march to the front line, for that invaluable device, the small box-respirator, is more than usually inconvenient when worn inside a tank. Later in the night a heavy thunderstorm broke; but by 2.30 A.M. the sky was clear once more.

At 3.10, on the very edge of dawn, the German front line between Hill 60 and Messines went up into the air with an indescribable shock and noise, as the nineteen huge mines exploded. Simultaneously the barrage fell through the dust-clouds upon the still-moving earth. With so tremendous a preparation, the first stage of the attack went like clockwork. Messines was carried by 7 A.M., and Wytschaete before midday. The tanks were seldom needed, and indeed were unable in most cases to keep up with the very rapid advance. One, however, by a combination of luck and skilful driving, was able to lead the Australian and New Zealand troops of the 2nd Corps the whole way to the second objective, a distance of two miles, in an hour and forty minutes. Another, the "Wytschaete Express," convoyed the Ulster Division into that village; and a third

lent very timely help at Fanny's Farm, beyond Messines,
where the infantry was held up for a time. In the meanwhile, the 24 reserve tanks had moved up to our original
front line, and in the afternoon climbed the ridge to lead
the assault on the final objective. The Oostaverne Line was
little damaged, by comparison with the shattered first and
second systems, and might have caused us serious trouble.
The tanks, however, reached the trenches ahead of the infantry, and so demoralised the defenders that the whole
position was taken at a light cost. During its consolidation, the surviving machines patrolled beyond it; and this
dangerous operation, which often exposes tanks to direct
artillery fire which they can neither avoid nor counter, led
on this occasion to one very gallant and useful piece of
work. Well east of Oostaverne, between that village and
the Ypres-Menin railway, stood Joye Farm, at the head of
a marshy little valley down which crawled a stream called
the Wambeek. Late in the afternoon two of the patrolling
tanks (both males of A Battalion) became ditched near the
farm, actually in front of our outpost line. All efforts to
extricate them before night having failed, it was proposed
to withdraw the crews. The Wambeek valley, however,
offered the enemy cover in which to mass his troops for
a counter-attack; and as the tanks would be of material
assistance in such an event, the men eventually were ordered
to stand by them during the night and resume unditching at
dawn. At 4 A.M., therefore, work was started again. One
tank was got out, and at once moved forward toward the
Ypres-Menin railway, where a counter-attack was in progress, but broke a track while attempting to cross the
metals. At 6.30 the Germans were seen to be gathering
along the Wambeek. Each tank could bring one 6-pounder
to bear on the valley, and the majority of their crews took
the machine-guns outside into shell-holes. The infantry
near at hand were asked for support and supplied with
ammunition, of which their Lewis-gun teams were deficient.
The enemy's attack was now developing; but although for

five hours he made repeated attempts to issue from the valley, in every case he was repulsed with heavy losses, inflicted largely by the 6-pounder and machine-gun fire of the two tank crews. At 11.30 our barrage opened again and finally dispersed the assailants.

In this battle the two tank battalions lost 3 officers and 16 men killed or died of wounds, and 26 officers and 73 men wounded or missing. Eleven tanks were disabled by direct hits; 48 were ditched, and 2 were hit after ditching. There were nineteen recorded cases in which they helped the infantry. The Mark IV.'s, with their lighter sponsons and other improvements, were shown to be far handier than the old type of machine. Apart from the obvious conclusions that tanks need not have been used at all in the first phase of the attack, and that the ground was thoroughly unsuitable for any combined effort on their part, the chief lesson to be drawn from Messines was one already taken to heart—the necessity, namely, of providing a more efficient unditching apparatus for use in such pulverised *terrain*. Many casualties would have been avoided, and many more tanks would have got into action and returned that night, if the long unditching spar issued shortly after had been in use during the battle.

The question of the advisability of using tanks at Messines raises another which it may be of interest to consider before we close this chapter. "The third battle of Ypres," says Colonel Buchan,[1] "was the residuum left to Sir Douglas Haig of the great plan of a Flanders offensive which he had conceived the previous winter. Events which he could not control had postponed it till too late in the summer." Here, as elsewhere, the writer implies that the dilemma in which we found ourselves was

---

[1] Apologies perhaps are due for the continual use of this book ('Nelson's History of the War') as a stalking-horse; but in spite of the difficulties attending its production, and its claim to be no more than a popular history, Colonel Buchan had exceptional opportunities of gaining information, and the work is in fact the only full and reliable account of the war as yet in print.

caused wholly by the failure of the French advance on Laon. Manifestly, the work of the Allied armies was interdependent; but the principle of assuming at all costs the perfection of our own dispositions can be carried too far. There was in any case a bold alternative to the Ypres offensive, which actually was proposed and might well have been adopted, even before the postponement of the latter compromised its prospects. This alternative was a tank attack on a large scale against the central portion of the Hindenburg Line—to take place after Messines. In other words, the battle of Cambrai was to be fought in the early summer, on the same lines as eventually were adopted in the late autumn. In the Arras battles the Mark I. tanks were used for the last time, and as none really were needed at Messines, the improved Mark IV.'s and the experienced personnel lost there might have been preserved for a greater occasion. The enemy's attention was drawn northward by the 2nd Army's victory. He began at once to transfer reserves to meet the obvious corollary of an attack from Ypres; and to foster this belief by various stratagems was no more difficult in June than in November. Meanwhile, let us suppose the four original tank battalions, reinforced in May by F and G, to be preparing at Bermicourt and Wailly for the secret blow far to the south. By the end of June, when the three brigades began to assemble in the Salient, it would have been possible to arm them with 100 tanks apiece—300 in all. (216 fighting machines were actually in Belgium for the battle of July 31st.) Our communications across the devastated Somme area were then so far complete (or could have been made so) as to permit of a rapid and secret concentration on that front, and the plan of attack adopted with such startling results on November 20th might have been anticipated in almost every detail, with this great additional advantage—twelve or fifteen fresh divisions, instead of six tired ones, could have followed the tanks. The ground was perfect, virtually untouched by war, and not likely to be affected seriously by rain. The enemy was unprepared. And of the possible obstacles, the fabulous Hindenburg trenches, whose rear systems were not even completed by midsummer, were the least to be feared.

Such was the scheme put forward and strongly urged by the supporters of the new weapon. If it did not seem to offer so glittering a reward as a victorious advance along the coast, its prospects of success were immeasurably higher. It would possess the elements for which tanks were designed—surprise and normal country. Apart from the ordinary difficulties confronting an attack out of the Salient, where the enemy was fully prepared for one, the effect of bad weather and gun-fire upon the ruined soil reduced every ambitious military operation there to the nature of a gamble. It is interesting to note that quite early in the year, after the reconnaissance made by the Heavy Section of the whole area, the ground north of Messines was declared utterly unfit for tanks; and far less rain than actually fell in August would have ruined our offensive. (As it happened, June and July, about when it was proposed to fight the alternative tank battle, were brilliantly fine.) Nor were the strategic prospects of a blow at Cambrai to be under-estimated. A success, of which there was every probability, would have threatened directly the great line of supply, running southward through Maubeuge, by which the German armies in Champagne were fed and clothed and armed. Such a threat was the object of the November attack, and of the second battle of Cambrai ten months later, when at length it was carried through to a practical conclusion.

This excursion into strategy and speculation may seem out of place in a book of this nature. But one of my main objects in writing is to show how a belated appreciation of the correct use of tanks in battle came to overset all the theories stereotyped by years of stationary warfare, and how the tactical beliefs held by the Tank Corps itself were ultimately accepted as gospel by the Army as a whole. Already there are signs of backsliding, and in a few years we shall be told that the war was won by cavalry. But regarding Cambrai as the great conversion (if only "for the duration"), it is both interesting and pertinent to discuss the earlier proposal, although it came to nothing at the time, and was only exhumed later as a sort of counsel of desperation. In the spring of 1917 there was little hope for it. The Belgian coast-line worked like a magnet, and there were infantry and guns in plenty to be drawn thither. The main argument against the attack farther south was, however, that too few tanks were available. Yet 300 at least could have been found, and only 370 went in eventually at Cambrai. No doubt there were other and better reasons. Whatever they were, they prevailed: our activities continued to shift northward, and soon men and guns and tanks were floundering in the morasses of the Salient.

CHAPTER VII.

YPRES: THE PRELIMINARIES.

I.

FROM now onward my own experiences with the Tank Corps in France will take up a large part of the narrative. I came out from England as a tank commander in G Battalion toward the end of May 1917. Only the personnel were on the boat, as by this time the tanks were shipped across in batches as they were completed, new battalions on their arrival drawing their quota from the park at Erin. F Battalion had preceded G by a week, these two units being the first to leave of those raised at home under the new establishment.

The month of June, notable for brilliant weather, we spent partly in the Bermicourt area, where my own company billeted in satisfactory isolation in the village of Pierremont, and partly at Wailly, where each company went for a week's driving practice. The combatant companies in the Heavy Branch were then numbered consecutively throughout the corps, and not by their battalions; so that G, as the seventh of the latter in alphabetical order, consisted of 19, 20, and 21 Companies—the last-named being my own. At Pierremont we led a very placid existence for a few weeks. We route-marched and drilled a little, toyed with Lewis guns, and played cricket: we suffered, not over gladly, the presence in our mess of two unshaven and lugubrious members of the Y.M.C.A. (which occasionally

errs in selecting its personnel) whom we knew only as
"Watch" and "Pray"; and eventually, with the rest of
the battalion, we marched over to Erin, about four miles
distant, to draw thirty-six Mark IV. tanks. We drove our
own twelve back to a park already established in the village.
At this time, however, I had no tank to command. There
were in my section three rather senior lieutenants, hailing
from the prehistoric Thetford age, who naturally secured a
tank apiece. The majority of the subalterns in G, including myself, had been commissioned from the ranks on the
same day some six months earlier, and joined the battalion
together, and their seniority necessarily was determined by
the alphabet. In consequence of this law the fourth tank
in the section fell to my friend and contemporary Brassington (killed a year later by Monument Wood, outside
Bapaume), since "Bra" comes before "Bro." On such
accidents of orthography, in the Army, may one's future
depend! I was left for the time being in command of the
fifth or reserve crew.

In the meanwhile Messines had been fought. We heard
the guns from Pierremont, and, a little later, learnt that we
should soon move up to the Salient ourselves to take part
in the forthcoming development of the offensive there. I
remember Torbett, the company commander, returning one
evening about this time from some conference, bringing
with him a large-scale map of the country over which the
battalion was expected to operate. Few or none of us had
seen the Salient then; and on this sheet, carefully layered
and thick with symmetrical villages and roads, it looked
quite attractive and very ordinary. I date from that event
an instinctive mistrust of maps depicting strange country
in war-time. I believe it would have helped us greatly in
this war to have had maps drawn especially to represent,
so far as was possible, the actual condition of the ground on
most battlefields. This should not have been difficult:
primarily it would mean inventing a series of entirely new
conventional signs for mud and shelled areas and obliterated

villages and roads, to take the place of the normal peacetime symbols of the cartographer, supplemented only by obscure legends which nobody reads. I have experimented with such a map myself. The ordinary production, showing every house and hedgerow and by-way in (let us say) Poelcapelle or Pozières, which simply had ceased to exist, was peculiarly misleading; and, so strong is habit, the more accustomed one was to handling maps before the war (an eccentricity not common, it is true, in the regular Army) the more misleading it became. Looking now at any sheet professing to represent the Pilkem Ridge and the Steenbeek Valley, and recalling what that atrocious neighbourhood really looked like, it is a marvel to me that we ever found our way about it at all. I am quite certain that in many cases loss of direction, or misstatements as to position in action—errors which were only too common—were due not to ordinary bad map-reading, although that also was prevalent enough, but to excusable inability on the part of an officer to reconcile the printed sheet with the actual appearance of the country: a difficulty that might have been mitigated in part by the use of some more appropriate system of cartography.

Toward the end of June the 1st Tank Brigade, consisting now of G and D Battalions, received definite movement orders; and a few days later an advance party of G, which I accompanied, moved by lorry to the Salient to prepare a camp. We reached our destination at Oosthoek Wood, beyond Poperinghe, about 3 o'clock of a blazing July afternoon, at the exact moment when a German aeroplane was attacking one of our observation-balloons which hung immediately overhead. There was a hideous racket of futile rifle and machine-gun fire: along the whole line of balloons stretching northward observers were descending in parachutes; and two dissolving spirals of black smoke above the trees showed where a couple of the fragile gas-bags had already been destroyed. As we tumbled out of our lorries, wondering what all the pandemonium was about,

the German pilot was in the act of diving down upon his
third victim, right above us. The two observers were still
floating uncomfortably earthward, and the mechanics on
the trolley below, at the edge of the wood, were working
frenziedly to lower the balloon, when the latter burst into
flames, shrivelled up like tissue-paper, and sank gently in
a rain of charred fragments beneath its own streamer of
smoke. The aeroplane, satisfied with a creditable afternoon's work, circled round and climbed toward the lines,
pursued, long after it was out of range, by useless and
indiscriminate small-arm fire and the equally ineffective
" Archie."

This was not the only untoward occurrence which had
disturbed Oosthoek that day. It appeared that during the
morning the whole wood, which was full of troops, had
been shelled, notably in that part where the 1st and 3rd
Tank Brigades proposed to have their camps. As these
attentions were guessed correctly to be only the precursors
of more, it was decided on the spot to send the personnel
of both brigades to some area farther removed from the
line. The tanks, however, would have to remain at Oosthoek. Our advance party, therefore, after spending the
night in the wood with the Reconnaissance Officers of the
battalion, who had been established there for a week,
moved back next morning to the vicinity of Lovie Château,
the headquarters of the 5th Army, where the camps of the
1st Brigade Headquarters and D Battalion already were in
process of erection.

Some account of the neighbourhood and general situation
will aid the story at this point. Oosthoek Wood, the centre
of our activities for the next four months, is a large and
straggling assemblage of trees extending in all over several
hundred acres, and lying in the middle of a triangle whose
points are Poperinghe to the south-west, Vlamertinghe to
the south-east, and Elverdinghe to the north-east. The
centre of the wood was within four miles of the nearest
point of the line, at Boesinghe on the canal, and about the

same distance from Ypres. It was bisected by a timbered military road (a splendid piece of work, capable of taking three lorries abreast) which ran from the direction of Lovie Château across the triangle to Vlamertinghe. Beside this road a double line of rails had been laid from Peselhoek railhead to a new and very conspicuous detraining ramp built at the entrance to the wood for the use of our brigade. Half a mile farther north a second ramp served the 3rd Brigade. (The 2nd Brigade was already in the area, having remained at Ouderdom since the battle of Messines.) A series of other woods diversified the country between Oosthoek and Lovie Château. The latter building, standing in beautiful grounds, was about seven miles from the line—uncommonly far forward, nevertheless, for an army headquarters. It was, indeed, in front of the 18th Corps Headquarters, close by. The whole of this low-lying and uninteresting region was under cultivation as far as Oosthoek itself; and there were people living in the farms on the western outskirts of that wood. The battered and unpleasant town of Poperinghe, although shelled intermittently and bombed at one time almost every night, was of course full of squalid shops and extortionate shopkeepers, most of them women. To carry on for three or four years a retail business under fire, within five miles of the enemy, implies a certain enthusiasm for gain; but perhaps the ordeal justified the imposition of high prices; and the ordinary Englishman's passion for buying rubbish is a direct invitation to it. The restaurants and tea-shops in the town—"Skindle's," "Cyril's," and the rest—swarmed all day with garrulous officers, and should have formed useful media of information for the Germans. As for the depressed and slatternly creatures in the farms nearer to the line, it was generally taken for granted that they were spies. The usual stories flew about of lamps flashing by night and cattle manœuvring suspiciously by day; and rumour was always shooting somebody. And if there was espionage, as there must have been, it had a mass of miscellaneous material to sift and report on. The whole country was crowded with troops. In the Salient alone there were two armies in one army area, Sir Hubert Gough having brought four corps from in front of Cambrai to take post on the 2nd Army's left. To his left again the 1st French Army had taken over from the Belgians the line between Boesinghe and Noordschoote; while Rawlinson's 4th Army had come in on the sea-coast in readiness for that flanking operation which never materialised. There could be no attempt to keep this huge concentration a secret, or at any rate there was none. Such a thing was not thought of in those days. Everything went forward deliberately on old-established lines, in full view of the enemy, who were in doubt only (and that not for long) as to the actual day of attack.

The decision to employ three brigades of tanks, or the whole of the Heavy Branch, had been come to in May, notwithstanding the adverse reports on the ground submitted by the Corps Reconnaissance Staff. From the first introduction of tanks in the field, the conditions with which they had to contend had gone from bad to worse. Ypres was the climax. The tanks were sent by scores, and then by hundreds, to drown ineffectually in a morass, and the very existence of the corps was imperilled by this misusage. The whole countryside was waterlogged: reclaimed from the sea, for even Ypres once had been a port, its usefulness and habitability depended in normal times upon an intricate system of drainage, for whose upkeep the farmers were responsible, and for the neglect of which they were heavily fined. This drainage had now been destroyed, or had fallen into desuetude and decay, over the whole area about the front lines. During our reconnaissances in July the deplorable results were not at first very apparent. The weather was fine, and the surface soil dry and crumbling: we walked, so far as it was safe, over what seemed to be solid earth covered with the usual coarse grass and weeds; and then, from observation-points in well-constructed trenches, peered out through our binoculars upon a barren and dun-coloured landscape, void of any sign of human life, its dreary skyline broken only by a few jagged stumps of trees. From this desolation clouds of dust shot up where our shells were falling. It was much the same as any other battlefield, to all appearance. But even then the duckboards under foot in the trenches were squelching upon water; and a few hours' rain dissolved the fallacious crust into a bottomless and evil-smelling paste of liquid mud. And rain was the least offender. It was our own bombardment which finished the work of ruin, pulverised the ground beyond repair, destroyed what drainage there was left, and brought the water welling up within the shell-holes as fast as they were formed. Long before any prolonged downpour had fallen, indeed after the hottest spells of weather, the little white discs on the aeroplane photographs were multiplying daily from end to end of the field of operations.

II.

The actual detraining of the tanks of G Battalion at Oosthoek Wood was accomplished without any serious hitch. It took place, of course, after dark, and spread over three successive nights, each company requiring a complete train. The workshops had already travelled up by road. My company was the first to arrive; and the Brigadier and staff, the Colonel and the company commander, Gordon, the company R.O., and myself, were at the ramp to meet it. We stood about there in the dark in some anxiety, for a night or two earlier a train of C Battalion's had been shelled as it drew in to the northern railhead. There had been stories of signal rockets going up in the neighbourhood as the train pulled in. The new white wooden ramps must have shown up clearly on aeroplane photographs, and no one had thought of camouflaging them. This night, happily, was exceptionally quiet; only a few heavy shells whistled far overhead on their way into Poperinghe. It was very dark, but fine, with a brilliant display of stars. It was also, I remember, uncommonly cold for July. The train drew in about eleven o'clock, creeping up so quietly that the dark bulk of the first tank, shrouded in tarpaulin sheets, was towering above the ramp before I knew anything about it. We had a party ready at hand for the business of chocking up, and these men fell to work at once while the tank crews unlashed and cleared away the sheets and started their engines. "Chocking up," by the way, was a process in use to save the springs of the earlier K.T. trucks, heavy T-shaped baulks of timber being wedged under the ends of each truck to carry the weight of the tank as it moved off. A later type of K.T. carried its own chocks in the form of screw-jacks beneath the buffers.

Everything went well until the eleventh tank refused to start up. Eventually it had to be towed off. In the meantime, Gordon and I had been leading the others to their allotted hiding-places in the wood. Parking tanks (especially Mark IV.'s) among timber at night is always a noisy and trying operation, resembling in sound and destructiveness the gambols of a herd of inebriated elephants. The tank-driver, unaided, can see nothing whatever, and has to be guided by the flashings of an electric torch, with which refinements of signalling are difficult and generally misunderstood. The trees, which appeared to be harmless and nicely spaced in the daytime, become endued with a malignant spirit and (apparently) have changed their positions since last seen. It was as black as a coal-pocket in Oosthoek Wood that night; and for an hour or so it rang with curses and exhortations and the crash and rending of ill-treated timber as tank after tank tried to swing this way or that and pushed down a young tree or two in the act. However, soon after one o'clock we had them all in, herded together more or less in sections, and the first arrivals were already camouflaged. Although the foliage was fairly thick, and probably would have formed an adequate screen, we were running no risks. The camouflage nets were suspended from the trees a few feet above the tanks, the sides being drawn down at a slant and pegged to the ground. All this was exhausting work in the pitchy darkness, and very trying to the temper. At the same time a party was obliterating the tracks we had made between the ramp and the wood. By three o'clock the work was done, and we lay down in and under the tanks to sleep for a few hours. Lorries were due to arrive at six to take all the personnel, except a guard, back to the camp at Lovie Château.

It was very cold, and personally I hardly slept at all. About five o'clock every one was aroused very effectually by the arrival of a high-velocity shell, which burst under the nose of a tank, made a small hole in another, blew half a camouflage net to tatters, and flung a haversack into a tree. We were still collecting our wits, and a few dishevelled figures were crawling out of sponson doors, when a second shell burst twenty yards beyond the first; and with that every tank disgorged its occupants in a hurry and all of us dived for shelter. There were various old pits and trenches in the wood, and within these we crouched for a short time, while the shells continued to arrive punctually at half-minute intervals. All of them except the first one fortunately burst beyond the tanks, although near enough for fragments to fly among the latter and over our heads. As the wood manifestly was no place for repose at the moment, we were ordered to leave it; and having collected the scattered parties (a proceeding interrupted periodically by the whistle of another approaching shell), we retired in some disorder upon the military road, near the ramp, where a party of negro labourers was watching the bombardment with marked uneasiness. The methodical gun, however, made no attempt to traverse or elevate: it continued to plant its projectiles around the same spot for another ten minutes, and then fell silent. Our only casualty was X. (as we will call him), who ran into a tank in the pardonable excitement of the moment, cut his forehead, and was removed within half an hour to the C.C.S. on the Elverdinghe road. There was no further shelling of the wood that morning. We had every opportunity of establishing this fact, as, owing to some muddle over the lorries, they were four hours late. Tired, hungry, and dirty, feeling acutely that no one loved us, we sat by that accursed military road until midday, when at length the transport appeared and carried us back to the new camp at Lovie.

During the two ensuing mights 19 and 20 Companies detrained in peace and were followed shortly after by D Battalion. F Battalion having also joined C, the 1st and 3rd Brigades were now concentrated near to one another, mustering between them (including supply and signal machines) nearly 170 tanks. Every day the crews of the four battalions marched down from Lovie Château to their work in the wood, returning after tea. By this time the Germans had acquired the habit of shelling Oosthoek in a rather desultory fashion every day. In the centre of the wood, where a number of camps and hutments clustered about some cross-roads, casualties became so frequent that the whole of the troops in the neighbourhood were withdrawn: the baths, canteens, and Church Army huts were closed down; and only a few details remained to dig themselves in and hope for the best. At our end the nuisance was less pronounced, although quite troublesome enough. In addition to our old friend the high-velocity gun, which, situated apparently somewhere near Langemarck, favoured us with its attentions almost every day, other pieces of ordnance took a hand occasionally; but in the 1st Brigade neither men nor tanks were ever hit. As the latter were packed together like herrings, one or two heavy projectiles among them might have done a lot of damage. The 3rd Brigade, less fortunate, suffered several casualties, five men being killed and five wounded in one morning. We used to debit this unpleasantness to the growing account of Sergeant Phillips. This gentleman (whose actual regiment, a Welsh one, I have forgotten), having been captured in a raid, proceeded to give to the enemy every atom of information in his possession. Most of it was fairly accurate. Among other things, he disclosed the presence and approximate numbers of the tanks hidden in Oosthoek Wood. This piece of treachery having come to the knowledge of our Intelligence Corps, a summary of the disclosures, together with a prophecy as to the offender's probable destiny if ever he returned to England, was ordered to be read out every week on parade throughout the Army. Now that the war is over, and the prisoners are returned, I have often wondered what really has happened to Sergeant Phillips. As he appeared to be a man of some intelligence, he probably has remained in Germany.

As soon as G Battalion was settled down at Lovie Château, reconnaissance of the area by tank commanders and N.C.O.'s was begun. Our part in the forthcoming attack had been decided upon a month before. We were working with General Maxse's 18th Corps on the left centre of the 5th Army front. General Elles was opposed to the use of tanks anywhere north of the Wieltje road; but the corps commander asked urgently for two companies, and guaranteed that his engineers would, if necessary, get them to the crossing of the Steenbeek at St Julien. The action of the tanks, nevertheless, was to be subsidiary to the infantry assault, as the battle was being conducted on the stereotyped lines which had failed so often before. 19 and 21 Companies of my battalion were detailed to the 18th Corps, 20 Company remaining in corps reserve. D Battalion, for the time being, was in army reserve. The object of the first day's attack was the capture of the enemy's first and second systems on the Pilkem Ridge, and the securing of the Steenbeek crossings. This was to be followed on the second day by a push for the third system and the Passchendaele Ridge beyond; after which it was hoped to break through in the direction of Thourout simultaneously with an offensive by the 4th Army on the coast and the landing at Middelkerke. Our advanced headquarters party of Reconnaissance Officers had already worked out routes to the front line, and collected much valuable information about the ground beyond. The first serious obstacle to tank operations north of Ypres was the famous canal. This forbidding and ill-omened waterway, lined on both sides by blasted and withered poplars, haunted by cemeteries, and sunk within high banks honeycombed with terraces of dug-outs, was crossed between Brielen and La Brique by a series of earthen causeways. Over one of these, known as Marengo, a few hundred yards north of the dismal region called the Dead End of Ypres, the tanks were to pass. The prospect was not inviting, as the whole canal was shelled on and off every day and night, especially in the neighbourhood of the causeways; and a single tank disabled on Marengo would hold up all behind it. There was no alternative crossing, all the others being engaged for the passage of artillery and supplies. Beyond the canal a maze of old and new trenches and wire climbed a gentle slope to the only eminence, if such it can be called, within the original salient, on the summit of which, about 2000 yards from the front line, the ruins of Frascati Farm lay hidden among some fine trees. From the farther edge of this timber nothing but a line of high camouflage netting, strung on poles, interrupted the view across the slight depression where the front lines ran to the Pilkem Ridge and the ragged outline of Kitchener's Wood behind the second German system. So long as one's body and legs are covered, one can look over a parapet with comparative equanimity; but it seemed to me always a strange thing to stand upright, and entirely unprotected, behind this fictitious screen of netting, and watch through its meshes the whole extent of the enemy's trenches over an area of several miles, with our shells bursting in clouds of dust about them. The front lines themselves, on the marshy ground of the hollow below, were on an average three or four hundred yards apart.

Along No Man's Land, just in front of and parallel to our trenches, ran an unhappy thoroughfare called Admiral's Road, down which, for two years and a half, neither admirals nor common folk (except the nightly patrols) had ever stepped. The German front-line trenches took in a number of farms—Mousetrap, Hampshire, Canadian, Krupp, and others; but these were only names upon the map. Even the remnants of the buildings had vanished utterly long before: there was not a brick remaining to mark the sites; nothing was left but foul water and mud and a few pollarded willows that somehow had survived the annihilating pestilence of high explosives. These Flemish farmsteads were surrounded almost invariably by moats and pools, and the water had now overlapped its ruined confines and inundated acres of ground on every side. And behind this barrier, along the crest of the Pilkem Ridge, another series of obliterated and waterlogged farms—Juliet, Oblong, Racecourse, Below—formed outposts to the second German system. Nor was this the end of these amphibious obstacles. Beyond the ridge lay what once had been the Steenbeek—a sluggish stream crawling between muddy banks, ten or fifteen feet in width and three or four in depth; now a strip of quagmire, believed to be impassable for tanks except at the ruined bridge of St Julien—an obvious defile marked down and taped to a yard by the German batteries. Nor, again, was this all. It was indeed only the beginning. East of the Steenbeek, Von Armin, commanding the 4th German Army, had extemporised for defence in a different manner a third series of farmhouses (in front of his third line), by filling their ruins with reinforced concrete. Similar strong-points on a smaller scale, known generically as "pill-boxes," were dotted thickly about the Pilkem Ridge; but it was in the area behind, out of our observation, that this type of pocket-fortress reached its climax of strength and ingenuity. Here also were the main-battery positions. The enemy had come to realise, after Arras and Messines, that any front line could be made untenable by a heavy bombardment, and that even the second line should be regarded chiefly as a means of delaying and disorganising the assault. The third line, covered by a forward system of strong-points, was the main zone of resistance, behind which, in comparative security, reserves could be massed for a counter-attack. Adapted, by the "pill-box" system, to the abnormal conditions of the Salient (where deep dug-outs, and in some places adequate trenches even, were out of the question), this was the first application of the principle of an elastic "defence in depth," as opposed to the rigid obstacle of such fortifications as the Hindenburg Line. Resistance hardened automatically as the attack progressed. The field batteries were kept well back. The scheme depended for success upon the quality of the defending infantry and machine-gunners, who must be equal to the task of holding isolated posts unsupported for a period long enough to disorganise and weary the assailants, and allow the counter-preparations to mature. Upon this personal factor, under the influence of tanks, the method broke down during our final offensive a year later; but at the end of 1917 the German *moral* was still high, and in the Salient the tanks had few chances of undermining it.

Such, then, was the position the two companies of G Battalion had to assist the infantry to capture. On our left the 14th Corps and General Anthoine's Frenchmen were attacking without tanks up the Ypres-Staden railway, and toward the dismal Forest of Houthoulst. South of our sector the 2nd and 3rd Tank Brigades were operating with the 2nd and 19th Corps respectively against Frezenberg and the frightful region beyond Hooge. Here the conditions were similar to those with which we should have to contend: if possible, even worse. The approach-marches of these brigades were complicated, not only by the canal, but also by two streams, called the Kemmel Beek and the Lombart Beek, over which five causeways had to be built. This work, as well as the construction of splinter-proof shelters, the filling in of smaller dykes and craters, the bridging of innumerable trenches, and every other form of engineering device necessary, was performed by the 184th Tunnelling Company, attached to the Heavy Branch for the operations. One section of this company worked with each brigade, and all rendered invaluable service.

III.

The third battle of Ypres was unique in the history of the Tank Corps in the facilities afforded for preliminary reconnaissance. A natural prejudice impels me to the conclusion that in this department, as in all the rest, the work of my own battalion was more thorough than that of most others; and undoubtedly some of the older units were inclined to think that because they had been in action on the Somme they knew everything about tank warfare. This was much as if the cavalry should believe Pinkie Cleugh to be the last word on mounted tactics—as sometimes it appears that they do. For much had been done and more learnt since Flers and Courcelette. In any case, all of us had exceptional opportunities for preparation in the Salient. It was a pity they were squandered on so unprofitable a battlefield. The 2nd Brigade had been in the area since Messines, and the Reconnaissance Officers of the other two had lived in Oosthoek Wood for a fortnight before the personnel arrived. By the time section and tank commanders were free to begin their individual surveys, a great mass of information had already been gathered and sorted out. Aeroplane photographs had been collected, special maps prepared, landmarks identified, and routes to the front line decided upon. And still there was ample time for every crew to become familiar (so far as was possible from a distance) with the deplorable country over which it would have to fight. For three weeks parties of officers, N.C.O.'s, and men of G Battalion went daily up the line. To begin with, each tank commander walked with his drivers two or three times over the penultimate approach route from Oosthoek Wood to Frascati Farm beyond the canal — a distance, by the circuitous way chosen, of about 10,000 yards. It was divided into two stages. It led by a narrow and winding by-way from the military road to Hospital Farm, on the northern edge of the wood, and thence along a track, known to the whole British Army as Rum Road, to a point north-west of Brielen village, where there was an enclosure surrounded by trees and overgrown hedges, which we called Halfway House. Here the tanks of 19 and 21 Companies were to spend X-day, or the day but one before the battle. During X-Y night they were to move forward again along Rum Road, past Murat Farm, across Marengo Causeway, and so to Frascati, lying up throughout Y-day under the trees there. The remaining stage of the approach-march to the front line at Forward Cottage was a mile in length. As it was impossible to walk over this in daylight, it was to be taped by the R.O.'s on the final evening.

The next preparatory step was the reconnaissance of the ground beyond the German lines. Parties of us would go by lorry to Reigersberg Château, a dismal modern building, greatly shattered, standing behind a high wall among trees a mile north-west of Ypres on the Brielen road. The whole of this region was thick with heavy guns, and there was a peculiarly obnoxious battery of 8-inch howitzers, hidden behind a hedge on the roadside opposite the château, which invariably fired with an ear-splitting blast of sound at the moment when one was standing by the lorry a dozen yards in front of the muzzles. As the Germans indulged in a good deal of retaliation in the neighbourhood, Reigersberg was no place to linger about. A section commander and an R.O. of F Battalion were blown to pieces one morning by a heavy shell which burst at their feet in the château grounds; and the gunners who lived there suffered casualties every day. Leaving this lugubrious mansion with some haste, therefore, we used to push forward on foot to another unhealthy spot, Bridge 4 over the canal. This was a timber structure for infantry and field-guns, built over the wreck of a sunken steamboat. It was constantly shelled, and I suppose at that time was hit on an average at least once a day; while if high explosive was not coming over, one could always expect a few bursts of heavy shrapnel above one's head. Owing to the causeways which blocked the canal lower down, the water here was stagnant and choked with weeds; but in fine weather, if the German guns were quiet, men usually were bathing in it; and, as somebody remarked, "it really became more like the Serpentine every day." Beyond Bridge 4 we entered the annihilated region of the real Salient. Along the high canal bank, with its terraces of sand-bagged dug-outs, named and numbered like suburban thoroughfares, stood the wreckage of a line of magnificent trees, the counterpart of that on the west bank. Half of these were mere splintered trunks or lay entirely prostrate, and those still erect were gashed and torn. They rose mournfully above the frightful welter of shell-holes and trenches, the litter of timber and rubbish, the rusted entanglements, and the patches of marsh lined with unhappy pollards, which sloped up gently to Frascati and the remains of La Brique. Our route from the bridge usually took us in one of two directions across this wasted land. Either we descended at once into trenches and made our way to various points in the reserve or support lines from which we could obtain a fair view of the Pilkem Ridge, or we walked above ground with some disquietude of spirit through Frascati and La Brique to Wilson's Post, a concrete observation-point on the forward slope beyond. This journey never was an unmixed joy. We had to pass through the garden of the last house (or, to be accurate, what had been the garden of what had been the last house) in La Brique. At one time the ruins of this building had been used as a machine-gun post. The Germans, having

YPRES: THE PRELIMINARIES 115

become aware of this, shelled it heavily, and the guns were withdrawn. The derelict house, however, was still an occasional target, and was yet another point where no sensible man lingered. Wilson's Post, a quarter of a mile in front, was a small two-storied tower embedded literally to its eyelids in the earth, its cranium concealed in willows and other shrubs. It was approached from La Brique by an unfinished trench about the depth of a roadside gutter. In the bottom storey, illuminated by a candle, an orderly sat over a telephone; in the upper chamber—about five feet square and reached by a ladder—a telescope peered through two shallow slits on the ground-level and swept from an angle the whole front over which my battalion was to attack. Sitting on a little bench with one's feet dangling over the trap-door, one could see the brown slope of the Pilkem Ridge, seamed with lighter-coloured lines which marked the enemy's trenches, the foliage of Kitchener's Wood appearing over the crest, and, away to the left, the debris of the estaminet called Boche Castle and a few clumps of skeleton trees which, on that obliterated countryside, served us for landmarks—English Trees, Marsouin Trees, Hurst Park, and that solitary but useful vegetable known to us as Lone Tree. (The fate of English Trees, marking the site of a vanished farm, was followed by us with peculiar interest, and odds were laid on or against their survival. Originally they were eleven in number, but our preliminary bombardment thinned their ranks, and the eclipse of one or another was sedulously recorded, and the vital information circulated throughout the battalion. About half a dozen, I think, all considerably the worse for wear, survived the ordeal, and may be standing yet.) Far beyond these outposts we could see the hazy woods about Pilkem and Langemarck and Poelcapelle. We were provided with sketches professing to depict all these features, and even such details as Langemarck Church and the Institute (whatever that might be) at Passchendaele; but no two of us could ever agree in identifying these remote buildings. Of far greater merit was a panorama, taking in our entire front, drawn from Wilson's Post by an R.E. officer named Brennan. This was of real service to us. One singular object, I remember, situated prominently on the ridge-top in front of Kitchener's Wood, puzzled us till the end. It was square in outline and of the size of a small cottage, only no cottage could be standing there and none was marked on the map. The map, on the contrary, misled apparently by a light railway which aeroplane photographs showed running out to it from the wood, marked it as an ammunition dump! This palpably was absurd, and was the result of some one making a guess without looking at the ground. Only a lunatic would erect a dump ten or twelve feet high a thousand yards from the front line and in full view of the enemy. I saw this mystery at close quarters for the first time on the afternoon of 1st August, when I was trudging homeward through the mud and rain with the remains of my crew, and then discovered it to be a large concrete machine-gun fort, covered with sheets of brown camouflage netting. It had been hit more than once, probably by the 9.2 shells with which we bombarded the enemy's second line; but these huge projectiles had only cracked the walls. The effect of the concussion inside, however, must have been terrible. A dead German, with wide-open blue eyes staring out of a grey face, was lying on his back half out of the entrance, and no doubt there were others within. I was in no mood for grisly investigations, and even my crew were too scared and exhausted to indulge the ruling passion for souvenirs.

Among the other attractions of La Brique and its salubrious neighbourhood were a couple of trees fitted with iron rungs and used as occasional o.p.'s, and a third dummy stump made of steel, inside which the observer insinuated himself. I never ascended the tallest tree, eighty feet high, and never had the least desire to do so; but I clambered once up the shorter one, which stood at the head of the ditch leading to Wilson's Post. I did not think that the view obtained therefrom was worth the trouble and anxiety involved. On another occasion a fellow tank-commander, Merchant, and myself were reconnoitring together from this point. He was up the tree and I was sitting at the foot of it, asking, like the lady in the poem, "Can you see anything, Sister Anne?" and wishing he would make haste. He might have replied, after Bairnsfather's hero, "They must have seen *me!*" For immediately after we both heard a familiar whistling crescendo, a sound whose disturbing quality time cannot stale nor custom wither—the shriek of an approaching shell. Merchant came down that tree like an acrobat; and our simultaneous arrival in the ditch coincided with that of the shell a few yards away. In point of fact, the wretched last house in La Brique, already adverted to, was again the object of unmerited suspicion. A succession of projectiles fell about it and about us, for the shooting was not very good, while we crouched on all-fours in the unfinished trench, and bobbed up like marionettes after each explosion to see how big a margin had been granted us. As this did not appear too generous, we withdrew presently to Wilson's Post, and there, a few minutes later, it began to rain gas-shells. Heaven knows what the Germans saw or thought they saw. Probably the whole business was mere caprice. There was no one but ourselves moving above ground for miles around, and we had been very circumspect, keeping under cover and refraining from flapping large maps about in the open after the fashion of some of these reconnoitring parties. Happily, the demonstration was short-lived. When it subsided we hurried back without undue ceremony through La Brique to Bridge 4, Reigersberg, and the waiting lorry.

While Reigersberg itself was no sanatorium, the village of Brielen, through which our transport had to pass on these excursions, became toward the end of July even more unpopular. Situate on one of the main thoroughfares into Ypres, with cross-roads running through it from Vlamertinghe to the canal, it was an obvious target, and under the continual impact of high-explosive shell it decayed very rapidly. In the autumn of 1916 it was still inhabited: by the following spring it was a mere avenue of empty ruins; and when I left the Salient in October '17, most of the debris even had been carted away as road ballast. And during our reconnaissances it was no uncommon thing to wait anxiously for an hour in the grounds of Reigersberg Château, with one eye upon the sand-bagged cellars there, watching the fragments of Brielen, two or three hundred yards up the road, ascending gracefully, at regular and frequent intervals, into the air.

It may be said that this sort of thing was child's play to the conditions endured in the line itself. And so, in one sense, undoubtedly it was. A walk to Frascati or St Jean and back was, on the face of it, preferable to a week's residence in either of those places. Yet I think that every one who knew the Salient in the summer of 1917 will agree that its most disagreeable feature, during what would be called inactive periods, was this persistent shelling of back areas. On any other front one felt moderately safe two miles behind the line, but never at Ypres. For troops in support there was no real peace east of Poperinghe. While the front trenches might be wrapped in quiet, shells would be falling all day in Brielen or Vlamertinghe or even in Oosthoek Wood. And the reason was obvious. The Salient was very narrow as well as very pronounced. As a purely military position it was absurd. A gun of quite moderate calibre, emplaced on either flank, could have fired right across the chord of the arc. At Boesinghe the enemy actually was north-west of Ypres: in front of Wytschaete, before the battle of Messines, he was south-west of it; and between these two points the distance was only seven miles. From the centre of a line drawn from one to the other, the Salient projected about four miles. Even after Messines the line of investment still ran through half a circle, and commanded, from the concentric Pilkem Ridge, almost all the

ground up to the canal. Within this enclosure, only half the
size of the city of Paris, the country was flat, marshy, and
intersected by minor streams and dykes; while the obstacle
of the canal caused all the main roads from the west, down
which our men and supplies must march, to converge on
the crossings at Ypres itself. On these roads, therefore, on
the points where they were cut by lateral thoroughfares, and
especially on the point of convergence, the hostile fire naturally was directed. And there were a thousand other targets
for less concentrated effort. Troops swarmed everywhere
from Ypres to the Belgian frontier; and in the forward area,
in addition to the camps of infantry and gunners, there were
hosts of engineers and labour men digging gun-pits, laying
roads and railways, putting up horse-lines and dumps and
water systems. Light and heavy trains moved up and
down all day. The Germans were perfectly aware of this
activity; and it was an unlucky battery that could not score
a hit or two in the course of twenty-four hours' speculative
shooting over so congested a countryside.

IV.

Our camp of bell-tents in the copse at Lovie Château,
where we spent our nights, was outside the normal area of
this unpleasantness. Poperinghe, of course, two miles to
the south, was shelled for half an hour or so every morning,
often in the evening, and occasionally at odd hours during
the day. The shells passed almost over our camp; and
while one was dressing or preparing to turn in for the night
one used to hear the whistle overhead and then the distant
crash and echo in the unfortunate town. And once we
were genuinely entertained by a crisis nearer at hand. An
enterprising 15-inch gun, probably travelling in luxury on a
train, took a few pot-shots at the 5th Army Headquarters
in the château itself. When one or two of these colossal
projectiles burst in the aerodrome across the road, the

army became alarmed, assumed hurriedly the unfamiliar steel helmet, and presently departed, bag and baggage, for Proven. The Germans, well informed as usual, learnt almost at once of this translation: the 15-inch gun was turned on the new refuge; and the Higher Command, choosing the most comfortable of two evils, came back to Lovie again, greatly to the annoyance of the Flying Corps, who in the meantime had occupied the château. The humour of this episode will be apparent to every one who has seen the vast paraphernalia accompanying a British army headquarters in the field—the scores of offices, the hosts of B.G.G.S.'s, G.S.O.'s, A.P.M.'s, clerks, orderlies, and interpreters, the attached French missions and Belgian missions, and missions from Liberia and Paraguay and the Great Cham, the numberless boxes of maps and crockery and returns and red-tape—all of which had to be conveyed in an armada of cars and lorries from Lovie to Proven and back from Proven to Lovie again within a fortnight. If three domestic removals are as bad as a fire, two moves of an army headquarters can be compared only to an earthquake. After the second hegira, the enemy, feeling no doubt that a continuance of this barbarous treatment (if it ever came to light) would bring down upon him the just execration of the civilised world, diverted his gun to more appropriate targets, and fell back upon an accepted method of irritating such exalted quarters—namely, bombing.

Bombing, indeed, was a very serious plague throughout the area that summer; and the subject raises an unpleasant question on which a few words must be said, both on general grounds and because it affected the tank units in a peculiar degree. There can be no two opinions as to who held command of the air (to use the cant phrase) in the Ypres sector in 1917. Our photographic and gun-spotting machines continued to perform their dangerous and thankless tasks with unfailing skill and courage, as they have throughout the war; but their work required experience, its results could be checked, and it was therefore in the hands of the best type of officer. The so-called scouts or fighting-machines, unfortunately, came in a different category. In this branch the Germans appeared to have things very much their own way. During the Somme battles the losses in the Flying Corps were extremely heavy, and fell naturally upon the class of pilot which could least be spared. Afterwards, with the continual growth of the corps, there began that wholesale raking-in of officers from the highways and byways, and from the very junior ranks of garage and bicycle-shop assistants—a policy which has steadily undermined the efficiency and credit of the force. The pay was high, and the opportunities for shirking unpleasant duties exceptional. It is not for nothing that the present R.A.F. is called the Hot Air Force, and has acquired a reputation in the Army sufficient to damn any organisation that is not exploited continually for commercial reasons by a wealthy newspaper syndicate. This is not a mere question of envy or rumour: the facts of the decline are patent and well known; and to clinch them one has only to recall to mind the type of flying officer (dressed like an attendant at a cinema theatre, and usually behaving as such) who swarmed in the London bars and in the clubs in France, and who afterwards swarmed in Germany. Half the subalterns to be seen did not wear even the observer's single wing—and, to hazard a guess for once, had no desire to wear it. All cannot have belonged to the equipment branch. I am sorry if remarks of this kind seem to do injustice to many gallant and capable pilots. At the close of the war there were, I believe, something like 30,000 officers in the R.A.F. A third of these may have been, and probably were, thoroughly efficient; but there remained a heavy balance of the untrustworthy; and it was for the hard work and devoted sacrifices of the minority that this discreditable residue received especial privileges and honours, and was allowed a general licence of behaviour exceeded only by that of colonial troops, who at least had the excuse of brilliant service in the field. The evil itself was fully recognised in the corps, and it is high time some protest was uttered against the unscrupulous nonsense which has flooded our newspapers for the past few years. The point, however, that I wish to bring out at the moment is that the results of employing bad material for tasks requiring a peculiar degree of nerve and a strong sense of responsibility were seriously felt for the first time at Ypres in 1917. The old Somme fighters were dead or captured; and now the back areas of the Salient were infested day and night by German bombing squadrons. The Germans, presumably, picked their aviators as they picked their machine-gunners. They did not lose their heads after a costly battle and rush to commission thousands of Berlin counter-jumpers, who might be excellent in the ranks but were useless as officers. The difficulties of countering night attacks by aeroplanes were obvious; but it was humiliating as well as unpleasant to have a dozen enemy machines sailing over the lines two or three times a day, bombing camps and towns, destroying balloons, driving off the slow and helpless gun-spotters and photographers (and their escorts), and obtaining into the bargain much valuable information. During four months in the area, while this infliction was occurring almost every day, I saw only one German aeroplane brought down behind our own lines; and this was destroyed, above two of our aerodromes, by a couple of French pilots. Possibly our own squadrons were simultaneously bombing Roullers or Menin. One hopes they were. But every aerodrome was crowded with fighting-machines, which used to perform tricks overhead when all was quiet, but made no apparent attempt to cut off the enemy's raiders. One corps commander informed the squadron attached to him that if he did not see it do more useful work, he would make every pilot fly for two additional hours a day.

I have written enough, perhaps too much, on this unsavoury topic. And it may be asked—What has all this recrimination to do with tanks? It has, in point of fact, a great deal to do with them. Tank warfare can be assisted

or hindered to a marked degree by aeroplane co-operation
or the lack of it. A man or a tank, or even a column of
troops, can often elude observation from above merely by
remaining still. It is movement which betrays. Infantry,
moreover, can always take cover rapidly; but it is impossible
to camouflage a tank in the open in a few seconds. In consequence it is inadvisable to move tanks during daylight
near the front line, if any of the enemy's aeroplanes are
likely to be about. In the Salient they were always about;
and things had got to this pitch—that although we were
hidden in a wood, with clearings close at hand where we
could have tested our machines secure from direct observation, *during the whole month of July no tank was permitted to
move a yard except by night.* At any hour of the day some
German aeroplane, unmolested except by "Archies," which
were more dangerous to us below than to the pilot, might
come flying low over Oosthoek. In my own case, a fortnight
before the battle I took over a new tank just arrived from
Erin by night, and driven into the wood by another crew.
I had no opportunity of testing it under way until we actually moved off on our approach-march to Halfway House on
the evening of 29th July. As was to be expected of a brand-
new machine, one or two mechanical parts were then found
to require slight adjustments. A slipping clutch, which
would have been discovered and remedied in a few minutes
during a preliminary trial, gave considerable trouble, and
held up all the tanks behind me for some time.

Secondly, contact aeroplanes can be of the greatest use
in battle by reporting the situation of tanks, of which
battalion and company commanders can have little or no
knowledge. Infantry send back runners; but tanks, except
for their pigeons, reserved (when available at all) for use at
definite objectives, have no means as yet of communicating
their whereabouts or condition once they have crossed the
front line. In view of this, arrangements were made with
the Flying Corps for tanks to carry certain permanent marks
which would attract the attention of contact-pilots. Every

machine had its number painted in large black characters on a white ground on top of the cab, and carried in addition a square of white cloth to be tied on the roof when ditched. The duty of a contact-pilot, as everybody knows, is to fly at a sufficiently low altitude to discover the position of his own infantry, and a tank, even without any distinguishing marks, is more conspicuous than a row of mud-plastered human figures. But no reliable information, so far as my battalion was concerned, ever came through from this source: in fact, I do not think the position of a single tank was reported. Most of them, of course, were ditched during a large part of the day, and possibly the other tank commanders acted as I did. When I found myself hopelessly bogged on the Pilkem Ridge, the last thing I dreamt of doing was to hang out my conspicuous square of cloth. I was at some pains even to obliterate with mud the number on my cab. I was convinced that if any aeroplanes flew low above me, in all probability they would be Germans. And in fact many ditched tanks, lying well behind our infantry, were attacked by the enemy's pilots, who machine-gunned the crews as they struggled with booms and shovels to get under way again.

The foregoing may seem rather a lengthy and unnecessary digression, but it is a poor book which one cannot write in one's own way. And war, after all, cannot be made or described (as some think) in water-tight compartments. Each arm is dependent upon the rest, and sees much of their work. And a fairly long and varied experience has driven home to most civilian soldiers like myself certain conclusions regarding the various branches of the British Army in Europe. The cavalry, since 1914-15 (when they fought on foot) have been utterly useless, in part because they will not see things as they are; the Flying Corps, since 1916, has declined steadily in quality and value; but throughout, for the infantry, the gunners, and the engineers, on the whole no praise can be too high.

CHAPTER VIII.

YPRES: THE 31ST JULY.

I.

ALL spare officers and crews had taken part in the reconnaissance of the Salient, for they might be called upon at any moment. And, as it happened, one of the original tank commanders in my section fell ill about the middle of July, whereupon I stepped into the vacancy.

His tank was also *hors de combat* with a broken-down engine. It being impossible to repair it in the time available a new machine, with two or three others required by the brigade, was on its way from Erin to replace it, and this I was to take over on its arrival. The night it detrained, therefore, I accompanied Kessel, my section commander, to the Oosthoek ramp. The event was marked by one startling occurrence. Earlier in the evening the Germans had been industriously shelling the far end of the wood with shrapnel; but everything was quiet when the tank train pulled in soon after ten o'clock. It was a very dark night. Before eleven, however, my new tank was parked up and camouflaged in the wood to the north of the military road. The rest of the company's tanks were a quarter of a mile away, on the south side. Lorries had come up to take the men back to Lovie Château, and we were standing by them, waiting for a few laggards, when a very large ammunition dump near Hospital Farm, half a mile to the northward, was hit and exploded. It was, I suppose, one of the biggest dumps in the Salient—a towering accumulation of every size and type of shell, together with thousands of cases of S.A.A., rockets, grenades, Very lights, and other inflammatory stuff—and even from where we stood the effect of its destruction was prodigious and alarming. A great red glare blazed up suddenly above the trees, broadened, and grew higher; volumes of blood-shot smoke, streaked with rockets, covered half the sky; and presently, through the pop-pop-pop of exploding rifle ammunition and the louder detonations of shells, we could hear the crackle of burning timber as the neighbouring trees themselves caught fire. In this lay a serious menace to the tanks, for the wood, although straggling, was continuous. It was not long before we could see the distant flames through the trees in front of us. In the meantime, preceded by magnificent eruptions of fire and sparks, there had burst two terrific explosions, whose concussions shook the ground, hit us like blows, and flung fragments of white-hot metal on to the military road. Happily, what little wind there was blew away from us, and the fire made no appreciable gain in our direction; and after standing by until midnight, prepared to drive the tanks out of the wood if necessary, we decided that we might go home. It was surprising that the Germans (so far at least as one could judge amid the prevailing uproar) refrained from stimulating things in general by a little judicious shelling. The glare of the great conflagration, which lit up the whole Salient, must have been visible from Courtrai. It was still blazing and exploding as we left; and two hours later, at Lovie Château, four miles away, I heard another series of crashing detonations.

The following morning I marched my crew down to the new tank. I decided naturally to take with me my own men, with whom by now I was well acquainted, in preference to the strange drivers and gunners whose officer I had replaced. The latter, I think, were as disappointed as my own crew was pleased by this translation; for throughout the battalion the spirit in the ranks was admirable. Most of the N.C.O.'s and a large proportion of the men came from the original F Company of the Heavy Branch, and very few of them (in my crew, for example, none at all) had ever seen a shell burst until they came to the Salient; and while it is true that soldiers often look forward to their first battle with a confidence born simply of ignorance, and deteriorate in *moral* as their experience of horrors increases, the personnel of the Tank Corps maintained to the end a conspicuously high standard. And to go into action in a tank, as I hope to show, is not the bed of roses some rash people used to think it. I put this consistent excellence down in part to the class of man which the corps attracted.

There was plenty of work to be done when I took over G 46, whose more intimate name—transferred from her disabled predecessor, and none of my choosing—was "Gina." (The tanks and each battalion were christened with names beginning with the initial letter of their unit. Thus we were all "G's." "Gina," appropriately enough, was a female; but in fact it seems natural to speak of all tanks as feminine, as if they were ships.) I have said already that no movement was permitted in Oosthoek Wood, and that in consequence it was impossible to test the transmission of my new command. Engines could be run quietly, however; and my first driver, a boy named Johnstone from the Armstrong College at Newcastle, who was one of those fortunate beings with a *flair* for anything mechanical, tinkered away affectionately at the magneto and other parts until the engine of G 46 ran like a dream. Throughout her short military career it gave no trouble of any kind until the water on the Pilkem Ridge got into the clutch and put the whole thing out of action at once and for ever.

Most of the novelties in the Mark IV. have been described already; but I have omitted so far any account of the new unditching gear tested by us for the first time at Wailly, and now to be used with a vengeance in the Salient. In place of the two short torpedo spars, each tank was now fitted with a single squared boom, about twelve feet long and strengthened with steel. It was a most heart-breaking affair to man-handle, for it weighed nine hundredweight; but for its particular work it was highly efficient. A pair of longitudinal rails lifted it clear of all obstructions on the roof, and when not in use it lay at right angles across these just above the spud-box fitted on the stern of the tank, its ends projecting a couple of feet on each side of the latter. Originally, the boom was lashed in place; but afterwards clips were provided to secure it to the rails. When required for unditching, it was attached to the track plates on either side in the same manner as the old spars, by a pair of chains and clamps. This attachment could be effected by a couple of men standing behind the tank, usually the most sheltered spot. On its completion the heavy boom was carried forward along the rails as the tracks revolved, slid down on to them in front of the cab, and was then pulled under the tank, where its great length and stiff resistance transversely to the direction of the latter's movement enabled the machine to climb out of almost any position. This boom was tested first in the sodden area of Messines, after that battle; and it was in use with all heavy tanks to the end of the war. Its only disadvantage—an inevitable one—was its weight. Added to that of thirty or forty iron spuds or shoes, it completed an extra load of a couple of tons; and on occasions when the heavier Mark IV. males became badly ditched it was found that the engine was not powerful enough to overcome this handicap. I have seen a boom on a tank lying at a rather acute angle refuse to move at all. But for all normal cases of ditching it was invaluable.

In those days tank equipment was devised and issued on a lavish scale. One took over with the machine a vast assortment of instruments calculated to soften the asperities of a very cramped and uncomfortable mode of warfare, and calling to mind the fittings of H.M.S. *Mantelpiece*. If we had no zoetropes, excellent carriage clocks, mounted in heavy brass, were the perquisites in more senses than one of every tank commander. The number of these clocks destroyed by shell-fire was so abnormal in the Salient that after that deplorable campaign the issue was stopped, it being felt that the residue of timepieces in stock would serve a more useful purpose and lead a safer life in the numerous offices of Central Stores and Workshops at Erin. A haversack full of splints, shell-dressings, iodine, and other sinister medical comforts, quite passable binoculars, electric hand-lamps, signalling shutters, six periscopes, and an ingenious device like a pair of pantomime braces fitted with batteries, switches, and red and green lights, to be used in guiding tanks at night, were also among the treasures thrust upon us in a very open-handed manner. But this halcyon age did not endure for long. Vulgar considerations of waste and expenditure supervened. Before the end the whereabouts of every spanner and split-pin became a cause of acute worry to us all. It should be unnecessary to add that this era of suspicion brought with it a veritable spate of new Army Forms—T.K. 5's and T.Q. 17's and so on—continually superseding each other and never by any chance filled in correctly. We were already in possession of immense log-books, atrocities known as battle history sheets, and pigeon-message forms. A fully-equipped tank, in short, was a combination of a battleship, an ironmonger's shop, an optician's, a chemist's, a grocer's, and a Government office. We only wanted a typewriter to round off the outfit.

I do not remember the exact date on which I took over G 46 and her belongings; but it must have been between the 15th and 20th of July. The battle, fixed originally for the 25th, had already been put back three days. The final postponement, to the 31st, was made known only at the last moment. In these circumstances there was not too much time for all that had to be done. The whole tank required to be washed down and scrubbed, for she came straight from the workshops in a filthy condition. The six Lewis guns had to be cleaned, and the 276 drums filled with ammunition. Track plates, spuds, camouflage nets, petrol, oil, and grease had to be procured from the advanced stores and dump beside the ramp. At the same time further reconnaissance was carried out, and we all went to see the large-scale model of our sector of the attack which the 18th

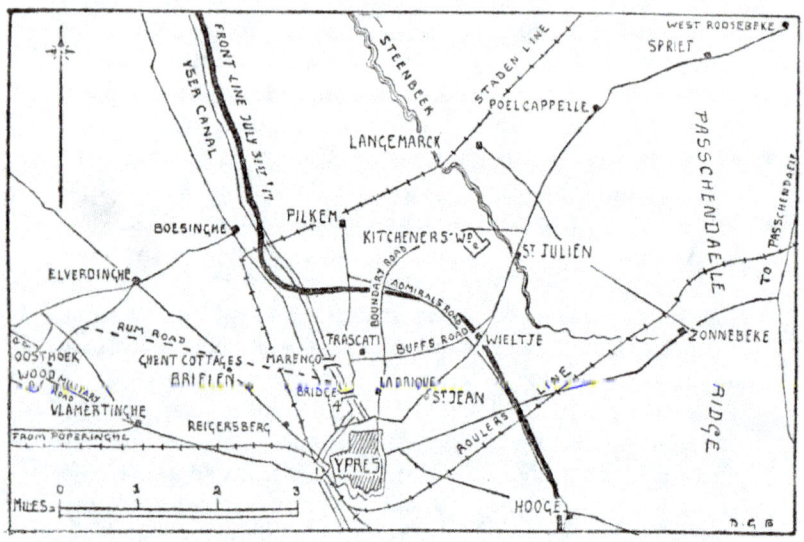

Third Battle of Ypres, Aug.-Nov. 1917.

Corps had built out of sand and brick rubble in the centre of the wood. I cannot honestly say that this ingenious curiosity was of much help to us. Here, however, some sort of liaison was effected with the infantry with whom we were to work. Meanwhile, back in camp at Lovie Château there were conferences with Reconnaissance officers and discussions with company commanders after dinner. Aeroplane photographs were studied, and special tank charts composed. (Every tank commander, so far as was possible, made his own chart on a scale of 1/5000.) Then there was

the question of supply to be considered. All crews took
into action two days' ordinary rations in addition to the
emergency ration; but this food was supplemented by a
few delicacies considered suitable to the festive occasion.
Thus most of us carried also oranges, lemons, chocolates,
and biscuits, one water-bottle filled with rum, and a bottle
of whisky. Personally, I took two bottles of whisky, and
was extremely thankful that I did.

Turning to the operations themselves, the 18th Corps
was attacking on a front of two divisions: the 51st Division
on the left and the 39th on the right. The two companies
of G Battalion were allotted as follows: 19 Company, with
my own section—No. 10—of 21 Company (16 tanks in all)
was to advance in two waves with the 39th Division. The
two remaining sections of 21 Company (8 tanks) worked
in a single wave with the 51st Division. The task of these
troops was to carry the German first and second systems
on the Pilkem Ridge and then secure the crossings of the
Steenbeek. The positions of these crossings, at or near
St Julien on the 39th Divisional front, determined the dis-
tribution of the tanks, it being the business of the second
wave on the right to endeavour to get over the stream and
help the infantry of the 118th Brigade to consolidate on the
far side. My section, in the first wave, received the following
orders:—

> "After crossing the German front line, No. 10 Sec-
> tion will split up. The left-hand pair, G 45 and G 46,
> pass to the north of Kultur Farm and take the northern
> end of Kitchener's Wood, giving special attention to
> Boche Castle and strong-point; then proceed round
> the wood and mop up in conjunction with the infantry
> until the barrage at line S lifts at zero plus 4.1, when
> they will advance with the infantry, giving special
> attention to Regina Cross. The right-hand pair, G 47
> and G 48, passing to the south of Kultur Farm, will
> take the southern end of Kitchener's Wood, and on
> the lifting of the barrage on line S at zero plus 4.1, will

devote their attention to the strong-point at Alberta, and push forward at the discretion of the commander towards Hugel Hollow.

"As soon as the infantry are consolidated on the Steenbeek Line, tanks will rally at C 11 d 20.90 (north of Alberta)."

I despair of making any one unfamiliar with the Salient understand what lay behind these clear and apparently simple instructions. Some of the difficulties before us will be described in the context. I will remark here, however, that every tank had to cross the enemy's front line by a single narrow gap between two flooded areas which marked the sites of Hampshire and Canadian Farms—themselves utterly demolished. We were warned that this front system was likely to become a serious obstacle. Lying in a hollow, always wet, it was to be subjected to a terrific barrage, which would destroy it completely, break down the revetments and all such firm surfaces as parapets and parados provided, and, in short, reduce the whole line to a grisly conglomeration of mounds of mud and pools of water. And once across, things would become even worse. For sixteen days before the attack the whole Pilkem Ridge was blasted by heavy-calibre shells. The amount of artillery we had concentrated in the Salient was unprecedented. Three thousand guns, I believe, were in position on that restricted front. Round about Brielen, Vlamertinghe, and the château called Les Trois Tours, batteries of 6-inch, 8-inch, 9.2-inch howitzers, and 60-pounder guns lined every hedge: down both sides of one narrow track that I remember one passed them every few yards; and when the preliminary bombardment was at its height it was sheer torture to be in the neighbourhood. As a result, everywhere behind the German line the water was welling up and spreading until the whole surface was a mere crust that would dissolve at a touch. The final barrage at zero, which as usual was to fall at dawn, would finish the work. The enemy's second line, along the crest, was to be deluged

Kitchener's Wood and German Second Line. Photo taken July 3, 1917, showing position of Tanks G 45 and 46.

with 9.2's; while 15-inch railway guns had been shelling for some days the strong-point at Boche Castle, for which my own tank was to make. Imagine a country like the Lincolnshire flats, or the valley of the Kentish Stour, or any other piece of reclaimed and water-logged land in England, subjected, at the end of three years' systematic annihilation by high explosives, to this three weeks' wild crescendo of destruction, and some idea may be gathered of what the area behind the hostile front had become even before the downpour on the 31st, and after added the ultimate touches of disintegration and horror and misery.

The probable conditions awaiting us were known to all; but none of our conjectures equalled the reality. Before the battle we were more concerned over what proved in the event a comparatively minor evil—the difficulty we should experience in finding our way to our various objectives. The view from inside a tank, as one cannot repeat too often, is restricted and misleading. Once we had crossed our front line, the few miserable tree-clumps which we had studied from a distance might appear very different near at hand. They might have been destroyed, or we might fail to see them at all. The one unmistakable landmark, Kitchener's Wood—a plantation, still in fair condition, some 700 yards in length—was actually out of sight until we had climbed out of some dead ground at the foot of the ridge; and with the dust and smoke of the battle the first hour after dawn was certain to be dark and confusing. As our compasses were thoroughly unreliable, there was a danger of losing direction at the very start. A few tanks, indeed, quite excusably did so. And throughout the day, all over a battlefield whose utter bewildering sameness no words can express, there was much groping and guessing and general uncertainty. One of G Battalion's tanks wandered right across two corps' fronts. But on the whole our lengthy and sedulous coaching was very triumphantly vindicated: routes were maintained and objectives reached with surprising accuracy and punctuality. Delays in most cases were due to the appalling state of the ground, some tanks having to be unditched two or three times before they got into action at all.

II.

If the belief still lingers that the British soldier, keen and willing as he is, always goes into battle (as the Ollivier Cabinet once went to war) with a light heart, it must be due to too much reading, in trashy books and journals, of the productions of half-educated persons with a bias against truth. For very few men, of whatever race, can even approach the front line in these scientific days with any real equanimity of spirit. The processes by which one can be hurt are too many and various, and impend too nearly to permit of it. No healthy being likes the idea of being killed or mutilated. A common sense of subordination and comradeship, the fear of being thought afraid, and the power of habit, take one further than all the high-flown cant about glory and the joy of battle. And indeed if we all went into battle with a light heart there would be no merit in the thing: such tokens as medals and ribbons would lose what small significance they still possess; and we should be more (or less) than human.

It is during the days immediately before a long-expected action that men show in their several ways that they are, on the contrary, very human indeed. The strain which perhaps for weeks has been there is suddenly increased. Nerves begin to wear, tempers to rise, uncomfortable moods to supervene. Only the very young and inexperienced sometimes are superior to this failing. I know that most of us in the camp by Lovie Château grew rather irritable and contentious toward the end of our period of waiting. The depressing influence which seemed always to brood over the Salient, and the feeling that we were embarking upon a novel and gigantic gamble, were enough to account for it. The weather had been uncertain, and about the 24th rain fell heavily. The camp, pitched in a wood amid choking undergrowth, became steamily moist, smelly, and unhealthy. Every two or three hours during every night the enemy's aeroplanes came over and bombed the neighbourhood thoroughly. There was the usual futile racket and excitement, with searchlights wavering, shrapnel sparkling and descending on our heads, and tracer bullets soaring up in streams in every direction but the right one. This became so much a habit that we grew accustomed to it; and we used to lie in bed amid the uproar and wonder sleepily if it were better to put our steel helmets over our faces or our stomachs. The tank park in Oosthoek Wood suffered from the same persecution, to which there seemed to be no adequate reply. So far as I remember, we were lucky enough to escape casualties from this cause; but other people were not so fortunate. I recall one ghastly incident of this period, because my crew was on guard fifty yards away when it happened, and might well have been involved in the disaster. A battalion of Northumberland Fusiliers, coming out of the line one evening, bivouacked beside the military road close to our tanks. They had réveillé at three o'clock in the morning, preparatory to marching off to rest billets, and at that dangerous hour very foolishly lit candles and waved lanterns about in the wood. The usual German aeroplane was at hand. It dropped two heavy bombs very neatly into the bivouac, and in an instant killed or wounded over a hundred men.

The effect of these powerful bombs, provided with light fuses which detonated at a touch, was terrible; and it would be thought that any one who once had seen the victims of a raid would be circumspect for ever after. Yet troops, even after considerable experience, were often extraordinarily stupid in this matter of hostile aircraft. Another north-country battalion — Tynesiders, I believe — was in camp near Elverdinghe about this time. Two or three German aeroplanes flew low over the camp in broad daylight. Instead of keeping out of sight, the whole battalion rushed out to see the raiders. The latter might have overlooked the camouflaged tents and huts, but the sudden appearance of a mass of white upturned faces caught their attention at once, with the inevitable result. A few bombs were released, and the crowd of spectators became a shambles. The Tynesiders lost 140 men in as many seconds.

Toward the end of July the shelling of Oosthoek and other likely places also increased in volume. The enemy was perfectly aware of the imminence of the attack, and also, as it appeared, of the original date and the first postponement; and the back areas suffered in consequence. The red dust floated over Ypres all day. Poperinghe received increased attention, and was bombed heavily into the bargain. The canal became more than ordinarily unpleasant. But the German artillerists, in addition to persecuting these obvious targets, had a system of plastering with shells certain empty areas which appeared to offer no attractions to a gunner. This wasteful method gathered in no doubt a few stray victims, but at a disproportionate cost in ammunition. The forward region, about Frascati and La Brique, was perhaps more naturally a favourite one for this blind "area" shooting, for field batteries were hidden among the willows; and the enemy's increasing suspicion of this neighbourhood caused us a good deal of annoyance during our final journeys on reconnaissance. I remember how Kessel, Merchant, and I, having been up the line one morning, were sitting under a hedge near Frascati, eating bully sandwiches and discussing (of all things) the fourth dimension, when we found ourselves the unworthy centre of one of these displays of hate. To us it seemed purposeless and uncalled for to a degree. There was no working party in the neighbourhood; no one, indeed, was in sight anywhere, and the batteries, some distance away, were not firing. But high-velocity shells arrived in streams, and when we were

back, very thankfully, at the canal, the dust-clouds were
still rising busily in the desert waste between us and the
farm.

During these last days our preparations in Oosthoek
Wood were completed. The fighting tanks were ready
for action. The supply tanks—two per company—were
filled up with petrol, oil, and ammunition; limbered
waggons drawn by mules were attached to us to work
between Frascati and the base, and we had also one
wireless and one cable-laying tank. Oranges, chocolates,
and whisky had been collected. We had received barrage
maps and time-tables, and had visited the headquarters of
the various infantry units with whom we were to work.
Merchant and myself, with G 45 and G 46, were co-operating with a battalion of the Rifle Brigade. This had moved
up to a bivouac on the edge of Oosthoek, and I walked
over one morning to discuss the attack with the Colonel
and his officers. They were very anxious about some
alleged wire in front of the Steenbeek, which I undertook
to crush for them if I ever got so far. In the event I got
nowhere near it, and I was of little or no use to these
infantry. I am afraid that not many of the officers I met
that morning were left after the battle, for the 117th
Brigade, to which the battalion belonged, suffered cruelly
on the 31st.

III.

During the night of the 24th-25th July the tanks of
21 Company (less No. 10 Section) moved from Oosthoek
Wood to Halfway House. On the 24th I had been working
late with my men on G 46, making the final preparations
for our own departure the following evening, and as we left
the wood about seven o'clock we met the eight crews
marching in to their tanks. Their move was attended by
one disaster. The night was exceedingly dark, rain had
been falling, and the surface of the narrow winding track

which I have described as leading through the wood to Hospital Farm had become greasy and treacherous. A male tank, swinging too far to avoid a tree, slid off the cambered road into the wide moat which surrounded the farm. The water rose a foot above the floor boards, instantly putting the engine out of action. As nothing could be done that night, the tank (whose roof was barely level with the road) was camouflaged and left, the crew bivouacking close at hand. The remainder pushed on, and after being harassed by some shelling which fortunately did no harm, parked up under the bushes at Halfway House. Owing to the postponement of the attack for another three days, the sunken tank, having been towed ashore the next night with infinite difficulty, was got running again in time to rejoin the company before the latter moved on to Frascati.

About five o'clock on the afternoon of the 25th I was having tea with Kessel, Merchant, and some others under the lee of a tank. We were due to start our own move at nine that evening. Having already consumed our own tea ration, we were drinking an extraordinary mud-coloured beverage infused from one of those compressed concoctions, strongly resembling tobacco, which friends and relations used to send out as being especially suitable for active service. Possibly the sinister influence of this drug was accountable in part for the fact that none of us were looking forward to the forthcoming approach march with the proper military enthusiasm. It was true that the day was humid and depressing; that the wood was squelchy underfoot and smelt like a badly-kept mausoleum hurriedly washed in petrol; and that some of 21 Company, having returned in lorries from Halfway House for a few hours' rest at Lovie, had brought discouraging reports of the route and the general conditions nearer to the line. Brisk shelling was in progress. The tanks of another battalion, uncomfortably embedded among heavy howitzers under the trees of Les Trois Tours, had come in for the enemy's counter-battery

work and had passed an extremely unpleasant night. I will
not speak for the rest of us, but I know that I, for one, was
greatly relieved when our tea was interrupted by the arrival
of a runner with the order cancelling our move. Owing to
the effects of the rain, the attack had been put off once
more until the last day of the month. In the long-run
it is obvious wisdom to get thankless duties over and done
with as soon as possible; and the Army's inveterate habit
of issuing eleventh-hour instructions is better indulged in
advancing than in postponing battles; but at the time one
does not always reason so philosophically. Also one feels
a little more like the gay and careless warrior of the newspapers at certain junctures than at others. Somehow we
had not felt either gay or careless that afternoon. And
now we could go back to bed like Christians or reprieved
criminals, and spend a further three days of grace revising
once more our testamentary dispositions (if any) in comparative safety and comfort.

A thoughtful act on the part of the Intelligence Branch
marked this interval and helped to amuse us. I have
spoken already of the sketches of church towers and other
remote landmarks with which we had been provided. There
was now issued to each tank commander, with every circumstance of urgency, a minute drawing about the size of
a blue Mauritius postage-stamp, depicting the tower and
spire of Hooglede Church. No one knew where Hooglede
was, or had ever heard of it. It was generally believed to
be near Brussels. Research on the map eventually discovered it to be a village north-west of Roullers, some nine
miles beyond our farthest objective for the first day. As
a sign of optimism in high quarters this valedictory gift
was appreciated; but, being under no delusions ourselves
as to the difficulties before us, we felt that there was small
hope of our visiting the place in the immediate future.
In the event, of course, after three months' hard fighting
the British Army was still six miles away from Hooglede,
and did not reach it for another year.

Yet, curiously enough, as it happened, there seemed for a few hours a possibility of Hooglede and many other distant villages coming quickly into the scheme of things. For one effect of the last postponement of our attack was to mislead the enemy to a certain extent. Still anticipating it on the 28th, he withdrew his troops the night before from 3000 yards of his front line on the canal opposite Boesinghe. The Guards and French immediately crossed the canal, occupied the abandoned trenches, and during the night constructed seventeen bridges. Subsequent attempts to eject them were repulsed. This affair started a fine crop of rumours about a more pronounced retreat along the whole front. But the Germans had no intention whatever of retreating. The evacuation of the canal trenches either was a blunder or had been designed as a trap, and evidently was regretted. Our movements, therefore, were carried out as arranged; and on the evening of the 28th, about dusk, the tanks of 19 Company and my own section began their approach-march to Halfway House.

No one ever troubles to inquire how tanks are brought up to a battlefield. They are there, miraculously, at zero, and that is enough. Approach-marches are usually described in a few words, and their details taken for granted. Yet they can be, and often are, the most exhausting and nerve-racking feature of tank operations. They have to be undertaken at night. Lights must be shown very sparingly, if at all, even inside the tanks. The glow of a cigarette, or a white handkerchief or map, are often all that an officer can use to direct his driver. The early stages of a march are made commonly over roads and tracks, both for help in guidance and to avoid leaving spoors which hostile aeroplanes could observe or photograph; and the breakdown of one machine on a bridge or in some street or defile may hold up all the others behind it, to say nothing of any traffic on the route. Notwithstanding the greatest care in constructing time-tables, no trek is complete that does not involve meeting and consequent trouble with transport.

Light railways, timber-tracks, bridges, ground-lines, pipe-lines, air-lines—all these must suffer, in spite of precautions. The rate of progress will be maddeningly slow. Although even a Mark IV. could move at a fair speed under normal conditions, it is impossible to maintain anything like this when moving a dozen or two by night into battle. There will be frequent halts to let those behind close up. It is almost certain that somebody will become ditched, or break a fan-belt, or get on fire, or fall into trouble of some kind. Such accidents, trifling in a peaceful daylight trek, become agonising amid the circumstances of an approach-march by night, when repairs have to be effected in the dark, and when prolonged delay may be fatal. In many cases all ranks will have been working most of the preceding day. They will be up all night. Probably they will work again during part of the next day, and will be moving once more throughout a second night. They are lucky if they can obtain any genuine rest during the few hours allotted for that purpose. Those hours are sure to be spent in the forward battery area, liable to be shelled or gassed at any time, and always intolerably noisy. And as the tanks approach the front line there is an increasing likelihood of their coming under shell-fire which they can neither dodge nor counter. An infantry column so caught can at least scatter or take cover; but the tank crews remain boxed up in their crawling machines, committed to a definite route which may lead into the heart of the trouble, seeing and hearing little or nothing, but imagining much, and with none of the stimulants of action to sustain them. Probably their officers are compelled still to walk outside as guides. Add finally to all this the inevitable strain and anxiety involved in the general situation; the actual physical labour attending all work connected with tanks; the extreme heat endured for hours by the crews; and it will be apparent that the latter are not exactly fresh when the time comes to go into action.

Justice has never been done to this side of tank warfare,

or to the Corps' achievements in respect of it. Before every one of the hundred actions in which tanks have taken part, some such ordeal as I have described, with variations for better or worse according to circumstances, has been undergone. Excluding the very early days, when everything was against the new unit, the occasions on which the great majority of every section or company detailed (often at the last moment) for action did not arrive at the front line in time were extremely rare. Far more often than not every machine arrived in time. The climax of this efficiency was reached in the last battle before Amiens, on the 8th August 1918, when out of 435 tanks collected hastily from all over France, 430 started in front of the infantry at zero. But even the infantry never fully appreciated, because they were never made to understand, the amount of sheer labour and persistence put forth on their behalf. They called for tanks from somewhere at three or four hours' notice—and the tanks came. And that, after all, was what chiefly mattered.

Our trek to Halfway House was accomplished with only one serious hitch. On account of the accident to the tank at Hospital Farm, we were to avoid that place by taking a parallel track through the wood which increased slightly the length of the route. My section was to lead. About an hour before we started something went wrong with the differential of Merchant's tank, and he did not leave with the rest. When, about nine o'clock in the evening, the other two tanks of No. 10 pulled out from the trees south of the military road and swung on to the timbered thoroughfare, G 46 was waiting on the north side to fall in behind. 19 Company followed after me. Spectators from the infantry bivouacs now springing up again in the wood lined the roadside to watch the long line of tanks moving off in the dusk, but all wheeled traffic had been stopped or diverted for an hour. Before that period was up all the fifteen tanks had left the road, and were proceeding northward along the lane under the trees. The night was misty but clear, and lighted brilliantly with stars; but there was

no moon, and in the wood it was very dark. To guide
my driver as I walked in front of G 46, I had a half-folded
map thrust under the belt and cross-strap on my back.

It must have been nearly midnight when I cleared the
wood at the point called Dirty Bucket Corner, and swung
to the right along a road leading eventually to Vlamertinghe. In the open one could see very clearly. The leading tank (M'Elroy's) of 19 Company should have been close
behind me, but there was no sign of it or any other.
Entirely unknown to me, a singular accident had happened.
A few hundred yards farther back in the wood we had
crossed a broad-gauge military railroad. As M'Elroy's
machine was actually astride the metals a light engine
came down them at a fair speed, struck the tank broadside
on, pushed it into a hedge, and was itself derailed. The
tank was uninjured, except for a bent plate on the sponson,
but several of the crew were cut about, and all were badly
shaken. M'Elroy himself, being outside, was unhurt. A
considerable delay ensued, the light engine having to be
towed out of the way, or back on to the line; and the tank
was left by the roadside while a spare crew was sent for.
In the meantime, knowing nothing of all this, No. 10 Section had carried on. It was not for another hour that
19 Company overtook me again. We had then left the
Vlamertinghe road, and were on Rum Road itself, nearing
our destination. The clutch on G 46, for reasons already
explained, had not been tested, and was slipping badly;
and I had to halt for ten minutes or so while it was
adjusted, thus letting several of the following tanks pass
me. This was our last delay. Alden and Brassington, in
front of me, already were parking up their tanks at Halfway
House, where the rest of 21 Company's machines had been
lying for three days; and here I soon joined them. Everything was quiet in the neighbourhood, except for the eternal
uproar of our own artillery; but we learnt from the guard
that Les Trois Tours, whose trees we could see dimly, had
been shelled again that evening. It was at this juncture

that we were astonished by the arrival of Merchant's tank, which we had left in Oosthoek Wood with its differential casing removed. The repairs had been effected very rapidly, and the tank had then covered the whole route on fourth speed, actually overtaking us in little more than an hour. The enclosure at Halfway House was rectangular, and to enter it we had to cross a wide ditch, choked with ferocious brambles, and break through a towering hedge. My section was to lie up under some long neglected fruit trees and another hedge on the far side; and a good deal of manœuvring—infuriating work in the dark with the Mark IV. secondary gears—was required before we were satisfactorily hidden. Camouflage nets had then to be strung up to the trees, pegged down, and supplemented by foliage. All ranks, as fast as their tanks were secured for the night, helped to efface our tracks through the hedge and across the enclosure. The work was finished about 2 A.M., and, leaving two men per crew and one officer per section with the tanks, the rest of us trailed thankfully back to the beginning of Rum Road, where lorries were waiting to carry us to Lovie for a final rest in camp. Such arrangements for one's comfort, it may be noted, were peculiar in my experience to this operation alone. They were made possible by the length of the route, and could be applied only to this short initial stage. Usually they are out of the question.

The ensuing evening, that of the 29th, we returned by lorry to Halfway House at dusk. The dangerous part of the journey, including the crossing of the canal, had now to be accomplished. Rain had fallen again, the sky was clouded, and the night promised to be a black one. It was indeed already very dark when 21 Company pulled out of the enclosure. A section of 19 Company followed, and then my own. My exasperating clutch, although it had been tightened up during the day, proved to be still refractory. I was obliged to halt again after a while to make a further adjustment; and as the operation was not

a lengthy one, I asked the tank commander behind me
(Lynch, who was killed thirty-six hours later) to wait, as
I wished to maintain my position in the column. We
were off again, in fact, very shortly after. But at this
stage every one was becoming anxious and irritable, and
the stoppage brought exalted personages raving about
G 46, clamouring for it to proceed. As it happened,
haste would have helped nobody, for about this time
serious disaster overtook the section in front. Our route
left Rum Road a quarter of a mile from the canal, and
took thence a narrow track leading direct to Marengo
Causeway. This track was bounded by a dense hedge,
with trees, on one hand, and by a deep ditch on the other:
its surface was greasy after the rain, and the two leading
tanks of 19 Company slid off into the ditch. They still
blocked the track, and until they were got out no one
could advance. I soon caught up this paralysed advance-
guard, where crews were labouring with booms and shovels,
and officers were peering at their watches and whispering
anxiously. Henriques, the Reconnaissance Officer of 19
Company, came to me muttering that "things were very
serious." As indeed they were, for the nights at the end
of July are short: it was already nearly one o'clock; and
it was essential for us all to reach the shelter of the trees
at Frascati before morning. If dawn found any tanks in
the open east of the canal, all sorts of calamities would
have ensued. The whole offensive would have been
jeopardised, as our presence so far forward must have
advertised its immediate onfall to the enemy, to say
nothing of the consequences to ourselves. Added to these
apprehensions for the morrow, there fell the present fear
that at any moment the Germans might begin to shell
the canal and its approaches. Their gunners had been
very quiet so far that night; but if they chose to indulge
in their favourite pastime while our fifteen tanks were held
up in a line, a couple of hundred yards from the Causeway,
the results probably would be highly unpleasant. Very

fortunately, nothing happened, and the difficulty was overcome. The ditched tanks got themselves out, and we crawled one by one on to Marengo Causeway, which 21 Company had crossed safely half an hour before. Here again our luck held: at this most critical point in the whole route not a shell fell to disturb us, and the whole column, passing over without mishap, entered the dismal wilderness of old trenches, wire, smashed trees, and shell-holes on the farther side. From here onwards our route had been taped by the R.O.'s, and but for this assistance half of the tanks must have ditched themselves or lost their way. The broken ground, which had looked nasty enough by day, became appalling in the pitchy darkness; and I recall this final stage of the journey as a long black nightmare of fatigue and apprehension. There was no track, and in many places even the tape had vanished, displaced or buried by the leading tanks. Over the communication trenches still in use narrow wooden bridges had been built, and these required skilful negotiation. As I walked in front of G 46, knowing that all my driver could see of me was the faint white patch on my back, I was continually falling into shell-holes, tripping over debris, or getting hung up in wire; and with the tank lumbering blindly along a few feet behind me, these accidents put me in infinite terror of being run over. At least one tank commander, Alden, had in fact a very narrow escape from death or injury that night through becoming entangled in a mass of wire. His tank cleared him by inches while he was still struggling to get free, and then the track caught the wire and pulled him helplessly after. He was being carried on to the roof when the driver somehow discovered what had happened and pulled up.

The enemy now began to interfere, to add to our discomfort, by bombarding the whole neighbourhood fairly heavily with gas shells. There was a battery of 4.5 howitzers firing in the open close to our route, and possibly this was his target. Very fortunately we had been

issued with a special type of box-respirator, in which the
goggles and mouth-mask were separate, and thus were still
able, at a risk to our eyes, to see our way—more or less.
With the ordinary fixed eye-pieces it would have been
next to impossible to see anything at all. As it was,
we were merely extraordinarily uncomfortable and anxious.
The Germans threw over little or no lachrymatory gas and
no mustard-oil, which then was just coming into fashion;
but we could not be certain about the latter, as it has no
smell; and it was the reverse of pleasant to have to
stumble along in the dark with our eyes exposed to what
might have been doses of this atrocious decoction. All
around us, for about half an hour, there sounded the soft
detonations peculiar to gas shells. And in the middle of
the bombardment, either through this or some other agency,
a pile of cordite charges by the howitzer battery caught fire
and flared brilliantly for a few minutes. I was passing in
front of the guns at the time, and I could see that one of
them had been hit, and was lying out of action with a
broken wheel; while at the others the gunners still toiled
in the glare like black automatons. Behind them the unhappy shattered trees along the canal bank were illuminated
eerily, and in front of me a line of tanks was visible dipping
and rolling over the shell-holes. I was afraid that this brief
conflagration would draw some heavy retaliation from the
enemy, but he contented himself with gas; and while the
fire lasted it was of service to us in lighting up our route.
Even the gas-shelling presently ceased; and with no further
adventures beyond periodical stumbles and searches for the
tape, we found ourselves at length under the black shadow
of the Frascati trees. We were only just in time. Dawn
was breaking as the last tank drew in; and we had taken
nearly seven hours to cover 5000 yards.

IV.

Frascati Farm stood just east of the road which ran, parallel to the canal, from Pilkem through La Brique to Ypres. The trees about the farm, their scars then concealed in part by heavy foliage, came down to the roadside; and to the right of them, as one approached from the causeways, a gap in a hedge gave entrance to a shell-pitted field. Our tanks, having been led through this gap, now lay parked up, nose to tail, against some immense overgrown bushes which lined the southern edge of the timber. The camouflage nets, joined together, stretched over the whole long line. As day broke we could see some very new shell-holes in the field; and we learnt that the place had been shelled that night while 21 Company was moving in. One officer had been hit in the leg, but insisted on staying with his tank and taking it into action—a piece of plucky quixotry which kept him in hospital afterwards for many months.

We spent that day, the 30th, in attempts to get sleep or at least rest under the tanks and camouflage netting. The weather was nondescript and depressing—a lowering sky threatened rain, but none fell. Throughout the day German aeroplanes came and went with impunity above us, and periodically shells whistled over the trees and burst in black plumes of earth beyond the hedge along the far side of our field, between us and Ypres. None, happily, fell any nearer. Of Ypres itself, on the low ground about a mile away, the higher ruins, dominated by the ragged tower of the Cloth Hall, were just visible above the hedge top. The town was being shelled continually, so that at times quite a haze of the familiar red-brick dust floated over it. The uproar of our own artillery seemed less intense, perhaps because we were now in front of the most advanced field-guns.

During those hours of waiting the incident I remember most clearly was a discussion we had at lunch-time on the

subject of English country places we had known. It seems
now an odd thing to have been sitting there, in that forlorn
region, our backs against a tank, peering through the camouflage netting at the shells bursting in Ypres, and comparing
the peaceful beauties of Sussex and Cornwall and the Eastern
shires. Of the little company of us gathered there, Kessel
was a Cornish man whose work was in the north; Merchant
was an East Anglian from India; Brassington came from
the valley of the Eden; and Alden and myself were by way
of being Cockneys of French extraction or interests. Between us we had seen a fair part of England, and there
was a peculiar fascination, in the circumstances, in recalling
pleasant holidays and journeys achieved in those remote
days when soldiering was the last of all human professions
we ever expected to adopt. All of us, I think, as very normal
unheroic people, would have given a good deal then to be
back in our own country.

A little later, toward tea-time, Major Fernie, then commanding 19 Company, appeared on the scene to wish us
good luck and issue final instructions. Company headquarters during the battle were to be established in the dug-
out at Hill Top Farm, a pile of rubble and sandbags about
a fragment of wall which stood up like a huge tooth midway
between Frascati and the front line. Throughout the expansion of the Tank Corps the company has remained the
unit of battle; the battalion is virtually a brigade, and
advanced battalion headquarters lives during operations
with the infantry division or army corps concerned. In
this case Colonel Hankey, a few hours before zero, established himself at the 39th Divisional Headquarters in
Oosthoek Wood.

As dusk fell we began to clear for action. We filled up
with petrol from the dump among the trees and piled there
all camouflage nets, tarpaulins, and spare kit. A tank prepared for action, cluttered up as it is with necessary stores
and ammunition, has no room for other impedimenta. The
crew, wearing ordinary workshop overalls, take with them

only revolvers. In the middle of this work the enemy, who had left us in comparative peace all day, started to shell the neighbourhood with gas; and for some time we had to carry on handicapped by box-respirators. The tedious business of fixing spuds occupied the last hour before the move. Spuds were always carried in the box on the roof until the last possible moment, as any hard surface, such as that of a road, crushed them and put a dangerous strain on the hard steel track-plates. Each tank carried forty-four of these iron shoes, of which we had to clamp on about thirty that night at Frascati—a laborious process with stiff nuts and bolts, and an inadequate supply of spanners. My crew and I were able to fix only half of our quota in the time, and the remainder we flung into a ditch under the bushes, where for all I know they lie to this day, unless they have been discovered by some puzzled Belgian labourer.

At 10.45 all engines were started up, and at 11 o'clock we moved off. One tank of 19 Company developed some internal trouble and was left behind. The trek for a long time was devoid of any incident. The Reconnaissance officers led: my section was now the last in the line; and I simply followed the tank in front of me. I can remember nothing that happened until we reached Hammond's Corner, a road junction near Hill Top Farm and about a thousand yards from the front line. We were so well ahead of time that we halted for an hour at this point. The night was very quiet, for there was a lull in the gun-fire. The sky was clouded and dark; but unceasingly, around the curve of the Salient—to our right and left and even in our rear—the Very lights rose slowly and hung for a space and faded, their diffused radiance reflected in the crater pools and imprinting continually along the horizon ephemeral silhouettes of naked and eerie trees. The Germans were using then a very pretty variant of this illumination (or so I suppose it to have been), a kind of slow rocket that soared up obliquely in straight bars of brilliant light, one below the other. In fact the Ypres salient, depressing in its utter ruin in the day-

YPRES: THE 31ST JULY

time and infinitely dreary and forbidding toward dusk, assumed an inhuman beauty when night had fallen and this semicircle of wavering incandescence began its deliberate and irregular rise and fall.

I was still leading G 46 from outside when we halted; and after a while I pulled myself up on to the towing shackle in front of the tank to talk to my driver through his flap. I was so tired that in this attitude, sitting on the unsympathetic shackle with my head on one track and my feet on the other, I fell asleep. I was told afterwards that several shells burst about us and exploded a small dump near at hand, but I slept through it all. Just before we moved off again a machine-gun barrage was started to cover the noise of our approach to the front line. I now got inside the tank and took the brakes beside Johnstone, as with the help of the continual stream of Very lights it was become quite a simple matter to follow the machines in front and even to see from the cab the tape which the R.O.'s had laid down earlier that night. Having still ample time, we crawled forward now at a snail's pace, and eventually pulled up once more a quarter of an hour before zero—which was at 3.50 A.M.—at a point 300 yards from Forward Cottage, where we were to cross the front line. As we were not required to overtake the infantry before the second German system was reached, we were to start at this interval behind them. While we waited, the thought struck me forcibly (and has recurred with every later tank action in which I have taken part) that if the enemy had used a few mobile searchlights at intervals throughout the night, sweeping the area immediately behind our line for a minute at a time, he could hardly have failed to discover us sooner or later. Now, for example, the twenty-three tanks, covered from view only by the darkness, were drawn up in line ahead on a forward slope little more than a quarter of a mile from his nearest trenches. The presence of these machines in the Salient was well known to him, and the attack had been awaited for days. A number of searchlights on motor-trucks, as used for anti-aircraft work, might have been brought up to the summit of the Pilkem Ridge at many points; and if employed with discretion for short periods and moved continually, our gunners would have found it very difficult to hit them; while once our tanks had been seen and held in the rays they might have been knocked to pieces in a few minutes. At Ypres, it is true, the Germans (with some justice) were not greatly afraid of tanks; but in later battles, particularly during the final autumn of the war, when elaborate road systems in fair condition ran behind the armies, the value of mobile searchlights for countering expected tank attacks would appear to have been so considerable as to justify any sacrifice involved. But on no occasion, so far as I am aware, were they used for this purpose. In the course of our last advance successive assaults, which might have been disorganised and possibly ruined by a premature discovery of tanks moving up, were allowed to come as a surprise.

The ultimate minutes before zero passed without event. With the aid of the Very lights I endeavoured once more to read the map which hung in front of me, and peered continually at my clock. A tot of whisky was passed round the crew. The engine, just ticking over, drowned by its throbbing the noise of the machine-gun barrage, which still continued. In front the long line of tanks stood motionless on the gentle slope. And so, in a dim-lit silent world we waited for the moment of attack.

CHAPTER IX.

YPRES: THE 31ST JULY (*continued*).

I.

I HAVE been told that the gigantic clap of sound produced by the simultaneous discharge of two or three thousand guns at zero that morning was a phenomenon never to be forgotten by those who heard it. But I do not remember hearing it at all. Enclosed in a vibrating box of steel, the subdued throbbing of my engine drowned even this apocalyptic crash. And this effect of silence—for we were all so accustomed to the local noise of our machinery that it may be said we were unconscious of it—made yet more wonderful the really astounding display of pyrotechnics which in a second blazed up around the whole arc of the Salient. At 3.49 A.M., when I looked at my clock for the last time, the night was dark and misty and very still. Heavier clouds had rolled up, and there was no sign of the dawn. Only the pistol lights still soared and died away about us. Precisely at 3.50 two or three thousand shells of every calibre burst virtually together in two great semicircles on or over the enemy's first and second lines—ten miles or so of sudden flame and horror. A few hundred yards in front of our leading tank the very earth seemed to erupt. It spouted fire and fragments like a volcano. The mist which hung over the trenches in the little valley was rent to tatters in a blaze of orange light, while hundreds of shrapnel-bursts sparkled above, and the drums of thermit poured down their molten oil like burning rain. Far behind, where the 9.2 barrage fell along the crown of the ridge, great tongues of flame leapt and wavered in volumes of scarlet smoke. And from out of this instantaneous inferno arose strings of green and crimson rockets — the S.O.S. calls of the enemy. It was the apotheosis of the artillery barrage, although no one suspected it then: the greatest blast of gun-fire ever concentrated at once on any battlefield, and, so far at least as the British Army was concerned, the last of its kind. The next offensive battle, at Cambrai, was to inaugurate a new order of things.

From Hill Top, or Frascati, this great curve of spouting fire must have been a magnificent spectacle, and the sudden shattering noise of it appalling; and I was so fascinated by the small part of it which I could see that I forgot entirely to start the tank. The whole of my crew was crowded forward behind the driver and myself, craning over our shoulders to watch through the flaps such a display of fireworks as they had never dreamed of. Realising suddenly that the interval between G 46 and the tank in front was increasing, I touched Johnstone on the arm; and the roar of the engine deepened as, with a slight jerk, we also began to move. Already the glare of the bursting shells, still raining down upon the zero line, was dulled by a pall of smoke and dust. The spectacular glory of the barrage was at an end. Within a few seconds it was due to lift forward at a rate of a hundred yards every four minutes. But it still showed as a flickering haze of light across our front; and against this one could see the long line of tanks moving downward to Forward Cottage, about which point groups of dark figures were standing on the parapets or walking carelessly forward across Admiral's Road toward the German trenches.

It seemed a long time before G 46 reached these trenches. There were, in fact, continual stoppages as the tanks in front struggled to find a crossing in the

narrow gap between Hampshire and Canadian Farms.
At length, after a particularly long halt, I swung out of
the line to the right to make, if possible, a passage for
myself. We were then somewhere in the middle of No
Man's Land. Dawn had broken—a miserable grey twilight
behind heavy clouds; and the creeping barrage, with its
following infantry, was already far up the ridge. It was
when we drew up to the German front line that the cause
of these irritating delays became painfully obvious. We
had anticipated difficulties here, but the reality was worse
than anything that I, for one, had imagined. The front
line was not merely obliterated: it had been scorched and
pulverised as if by an earthquake, stamped flat and heaved
up again, caught as it fell and blown all ways; and when
the four minutes' blast of destruction moved on, was left
dissolved into its elements, heaped in fantastic mounds of
mud, or excavated into crumbling pits already half full of
water. There cannot have been a live man left in it. At
our point of crossing there was nothing to be seen which
remotely resembled a trench: before us yawned a deep
muddy gulf, out of whose slimy sides obtruded fragments
of splintered timber, broken slabs of concrete, and several
human legs clothed in German half-boots. Immediately
beyond, a veritable lagoon, fringed by a few stripped and
blackened willow-stumps, marked the site of Hampshire
Farm. Infantry were strolling about here in a very casual
manner, smoking, eating, and ferreting for souvenirs. The
battle seemed a long way off. The morning was so dark,
and the murk of mist and smoke so thick upon the ridge,
that one could see only a few hundred yards in front. I
was determined not to get ditched so early in the day if
I could avoid it; and for five or ten minutes we hung over
this black chasm, backing, swinging, nosing about in vain
for a likely crossing. We were rather too much to the
right of our proper track, but the ground everywhere was
so broken and treacherous that there was little choice. We
had made several tentative efforts, but had shied each time

at the prospect of crumbling and slithery mud-heaps in front of us; and I was about to leave the tank to search for a crossing-place myself when Kessel unexpectedly appeared outside. With his help we got over, at a point where some revetting-stakes and wire still survived, holding the soil together and providing a quasi-stable surface for the tracks to grip.

Once across, Kessel scrambled in through one of the sponson-doors, and as we lurched warily round the lagoon he informed me by shouts that all this was "great fun" (a point which had escaped me), and that poor Brassington was bogged hopelessly somewhere near at hand. We were now climbing out of the dead ground in which the front line had run. The light was improving rapidly, but so dense a screen of smoke and mist hung over the ridge that no landmarks were visible. In front of me a line of tanks—the leading section of 19 Company—was moving obliquely to the right. Nearer at hand was one on fire, and a second apparently ditched. No shells seemed to be falling in our neighbourhood, but far ahead a flicker of light in the fog showed where our barrage continued its annihilating progress up the slope. Indistinct groups of figures moved about in the gloom—signallers laying lines of wire, platoons in support digging themselves in, stretcher-bearers, runners, and walking wounded trailing back to the aid-posts. The damp air reeked of the pungent gases of high explosives. The ground, although one intricate net of shell-holes, grew firmer as we left the infamous region about the front line; and, with skilful driving, we were able to make fair progress without running extravagant risks. Johnstone, indeed, drove extraordinarily well. The great trouble at first was to find our right direction, for all our famous groups of trees were still invisible, and Kitchener's Wood was veiled completely by the smoke and dust of the barrage. The German trenches which we had studied on the map were blown to pieces and unrecognisable. One could see nothing anywhere, in fact, but a brown waste of mud blasted into ridges and hollows like a frozen sea, littered with debris, and melting on all hands into the prevailing haze. The gradient of the ridge was too slight to be a guide under the circumstances; my compass was chasing its tail and behaving generally as if it was drunk; and, after we had swung a dozen times to avoid the more dangerous craters that lay in our way, we might have been heading in almost any direction. It was therefore with some relief that Kessel and I detected presently, in the smoky distance, a familiar object that both of us, like Captain Reece's washerwoman, long had loved from afar. This was Lone Tree — a rotund bushy shrub near Kultur Farm, whose exceeding merit it was to look the same from every point of view. It was unmistakable; and now, happily preserved amid the universal ruin, it still stood, a little battered and entirely denuded of foliage, as a signpost on the way. Very shortly after the ragged tree-tops of Kitchener's Wood came also into view.

About this time Kessel scrambled out, leaving behind him various impedimenta, including a haversack and the section flag — this last an emblem of red and green, the battalion colours, with a large white "10" sewn on to it. I could now see Merchant's tank, apparently in trouble, in a sort of marshy gully to my right front; but a little while later he passed me again, going in great style. Time was slipping away: it was nearly five o'clock, and already we were late, owing to the delays at the front line. We were not far, however, from our first objectives—Boche Castle and the German second system in front of Kitchener's Wood, where I still hoped to overtake the infantry. The heavy howitzers had now lifted to the Steenbeek and beyond, and the creeping barrage was crashing in the wood itself, above which hung clouds of smoke. The enemy's counter-barrage, falling in the beginning on our front and assembly trenches, had developed into a heavy but promiscuous bombardment of the western slope of the ridge; and for the first time since zero,

I saw the sinister black fountains of earth spouting up in front, and heard the occasional rattle of fragments on the roof of G 46. It was, presumably, one of these pieces of shell, or perhaps a shrapnel ball, that cut the lashings of my unditching beam about this time. As we dipped our nose into a shell-hole the beam slid down over the cab on to the ground. Stopping at once, I got my whole crew out to recover it; but to lift on to the roof again 9 cwt. of steel and wood in so unhandy a form was beyond our powers; and the occasion being urgent, I decided to abandon the thing rather than waste time in manœuvring the tank and fixing the clamps or other tackle.

We obtained a more comprehensive view of the outer world during this excursion, but there was little to be seen. The battlefield wore that melancholy and deserted air characteristic of modern war. Acres of foul slime below, dark and heavy clouds hanging low overhead, odours of gases and corruption, a few tree-stumps, a few bodies lying crumpled in the mud, half a dozen tanks labouring awkwardly in the middle distance, and the shell bursts shooting upward like vast ephemeral mushrooms — and that was all. There was hardly a sign of life in all that mournful and chilling landscape. The dark but busy interior of G 46, crowded with humanity, was homely by comparison and infinitely quieter. War has been translated into terms of sound, and the racket of gun-fire was appalling. Coming from inside a tank, where one heard nothing but the familiar roar of the engine, this eternal throbbing blast of noise deafened and bewildered. Overhead the shells were rushing in a torrent with a continual cry like that of a gale among trees — "whee-u, whee-u, whee-u, whee-u . . ." For the first few minutes, until I can become used to it, any loud and sudden noise (and this was worse than any ever heard before) always renders me virtually imbecile, almost incapable of coherent thought or action; and I was heartily glad to clamber back again to the company of decent mechanical reverberations to which I was accustomed.

We moved on once more. I can remember very little of our normal progress beyond a general impression that the ground everywhere was atrocious, and that Johnstone's driving was exceptional. We passed over a ruined trench, which a line of men was labouring to convert with pick and shovel; and once we came upon a wounded infantryman lying at the bottom of a shell-hole which we were about to cross. We stopped instantly and swung to avoid him, but in the act of changing the secondary gears the tank lurched forward a foot or two and hung over the very lip of the crater; and I shall not easily forget the terror in the man's face as he watched the huge machine rearing up fifteen feet above him, about (as he supposed) to crash down upon him with all its thirty tons. It was about 5.15 when we drew near to the site of the estaminet called Boche Castle. On our right was the dark mass of Kitchener's Wood, its trees blackened and mangled and almost bare of leaves. No living soul was to be seen, and it was plain that the infantry had carried the strong point itself, and the whole of the German second line in this neighbourhood, and had already pushed on toward the Steenbeek. The trenches ran generally along the western edge of the wood, but a few hundred yards from the northern end of it they turned westward through Boche Castle and Hurst Park toward Pilkem. I have spoken of an estaminet at Boche Castle, but of course this building, where a few years before the Walloons had drunk their indifferent beer, had been reduced long since to a pile of rubble. Amid this debris the Germans had constructed a concrete tower, which commanded the whole face of the ridge. I have mentioned also that this interesting innovation had been shelled by our 15-inch guns. The effect of this bombardment was extraordinary, for in that moist and ruined soil the huge projectiles had penetrated to a depth of fifteen or twenty feet before they exploded; and the result was a congeries of immense craters, which I believed to be caused by mines, until I reflected that no mine-shafts could have been driven so far. The mebus itself had been uprooted bodily, like a plaything, and now lay flat upon its side, cracked, but still more or less entire —an advertisement of the resisting powers of reinforced concrete.

From this and other indications (*e.g.*, the absence of dead or wounded on the ground except at one spot, to be noted later), it was clear that there had been no very serious fighting about this point; and indeed the first impact of 9.2's at zero, followed later by the lighter creeping barrage, had virtually obliterated the whole system in front of the wood. It was no easy task for a tank to thread its way among these vast excavations about Boche Castle, and things were complicated by the presence of a large patch of boggy ground there which had also to be avoided. As we proceeded, we discovered that Merchant's tank, less fortunate than our own, had become ditched in one of the biggest craters, where it lay at a most uncomfortable angle, looking very much like a drowned beetle in the bottom of a wine-glass.

Our own ultimate disaster was near at hand. There ran out of the salient the dismal remains of a thoroughfare known to us as Boundary Road, which, after crossing Admiral's Road in No Man's Land and then the German front line, zigzagged past the reserve trenches at Kempton Park and Gatwick Cottage to Hurst Park and Boche Castle itself, from where it hugged the north end of Kitchener's Wood before descending the reverse slope to a culvert over the Steenbeek. Up this latter part of it was laid a light railway, as disclosed by aeroplane photographs, and duly recorded on the map. Information from prisoners led to the belief that this road was mined; and Merchant and I had been warned time and again on no account to move along it. We were to cross it in the neighbourhood of Boche Castle, proceed parallel to it on the north, and

recross it beyond the wood, thus reducing to a minimum
the risk of striking one of the mines. The road itself, when
I arrived at it, was indistinguishable from the surrounding
mud; but the twisted metals of the light railway betrayed
its site; and in accordance with my instructions, without
thinking twice about it, I drove straight over it at a point
midway between the wood and the prostrate mebus at
Boche Castle. I then swung to the right and moved
forward parallel to it. As written down, this manœuvre
sounds a simple one; but already another peculiarity of the
Salient was disturbingly manifest. Owing, as I suppose,
to some arrangement of strata—the same phenomenon is
to be found in parts of Dorsetshire, among other places—
the water with which Flanders is too abundantly provided
collects on top of the ridges as well as in the adjacent
valleys. The boggy patch on the other side of Boche
Castle before mentioned was a symptom of this eccentricity.
And across the vanished road the conditions became at
once appalling. The ground was one network of big shell-
holes, and every one was full of water. There was no
escaping it. On all hands lay these brimming pools,
divided only by a sort of mesh of semi-liquid mud. I
tried at once to get back to the road, preferring the possibility of mines to the certainty of being ignominiously
engulfed, but in that amphibious world the engine was not
powerful enough to induce the tank to reverse or swing.
She would only plough her way slowly forward through
the mud. The end was inevitable. We covered (and this
in itself was something of a miracle) about two hundred
yards of this quagmire, forcing our way through it rather
than over it. It was during this final lap that I heard
my left-hand pair of gunners open fire with their Lewis
guns. Knowing that we were still behind our infantry, I
induced them to stop by hammering the nearest man on
the back; and it was not until some time later that I learnt
the cause of their firing. All this while we tried continually
to swing back toward the road, a hundred yards away, but

L

the tank was sunk in mud to her belly, and would move only in the one direction. We arrived at length at a point abreast of the far edge of Kitchener's Wood: water lay everywhere about us; and immediately in front were two or three large shell-holes, full to the brim. It being impossible to avoid them, G 46, like a reluctant suicide, crawled straight into the first, which we could only hope was shallower than it appeared to be. The water rushed in through the tracks and sponson doors, covered the floor-boards, and flooded the sump: the fly-wheel thrashed through it for a second or two, sending showers about the interior; and then the tank, not having been constructed for submarine warfare, gave up the struggle. The engine raced with an increased but futile noise, for the wet clutch had ceased to grip, and we did not move.

It was nearly six o'clock, and the rain had begun to fall. To take stock of the situation we had to climb out through the manhole in the roof, the water having risen to such a height above the floor that we could not use the sponson doors. Once outside, it was manifest that there was nothing to be done. The lost unditching beam would not have helped us with the clutch half under water. The tail of the tank just touched the muddy rim of the shell-hole, but on every other side the great pool extended for several feet. The accompanying photograph, although taken a couple of months later, after the tank had been hit on one track and elsewhere, shows her exactly as she lay at that moment, and as we left her the following afternoon. A hundred yards to our right was the northern corner of Kitchener's Wood. Three or four hundred yards to the left was a ruined building, converted with concrete into a machine-gun post, which was known as Von Werder House. This was not visible until one stood on top of the tank, for the latter was sunk deep in the shell-hole, and was screened also on this side by the tattered remnants of a hedge. A quarter of a mile in front of us the ridge fell away toward the Steenbeek, and over the edge we could see the tops

Tank G 46 as I left her (except for hit on track), August 1, 1917.

of the trees which lined the banks of that stream; while
to our rear, beyond a row of wrecked sheds made of timber
and corrugated iron, rose the white pile of rubble and
concrete where Boche Castle had stood. Occasional shells
burst along the ridge. The shriek of our own projectiles
rushing overhead was continuous, and the actual throbbing
blast of gun-fire a torture to the nerves; but not a living
soul except ourselves was within eyesight. I did not know
how far our infantry had progressed, but supposed them to
be somewhere near the Steenbeek. A heavy rattle of rifle
and machine-gun fire sounded out of the valley. Nearer
at hand, but invisible, one or two Vickers' guns were in-
dulging in overhead fire.

Having satisfied myself that the tank was bogged beyond
immediate repair (a fact, indeed, so obvious that no consideration was needed), I sent my crew inside again and
started to walk back to Merchant's G 45, lying in the big
crater by Boche Castle, where I expected to find Kessel.
The distance was about five hundred yards. It was now
raining heavily, and walking was reduced to a maddening
process of dragging one's feet through deliquescent mud,
sliding into shell-holes, and crawling, sometimes on all-
fours, laboriously out again. As I drew near to Boche
Castle I crossed what was left of the support trenches of
the German second line, and here, lying face downward
side by side over a fragment of parados, were the bodies of
six British infantrymen, all shot through the head—killed
together as they were in the act of climbing out of the
trench. I was to become only too familiar with these
unfortunates in the course of that day and the next. A
little farther beyond was the series of great craters about
the strong-point. On reaching the lip of the one in which
G 45 still lay engulfed, I saw Kessel, Merchant, and the
crew grouped far below me round the tank. They instantly made violent signals to me to come into cover, and
I slid down the side of the crater with some precipitation.
Believing that all the enemy must have been driven off the

ridge in our neighbourhood, since the infantry was out of sight ahead, I had taken no precautions in walking across beyond listening anxiously for the whistle of unfriendly shells; but on arriving, muddy and breathless, among the others in the crater bottom, I learnt that all this while there was a German machine-gun still in action in Von Werder House, then nearly half a mile behind our front. Its very gallant gun-crew (I never knew if there was only one man there or more), cut off by the annihilation or flight of the defenders of the second line, apparently went to ground until our attacking waves had passed by, only to reappear afterwards and begin sniping conscientiously at any one who came within range. This sort of conduct always seems to me the height of heroism or fanaticism, for the ultimate fate of such isolated rearguards is certain. In all ignorance I had walked right across the front of this gun within a few hundred yards of it, and I can only suppose that at the time the gunners were occupied at a loophole on the other side of the mebus. It appeared that Merchant had left his true course, and so become ditched in the crater, in an attempt to reach and silence this nuisance; and when I returned later to my own tank I learnt that it was the "tap-tap" of bullets on the armour, no doubt from the same source, that had provoked my gunners to open fire. And I imagine that the six dead infantrymen whom I had just seen were also among the victims of Von Werder House.

Having reported to Kessel the hopeless situation of G 46, I was told to evacuate her, leaving, however, two men as a guard. This was in accordance with orders, and was in one sense a very necessary provision; for it had been found that any ditched or disabled tank left unguarded was sure to be stripped within a few hours of every removable part. But the duty, never popular, was likely to be peculiarly dangerous in the Salient, on account of the persistent shelling to be expected there. Near Mousetrap Farm, a day or two later, four men were killed while guarding a

couple of derelict tanks, after which the practice of leaving
such guards east of the canal was abandoned. And the
position of G 46 was exceptional. She lay so near to the
Steenbeek, our final objective for that day, as to be in
imminent danger from any counter-attack, and she was,
in fact, farther forward than any machine left within our
lines. She might be seen from the next ridge, and her
neighbourhood, whatever else happened, probably would
be shelled heavily. Under these circumstances, much as
I disliked the prospect of remaining in her myself, I felt
that I could not leave two of my crew alone there; and
I determined, therefore, to form one of the guard.

Merchant's tank was as immovable as my own. Its
engine had failed in an attempt to pull it out of the big
crater, and it now lay at a highly uncomfortable angle, its
nose pointing obliquely upward and its floor so tilted that
one could not stand inside. Fortunately for the crew, the
crater was comparatively dry for the Salient. It was
merely a mud-hole—that is to say, without much water in
the bottom. I remained here for about half an hour, talking to the others, for I confess I was in no hurry to begin
my return journey. Most of us, I think, are great cowards
when we are alone and have no gallery to play to, and I
did not relish the idea of exposing myself again to the
occupant of Von Werder House, who might not overlook
me a second time. When at length I moved off, I took
rather elaborate precautions, keeping under cover when
possible, running across the open spaces, and making a
wide circuit through the moist and reeking undergrowth
of Kitchener's Wood. It was an ignominious performance,
and I am not proud of it; but I could not forget those six
men lying in a row with bullets through their heads. And
as it happened, the machine-gun was now permanently
silenced. When I came out from the wood upon the ruined
road abreast of my tank, prepared to duck or run for it, I
saw a party of kilted infantry, belonging to the supporting
battalion of the 117th Brigade, gathered round Von Werder

House. Presumably the plucky German gunner had been killed. Scrambling back into G 46, I told my crew (sitting dismally immersed to the knees in water and oil) to draw lots for the doubtful privilege of remaining behind with me. The duty fell to my second driver, Swain, who successfully dissembled his joy. The others began to collect their kit, most of which was under water, for in a tank everything gravitates eventually to the floor. These men would have to carry with them also the six Lewis guns and the compass, and their journey through the shells and rain and clinging mud to Frascati, thus encumbered, promised few pleasures. There was still a job of work for them to do before they left. I wished to camouflage the tank to some extent with mud and branches, and especially to obliterate the conspicuous number painted on the roof of the cab. (I have explained already my reasons for this diffidence.) At this work we toiled for half an hour, slipping and splashing in the surrounding pool; but the rain, now falling in sheets, washed the mud away almost as fast as we shovelled it on, and we had to depend upon the relics of the adjacent hedge. It was nearly nine o'clock when my corporal, Mitchell, and the other five prepared finally to leave the tank. At this juncture another tank appeared, homeward bound, round the corner of Kitchener's Wood. It was one of 19 Company's, commanded by Maelor Jones. It had been across the Steenbeek into St Julien, where it had been attacked by infantry with hand-grenades, and Maelor Jones himself had shot a German N.C.O. with his revolver through the flap. He was now struggling home with a badly leaking radiator. I do not remember how he came to be so far off his direct route, which was south of the wood, a mile away. I gave him all my spare water, and also put into his tank my six Lewis guns, to save my crew this extra burden. When he moved off again he contrived to navigate the lake district about us without disaster; but eventually (as I discovered later) came to a standstill, with an empty radiator, half a mile beyond Boche Castle, where

the tank was hit soon after. At the same time my six men
left me for Hill Top Farm and Frascati, with orders to
report to the company commander at the first-named place.
Swain and I remained alone in G 46, with a prospect (at
the best) of indefinite discomfort before us. The only thing
remaining for me to do was to despatch my two pigeons
with duplicate messages, giving my exact state and
situation.

II.

The tank, as I have said, was almost knee-deep in water.
The rain dripped in steadily through the imperfectly fitting
armour-plating of the roof. And about this time the
enemy's shelling, scattered hitherto in a desultory fashion
over his lost positions, settled down to a sustained and
heavy bombardment of the whole crest of the ridge. It
fell with particular intensity on certain areas, of which
our own deserted and impracticable neighbourhood unfortunately was one. Possibly the Germans thought we
were using or repairing the road; but except for one
platoon of infantry, ploughing along it in single file on
either side, to avoid (as I suppose) the legendary mines, I
never saw a living soul upon that obliterated highway, and
very few anywhere else about us. Whatever the reason,
from about ten o'clock on the morning of the 31st until I
left the place at four in the afternoon of the following day,
a period of thirty hours, 5.9 shells fell about us without
intermission at the rate of one every minute. The particular gun or guns responsible for our little sector maintained
with Teutonic exactitude the same invariable line, represented approximately by G 46 on top of the crest, Boche
Castle 300 yards in rear, and Merchant's tank 200 yards
beyond that; and the feature of this apparently senseless
expenditure of metal was the fact that neither tank was hit
during this time.

It might appear the obvious remedy, in these circumstances, to have left the half-drowned "Gina" for some other shelter a few hundred yards away. But there was no shelter to be found, or I could find none. Trenches had been beaten to a muddy pulp; dug-outs, if they existed, were undiscoverable in the prevailing devastation; water lay everywhere; and shells were falling almost as thickly in Kitchener's Wood and about Von Werder House as in our immediate neighbourhood. The tank at least offered protection against splinters, and, apart from a few leaks, against the ceaseless downpour of rain. It held our food and other possessions, which were kept moderately dry. And it is a well-known, if illogical, truth, that any overhead cover is better than none. A parasol would give one infinite comfort in battle. G 46, nevertheless, was not an ideal home. She vibrated periodically from the concussions near at hand: every fifteen minutes or so came an explosion so close that lumps of mud pattered heavily upon the roof; and once or twice the whole thirty tons of metal seemed to jump bodily. With the engine silent, one heard the crescendo of every approaching shell, and had ample time to speculate on its point of arrival. It is one thing to be shelled in this manner when you are actively engaged in some work which helps to occupy your mind: it is altogether another to have to sit through two days and a night of it within a few feet of thirty or forty gallons of refined and expensive petrol, with nothing whatever to do but wonder what exactly will happen when you are hit. It was natural to dwell upon the fact that a 5.9 projectile goes through a tank's armour as if it was paper, and then bursts inside. Thirty hours of this life, in short, became in the end a little wearing; and I hope sincerely never to repeat the experience.

Yet of all that long period, which seemed so interminable at the time, I found afterwards I could remember very little. When Swain and I were left alone in the tank, we proceeded to make ourselves as comfortable as circumstances allowed.

Swain curled himself up in the driver's seat. I sat with my
shoulders against the front of the cab, using a tin box of
Lewis-gun ammunition as a back-rest. Half of the engine
cover, laid over a couple of oil-drums which rose well above
the water-level, served to keep my legs out of the flood.
Both of us, of course, were already soaked to the skin and
plastered with mud, so that the steady trickle of rain from
the roof mattered little to us. For the first hour or so I
think we were asleep, too tired to worry about the manifest
increase in the shelling about us. Toward midday we ate
a cold and uninspiring lunch of bully and sardines, supplemented by whisky. These delicacies lived close at hand in
lockers on each side of the cab, room for which, and also
for a small drinking-water tank, had been made in the
Mark IV. by the removal aft of the petrol supply. Our
drinking water, unfortunately, was rather mature, there
having been no opportunity of refilling the tank since the
postponement on the 24th. On all counts I congratulated
myself on the two bottles of whisky. We were now fully
alive to the fact that shells were bursting very near G 46
with great regularity, and so far as I was concerned
further sleep proved to be out of the question. After each
periodic whistle and explosion, I peered around through the
revolver ports in the cab to see where the resultant cloud of
black smoke was hanging, and usually discovered it unpleasantly close. It may have been about this time that
the infantry I have mentioned came up the road past the
edge of the wood. They deployed into open order and
halted for a few minutes; and having left the tank to learn
something about the general situation, I found the subaltern in command sitting with his sergeant in a comparatively dry shell-hole. They could tell me very little,
however. The firing line, which they were moving to
support, was believed to be along the Steenbeek, about
800 yards in front of us. The rattle of machine-guns in
the valley was more persistent than ever. The Vickers on
the ridge had fallen silent or gone forward, and from the

loud throb of gun-fire behind us it was clear that field batteries had, in some miraculous manner, been got over the German front line and through the slough beyond. I returned to the tank as the infantry platoon began its stumbling progress forward again; and the last I saw of it was a scattered line of figures disappearing beyond the brow of the hill. This was the only formed body of troops that came within sight during our stay on the ridge.

The next incident I remember was the startling return, about 4 o'clock, of Corporal Mitchell and three others of my crew, who had left us six hours earlier. It appeared that having reached the dug-out at Hill Top Farm, after losing their way several times and enduring other unpleasant vicissitudes, the original six had reported to the company commander there, only to be told to return and stand by the tank, a complete reversal of our original instructions. Orders to this effect had been sent to Merchant by runner immediately on receipt of a pigeon message from him announcing his hopeless situation; but the runner, having intercepted this crew just as it was starting for home, had returned without bringing on the order to me. In any event, nothing was to be gained by leaving the two crews, except a certainty of more casualties if either tank should be hit; and trained tank personnel was never so easily come by that it could be risked without a proper cause. The crew of a tank left derelict on or near the front line can often be of use by getting out and helping the infantry with Lewis guns, but we were respectively half and three-quarters of a mile behind. I had sent my guns back, perhaps rather foolishly, by Maelor Jones, and both machines were so placed that they would be of little or no help in repelling a counter-attack. In short, this clearly was a case where the section and tank commanders on the spot ought to decide on the best course of action. As for my own men, this development entailed for them the additional fatigue and danger of the two-mile tramp back from Hill Top to the tank. They started to return at once. Almost immediately

one of the gunners was hit in the head by a shrapnel bullet,
and a second man was left with him to help him to the
nearest dressing station. The other four eventually rejoined me after six hours' continuous struggle through slime,
rain, and shell-fire, and they were so famished and exhausted
that, although a certain amount of petrol was floating about
in the tank, I went to the risk of lighting a primus stove in
one of the sponsons in order to make them some tea.
Braced with a little rum, this drink, like godliness with
contentment, was great gain. It was no easy matter now
to pack six men inside G 46 above water-level, but with the
aid of engine-covers and petrol and oil-tins, the returned
wanderers contrived somehow to fit themselves in.

Shortly after this I paid a visit to Merchant. Never an
attractive expedition, as it involved a good deal of wading
to begin with and subsequent periodic dives into the mud
to dodge shell fragments, this occasion provided me with
a quite superfluous thrill. Hearing suddenly the alarming
crescendo of a 5.9 coming apparently straight at my head,
I dropped in a hurry just as it landed within a very few
yards of me. Fortunately it plunged some ten feet down
into the semi-liquid ground before it burst, so that beyond
a bad shaking and a temporary immersion beneath a perfect
deluge of mud, I was none the worse. A little dashed by
the incident, however, I ran (or attempted to run) the rest
of the way, and of course almost fell over the six dead
infantrymen lying so neatly spaced in front of Boche Castle.
I was glad to get down into the fallacious shelter of
Merchant's gigantic crater, where I found his crew brew-
ing tea on a primus in the rain. They had with them two
German prisoners commandeered to help in a last hopeless effort to dig out the tank. One of these men was
dazed, speechless, and useless; and it was supposed that
he was suffering from shock until some one discovered that
the poor wretch had been hit in the stomach. Heaven
knows how he managed to stand upright. He vanished after
a while, probably to die miserably in some shell-hole; and

his comrade, having been made to understand with difficulty that his services were no longer required, hurried off toward the rear with every symptom of relief. Merchant, I found, had received no further orders, nor indeed any news whatever, and he and his men were as weary of this mode of life as I and mine, although spared our amphibious discomforts. His N.C.O., Sergeant Meyrick, a splendid type of long-service soldier from the R.F.A., had the beginnings of an attack of fever, and was shaking like St Vitus, while his first driver, Waller, was also ill. (Both these men came to be associated with me, in circumstances peculiarly creditable to them, in our next action, when I learnt thoroughly to appreciate their merits.) While I was in the crater at this time a number of shells burst so near to us that we left the tank in an endeavour to find shelter elsewhere, but we soon abandoned the search. As in my own case, the derelict machine remained the most attractive of the several unsatisfactory alternatives. I may point out once more that this instinctive desire to leave a ditched tank when shells are falling about it arises from the fact that the protection the tank offers against splinters is heavily outweighed by the knowledge of what almost certainly will happen if it receives a direct hit, especially from such a projectile as a 5.9. The terrific explosion in the restricted space, the whirlwind of flying white-hot metal, and the inevitable fire which follows, leave the crew with a poor hope of escaping, as was proved in several tragic instances that morning; whereas in the open, lying flat behind a lump of mud, the probabilities are all the other way. I think it was the rain and the general wretchedness of things outside, as much as the total lack of any standing cover, which induced us to remain throughout inside our tanks.

Having spent about half an hour with Merchant, I started on my return. In spite of a fixed intention of avoiding the six corpses on my route, I ran into them once more, but arrived at my own watery home without further unpleasantness. Inside G 46 the tide appeared to have risen in my absence.

It would be tedious to inflict in detail my fragmentary recollections of that evening or of the interminable night which ensued. The conditions may be pictured as before. The rain fell heavily, unceasingly, like fate. The water within the tank rose slowly but perceptibly, and the shells exploded about us with the punctuality of unwelcome guests. After each shriek and detonation which sounded more than usually close to us, I would see the dim faces of my crew turned rather anxiously toward me to see how I took it. It seemed then advisable to make some silly joke, which, although it should have deceived no one, helped apparently to ease the tension. And this experience, recurring frequently through many hours, impressed me forcibly with certain truisms lying, as I imagine, behind all theories of military conduct and training, of which the chief was the moral value of responsibility to others. If I had been left alone in the tank, with nothing to think of but my own predicament, I should have dwelt upon this until it became unbearable. Probably I should then have run away. As it was, however, my main business necessarily was to set a fairly decent example to the men who relied on me and for whom I was responsible. In other words, it was their presence and obvious dependence upon my behaviour which governed the latter, while conversely this influence reacted upon them to the extent that my artificial optimism and rather feeble jokes set up some sort of standard which they felt obliged to imitate. We were all equally afraid, but so long as we were all equally ashamed to admit it we could carry on. The point of interest in our case, otherwise very ordinary, was the fact that a number of men who never in their lives before had been in any serious danger were now called upon in their first action to endure a test exceptionally trying to nerve and courage: to sit, during a day and a half of persistent heavy shelling, passive, idle, and helpless in a flooded steel box on top of gallons of inflammable spirit, protected overhead by nothing more than a thin plate which a substantial sledge-hammer would have dented. I have said all this before, and it may appear scarcely to warrant the previous digression, but I will not labour to excuse the latter. It represents the reflections which occurred to me afterwards. No doubt they have occurred to millions of others since the first prehistoric battle; and the whole thing may be summed up in the axiom that, when in doubt or tribulation, it is a very material help to be forced to act a part.

That night was peculiarly unpleasant. Owing to our position on the crest it was inadvisable to show any adequate light. (It must be remembered also that we were entirely ignorant of the day's events. For all we knew the Germans might have regained ground elsewhere on the ridge from which the tank was in view at short range. One can learn nothing from a mere inspection of a modern battlefield, for there is nothing to be seen.) Normally, tanks are lighted by small electric festoon lamps hung under the roof, but in G 46 these were now out of action, the accumulators being under water. In any case, I should not have used them, as even with everything shut down the light escaped through numerous small chinks around the gun-ports and shields. The more powerful hand-lamps were tabooed for the same reason. There remained only the pair of coloured bulbs on the signalling belt, of which the green, besides making us look as if we were in the last stages of decomposition, was too brilliant to please me. The feeble glow of the red bulb, however, could hardly have been seen by some one standing close outside. I had to employ it sparingly, as I did not know how long the small battery would last, but when at intervals I switched it on the effect was rather curious. The dull crimson light was reflected in the water beneath us, the rain-drops collecting along the joints of the roof shone like rubies, and the complication of exhaust-pipes and ammunition-boxes above the engine cast over half the interior a great wavering shadow, in

which I could see dimly the faces of my crew, huddled in
the sponsons and about the differential. Between these
theatrical glimpses we lived in pitchy darkness, talking a
little, sleeping hardly at all, feeling acutely the bolt-heads
and angles in our backs, drinking a periodic tot of whisky
(for we were soaked and chilled), listening to the rain and
the shell-bursts and the occasional ominous patter of mud on
the roof, and praying for the dawn. When at length it
broke, dreary and weeping, and we could see once more the
too familiar landscape, the latter was as desert and uninvit-
ing as before. There was more water about, and a large
shell-hole in front of us was brimming over into ours. We
lit the primus again, regardless of possible consequences,
and rummaged about for our somewhat sodden victuals. A
good deal of food, including several loaves, was submerged,
and our two days' rations began to look small.

The morning was a repetition of the previous day. The
rain fell as if it had never rained before, the shells whistled
and crashed, and, for all that we could see, we might have
been in the Ark on Ararat, whose situation indeed must have
borne many points of resemblance to our own. We had
even despatched our doves, or pigeons. But there were no
high explosives on Ararat. About 11 o'clock I ventured
forth again rather reluctantly, and stumbled over the mud
to call on Merchant. For the fourth time I encountered
on the way the six infantrymen, now showing unequivocal
signs of having been dead for a good many hours. In the
big crater I found neither orders nor news, although there
had arrived a very superfluous visitor in the person of a
salvage officer, come to lend us the assistance of his in-
tellect toward the business of extricating our tanks! To
Merchant he offered some hints on the use of sleepers,
hints whose value was impaired by the fact that no sleepers
were to hand. When I returned to G 46 I took him with
me, as I wanted an independent report on the tank which
hitherto no one had visited. He was not impressed favourably with the neighbourhood, perhaps because we arrived

just in time to dodge a salvo of 5.9's; and having advised me to bale out my shell-hole with petrol-tins (!), he left in a hurry. I never saw this useless individual again, and I have forgotten his name, but I took an instinctive dislike to him.

Merchant and I agreed at this meeting that if no orders had reached us by four that afternoon we would lock up the tanks and march back to Frascati. Accordingly, after a second visit to him in the afternoon, when I found him still without any news, I returned once more to make my own final arrangements, by which time I was coming very thoroughly to hate this solitary journey with its inevitable accompaniment of shells and rain. My crew collected their kit (in most cases it was under water), and we filled our haversacks and pockets with the unspoiled residue of our rations and with the small equipment which had to be salved—the clock, periscopes, lamps, &c.—and just before four o'clock we climbed very thankfully out of the manhole and padlocked it behind us. Only a beaver or an Indian pearl-diver could have got at the sponson doors: any child, on the other hand, could have broken the padlock. But that was not our concern. It was impossible to pretend sorrow at parting from G 46: our main apprehension, indeed, was that sooner or later we should have to return to her.

Merchant and his men were ready to move when we reached the crater, and we set off together on our dreary trudge back to Frascati. We each took our turn at carrying his four Lewis guns. Enough has been written of the discomfort of marching anywhere in the Salient in bad weather, and I will not dilate upon this hegira, of which, in fact, I remember very little. One odd incident, however, sticks in my memory as worth recording. As we struggled past the front of Kitchener's Wood, where the German shells were still crashing, and approached the big camouflaged mebus which I have mentioned in an earlier chapter, a flock of little black-and-white birds flew out from the

trees and followed us for some way, fluttering about our
legs and twittering and squeaking in a very agitated manner.
I can only suppose that they came to us, the sole living
creatures to be seen, for company and protection, their
natural fear of mankind overcome by the greater terror of
that reeking wood, resounding with the crashes of exploding
shells and falling trees. It was a singular circumstance, but
I was too tired at the time to give much thought to it or
even notice what birds they were. Possibly they were
swallows. After following us in this fashion for perhaps a
quarter of a mile, they disappeared.

We were making our way obliquely across the front of
the wood toward the Wieltje-St Julien road, which was to
have been put in use immediately after the advance. It
was out of our direct route, but with the rain still falling
in torrents and the elemental mud something beyond the
power of language to describe, any sort of stable surface on
which to walk was an attraction. Tired and burdened as
we were, we could not face a struggle of two or three miles
through pure slime. And presently signs of human and
friendly activity were at length visible. We passed a few
18-pounders buried in shell-holes or hidden behind pollard
stumps. A little later a line of moving figures and vehicles,
marking the road, came into view through the rain. We
found the road congested, in fact, by opposing streams of
mule trains and ammunition limbers, bringing their loads
up to this new battery area and then returning for more.
Nearer the crest, about the mebus called Cheddar Villa and
the ruins of Vanheule Farm, it was being shelled heavily.
Its extemporised surface of brick-rubble and timber was
swimming in liquid mud which wheels and hoofs sprayed
liberally over us. Dead animals and abandoned limbers lay
clustered on either side. We struck it at a point where it
crossed the unrecognisable debris of California Reserve
trench, the third line of the German front system, and just
here another hastily renovated track, also choked with
traffic, forked westward over No Man's Land to Hammond's

Corner, where we had halted before the attack. This branch, called Buffs Road, subsequently was timbered almost throughout, and, with the continuation through St Julien, came to be known only too well by all ranks of the 1st Tank Brigade. We stumbled and splashed along it, involved in endless lines of mules and horses, toward Frascati, which dilapidated haven, loathed by all two days before, now beckoned to us like home. We reached it at length, to find it transformed out of all knowledge. Its shell-pitted fields, last seen deserted, swarmed with men and animals; engineers and labour troops were digging and building, rows of horse-lines had sprung up, dumps were accumulating, and a dressing station was established under the trees. The small ruined lanes behind were packed with ammunition trains and ambulance convoys, and always an endless tide of soaked and muddied transport flowed by the outskirts toward the front line. Around La Brique, where we had been used to venture with such misgivings, 60-pounder guns were firing noisily, while behind them rested the novel gun-carrying tanks which had brought them into action.

III.

In some iron and timber shacks in the middle of the trees, by our own petrol dump, we found Kessel, Winters (second in command of 19 Company), and various details, including Deakin of my own crew, who had been left behind at Hill Top with the wounded man. Every one looked tired and dirty, and had a three-days' growth of beard, but they were perfect d'Orsays by comparison with our disreputable party. Winters, who was in command on the spot, had some dutiful misgivings as to the strict propriety of our leaving our tanks without orders, and even suggested that we might have to return to them; but Merchant and I held forth so vigorously on the subject that this idea died a very rapid death. Our men, in fact (to say nothing of

ourselves), were dead-beat; while it was because our
remaining with the tanks was so palpably useless that we
had come away. The disadvantages of being attached
temporarily to another company were manifest throughout
this affair. No one in 19 Company took much interest in
No. 10 Section. It appeared that the company commander,
without worrying at all about us, had gone back to Lovie
to sleep on the previous evening with the rest of his own
people, although their tanks, with one exception, were also
ditched at various points about the battlefield. He had not
been seen since. Kessel, having been in charge at Frascati
during the greater part of the day, had been unable to come
out to us as he had intended. In short, if we had not taken
matters into our own hands, there appeared really to be no
reason why we should not have been left indefinitely on the
ridge without rations or orders.

Having seen the men settled down with some hot food,
Merchant and I looked after ourselves. I remember very
vividly the excellence of a mess-tin full of scalding stew
which Kessel's servant procured for me. During this meal
we learnt some of the details of the previous day's fighting.
Considering the conditions, our two companies had done
uncommonly well at a light cost. Most of the tanks got
into action. The two sections of 21 Company on the left
had taken the 51st Division to its final objective on the
Steenbeek, losing one section commander, one tank commander, and about half a dozen men wounded. Of my
section, attached to 19 Company, the misfortunes of three
tanks were known to us. The fourth, Alden's, had a happier career. It reached its objective at Alberta, beyond
Kitchener's Wood, assisted the infantry to capture this, and
then, proceeding onward, passed inadvertently through our
stationary barrage and engaged in a unique duel across
the Steenbeek with a light railway train carrying a small
gun, which it drove away. Alden received the Military
Cross for that morning's work. Meanwhile, on his right,
19 Company had attacked in two waves up the St Julien

road. Four or five tanks of the second wave got across the half-ruined bridge and into the village. One, Jordan's, actually pushed on as far as Springfield, a fortified farm on the Langemarck Zonnebeke road, but the infantry could not follow. This tank, with Maelor Jones's, alone of those which crossed the stream, returned to the west bank. The others were all disabled by artillery fire or ditched. Poor Lynch ran upon a 5.9 howitzer firing as a field-gun over open sights, and he and his whole crew were killed by a shell which came through the front of the cab and burst inside. The following year, when I was near Bethune, I met a chaplain who had seen this tank a couple of months after it was hit. He had found the skeletons of the crew still lying among the shattered machinery. This complete destruction of a crew represented the majority of fatal casualties in the battalion that morning. There were in addition, in the two companies, four men killed and seven officers and nineteen men wounded.

Having acquired this information and consumed large quantities of stew, Merchant and I assembled our crews again and trudged off to Reigersberg, where a lorry from the camp was due to arrive at six o'clock. In the dismal château grounds a 15-inch howitzer was now firing from a railway truck, the 8-inch weapons which had helped to make the place so unhealthy having moved a mile or so farther forward. The journey back in the lorry was a slow business, for the roads were jammed with transport, and it was after eight when we arrived at Lovie again.

CHAPTER X.

THE "HUSH" OPERATION AND THE COCKCROFT.

I.

THE result of the first day's fighting at Ypres was on the whole satisfactory. The left of the attack had been quite successful. The French, Guards, and 51st Division had carried their final objectives, and the French had even gone beyond theirs. But from St Julien southwards things had not gone so well. Repeated counter-attacks during the afternoon and night drove our infantry out of St Julien itself, and away at Hooge the net result of twenty-four hours' terrible fighting was a very small gain indeed. The 2nd and 3rd Tank Brigades, operating in this southern sector, suffered heavy casualties, although the average time during which their machines were in action was comparatively short—five hours in the case of the 2nd Brigade and seven in that of the 3rd. The same average in G Battalion, the only representative of the 1st Brigade, worked out at sixteen hours. The two southern brigades sent in between them 94 fighting and 13 supply, signalling, and cable-laying tanks—a total of 107. Thirty-three were disabled by shellfire, a similar number remained ditched at the end of the day, and 22 had mechanical breakdowns. This last figure appears extraordinarily high. Nine officers and 27 men were killed, 29 officers and 168 men were wounded, and 8 men were reported missing—in all, 241 casualties out of some 800 of all ranks who went into action. In many cases valuable help was given to the infantry, especially by the 3rd Brigade (C and F Battalions), working with the 19th Corps against Spree and Bank Farms, Beck House and Capricorn, and Frezenberg. The 2nd Brigade was hampered by the appalling state of the ground in the Hooge area. Most of its tanks were late in coming up, and the infantry in the meanwhile having been checked, machine after machine was hit in the narrow defiles by which they endeavoured to get forward. Our counter-battery work, thorough as it appeared to be, failed completely in this region to keep down the German artillery fire. The two tank battalions, A and B, lost more tanks and men than the other two brigades together.

Individual tank actions during this day presented, one and all, similar features, and I shall not consider them here. The machines dragged themselves laboriously through the mud, became ditched and extricated themselves, and then probably became ditched again. Crews, while in the open during unditching operations, were much harassed by machine-gun fire from low-flying aeroplanes. There were fifty-one recorded cases in which tanks assisted the infantry. Sixteen of these were credited to our two companies on the left, and there can be no doubt that G Battalion, in its first action, carried off such honours as the Heavy Branch gained in that dismal battle. Whether this performance was due to the ground in our sector being a trifle less atrocious than elsewhere (although in all truth it was bad enough), or whether, as one likes to think, it was due rather to the excellent training and spirit of the battalion, must remain a matter of personal opinion. It is certain, however, that our discussions with the infantry beforehand led to a standard of co-operation in the field which does not seem to have been reached in other cases. On several occasions the infantry directed our tanks on to objectives, or called them up from a considerable distance; for we had brought their officers to understand that the view from a

THE "HUSH" OPERATION AND THE COCKCROFT 183

tank is so restricted that without such help half its value will be wasted.

'Weekly Tank Notes,' a concise history of the corps issued recently from the Headquarters in London, sets out the main lessons to be drawn from this day's fighting, as follows: "The unsuitability of the Mark IV. tank to swamp warfare; the danger of attempting to move tanks through defiles which are swept by hostile artillery fire; the necessity for immediate infantry co-operation whenever the presence of a tank forces an opening, and the continued moral effect of the tank on both the enemy and our own troops." This last was exemplified very strikingly in the case of one of 21 Company's tanks, which led the 51st Division to the Steenbeek, and helped it to establish itself there, without firing a shot. Successive German posts surrendered as soon as the tank came within range. As for "swamp warfare," the unsuitability for this of an experimental machine weighing thirty tons had been manifest to every one in the corps itself long before. But to infantry commanders, regular British officers with the conservative outlook and the prejudices common to their type, this consideration carried no weight. They had never liked this newfangled weapon. It was absurd, in their eyes, to attempt to introduce the tactics of naval warfare on land, and they seized upon the inevitable failures at Ypres as a happy confirmation of all their doubts. The three corps commanders concerned supplied the 5th Army H.Q. with their opinions on the work of tanks during the battle. Major Williams-Ellis, in his book, deals with this incident so effectively that I cannot do better than quote him.

"The three summaries were agreed that the courage and perseverance shown by tank personnel had been admirable. One corps, however, had given way thoroughly to the spirit of the time. They practically reported that tanks had been of no use to any one, and moreover that they were never likely to be. With the 30th Division they had been unable to deal with certain machine-gun emplacements; with the 24th they had been late—they always drew enemy shell-fire; and with the 8th Division one tank had even lost direction and been reported as firing on our own men. Another corps had found tanks helpful, and said all they could for them. Tanks had greatly assisted the Gordons and Black Watch at Frezenberg; they had dealt effectively with concrete dug-outs; with the 55th Division they had broken the wave of an enemy counter-attack at Winnipeg, and everywhere their moral effect on the enemy had been of great assistance. Twenty-four tanks had been put out of action by bad going or shell-fire.

"A third corps, with fewer machines, had in many cases reached their objective without being held up. The tanks had in these cases merely followed the infantry, but they reported that without tanks the capture of the strongly-wired position of Alberta would have cost the 39th Division dear, and that on the Steenbeek near Ferdinand Farm the enemy, who had bolted at the mere sight of a tank, had been 'dealt with' at ease with a machine-gun by infantry of the 51st Division. Upon these summaries and upon later failures the commander of the 5th Army was subsequently to base a generally unfavourable report upon tanks.

"The report may be condensed into a simple syllogism:—

1. Tanks were unable to negotiate bad ground.
2. The ground on a battlefield will always be bad.
3. Therefore tanks are no good on a battlefield.

"He added to this, that being no longer a surprise to the enemy, he considered that tanks had lost their moral effect, and had no value used in masses. This report was not officially presented for some weeks, but the Higher Tank Command must early have perceived the drift of affairs."[1]

[1] 'The Tank Corps.' C. A. Williams-Ellis.

THE "HUSH" OPERATION AND THE COCKCROFT

The prospects of the Tank Corps, in fact, were become suddenly very gloomy. I cannot say how near the corps came to extinction, or at least to drastic limitation, at this period; but by all accounts it came very near. All the prophets of evil were up and about and busy, saying everywhere, "I told you so!" The labour of three years, the sacrifice of many lives, seemed likely to come to nothing after all. A weapon which, properly applied, could alter the whole face of the war, was in imminent danger of abandonment because it had been used, in defiance of all authoritative opinion, amid conditions for which it was wholly unfitted. By a parity of reasoning the cavalry might have been threatened with abolition; for their patrols were supposed to be at hand to cross the Steenbeek, and not a trooper got even as far as the canal. And, when one comes to think of it, a state of mind which can hope that cavalry will be of any use whatever at such a stage of such a battle must be capable of the most astounding misjudgments. It was in this state of mind that too many senior officers, even after three years of shattering surprises and disillusionment, looked upon tanks or any other new thing. Faced by so obstinate a prejudice, now fanned into activity by the events of the 31st July, the position of the new arm obviously was precarious. It is possible also that the Treasury, always alarmed by the growth of a very expensive organisation, and encouraged by the fact that the Tank Corps, unlike the R.A.F., had few friends and no publicity agents, was backing up any proposals made at home for economical reform. In short, it looked very like becoming a question whether the corps would have another chance of justifying itself before its fate was taken out of its hands. For, in the meantime, at Ypres the rain still fell, the whole offensive came virtually to a standstill, and the mere idea of further tank operations in that dissolving world seemed ludicrous. One such attempt, indeed, was made, and ended as an inglorious but inevitable fiasco.

Before we come to this, however, and to the surprising

success which, following immediately after, re-endued the Tank Corps with life and hope, another and unique enterprise falls to be noticed.

II.

The most interesting phase of the third battle of Ypres, as originally planned, was never fought. This was the landing on the Flanders coast. Tanks were to have played an important and indeed essential part in the undertaking.

The landing was designed to take place in the neighbourhood of Middelkerke, a little *plage* midway between Nieuport and Ostend. The sea-front along the whole of this flat coast is protected by a high concrete wall, on the top of which runs the usual esplanade and roadway. On the other side of the road are the villas and cafés and *pensions* where, in happier days, visitors crowded during the summer and autumn. The whole esplanade now was all but hidden by barbed wire, and there was more wire along the beach; batteries were emplaced at close intervals along the wall; and the ground-floors and cellars of the lodging-houses were become concrete machine-gun posts. A landing here presented extraordinary difficulties, but the main problem before the assailants (assuming that all else went well) was how to haul field-guns and supplies rapidly over the concrete wall under fire. Infantry might be got ashore under cover of a smoke-screen and a bombardment from the sea; but infantry alone, even if it could capture that fortified esplanade, could not hope to hold it. Guns were essential, and, if possible, some other factor which would upset the enemy's *moral* and prevent him recovering from the initial surprise. For this purpose tanks, of all things, were to be employed.

The attacking force consisted of the 1st Division, several batteries of field-guns and 4.5 howitzers, a company or two of engineers, and nine Mark IV. tanks. To throw this

THE "HUSH" OPERATION AND THE COCKCROFT

considerable force ashore three immense pontoons or barges were constructed, each 700 feet long. These were taken over to Dunkirk harbour toward the end of July. On the night of the attack (which, as I have said before, was to follow the capture of the Passchendaele Ridge, provided that was effected within three or four days) these barges were to be pushed on to the beach by pairs of monitors, lashed together, one barge at Middelkerke itself and one on either side of that place. Each barge carried a brigade of infantry, several batteries, three tanks, and some motor-lorries. The landing was to take place just before dawn, covered by a dense smoke and ordinary bombardment from warships supplied by the Dover Patrol, which was in charge of the naval side of the enterprise.

The wall itself was a very serious obstacle. It rose to a height of some thirty feet, sloping up from the beach at an easy angle, but ending at the top in a vertical coping with a lip or overhang. A tank, fitted with special shoes on the tracks, could climb the slope easily enough, but the vertical coping was too high to be surmounted without additional appliances. To each tank, therefore, was fitted in front a massive detachable steel ramp, slightly wider than the machine, supported on lattice-work girders carrying a pair of wheels, and so constructed that it sloped upward from the inclined part of the sea-wall to the top of the overhang. When the tank reached the foot of the incline, the ramp would be lowered by tackle until its wheels rested on the concrete, pushed up against the coping, and there detached. The tank could then climb over it on to the esplanade. Afterwards this highly ingenious contrivance was to be used for the haulage of guns and motor-lorries over the obstacle, the tanks being fitted with special cables and attachments for this purpose. Another clever device was a system of wooden sledges carrying ammunition-boxes, the sledges being simply jammed on to a rope and hauled up by the tanks, releasing themselves automatically as they cleared the top of the overhang.

The actual disembarkation from the huge barges to the beach was effected by strong hinged gangways, which fell over the bows.

The troops detailed for this hazardous attempt were trained very thoroughly. The infantry, segregated for weeks in a camp near Dunkirk, practised repeatedly the whole attack with the aid of a concrete model of a section of the sea-wall. A similar model was built at Merlimont, where the special tank detachment, commanded by Major the Hon. J. D. Y. Bingham, and made up of volunteers from the original four battalions, climbed up and down with their machines, towed up guns and lorries, and demonstrated conclusively that this essential part of the enterprise was perfectly feasible. The ramps worked admirably. Major Bingham informs me that tanks made as many as 200 ascents of the model at Merlimont.

Had this attack taken place, it would have been profoundly interesting. Obviously it was an immense gamble. It bore many points of resemblance to the successful raid at Zeebrugge, with this great difference: it was intended not as a raid but as a permanent landing. Once troops and tanks were ashore, it is difficult to see how they could have been got off again if things went wrong. The great barges would have been blown to matchwood if they remained on the beach after daybreak, unless an extensive clearance of the sea-front was effected at the very start. The roadway above the sea-wall was none too wide, and there were doubts as to whether the tanks would have room to tow the guns, to say nothing of the lorries, up the narrow ramps. It was found afterwards that the lower storeys of the houses across the road were veritable fortresses of concrete. There were a hundred other obstacles to success which might arise, such as bad weather, premature discovery, or even a wind sufficient to dissipate the smoke-screen. And it seems probable that, well as the secret was kept in England, the Germans had some uncertain information about it. I believe that the camp near Dunkirk was bombed with quite exceptional

THE "HUSH" OPERATION AND THE COCKCROFT

thoroughness. The chances, in short, seem to have been very greatly against success, and failure would have meant a ghastly slaughter on the beach and along that narrow esplanade. On the other hand, whatever the Germans suspected, it does not seem likely that they possessed any exact information. Some sort of a landing somewhere on the Flanders coast was always a bogey to them. And after so prolonged a crying of "Wolf!" the prospects of a genuine surprise, if one could be effected, were very hopeful. Above all, if the German machine-gunners, buried in their concrete basements and discouraged by news of a successful advance at Passchendaele, threatening their whole coast-line, were to be confronted suddenly with tanks where no rational human being could expect tanks to be, a widespread panic was possible. One can imagine these men, deluged with gas and high-explosive and blinded by smoke, peering anxiously out of their loopholes for human targets, and seeing instead, huge and distorted in the gloom, tanks which seemed to have arisen from the sea. . . .

But this great experiment was never attempted. By our sanguine calculations, it was due for the 3rd or 4th of August. It was admittedly useless, however, to land a force at Middelkerke unless the armies from Ypres were in a position to do their share of the work; and at the end of the month, and for many weary weeks after, the armies from Ypres were still floundering in a morass a bare mile or two from where they started. Passchendaele and its insignificant ridge were not ours until November. And with the ruin of its parent enterprise, the conception of the Flanders landing, the great "Hush" operation, necessarily came also to nothing. Long before we had even a footing on the ridge, the amphibious attack had been abandoned. The infantry dispersed to more normal fields of action, the great barges lay derelict, like Napoleon's, in Dunkirk harbour, and the special tank detachment was disbanded. The scheme remains one of those unfulfilled but deeply interesting adventures over which any person of a speculative mind could write pages of inconclusive arguments.

III.

We will return from these cursory surveys of the whole field of operations to the small world of Oosthoek Wood and the camp by Lovie Château.

The morning after I rejoined from Frascati, the tank commanders left in our two companies—eight out of the twenty-three had become casualties—were interviewed by the brigade commander and his Intelligence officer, that same Major (then Captain) Williams-Ellis whose book I have quoted. For the next two or three days most of us were suffering from the reaction after the strain and fatigue of the approach-marches and the battle itself. For all tank personnel (and this applied to every other arm) the fighting at Ypres was by far the most exhausting and nerve-wracking ordeal undergone throughout the war. The dreadful conditions of ground and weather, on top of all the ordinary trials of warfare, brought every one to the limit of endurance very quickly. The hard labour involved in taking and fighting tanks anywhere was multiplied tenfold in the Salient; and after a severe action there, it was a physical impossibility for any crew to go in again until it had been given a complete rest. On other fronts the same tanks and men often were fit enough for a renewed march and attack after a few hours' sleep. In our case there was now little or nothing for some of us to do, for the two companies were left for the moment virtually without tanks. Of the twenty-three which went into action, one only returned the same day to the neighbourhood of Frascati. Four, which had received direct hits, were lying in the new No Man's Land around St Julien; others, like G 46, were derelict in positions where salvage work at present was out of the question; and the rest, half engulfed or mechanically crippled, or both, lay scattered about the west slope of the Pilkem Ridge. During the next fortnight most of these nearer machines were brought back to a spot known as Ghent Cottages, near Brielen, where the battalion had established an advanced base.

In the meantime it rained. The camp at Lovie, its leaky tents immersed in dripping shrubs and undergrowth, and surrounded by sodden parapets of sandbags as a protection against the persistent bombing raids, grew always more evil-smelling, steamy, and unhealthy, and those of us who had little to do became more melancholy every day. There was a time, some four days after the battle, when the reaction was at its worst, and when, personally, I felt I could cut my throat for twopence. An expedition up the line to retrieve my six Lewis guns from Maelor Jones's tank was a diversion, but not a strikingly attractive one. For once, it is true, it was not raining; I do not know why. We went by lorry to Salvation Corner, a miserable road-junction near the Dead End of Ypres, and thence walked once more over the familiar route by Bridge 4, Frascati, and La Brique. At Frascati, under the trees where our tanks had lain during Y-Z day, 9.2 howitzers were being "assembled"—if one may use this expression with regard to such imposing weapons. A few duckboard tracks had been laid over the tumbled waste of mud and water beyond, by which we proceeded with comparative ease for a part of the way. I was able for the first time to examine at leisure the ground over which we had advanced, and it appeared to me to be rather astonishing that tanks had got over it at all. A good number of dead were still lying about, among them a whole batch of Highlanders, I remember, near Hurst Park, and everywhere hung the horrible sweet odour of decomposing animal matter. Away on the top of the ridge the Germans, with a curious futile industry, were shelling with heavy metal the big concrete mebus in front of Kitchener's Wood.

Our directions for finding the tank were not too explicit, and even so large an object was easily missed in that distorted wilderness, where everything was mud-coloured. When at length we discovered it, we found it had been hit on one track. The guns were lying rusting inside amid a litter of tools, petrol-tins, and rubbish, and mud was everywhere. I had intended to go on to G 46, if the situation seemed propitious, to collect Kessel's cherished flag and my binoculars, which I had left somewhere under water, but the auguries were not favourable. The enemy began to burst heavy black shrapnel overhead. As no one else was within sight, I concluded that my little party probably was under observation, and the epidemic of high explosive on the crest appearing to spread at the same time, we made for home with all the speed of which we were capable, hampered as we were by half a dozen Lewis guns. Johnstone, who was not in good health, presently became so ill that I took his burden from him. It was while I was staggering along under this double load, gingerly circumnavigating craters and cursing the very name of the American Colonel who invented the weapons, that I stepped literally into an inglorious predicament. I tried foolishly to cross a well-churned artillery track, went into the soft mud up to my knees, and there stuck, absolutely helpless, with the wretched guns occupying both my hands and weighing me down, and at the same time totally unable to move my legs. It required the cautious assistance of most of my crew, helped by some providential gunners who brought bits of board, to get me out.

There ensued another week of rain, squalor, and depression at Lovie Camp. Our doctor was despatching officers and men by twos and threes to a rest-camp at Wormhoudt, just over the Belgian frontier, and I managed to get Johnstone away with one of these parties. He was not over strong, and he had never recovered from the strain of our thirty-six hours' vigil on the ridge following on that of driving for the best part of three successive

THE "HUSH" OPERATION AND THE COCKCROFT

nights and a part of the fourth day. Neither of my other drivers had his knowledge or skill, and during the latter stages of the approach-march, when he should have been resting, I had been obliged to call upon him. As it happened, he was still at Wormhoudt when the sudden call came for the Cockcroft operation. In the meantime the general outlook, from what we could deduce, was not encouraging. The great offensive, launched with so vast a preparation, had come to a sudden standstill at the very start. Fighting continued every day: there were minor attacks and counter-attacks all round the Salient, and we had blown our way once more into St Julien and into various other posts captured and then lost again on the 31st; but in essentials our line remained where it had been on the evening of that day. Already more than a week had passed since, by the original time-table, Passchendaele should have fallen, and now it was tacitly confessed that the whole ambitious plan (persistently described as a "residue" of something even greater, although before the end almost every division in the British Army was involved and decimated in it) had dwindled to a struggle, amid conditions indescribably ghastly, for that single ridge, which at one time was to have been but the starting-point for infinitely bigger things. Into this struggle the Tank Corps was drawn virtually to the last tank and the last man. We have seen what happened on the 31st, and how hopeless it was, even then, to expect decisive results from these machines in such a country. A fortnight later, when the ground was a mere slimy pulp, 20 Company of G Battalion moved up to take part, if possible, in a second serious attempt to advance.

This attack was fixed for the 16th August. 20 Company, which had been in corps reserve on 31st July, had since moved forward to our old park at Halfway House. On the 13th the twelve tanks started for Frascati. The ground everywhere was now in so appalling a state that one machine actually became bellied in Rum Road, a few hundred yards from the start. As she could not be got out that night, I was detailed on the following day to take my crew down and see what I could do, while her own people came back to camp for the short rest. We worked the whole afternoon, digging round the tank, which was sunk to the sponsons, and building a small causeway of timber and brick-rubble in front; and when her crew returned in the evening they were able, with the help of the unditching beam, to pull her out at once. But if this sort of thing happened on Rum Road, what would happen in the shelled zone? In fact, the progress of the company across the old trench systems and up the slope toward St Julien, during the dark hours of the 14th and 15th, was one long nightmare of ditching and unditching under shell-fire and gas. Four only got anywhere near the front line, and at length it was clear that even these could not arrive in time. When the infantry attacked, these four were still a mile behind. So far as the 1st Tank Brigade was concerned, this was the last attempt made to move tanks across country in the Salient.

The infantry assault was, in results, very similar to that of the 31st. The left, where Langemarck was carried by eight o'clock in the morning, was successful, but from St Julien southwards little or no progress was made. In this part of the field we had now come up against the main system of fortified farms and other strong field forts already mentioned. A cluster of these forts, just beyond St Julien, checked every attempt to debouch from the village up the Poelcapelle road; and until they could be carried no further general advance was possible, as our line now bulged out into an awkward little salient in the north. General Maxse, commanding the 18th Corps, was told that an attack on these forts would cost him 600 to 1000 casualties, without any guarantee that we should capture them in the end. The Lieutenant-General, who had more faith in tanks than some of his colleagues, for they had served him well on the 31st, consulted with the Brigadier of the 1st Tank Brigade.

THE "HUSH" OPERATION AND THE COCKCROFT 195

The position of the forts, disposed about a triangle of roads, was such that tanks could get close to them, and in some cases absolutely alongside, without necessarily venturing into the slough of mud on either side of the *pavé*. Details of the operation were accordingly hurriedly worked out. One company of tanks was to be used, and G Battalion, straitened for machines as it was, once more was called upon. This, at least, was a notable compliment, for D Battalion, one of the old originals, as it never failed to remind us by word and behaviour, had not yet been into action at all.

IV.

About midday on 17th August, Kessel, I, and several others were standing together in the marquee which served us for a company mess at Lovie, drinking the usual sherry and bitters, or something of the kind, before lunch. To us entered Paisley, second in command of the company. He held a sheet of paper, from which he proceeded to read. "The following officers will take over tanks this afternoon, fill up with petrol, oil, and ammunition, and be prepared to move at six o'clock." The officers named were Coutts, Claughton, Chaddock, Bubb, and myself. It transpired further that four tanks from 20 Company, and three from 19 also were to move: that we were to trek that night to Bellevue, on the old German front line, and again the night following to St Julien; and that we were going into action on the morning of the 19th. The charge of this composite detachment had been given to Major Broome, who had just arrived from the depot at Erin to replace Torbett, invalided home, in command of my own company. There were to be three section commanders, Kessel, Guy of 20 Company, and Wright of 19.

Sudden orders of this kind, when one has been contemplating a quiet afternoon with a book, are always somewhat disturbing. There ensued now the inevitable bustle, for

there was no time to lose, as we were leaving by lorry at
1.30. My first task was to make up my crew. I had lost
one man on the 31st, and now Johnstone was away; and
it was essential to get a good first driver in place of the
latter. I went immediately to find Sergeant Meyrick, the
section sergeant (already mentioned as Merchant's N.C.O.),
and told him what I wanted. He volunteered on the spot
to come himself as an ordinary gunner under my own
corporal. Meyrick was, I think, one of those rare people
who positively enjoy a battle, and, what was more valuable,
he was a peculiarly intelligent and competent regular
soldier, who had come out with his battery in the original
Expeditionary Force. For a first driver he recommended
Waller, of his own crew, who volunteered as promptly. I
was extremely fortunate in obtaining these two men.
Leaving Meyrick and Corporal Mitchell to arrange about
rations and other details, I reported, with the rest of the
tank commanders, to the Major for further instructions.
The first thing to be settled was the allotment of tanks
to one or two of us who had none. My own, of course, was
still lying by Kitchener's Wood; but by this time some six
or eight of the others had been got back to Ghent Cottages,
where they were parked under a hedge in various stages
of unreadiness or actual disrepair. We could just about
manage to provide five dependable machines. John Alden
being away at the Wormhoudt rest-camp, I was told to
take over his tank, G 47, or "Gitana," my second eponym
from the variety stage. The general idea and tactics of the
proposed attack were then discussed. At this time our
outpost line just skirted St Julien on the north and east.
A thousand yards beyond the village two important roads
cross one another—the St Julien-Poelcapelle road, pointing
almost due north at this point, and the Zonnebeke-Langemarck road, running north-west. A triangle, of which these
thoroughfares form two sides, has for its base a third road,
running eastward from St Julien and cutting the Langemarck road at Winnipeg. A fourth road, whose direction

THE "HUSH" OPERATION AND THE COCKCROFT

is also roughly east and west, bisects the triangle 250 yards from its apex. Around the sides, or within this symmetrical boundary, lay all, save two, of our objectives. Of the two exceptions, one, called the Maison du Hibou, was situate west of the triangle, and some 300 yards along the fourth or bisecting road; the other, the Cockcroft, was due north of this, a quarter of a mile from the apex up the Langemarck road. In the original scheme, four tanks were to devote themselves to these two objectives, while the remaining eight moved in line ahead along the roads right round the triangle, dealing with the other strong-points as they passed, and beginning and ending at St Julien. Very unfortunately, as it turned out, this plan was afterwards modified considerably, for what reason I do not know. The eastern side and base of the triangle were left for another day. Our work was confined to the two outlying forts, the Poelcapelle road, and a couple of farms at the apex. It was, in any case, an entirely novel operation in every respect, much resembling a naval action where a squadron of ships passes by and reduces a line of batteries. The tanks, if possible, were to keep strictly to the roads, as the neighbouring ground, watered by one or two small tributaries of the Steenbeek, was now reduced by rain and shell-fire to a swamp notable even in the Salient. The infantry was to follow on either side of the roads, one platoon to each tank 250 yards behind it, and was not to attempt to occupy the objectives until the tanks signalled that all was clear, or that they wanted help. The signal in either case was a shovel waved out of the manhole in the roof. There was to be no artillery preparation: the affair was intended as a genuine surprise; but at zero, which was 4.45 or dawn, an ordinary creeping barrage would come down, together with a heavy smoke barrage on the German third-line trenches, which lay behind the posts to be attacked. This was devised to blind the enemy's observation of what was happening. A large number of extra field batteries were brought up to supply this smoke-screen, much to the disgust of the weary gunners who manned them, and who had just gone back to rest. The infantry concerned were the 48th and 11th Divisions, the former a Midland unit. Our own arrangements for the attack and the particular objectives allotted to tanks will be better left until I come to deal with the Divisional conference held on the 18th, when we were told of the modification already referred to, and when all final details were decided.

Having obtained this rough outline of the scheme, we ate a hasty and uninspiring lunch; collected such articles as we thought we might require; were loaded in addition with maps, periscopes, compasses, and clocks; and departed by lorry at 1.30. Very fortunately the weather was fine, and remained so, by some miracle, over the next two days. On arriving at Ghent Cottages — a row of melancholy ruins on the Brielen road — I found that I had a great deal of work to get through in a very short time. G 47 having suffered from some mechanical trouble, it had taken Alden and his crew several days and nights to repair her temporarily and drive her back from Mousetrap Farm, where he had left her on the 31st, to her present quarters. Since then she had been in the hands of our workshops personnel. Although very dirty, she appeared now to be in good order mechanically, but she had to be greased up and filled with water, oil, and petrol. She was short of about a hundred Lewis drums (Alden must have used a fair amount of ammunition in capturing Alberta and engaging the German train), and many tools and spare parts were missing. This last calamity we considered, perhaps unjustly, to be inevitable when workshops had been about. I raided a supply-tank and replaced most of the deficiencies, while my crew cleared up inside, greased the rollers and stauffers, and cleaned the six Lewis guns we had brought with us from store. We had time for tea, and were ready to start when the first tank moved off just after six o'clock. I should have mentioned that there were only

eleven fit tanks at Ghent Cottages. Our twelfth machine—
a doubtful starter belonging to 19 Company—was on the
other side of the canal, where she had lain since the 31st
with a twisted extension-shaft and badly ditched into the
bargain. To such an impoverished state had the Salient
already reduced us!

The first stage of the night's journey was a short one.
As we did not wish to cross the canal before dusk, we
pulled up before seven o'clock at Murat Farm, close to
Marengo Causeway. I never saw any vestige of a farm
at this place; but there was a row of tall splintered trees
hung with camouflage netting, a few muddy enclosures
bounded by overgrown hedgerows, and the usual squalid
dug-outs and elephant-iron shelters. Behind one of the
hedges was a 9.2 naval gun on a railway mounting. The
brigade had formed a petrol dump here, and we took in
a final supply of the spirit. Although we had come such
a short distance the water in my radiator was boiling
furiously, and for some time we could not discover the
cause, until, with the help of Paramor, the engineer of
20 Company, who was ministering to the detachment, we
found that the workshops people had unscrewed a large
baffle-plate from one side of the copper envelopes and
omitted to replace it. The plate was lying on the floor
beneath an accumulation of oil-drums and water-tins. We
readjusted this by 7.30, when the eleven tanks moved off
again.

We now began one of the most wearisome and maddening treks I have ever undertaken with tanks. At first
everything went well. The evening was fine: the German
artillery was inoffensive, although our own was very noisy
and persistent; and we crossed the causeway and the bad
ground beyond without a hitch, for there was still light
to see by. We passed 19 Company's ditched tank, still
immobile and plainly in no condition to attempt even to
catch us up later. It was just getting dark when we
swung out of the wire and shell-holes on to Boundary

Road, with the trees of Frascati to our left. Boundary Road, as I have mentioned in the last chapter, eventually crosses the old front lines, passes the north end of Kitchener's Wood, and then descends to the Steenbeek. Our route now followed it as far as our old acquaintance Hammond's Corner, and thence by Buffs Road to the main St Julien highway. Both Buffs and Boundary Roads, presumably having been (at a prehistoric era) ordinary country lanes, had gone utterly to pieces under the impact of high explosive, and long stretches of them since our advance had been timbered. A tank on a timbered road can do a great deal of damage, especially if the driver is inexpert and swings too often. During this trek I had the misfortune to meet the R.E. officer responsible for the upkeep of Buffs Road at the moment when G 47 was swinging unavoidably round a bend, and when, to the accompaniment of loud rending and crashing noises, all the beautifully laid and clamped baulks of timber on our off or turning side were opening upward and outward like a fan. It was not my fault, as I hope he realised after a period of reflection. At the moment his language and despairing gestures seemed fully adequate to the situation, and I was too much occupied with my own troubles to spare much sympathy for his. For long before this we had begun to experience some of the vicissitudes which attend the movement of tanks by road at night anywhere near the front line. Our first encounter after getting on to Boundary Road was with one of our own machines on its way home, in charge of a young officer, Wayne, who had joined the battalion only the day before. To acclimatise him without delay, Wayne had been detailed immediately to bring in this tank from some unhealthy spot near St Julien, where it had been lying in the mud undergoing repairs since the last battle. By this time it was growing dark rapidly, and we now began to encounter the mules. I have never seen so many mules as we met that night. I did not know there were so many in

THE "HUSH" OPERATION AND THE COCKCROFT

the world, or that any modern quadruped could be so stupid. We had collided, of course, with the usual nightly ammunition trains, going up loaded to the forward battery positions and returning empty. Even a mule could not travel at night across country in the Salient, and there were only three or four roads for all this vast traffic. Buffs Road and its continuations rearward formed one of the most important lines of supply. It was well choked with opposing streams of mules and limbers, when into it turned our eleven tanks. The result, I hope, can be imagined: it was something beyond the power of polite language to describe. The night fell intensely black; one could see only a hundred yards or so ahead, and the world seemed to be full of mules. My tank was one of the last, so that the beasts were thoroughly disorganised by the time I reached them or they reached me. The latter state of affairs seemed the more normal of the two, for I was forced to stop continually for five or ten minutes at a time while limbers or pack-mules were pulled and pushed and cajoled past G 47. Occasionally there would supervene a thoroughly satisfactory block, when the road in front was filled from edge to edge, and, as far ahead as one could see (which was not far), by a seemingly insoluble congestion of animals and transport—the former heading to every point of the compass, some standing rooted as if stricken with paralysis, some bucking and kicking, some deliberately getting entangled in their own and others' harness, and a number wandering casually off into the mud on either side. I was sorry for their drivers, who must have had a perfectly abominable evening, but I was still more sorry for myself. I soon lost touch with the tanks in front. They were swallowed up in the nightmare ahead, wrestling with their own problems. I was expecting every minute the whistle of a shell, and I shall never understand why the German gunners, who were very prodigal of ammunition at that time, and who possessed, in the 5.9, the most accurate of created guns, did not devote themselves every night and all night to such arteries as the St Julien road. They would have found it far more profitable than the blind "area" shooting to which they were so addicted. I am speaking, of course, in the judicial spirit that comes with comfortable surroundings where 5.9's are not. There were nights and to spare when the Germans did shell the roads and turned them into shambles, and I shall be the last to complain because they omitted to do so that evening. Wedged for hours amid the stream of demoralised animals, the expectancy was bad enough. We were infinitely fortunate that it was not realised. For our progress up that road was in itself like some fiendish torture invented for animal haters by the S.P.C.A. Hour after hour went by, the night grew blacker and blacker, dawn, even, was drawing near, and still we were embedded in mules. Under the circumstances, no better obstacle to tanks could have been devised. We were entirely helpless. We could not drive over the mules, if only because they were controlled, in theory, by human beings, who (when they were not falling off) were blaspheming and raving in their saddles. We could not drive round them, because in the dark we did not dare to leave the road. We could only wait their pleasure. Like ships struggling against a violent current, we forged slowly, very slowly, ahead. I do not wish to appear to be exaggerating, and a trivial arithmetical computation will prove in a few lines what has taken me several pages to explain in words. From the point where we turned on to Boundary Road to our destination at Bellevue is roughly a mile and a half: it is actually 2500 yards. (I have just measured it on a large-scale map with a simple but ingenious instrument like a speedometer.) Judging by the light, it cannot have been later than 8.30 P.M. when I struck the road. When I turned off the road again at Bellevue, it was two o'clock in the morning. It had taken me five and a half hours to cover those 2500 yards—on a road. With no obstructions, the tank could have done it in thirty minutes.

If I have written flippantly about this journey, it did not strike me as being in the least amusing at the time. I walked outside, of course, throughout, and nothing is in itself more fatiguing than this sort of enforced crawl with frequent stoppages. Added to it was a consuming anxiety about shells and other things peculiar to an approach-march. Waller, who drove most of the way, must have been even wearier than I was. I do not remember how I discovered Bellevue, which was nothing but a name on the map, but I think I overtook the tank in front, thanks to some unexpected hiatus in the torrent of mules. Kessel was there, however, to guide me to a vacant space behind an exiguous hedge. The place struck me as being extraordinarily noisy. We were, in fact, surrounded by field batteries, all of which were very busily in action. The gun-flashes supplied our only illumination, and this was insufficient, as I discovered when I had fallen three times into a cesspool under the nose of my tank while helping to rig up the camouflage net. After this we lighted primus stoves, brewed ourselves some cocoa, wound up with a tot of rum, and then crawled inside with an optimistic notion of obtaining a little sleep. It was just on three o'clock.

CHAPTER XI.

THE COCKCROFT (*continued*).

I.

VERY few of us contrived to sleep before dawn. The 18-pounder, for its size, makes the most ear-splitting report of any gun, and there were batteries so near to us that their fire, which never ceased, kept the tanks in a continual state of vibration. The only pillow available for most of us was made of armour-plate, studded with bolt-heads, and now being hit by these concussions as if by millions of muffled but infuriated hammers. Under these circumstances any sort of rest was out of the question. Toward dawn, however, the bombardment slackened. I had just begun thankfully to doze when I was aroused again by some one shouting my name. It turned out to be the Major, who very thoughtfully had walked across at that unconscionable hour from Company H.Q. (established overnight on the canal bank) to take some of us back for a wash, a rest, and a meal before we attended a Divisional conference at midday. It was now just after five, and a bright sunny morning. When I joined the Major outside the tank, I obtained my first daylight view of our quarters, which were much as one might have expected. I do not know the cynic who named the spot Bellevue, but no doubt he had his reasons. It was the site, apparently, of a small farm— a building, at least, was marked on the map, although long since invisible to the naked eye; and it was happily situated in the original No Man's Land, close to the German front line, the remains of whose first trench, California, bounded this desirable property to the east. For the rest, there was a square of bedraggled hedge, entirely imaginary in places, behind parts of which the tanks, like so many ostriches, believed themselves to be concealed: the usual ground surface of mud, wire, and shell-holes; and in one corner a patch of unmitigated bog where a pond had been. Buffs Road, lined by sand-bagged shelters and dead mules, and now void of any sign of life, passed by the north side toward its junction with the main St Julien road at California Reserve. Beyond it, and to the east and south-east, rose the curve of the ridge, while behind us were the stump of wall at Hilltop Farm, the trees of Frascati, and the higher branches of the shattered avenue along the canal. The whole landscape, if intrinsically depressing, was very peaceful at that moment. No one seemed to be discharging any sort of lethal weapon anywhere.

It appeared that 19 and 20 Companies had made their own arrangements with their officers in the detachment, and only four of us, therefore, accompanied the Major back to headquarters. Bubb was left in charge of our tanks. As the Major was in excellent condition, and had not been up all night, we had an exhausting walk across country at the rate of about five miles an hour. Before six o'clock we arrived at that singular colony of sand-bagged dwellings which had grown up in regular terraces along the inner face of the eastern bank of the canal. The address of the two shelters appropriated to our use, if I remember correctly, was 9 and 10 Gordon Terrace. They commanded no view, except (across a two-feet duckboard walk) of the back of a similar terrace on a lower level, and their accommodation was limited. They were, in fact, the familiar structures of curved elephant iron, about eight feet high in the centre and perhaps twice as long, half the length being dug out of the canal bank, and the front part surmounted by a towering mass of sandbags. There were a couple of wire-beds and a table or two in each, and everywhere there were flies. One of these tenements was given over to our signallers, runners, and other details. Into its fellow we crowded as thankfully as if it had been the Ritz, and sat about on the beds and floor while kindly people brought us tea and bacon and bread. Kessel was there, and with him his invaluable servant, Taylor, who always seemed to have a hot drink ready at the psychological moment.

We passed the morning at Gordon Terrace, washing, shaving, and behaving generally like gentlemen of leisure, worried only by the malignant flies and the telephone, which conspired successfully to rob us of what we needed most—two or three hours' sleep. Shortly before midday, Claughton, Chaddock, and I left with the Major for the conference at the 48th Divisional Headquarters. Coutts was working by himself with the 33rd Brigade of the 11th Division, and had already gone off to hunt for his Brigadier, who was living in some remote dug-out east of the canal. Our destination was nearer at hand. There runs side by side with the canal north of Ypres a sluggish stream called, I think, the Yperlee. Overhanging this, there had been built into the western canal bank a series of dug-outs and shelters similar to those on the east side, and divisional headquarters occupied a quite commodious suite in this part, with a railed balcony projecting over the stream. Here were a great number of immaculate persons wearing red tabs; and scattered humbly among them, like poor relations, a few more workmanlike figures in steel helmets and privates' tunics—the officers of the two infantry battalions which, with ourselves, were going to do the fighting.

At these conferences one is always kept waiting, the delay usually being in strict ratio to the presiding General's dignity; and on this occasion it was nearly one o'clock before any of the actual performers were called upon. We spent the interval profitably in becoming acquainted with our infantry colleagues. I discovered the platoon commander of the 7th Warwicks who was to follow the fortunes of G 47. The Major was then summoned to consultation with the infantry battalion commanders, and we continued to stand patiently about and wonder when we were going to get any lunch. At length the conference was over: it appeared that none of us, except the Major, had been wanted at all; and we trooped thankfully back to Gordon Terrace, where we found Merchant and some other faithful souls who had come all the way from Lovie to bring us our letters and wish us luck.

The Divisional conference, all natural misgivings notwithstanding, had at least accomplished something: the scope and details of the attack were agreed upon—for how long of course no one could prophesy. The operation had been modified, as I have explained, until it took in only the western side of the triangle of roads. It was limited, that is, to the Poelcapelle road itself, the apex, and the two formidable works to the west and north-west of the latter. Nine tanks were to go in, the other two remaining in reserve at Bellevue. Tanks were detailed for objectives as follows, and were to move in this order:—

Coutts, with Willard of 19 Company, for the Cockcroft, the most distant fort to be attacked (it was a mile north of St Julien). Charles Baker and Kane of 20 Company, for Maison du Hibou; Morgan and Close of 20 Company, for Triangle Farm and Vancouver, at the apex; Claughton of 21 Company, for Hillock Farm, at the side of the Poelcapelle road, 400 yards south of Triangle Farm; myself for a row of fortified gun-pits lying almost opposite Hillock Farm, but well off the road, toward the middle of the triangle. Chaddock, with the ninth tank, was to follow me and make himself useful where possible. We were to cross the Steenbeek, not by the ruined bridge at St Julien, but at a point 100 yards to the left, where the engineers that night were going to lay fascines in the bed of the stream. As this necessitated our leaving the road for a short distance, rejoining it in the village itself, Guy and Kessel were detailed to tape the crossing after dark. Our battle headquarters would be established before zero at Cheddar Villa, a large concrete mebus by the roadside on the crest of the ridge, from where a good view was obtained over the whole area of the attack.

It was unfortunate that there were only two male tanks in the detachment—Willard's and Baker's. Six-pounder guns are of great service against these field forts, especially if the tank can get round to the rear of the latter, where the concrete is always weaker and where the entrance is situated. This weakness is intentional, as it facilitates a lost post's recapture with the aid of field-guns, whose shells penetrate the thin rear wall. As the Cockcroft was believed to be the most formidable of the St Julien forts, Willard with his 6-pounder was detailed to assist Coutts's female machine, but in the event Willard did not get into action. His tank was not running well, and from the first it was thought likely that Coutts might have to tackle the Cockcroft single-handed. Chaddock therefore, if required, and if he could pass the other tanks in front of him on the road, was to push on to Coutts's help. The Maison du Hibou, almost as powerful as the Cockcroft, was allotted for the same tactical reasons to Baker's remaining male tank, assisted by Kane.

Coutts returned from his interview with the 33rd Brigade while we were having lunch at Gordon Terrace. He was not in the best of spirits, as he had been impressed unfavourably by what he had seen of the infantry who were to work with him. As it fell out, his misgivings were justified. About this time Brown, the assistant Reconnaissance Officer of 21 Company, arrived with some aeroplane photographs and additional maps; and a little later Colonel Hankey and the Adjutant appeared with the battalion R.O., Hatton Hall.

We spent the afternoon lounging about near the dug-out, a dreary interval of waiting without any genuine rest. A slight shower fell, but toward evening the weather cleared again and gave promise of a fine night. At eight o'clock the

THE COCKCROFT

four of us started to walk back to our tanks by way of Buffs Road. Evening was always the most melancholy time in

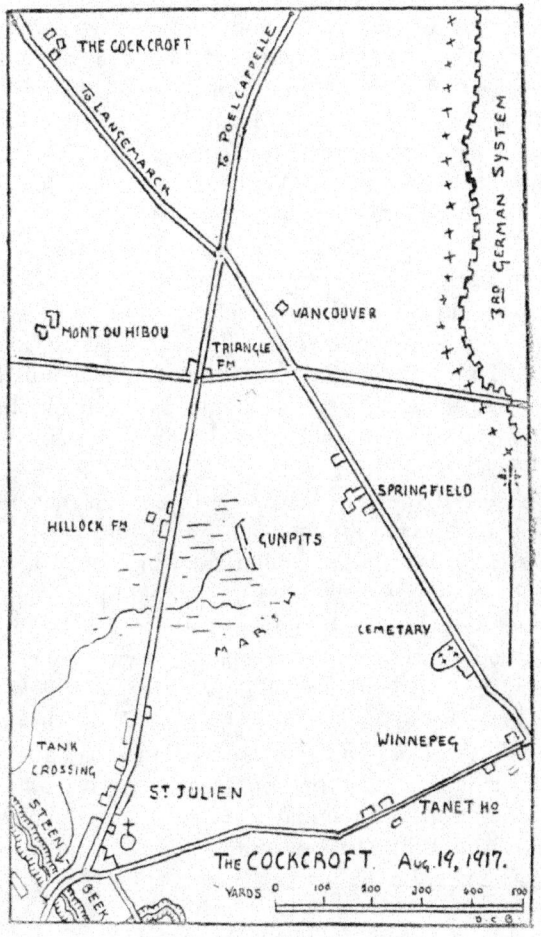

The Cockcroft, Aug. 19, 1917.

the Salient: the colours and mists of sunset serve only to emphasise the utter ruin of the country. At that hour no one was moving, for industry above ground began only

O

with the dark. The road wound on deserted in front of us, and on either side were only mud, sandbags, dead animals, and skeleton trees. Even the guns were silent. Impressed as we were with the unpleasant possibilities of the morning's battle, we compared reflections of a generally pessimistic tone as we tramped through the twilight, while the wilderness about us awoke to its nocturnal life; and looking back upon it, that walk appears as one of the least exhilarating I can recall. We had some excuse for dubiety, especially Coutts, who had the most difficult task of all and who mistrusted the people who were to support him. The whole operation before us confessedly was another gamble, of a novel and more than ordinarily hazardous nature so far as tanks were concerned. It had been an axiom in the corps, until the latter was plunged into liquid mud at Ypres, that in action tanks should avoid roads like the plague, for obvious reasons. In the present case, the field forts themselves did not worry us an atom; but if everything went wrong—if the smoke barrage failed or if the enemy by any means suspected in time what was happening—then our tanks, strung out along a highroad which they dared not leave, on which it was doubtful if two could pass each other, and which the German batteries on the next rise knew to a yard, stood every chance of being blown to pieces in a few minutes. Although as it happened our attack proved a complete surprise, and was successful in all essential details, those of us who remained on the road to the end escaped damage or destruction very narrowly; and subsequent operations on similar lines were mostly disastrous failures. And during that evening walk we could not foresee events—we could only imagine them.

II.

It was quite dark when we arrived back at Bellevue. Already some of the batteries in our neighbourhood had begun their night firing, and all round the Salient the cold white flares and Very lights were rising and glowing and fading once more. The tank crews had passed a peaceful day, sleeping during the morning and completing their battle preparations in the afternoon. They had been visited by the Chaplain, who brought them letters, newspapers, and cigarettes. He also held a Communion service before he left, a proceeding which provoked the Major to a characteristic utterance. " That's the worst of these *specialists*," he remarked a day or two later, "they're always butting in where they've no business to be!"[1] The Chaplain, in fact, had the temerity to wish to be of some real use on these occasions. He had accompanied the tanks of 20 Company on their dismal fiasco a few days before, and had done admirable work preparing food and hot drinks under shell-fire for crews whose machines were ditched, winding up by assisting to bring home a tank whose officer had been gassed. He was given the Military Cross for his work that day.

I found there was little, or nothing, for me to do before the time came for us to start. Meyrick and Corporal Mitchell had thought of everything, and G 47 was as ready to go into action as she ever was likely to be. The pigeons, even, had arrived, and our pair was stowed away in their basket beneath my seat in close proximity to the left-hand track-oiler, a conjunction which they seemed to find beneficial. I explained to my crew exactly what was required of us, but tactically our part in the affair was so simple that very little discussion was necessary. It merely resolved itself into a question of going up a road and, with a percentage of luck, coming down it again. In these final conferences one does not enlarge upon unpleasant contingencies. We examined the map and photographs inside the tank by the light of an electric torch, and then after the inevitable ritual of bully, cocoa, and rum, disposed ourselves for sleep, if such was to be had. We had still two hours and a half before we need be disturbed.

[1] See William III. and Bishop Walker at the Boyne.

The tanks were to be formed up in the road, in their fighting order, by 1 A.M. Guy and Kessel having gone on to tape the crossing over the Steenbeek, Wright was in charge of this stage of the proceedings. I must have fallen asleep, notwithstanding the noisy batteries and my vibrating steel pillow, because I remember him waking me prematurely to ask me some question which, at the time, I considered superfluous. I did not get to sleep again. At 12.30 I roused the crew, and we started the engine. Soon after this, Coutts and Willard, the leading pair, were moving on to the road, and before one o'clock all the nine tanks were lined up, their engines ticking over almost silently, ready to start.

We were away on the stroke of one, with three hours and three-quarters before us in which to get to St Julien, a distance by the road of only 2500 yards, or less than a mile and a half. The whole trek, however, was to be taken very slowly, and the latter part, from Cheddar Villa onward, must be covered at a mere crawl, for then we should be descending the reverse slope of the ridge without any covering noise except the normal night firing from our field batteries. It may be as well to correct here any misapprehension that shall have arisen from all this talk about ridges and valleys. These terms have only a relative significance, and the reader who is so fortunate as to know nothing of the Salient must not picture us climbing and descending a range of hills like the Pennines, or even like the Chilterns. It is necessary, however humiliating, to confess that the famous Pilkem Ridge, at the highest point attained by the St Julien road, rises no more than 81 feet above sea-level. The valley of the Steenbeek is only some 40 feet lower. In the country of the blind, however, the one-eyed man is king; and a geographical excrescence negligible anywhere else becomes a prominent feature in Flanders. The Steenbeek valley is a genuine depression, led down to by a level slope over a mile in length, and it carries sound as well as any similar if more pronounced depression elsewhere.

Once we began to descend, moreover, we were without any direct cover from view, for the night, although dark, was starlit and free from mist, and a few sparks from the exhaust of a tank would have been clearly visible from the German posts on the rising ground beyond the stream. Hence the various precautions entailed in our approach over this portion of the route. Not only must we crawl, but for tank commanders who, like myself, were walking outside, cigarettes even (one's chief comfort during an approach-march) very properly were forbidden.

Before we had been long on the road an irritating delay ensued, due to trouble in Willard's tank. The gases from his exhaust were escaping through the breathers in the engine-casing, and threatening to asphyxiate the crew. This fault having been remedied for the time being, we proceeded for some way without further incident, and presently topped the crest and began our cautious descent. The fall of the ground was so gentle that one might hardly have observed it but for other material evidence, unmistakable even in the darkness, that we were on a forward and not on a reverse slope. Up the western face of the ridge the road was clear of all obstructions. Such objects as dead mules and shattered limbers were pushed to one side. But once over the crest one began to encounter dead animals lying in the roadway, and also other shapeless forms that were not those of animals—in the common usage of the term. No one moved about on the road on this side during daylight, or lingered at night to clear anything away but the wounded; and as in the darkness some of these remains were indistinguishable until too late from the black mud on which they lay, while others, when seen in time, could not be avoided, one could only hope that no single spark of life still flickered anywhere among them. For after nine tanks had passed over them . . .

The sky being cloudless, the night, dark as it was, had not the same impenetrable quality as that of the 31st July, when I had last taken a tank down toward the German lines. I could imagine now at times that I could see a little mist over the Steenbeek below us, and even the vague outline of the farther ridge; and presently, when far away in the German rear a fire broke out, a short strip of skyline in the direction of Langemarck was clearly visible against the glow. In reality, however, one saw virtually nothing but the stumps of trees on either side, the faint shine of water in ruts and pools on the roadway, and the darker shadow of the tank in front. After a while came another halt, due to further trouble in Willard's machine. In our exposed position, any experiments with the exhaust were impossible, and he had to proceed eventually as best he could, with everything flung open to admit fresh air. The next event I remember was the appearance on the right of the road of a clump of ruined buildings—presumably Vanheule Farm. Away to the left the trees in front of Juliet Farm were just visible. Vanheule was only some 600 yards from the crest, but this distance seemed to have taken us hours. The time, in fact, was 2.30. And at this point the first really unpleasant interruption of our march occurred, with the whine and crash of a shell which burst somewhere behind the farm. Several more followed in our neighbourhood, and somehow it was additionally disturbing to perceive the flashes of the guns that were firing, apparently not so very far away. If we could see these flashes, one could not help the illogical suspicion that the gunners could see us. In any case, I decided I should be more happy inside the tank, as shell fragments have a way of travelling unexpected distances. I scrambled in accordingly, hoping devoutly that this sudden activity was a mere caprice, having no connection with our presence on the road. Once inside I could hear nothing, but I believe this shelling was a spasmodic burst directed vaguely at some suspected target near Vanheule Farm. We were not troubled again during the rest of our journey.

Owing to our deliberate pace and the several delays in the front of the column, most of the tanks had little time

to spare, after all. Coutts, unhampered, pushed on well
ahead, and was in St Julien a quarter of an hour before
zero, at which time the rest of us were crossing, or waiting
to cross, the Steenbeek. This stream, when I arrived at
it, presented in the growing light (for dawn was just about
to break) so forbidding a spectacle that I got hurriedly out
of the tank to lead the way across myself. At one time an
insignificant trickle of water a couple of yards wide at the
most, but enclosed between banks 6 to 8 feet high, the
pounding of our own barrage, followed during the past
three weeks by that of the Germans, had multiplied its
difficulties tenfold. There was little water to be seen now,
only a sort of boggy surface, several yards across, beneath
which the fascines laid that night by the engineers had
already disappeared completely under the weight of the
leading tanks. Some of these tanks were now climbing
a perfect precipice of mud on the opposite side, the black
nose of one pointing almost vertically upward against the
rapidly brightening sky in the east. Two, however, out of
the seven in front of me, had not got so far. Close to my
left was Willard's unfortunate machine, apparently ditched.
Behind this was a second tank, which I discovered afterwards to be Kane's. He had missed the tape, or attempted
to find a crossing for himself, and was ditched hopelessly
in consequence. I had little time for investigation, however,
for I was pounced on immediately by Guy, who was waiting
there to see all the tanks across—a most unattractive duty,
as the German barrage always fell on the stream. He
abused me roundly for being outside, pointed out the way,
and then pushed me in again. The fascines, it appeared,
were there, although invisible, and we crossed the stream
and mounted the farther bank without difficulty. A final
climb over the debris of a house, and we were in the main
street of St Julien on the stroke of zero. I did not even
pause there. As we swung left-handed on the brick-littered
pavé and saw the tail of Claughton's tank, with its large-
painted number, G 44, moving forward a few yards in

front, the yellow sky beyond was dotted suddenly with shrapnel bursts, a dense cloud of white smoke billowed upward from the far end of the village, and almost simultaneously there soared above this the red and green rockets from the startled German forts.

III.

I find that my memory plays me curious tricks on, or after, occasions of this kind. I gained a distinct impression, for example, that I moved down a street whose houses, although battered, were for the most part standing to a considerable height. It appears, however, that there was nothing standing in St Julien at all. The place was merely a series of rubbish-heaps. On the other hand, I remember with unnecessary accuracy certain objects lying amid the reddish brick-rubble and dust which covered the muddy road—a dead German soldier on his face, two of our own infantrymen, also dead (and not recently, to judge by appearances), a neat roll of wire-netting, half an iron bedstead, a decapitated mule, and, several yards distant, the mule's head. I do not know why I should have noted these particular items among the assorted domestic, military, and human debris which littered the street. St Julien had been systematically destroyed only within the last few weeks. Before that, being hidden from direct observation (unlike St Jean, its equivalent on our side), probably it was in fair preservation and in use for billeting troops on their way into or out of the line. I have an idea that there were a number of fragmentary articles of furniture lying about, perhaps dragged from the cellars to make hasty obstacles during the recent fighting in the place. It is curious how often such trumpery things survive the effects of a bombardment. You will see a house dissolved into its elements, and, amid the wreckage, some old bird-cage or an almost perfect chair.

The dawn seemed to have broken into full day with startling rapidity. The morning was bright and cloudless, and one other feature I somehow found time to notice and even to enjoy—the extreme brilliance of the yellow-green sky, streaked with green and crimson rockets, above the cloud of the smoke barrage in front. The smoke, however, was rising fast and drifting back down the street. A smoke-shell, falling short, burst in front of the tank, blinding us so completely that we nearly ran into Claughton's machine; and from that moment until I was in St Julien again on my way home I was never able to see more than a few hundred yards in any direction. There was no wind, and the smoke lay heavily in the best way possible for our purpose.

Through the village the going for tanks was good, as the greasy road was coated with brick-rubble and there were no pitfalls on either side. But once beyond the last ruins our troubles began. The Poelcapelle road is, or was, a characteristic, straight, continental highway, rising very gently uphill from St Julien, lined by fine trees, provided with a deep ditch on both sides, and paved in the middle. It had been shelled now very heavily for over a month by one army or the other, or both at once; and its condition was this. The central strip of *pavé* had withstood the shell-fire moderately well, but was badly broken in places by jagged holes. It was covered by a thick greasy scum, and as it was cambered, careful driving was needed if one wished to avoid slipping off. And to avoid this was essential, for the macadamised portions on either side had, for all practical purposes, vanished. They were blown away and merged in the ditches, forming deep gulfs a yard or two wide, out of which the stouter *pavé* stood up like a causeway. Of the double line of trees, half were down, and a large proportion of these victims lay across the road at all angles. Beyond the trees the country was quite impassable for tanks, and on the east side of the road, where my objective lay, was simply a swamp. A small tributary of the Steenbeek rose near my gun-pits, and since its bed had been destroyed by the shelling, its waters had welled up and spread over a wide area of ground from St Julien to Triangle Farm. This inundation was shown clearly on aeroplane photographs, and it put out of the question any attempt on my part, had I wished to make one, to leave the road. My only course of action was to remain on the *pavé* and engage the strong-point across the intervening 150 yards of quagmire.

We had to get there first, however, and this was a delicate matter. As we emerged from the village I saw Claughton's tank, 50 yards ahead, surmounting the first fallen tree. A big tree is an unpleasant impediment to a tank, as it is impossible to balance on the rounded trunk, and one comes down inevitably on the other side with a jarring crash. On the Poelcapelle road these trees became a dangerous obstacle, because in crashing down over them, with the nose of the tank falling from a great height and the whole thing entirely out of the driver's control, the machine was very likely to slip straight off the greasy *pavé*, which was none too wide, into one of the gulfs on either side. (This happened eventually, I believe, to Morgan's tank when he was trying to draw closer to Triangle Farm.) There also was a danger of breaking a track-plate on the stones. The angle at which the trees could best be taken, lying as they did in all directions, required to be judged, and when this was done they might move suddenly under the tracks and precipitate a crash at the wrong moment. Negligible, in short, as they would have been on a good road, in the circumstances they caused us all a great deal of anxiety. Everything depended on the drivers; and the fact that all seven tanks reached at least the close vicinity of their objectives was a distinct feather in the cap of every one of these admirable men. Waller drove G 47 over a succession of trees without a semblance of trouble. Everything loose inside, of course, including the crew, fell helplessly about each time we crashed; but this was a part of the ordinary day's work. The pigeons, as I have remarked before, bore this repeated experience, which must have seemed to them like a series of earthquakes, with as much equanimity as anybody, although their basket usually was dislodged and upset.

All this time I was peering out for some sign of my gun-pits. The smoke was still very dense, and visibility a matter of a couple of hundred yards. G 44 sometimes faded to a mere blur in front. The first recognisable feature I saw was a wide sheet of water to the right of the road, which I took correctly to mark the actual course of the flooded stream. Immediately after, my right-hand pair of gunners, Sergeant Meyrick and Carter, opened fire. It appeared that they had sighted not only the gun-pits but also some figures moving out from them carrying a machine-gun. I could still see nothing from the flap in front, but on craning over Waller's head and opening a revolver loophole on that side of the cab, I discovered at once a row of high mounds, looking enormous through the smoke, about 150 yards from the road. It had been obvious from an inspection of aeroplane photographs that these pits had been constructed for heavy guns, but I had not expected to find them so conspicuous. Further investigation was curtailed rather summarily by a rapid " tat-tat-tat-tat " upon the side of the cab, indicating two things: (*a*) that some one in or near the gun-pits was firing at us with a machine-gun; and (*b*) that if he could see, and was aiming at, my revolver loophole, he was making remarkably good shooting, and must be blessed with far better eyesight than I could claim. It is true that by this time the German machine-gunner knew all about tanks, while we must have presented a fairly clear-cut target. I closed the loophole instantly, and telling Waller to hold G 47 in her present position, broadside on to the strong-point, proceeded to fish about in the locker for our periscopes. It is impossible to see anything on a flank through the front flaps, nor, if one can use them, is it advisable to do so under machine-gun fire. We carried six periscopes, drawn in a hurry from store before we left camp. It was only when I had pushed all six through the hole in the roof, and had failed utterly to see anything through any one of them, that I remembered that we had lashed our camouflage net on top of the cab. Normally the net is carried on the spud-box in the rear, but it is then very apt to be shaken on to the red-hot exhaust-pipe, when it catches fire. I had a horror of fires on a tank, and was determined on this occasion to put the net in some safer place, forgetting that I might want to use the periscopes.

During this time Meyrick and Carter had continued to fire busily, and there was a periodic clatter of emptied Lewis drums on the floor. The tattoo on the cab having ceased, I resorted again to the revolver port. There was not a sign of life about the gun-pits, but so long as the smoke continued to hang over the ground they might have concealed a battalion of infantry for all we could see. My gunners, in addition to claiming the destruction of the party seen to run out in the beginning, asserted that their fire was hotly returned; and the lead splashes on G 47's exposed flank proved that there was some truth in this contention; but my belief is that the garrison of the pits abandoned them after the first few minutes—a fact which, if true, in no sense detracts from the spirit and general excellence of our performance. And as we had no means of telling what had happened, we could only continue firing until the situation (and the light) became clearer. After a while I moved the tank a short distance up the road, with the slight hope that I might find a patch of ground firm enough to justify our attempting to get to closer quarters; but between us and the enigmatic gun-pits the swamp lay everywhere.

In all, this curious duel lasted for about a quarter of an hour. While it proceeded I could see Claughton's tank, a little way ahead, motionless alongside the ruins of Hillock Farm, which abutted on to the road. His guns appeared to be firing point-blank through what was left of the windows.

Beyond him was nothing but smoke, in which the leading tanks were swallowed up. While I watched G 44, and while my own two guns were still in theory dealing out death and destruction to the gun-pits, I saw Claughton's shovel, that grotesque symbol, waved triumphantly out of his manhole. Hillock Farm, presumably, had fallen. Out of my left-hand loophole an extended line of infantry was visible crawling forward with extreme care through the mud beside the road—evidently Claughton's supporting platoon moving up to take over the farm. And very shortly after this, welcome portents became manifest about my gun-pits. A great plume of smoke and mud shot suddenly upward beside them, and then a second plume, and a third. Others followed, appearing in some cases to rise out of the mounds themselves. The Germans were shelling their lost property (and with remarkable accuracy, as it must still have been invisible to the gunners), a fact which could be taken as evidence that it definitely was lost, for if any of the garrison remained there, they would not give much trouble while they were being bombarded by their friends. I indicated the "cease fire" by the usual method of thumping my nearest gunner on the back, and then clamoured loudly for the shovel. The Germans were only shelling the pits at the moment, but there was no knowing in what direction they might not extend their activities; and as the smoke cloud was thinning palpably, I did not wish to remain stationary on the road longer than was necessary. I had a rooted dislike to stationary tanks in action.

We waved our shovel and peered out of every opening for signs of our following infantry. Failing to detect them, I told Waller to swing the tank round, in order that I could get a better view backward, and also be in a position to start for home. Although I had definite orders to return the moment my objective was secured, I had thought of pushing on to help Coutts in his single-handed attempt on the Cockcroft, but a glance at the *pavé* negatived this idea. It was too narrow to permit of my passing Claughton's tank, now also in the act of swinging round. For the same reason, Chaddock, who had a roving commission, and who wished to go on to Coutts's help, could not pass G 47. There was nothing for it, therefore, but to return as soon as the infantry were in the gun-pits. The business of swinging on the narrow greasy camber of the *pavé* was not easy, but Waller accomplished it with his usual skill, and I found myself presently facing Chaddock's tank and waving to him out of my flap. He was about twenty yards behind me, and his guns also had been firing at the gun-pits. A line of infantry was now visible close at hand, the men crouching in a sort of drain which ran outward from the road. I beckoned to the nearest man, who was kneeling behind a fragment of wall by the roadside, and on his running cautiously to the front of the tank I learnt that these people were the second wave of my supports. The leading platoon had moved on to the gun-pits. Our work, therefore, was done. Chaddock, in his turn, was edging carefully round on the *pavé* to start for home; Claughton was close astern of me; and in a few minutes the three tanks were making for St Julien again at their best speed. None of us knew what had happened to the other four in front.

The time was 5.45, the sun was up, the smoke and dust about the village had vanished away, and as we crashed once more over the fallen trees, I could see to the left, between St Julien and Winnipeg, two of 19 Company's disabled tanks lying where they had been hit on the 31st of July. At this time, although I did not know it, the German batteries had at last turned their guns upon the road. Possibly we were now in sight as we jolted down it. Three or four shells burst clean on the *pavé*, between G 44 and my own tank, so that Claughton thought we had been hit, but we heard nothing of this until after. It appears to have been a narrow escape for both of us. In the street of St Julien we were able to push on at top speed, until I remembered that I had not despatched the necessary pigeon-message. We slowed up while I wrote it, thus letting in Claughton, who passed us at a great pace. I have in front of me now my copy of Army Book 418 A, containing the carbon duplicate of that historic document. It is all but illegible. Having released the bird, we put on speed again and made for the Steenbeek crossing.

That unpleasant spot appeared less formidable in daylight, but it was to provide us with a final nerve-wracking incident before we finished with it. As we mounted the ruined house again and looked down upon the muddy gulf below, it was congested with tanks. Willard, with his asphyxiating box of tricks, was still in much the same position as when I had passed him before zero — hours ago, as it seemed now. He had contrived, however, to unditch himself partially, and crawl a few yards forward, so that he almost blocked the narrow crossing. Close beside him was G 44, clawing its way precariously round. Behind was Kane's tank, still in its old place, while Chaddock, who had got across in safety, was close to Kane. I had begun to descend toward this congregation before I realised that it was going to be very difficult to get past Willard. The passage where lay the buried fascines was only just broad enough to take a tank, and on either side was the bog which represented the true bed of the Steenbeek. We slid down the bank rather more rapidly than I intended, and brought up nose to nose against Willard's tank. We tried to swing, and failed. We tried to reverse, and failed again. It was a repetition of our experience at Kitchener's Wood. We were sunk too deep in mud to permit of any movement but a forward one, which was rendered impossible by the tank in front. External measures were necessary, and I led the way outside. It was then that I discovered that the village behind us, and also the Steenbeek itself, were being shelled heavily. We had stopped, in fact, on the line of the German counter-barrage, which fell automatically along the stream,

particular attention being paid to the neighbourhood of St
Julien. This was an unfortunate circumstance, and I do
not think any of us can ever have worked harder, or more
apprehensively, than we did in the course of the next twenty
minutes. Chaddock and Claughton by this time had got
clear of the imbroglio, although the former, deciding for
some reason not to return to the road, got himself ditched
hopelessly farther on. Willard and some of his crew appeared from his tank and asked for assistance in starting
up the engine. They all seemed rather dazed and helpless,
from the poisonous exhaust fumes, as I supposed; and finding them still standing about in the open after I had sent
two of my men to help, I pointed out to Willard that they
would be very much safer inside, fumes or no fumes.
Heavy shells were exploding about us much closer and
more frequently than was pleasant, and fragments flew
whining overhead continually. Twice we were deluged
with brick rubble from the remains of a house on the
bank above. Presently Deakin was hit in the back by
a flying piece of brick, which knocked him down; but
as it struck a buckle of his equipment, it did him no
harm. All this time we were labouring feverishly, digging
away the mud piled against one side of the tank, as it prevented her swinging, collecting bits of timber, boughs of
trees, bricks, and other rubbish, to form a holding-surface
beneath her, clamping on the unditching-beam, and remov-
ing the camouflage net from the cab, where it interfered
with the beam's action. These varied pursuits took up a
considerable amount of time, as any one who has engaged
in them will believe, and we were interrupted periodically
and impelled to shelter against the tank by the sudden
rush and explosion of some more imminent shell. Altogether, this job must have taken us nearly half an hour,
for a premature attempt to swing G 47 failed, and we had
to back her again and continue our work. At length we
had prepared what seemed an adequate base for her
manœuvre, and I pushed most of the crew inside again

and beckoned to Waller to come on. As the heavy unditching-beam fell over the nose and jammed beneath the
tracks against our rubbish-heap, and the tank climbed over
it until she was almost on the point of balance, I signalled
to him to swing. She came round, to my intense relief,
dragging the beam with her, and cleared the nose of
Willard's machine. All was now plain sailing. Three of
us unclamped the beam as it came up, like Caliban, filthy
and dripping, over the tracks behind, and made it fast; and
the tank climbed easily over the mud slope toward the road.
I could do nothing to help Willard or Kane. The former,
indeed, as his engine was running again, could effect his
own salvation now that I was out of the way. I scrambled
up the slippery slope after G 47, and hoisted myself on
board as she increased speed on the level ground between
the Steenbeek and the road.

IV.

The remainder of our return journey went without a
hitch. No shells were falling west of St Julien, and we
rolled along the deserted road at a good pace and at peace
with all men. We had that sense of exhilaration (rare in
the Tank Corps at Ypres) that follows after the successful
achievement of a task, however small. As we neared the
top of the ridge, Meyrick and I got outside again and
looked back over the valley, but we could see nothing of
interest. Our own artillery was still busy, as was the
enemy's, and a haze of smoke hid all the farther end of
the triangle and the ground beyond. There was no sign
of any of the other tanks. As we passed Cheddar Villa,
Kessel ran out to congratulate us and hear our news. He
was without any detailed information himself, beyond the
fact, conveyed by telephone, that the whole operation had
been a remarkable success. He and the other watchers at
Cheddar Villa had seen through their glasses the German

troops abandoning their third-line trenches (which nobody had approached), and streaming away over the farther crest. A little later we passed Bellevue, and found it deserted, the two reserve tanks having been ordered to return. From the battery positions in this region, gunner officers came out to inquire anxiously about the efficacy of their smoke-barrage. Being able to assure them, from ocular evidence, that it had been little short of blinding, I became extremely popular, and was dragged off to the nearest dug-out for a very welcome whisky-and-soda.

Farther down, in Buffs Road, we met with one or two delays. Traffic was on the move here, and my radiator started to boil again. Somewhere about this time we came across Chaddock, carrying a Lewis gun and helping one of his crew, who had been hit by a shrapnel bullet in the leg. His tank, it appeared, was ditched near Juliet Farm. I took the wounded man and the gun on board, and deposited the former at a dressing station lower down the road. Owing to these and other brief stoppages, it must have been nearly 10.30 when we drew near to the canal. I halted the tank by Marengo Causeway while I went to report at Gordon Terrace. At our headquarters I found the Colonel and Adjutant with the Major, all in a very Christian frame of mind and full of felicitations, messages having arrived from both infantry and tanks reporting the capture of all objectives at a ridiculously low cost. The infantry casualties, up to the date of the last message, totalled a dozen wounded. I was beginning to realise by now that between us we had accomplished something rather exceptional that morning. It transpired, however, that our four leading tanks were ditched, and no further news had come through as to the fortunes or whereabouts of their people.

I was told to proceed with G 47 to Murat Farm, where a fresh crew would take over the tank. I rejoined the latter, and we began the last stage of our journey. All my men were thoroughly exhausted, and Waller in particular, as he had been driving for seven or eight hours. But in view of my experiences during the latter part of our homeward trek from St Julien, where my second and third drivers had been in charge alternately, I felt obliged to ask him to complete the run. (It was a misfortune that at Ypres there were no facilities for driving practice for second and third drivers. Tanks hardly moved except when going into action. The first drivers usually were highly skilled men, but between them and the others there often was a great gulf fixed, which we had no opportunity of reducing by a little regular training.) I took the brakes, and with poor Waller almost falling asleep in his seat, we crossed the causeway and parked up eventually under a hedge at Murat Farm just after midday. One minor *contretemps* rounded off the performance. We proceeded as a matter of routine to camouflage the tank. The little canvas tags sewn profusely over a camouflage net are dyed in some highly inflammable green paint, the cause of innumerable fires. Our engine having been running continually for twelve hours, the whole machine was like an oven, and the exhaust-pipe on the roof all but red-hot; and the net instantly caught alight. We had to use every pyrene extinguisher we carried to keep the flames under before we had pushed the last smouldering fragments over the side. I was standing on the roof stamping out a few stray embers and blaspheming about war in general to Allerton, of 20 Company, who had just appeared, when my nerves received a final shock. The 9.2 naval gun on the other side of the hedge, whose existence I had forgotten, fired with a frightful detonation and nearly threw me off the tank.

Our tribulations were now, however, at an end. It is true that I missed the lorry which took my crew back to Lovie; but after waiting for some time at Essex Corner, on the main road beside the canal, for any vehicle which would take me on my way, I was picked up by Major Fernie in his car and arrived at the camp, fast asleep, at tea-time.

V.

Leaving for the next chapter a consideration of the causes which gave to the Cockcroft operation a significance out of all proportion to its scope, I will describe briefly the general result and the fortunes of the other tanks. The accounts hitherto published are inaccurate.

Coutts, who gave the "star turn" of the performance, was reduced as we have seen to tackling the Cockcroft itself single-handed with a female tank. This fort was an extremely powerful and massive affair of concrete, erected in the ruins of some farm buildings. It held a garrison of something like 100 men, with a number of machine-guns, and was further protected by wire and outlying posts. The concrete of the walls and roof would keep out any projectile below a 9.2 howitzer shell, being in places eight feet thick. A formidable stronghold of this nature bears as little resemblance to the ordinary light "pill-box," containing half a dozen men, as does a first-class fortress to a semi-permanent redoubt, and if held by a determined garrison in combination with similar forts, could check a large force indefinitely, as indeed the Cockcroft and its fellows had conclusively demonstrated. A 6-pounder tank, provided it could place itself against the weak rear face of such a fort, might compel its surrender; but a female tank, moral effect apart, was in fact as helpless against it as a platoon of infantry, although less vulnerable itself. Nevertheless, when Coutts, by leaving the road, managed to get within 50 yards of the Cockcroft before becoming ditched, the large garrison abandoned it after a brief defence. As an instance of a tank's moral effect this was the more remarkable in that the infantry of the 33rd Brigade, confirming all the tank commander's previous misgivings, failed signally in their duty of supporting him. No attention was paid to his signals announcing the evacuation of the fort. His sergeant was sent with a message to the same effect, but still the infantry

did not come on. Eventually Coutts himself went back
under machine-gun fire and through the German barrage,
found the officer commanding the supporting battalion, and
urged him to send his men forward: after which a move
was at length made and the Cockcroft occupied, with no
more than two or three light casualties. Coutts and his
crew, after failing to extricate the tank, formed Lewis-gun
posts at the request of the infantry, and only returned in the
late afternoon.

The Maison du Hibou was scarcely less formidable than
the Cockcroft, and consisted of two storeys of solid concrete,
garrisoned by about sixty men. It was attacked by Charles
Baker with the only remaining 6-pounder tank. The fort
stood some way off the road, in the middle of a perfect
morass; but Baker, finding he could effect little from the
pavé, plunged into the mud and was able to crawl round
to the rear before, like Coutts, he also became bogged.
One 6-pounder, however, now bore on the entrance of the
Maison du Hibou at short range. Thirty or forty rounds
were fired into the door. Most of the garrison came running out, and thirty were shot down or captured by the
infantry of the 48th Division, who followed up in excellent
style. The tank being immovable, Baker formed Lewis-gun posts with the infantry until the afternoon. One of
his men was killed.

Morgan and Close, engaging Triangle Farm and Vancouver at the cross-roads in the apex, met with a good
deal of trouble. Morgan's tank proved to have defective
plating, and the German armour-piercing bullets filled the
interior with flying splinters. With his help, however, the
infantry got into Triangle Farm, which was not so powerfully constructed as some of the other forts, and shot or
bayoneted the garrison, who had been resisting stoutly.
Morgan then attempted to go to Baker's assistance, but
became ditched through slipping off the greasy road. He
was in a position to fire into the back of the Maison du
Hibou, and his Lewis guns accounted for a number of the

escaping garrison of that place. Having unditched his tank after a while, he returned to St Julien by midday.

Close had a variety of adventures, including that of being taken prisoner for a time. His tank also was permanently ditched somewhere near Vancouver, but its influence seems to have been responsible for the abandonment of the strong-point. Close himself did not appear again until the next day.

Claughton, whose tank I had watched, had no trouble with Hillock Farm, whose garrison fled the moment he ranged up alongside and opened fire. My own experiences with the gun-pits I have already described at unpardonable length. I may add that my two right-hand guns fired 1200 rounds between them, but I never heard evidence as to what damage, if any, they effected.

All the four leading tanks came under excessively heavy machine-gun fire from posts outside the strong-points. Morgan's machine, which was the only one we had the opportunity of examining, had large areas of its armour plastered a whitish-grey with lead splashes, and the armour-piercing bullets were driven almost through the defective plates. He and his crew suffered a number of tiny wounds in their faces and hands from steel splinters. These counted as casualties, and made up more than half of our very trifling list, which totalled two men killed and one officer and ten men wounded. The infantry casualties, however, were even more remarkable for their insignificance. The two Warwick battalions (of the 48th Division) which were working with every tank except Coutts's, followed up in an admirable manner throughout; yet the whole operation, in which the equivalent of a brigade took part, which resulted in the capture within ninety minutes of six formidable strong-points and a gain of 600 yards of ground on a mile front, and in which the enemy must have lost several hundred men killed, wounded, and prisoners, together with some fifty machine-guns, was carried out at a cost to the infantry engaged of fifteen men wounded!

CHAPTER XII.

FROM THE COCKCROFT TO CAMBRAI.

I.

It is no exaggeration to say that even those of us who had played the most modest part on the 19th August awoke the following morning to find ourselves famous—at least in the not inconsiderable world controlled by the 5th Army. The astonishment and interest evoked by this single little action were a measure of the perplexities confronting the Higher Command in the Salient. In any series of operations the casualty list may become a governing feature, as it must always be an important one. There are limits to the price which may be paid for any gain, and there are limits to what any troops will stand. The most highly-trained infantry, save in exceptional circumstances, cannot be expected to maintain their offensive spirit after sustaining a succession of crippling losses for no very apparent result. In mid-August our casualties at Ypres had not approached the frightful total they were to reach before the end, nor perhaps were they as high proportionately as in October or November; but they were becoming very serious, if only because to the subordinate ranks, who were suffering them, they seemed to lead nowhere and promise no cessation. One murderous attack against wire and concrete, if it gained a little ground, meant only increased misery for those who were left, followed, the next day or the next week, by another murderous attack against more wire and more concrete.

One had only to look at the faces of infantry going into the line before an assault, or even for ordinary trench duties, to realise how the strain was telling. At this time our most precious assets, the journalists, after walking through a cavalry camp thirty miles behind the front or watching a brigade in rest going out with its bands for a route-march, were writing to their newspapers about the cheery faces of our fighting men, the grim delight they took in shells and slaughter, and the pusillanimity and general idiocy of the enemy. A phrase which appeared in some journal (it referred to Cambrai, but will serve in this digression) was bandied about our camp for a long time, as being characteristically imbecile. The writer, speaking of a unit which had received sudden orders to move, remarked that "the men hurried from the baths, fearing that they might miss the fight!" For weeks after, any one seen moving hurriedly was accused of fearing to miss the fight. This sort of rubbish may conceivably have served some useful purpose in England; but it made extraordinary reading in Flanders, where, after only a few weeks, there was growing upon every one the feeling that this offensive, with its peculiar horrors due to weather and terrain, was becoming another and more dreadful Somme, remorseless and everlasting. And if the Higher Command still cherished brighter hopes, they cannot have contemplated the future without anxiety. They must have realised that Von Armin, or whoever was responsible for the interminable series of pill-boxes and concreted farms, had devised a method of defence which in such a country, and in combination with the barriers that our own artillery was augmenting daily, deserved at least as much credit for our discomfiture as that convenient public scapegoat, the rain. Without any rain at all, there would still have remained the problem of how to surmount quagmires and reinforced concrete bristling with machine-guns. And then had come what seemed a sudden and quite startling gleam of light. Here was a group of these pestilent fortifications which had held the 18th Corps in check for

three weeks. Attempts to get near them, even, had resulted
in sanguinary repulses. A serious attack on them, it was
estimated (and it may be noted that such estimates usually
are conservative), would cost from 600 to 1000 casualties,
and would be a doubtful speculation at that. And this was
only the beginning — a little preliminary clearing away.
There was the untouched German third line beyond, and
behind that again more forts. . . . But now, in an hour and
a half, all these initial bogies had tumbled down like nine-
pins, at the ridiculous cost of fifteen wounded infantrymen
and a few Tank Corps personnel. To men habitually dealing
in returns and states and figures of every kind, arithmetic
makes the most potent appeal. The grander the scale, the
more they are swayed by it. It represents, at least to their
minds, a concrete fact from which there is no escape.
They cannot fail to understand it. It is inevitable in an
army that plain figures must often be the solvent of a
doubtful point. A thousand men are always a thousand
men. Here, then, was a simple comparison of numbers
which must have been very startling to some of the staffs
concerned. Here was a plain statement: in the one column
an estimate of 600 to 1000, in the other the actual expenditure—15. Generals and G.S.O.'s who knew nothing about
tanks, who never had attempted to comprehend their
tactics, but who had seen them lying bogged in scores
about the Salient, must have felt that a miracle had happened. It was unfortunate that some of them, still wider
from the mark, mistook it for a conjuring trick, which could
be repeated indefinitely.

   I have laboured this point because the Cockcroft action,
insignificant in itself and forgotten long ago, did actually at
the time arouse remarkable interest in the Army as a whole,
and because it affected permanently the future of the Tank
Corps. It was by far the most complete success achieved
by tanks up to that time. It proved conclusively their
potentialities as economisers of life—a point upon which
their advocates had been insisting from the beginning. It

was a striking example of their moral effect. And because it was all this, it helped undoubtedly (although to what exact degree I cannot say) to determine the whole future of the corps, then hanging in the balance. Dozens and scores of tanks were thrown away in the Salient after the Cockcroft with no adequate return for the sacrifice, but there was no more overt talk of abolition or even of reduction. It was not a mere coincidence that on 6th October an actual programme of expansion to 18 battalions, already rejected in June, was confidently put forward again. It was approved in a hurry immediately after Cambrai in November; and indirectly the Cockcroft led to Cambrai.

II.

While the first glad rapture lasted, G Battalion basked in a rare blaze of popularity. To any one of a cynical turn of mind—and I think that prolonged experience of the Army induces that spirit in most people of moderate acumen—the days immediately following the action must have provided much quiet amusement. The very morning after, while those of us who had been the innocent actors in the scene were making up for lost time in bed, the camp was thronged with exalted visitors. A deluge of congratulatory telegrams descended upon the Colonel. Most significant of all, perhaps, Mr Beach Thomas, of the 'Daily Mail,' felt impelled to leave the seclusion of the Ternoise Valley to gather copy among our tents at Lovie. The actors, however, all being in bed when he arrived, he was captured very fortunately by 19 Company, who immured him in their mess until he had to leave. Their only representative in the caste, through no fault of his own, had never got into action at all; but this fact was no bar to their imaginations, and they supplied the journalist with what must have been a very highly-coloured version of the facts. The result, to our great joy, appeared a few days later in the 'Times' and the 'Daily Mail,' in an account of a most extraordinary and Homeric conflict in which the inevitable "leviathans" figured prominently, but in which, oddly enough, those of us who had been there were unable to recognise a single detail.

The most gratifying tribute came in the form of a Special Order by the 18th Corps commander, General Maxse, addressed to G Battalion, in which he thanked all ranks for their efforts, and frankly attributed the success his corps had attained at such a trifling cost entirely to the tanks. I regret having lost the copy I made of this letter, which was quite exceptional in form and substance. Hardly had we digested these unusual compliments when it was intimated that the Army commander, General Gough, wished to see some of the officers and men who had been in action on the 19th. Five of us, therefore, paraded with our crews the following morning near the old tank park in Oosthoek Wood. A curious but characteristic incident marked this ceremony. Coutts, with his crew fallen in behind him, was on the right of our little line: I was next to him. As the General approached, his Staff quite obviously shepherded him past Coutts and diverted him on to me. With his first question I realised the reason for this manœuvre. He asked me if the infantry had supported me properly. I was able to testify, quite honestly, that they had; and Morgan, Close, and Baker, who were the other three present, could give equally satisfactory answers. Some rumour must have reached the Staff about the trouble at the Cockcroft, and Coutts, who might have made damaging revelations, was given no opportunity to speak. It was a little thing, but instructive.

As a final result of the action, so far as we were concerned, Coutts, Baker, and Morgan received an immediate award of the Military Cross. In the meantime an attempt had been made to repeat our success, on the principle of the conjuring trick. Of the strong-points in front of the 18th Corps there still remained intact those along the eastern side of the triangle, the Zonnebeke-Langemarck road. There can be little doubt that we could have accounted for these places on the 19th, especially if the two reserve tanks had been brought in. The Germans were then completely surprised, in ignorance of what actually was happening (on account of the very effective smoke barrage), and, for the time being, thoroughly demoralised. They were even running from their third-line trenches, as has been recorded. If the original plan of attack had been allowed to stand, there was nothing, barring accidents, to prevent Claughton, Chaddock, and me, with the reserve tanks, from pushing on from Hillock Farm and the gun-pits right round the triangle, and capturing also Springfield, Winnipeg, and the other forts near them—all of which lay on the road. The task, however, had been left unfinished; and on the 22nd a company of D Battalion, with the necessary infantry, went in to complete it. The attack was designed on the lines of our operation. At the same time tanks from the 2nd and 3rd Brigades advanced with the 2nd and 19th Corps on the right against similar forts and subsidiary works on their fronts. The result was not very encouraging. The Germans this time were wide awake, and the stratagems which had proved so successful in effecting a surprise on the 19th could hardly be expected to deceive again so soon after. In some cases also where tanks reached their objectives, the infantry was unable to follow. On the right, part of Glencorse Wood was carried with the help of four tanks. On the 19th Corps front, where even the roads had been almost wholly blown away, the tanks of the 3rd Brigade could do little and the infantry less. One very remarkable feat, however, was accomplished by a tank of F Battalion. This machine, on board of which was the section commander, Richardson, was detailed to attack a field-fort called Gallipoli, south-east of St Julien. The infantry were to follow behind in the now accepted fashion. They did not follow; and the tank became ditched in what virtually was No Man's Land, although the phrase had lost

some of its definite connotation in the fighting for these
isolated forts. The tank was so far ahead of our line, in
fact, that it was believed to be captured, and a steady fire
was opened and maintained on it from rifles and machine-
guns. The Germans, of course, were firing on it from the
other side. The tank commander was wounded almost at
once, and Richardson took command. This was on the morning of the 22nd. The situation continued the same through
out the day, the crew being unable to evacuate the tank owing
to the fire from our lines. At the same time they were able
with their own guns to break up several German counter-
attacks which were gathering behind Gallipoli. At night-
time the Germans closed on the tank, and eventually
brought a machine-gun to within a few yards, and even
climbed on the roof. Our own people, imagining the tank
to have been converted into a hostile strong-point, continued to fire briskly in its direction. It was still holding
out the next morning, however, and continued to defend itself
during the day—the 23rd. Signals to our own line were
attempted, but produced no result. A second night supervened, and again the Germans closed in with machine-guns
and grenades, but failed entirely to subdue the defence.
These attacks, in fact, caused them considerable losses.
But when day broke on the 24th, the situation inside the
tank was becoming serious. One man had been killed,
every other member of the crew except Richardson himself
was wounded, and food and ammunition were running short.
The condition in that restricted space, with one dead man
and several badly wounded lying among the others' feet in
blood and oil, must have been appalling. Yet for another
whole day the tank held out under the double fire. Any
attempt to signal to our people was made dangerous by
their misdirected zeal, and was never understood. This
could not continue. At any risk the infantry must be
made to realise the true state of affairs; and after dark a
man contrived to crawl back to our front line under a
constant fire from both sides. The situation was now

made clear to our troops, and their fire ceased. Richardson was able to evacuate all his wounded men without mishap. The tank had been held for seventy-two hours under these extraordinary circumstances, had killed or wounded a great number of the enemy, and had disorganised at the outset several budding counter-attacks — a feat without parallel, and one which well merited the special complimentary order issued from Tank Corps Headquarters. Richardson received the D.S.O., and the tank commander the M.C.

Returning to the operations on the 22nd, we find D Battalion's tanks moving up by our old route through St Julien. The road was no longer as quiet, however, as it had been four days earlier. On the night of the 20th, in particular, it was shelled heavily, and four of the tanks were hit and disabled during the approach-march. Four of ours from Ghent Cottages, being the nearest reserve, were sent up to replace the casualties and handed over to D Battalion crews. The action which followed was moderately successful, Winnipeg and Springfield being carried; but the losses in infantry and tank personnel were heavy, and a large proportion of the tanks were ditched and abandoned. In all the attacks on the 22nd, every tank which left the roads became instantly bellied, some sinking into four or six feet of water. Out of thirty-four machines employed on the three corps' fronts, eighteen were lost from this cause and six were hit by shell-fire.

It will be unnecessary to describe in any detail the further operations in the Salient in which tanks took part. They provide the same dreary experiences, were almost uniformly unsuccessful, and possess no novel tactical features for consideration. They should never have been attempted. By this time E Battalion had come out from England and joined the 1st Brigade, having its camp at Lovie and its tanks in Oosthoek Wood, and before long it also was flung into the hopeless struggle with the elements. After a series of minor affairs on 23rd, 26th, and 27th August, in which a few tanks of the 2nd Brigade were involved and inevitably

FROM THE COCKCROFT TO CAMBRAI

lost, without accomplishing anything at all, a pause lasting for nearly a month ensued in the general operations. We were still in front of the original German third line, and guns had somehow to be got forward and arrangements completed for another formal assault. The weather improved in September, but this made little difference to the state of the ground, which was broken up by shell-fire as fast as it attempted to dry. The attack took place on 20th September, extending from the extreme right of the Salient (where the 2nd Army had now taken over a part of the 5th Army front) to the north of Langemarck. Tanks were to operate as on 31st July, following up the infantry to deal with the fortified farms along the second and third objectives. This was a reversion to the old bad manner, and in the event was almost a complete failure, although the tanks endeavoured to keep to the roads. Four machines sent in by the 2nd Brigade went to swell the crowd of derelicts in the quagmire by the Menin road, known as the "tanks' cemetery." Of nineteen tanks from E Battalion, thirteen were ditched and four hit; while only three out of fifteen from D ever got near the fight at all. The Germans had grasped very quickly some of the lessons of this road fighting, and trees had been felled across the roads in such a position as to offer the greatest obstruction to tanks. On the night of the 22nd-23rd, D and E Battalions tried to get one tank apiece into action by dawn and failed. A further attempt on the 26th met with the same fate. In the meantime the infantry attack had succeeded to the extent that our line was advanced everywhere to an average depth of 1000 yards, and minor operations on the 18th Corps front during the last days of the month brought us to the outskirts of Poelcapelle. On October 4th this village was captured. By heroic exertions some tanks of D Battalion were at last able to render substantial help, forcing the surrender of Gloucester and Terrier Farms and entering Poelcapelle itself with the infantry. On the same day a section from A Battalion was in action farther south, and

Captain Robertson, who was in command, died and was awarded a posthumous V.C., after what has been well described as "one of the most patiently courageous actions of the war." His tanks had to cross a bridge over a stream called the Reutelbeek, and drive the enemy from positions on the farther side. For three days and nights Robertson and his servant (who won the D.C.M.) went to and fro over the ground, reconnoitring and taping routes, always under heavy fire. They returned from their last trip at 9.30 on the evening of the 3rd, and Robertson at once began to lead the tanks forward. For seventy hours already he had been almost continually under fire, without rest of any kind. He led his section to the assembly point, and the weather being misty and the ground execrably bad, went on again with it at zero, still walking in front. Amid increasingly heavy shelling he guided his tanks down to the bridge, across it, and on toward a road which would take them, beyond any chance of error, to their objectives. The tanks, now visible to the enemy and far ahead of the following infantry, drew a furious hail of rifle and machine-gun fire; and Robertson, having brought them to the road and launched them to the attack, was shot through the head. "But the tanks went on, and succeeded in their mission. The object for which Captain Robertson had so deliberately sacrificed his life was achieved."[1]

The attacks at Poelcapelle and on the Reutelbeek, on the same morning, were the only successful tank actions in all the dreary weeks since mid-August. The 2nd and 3rd Tank Brigades were now withdrawn to refit. The 1st Brigade was to make one more attempt and to suffer the most calamitous failure of all.

On the 7th October, tanks of D Battalion were to have attacked certain forts along the Poelcapelle road, beyond the village. One became ditched, however, blocking the road, and before a way could be made round the derelict it

[1] 'The Tank Corps' (Williams-Ellis), from which the whole incident is paraphrased.

D Battalion Tank ditched on remains of Poelcapelle Church, October 4, 1917.

Poelcapelle Church before the advance in August, September, &c., 1917. (German Photo.)

was too late to go on. Two nights later eight tanks of the
same battalion left St Julien (where they had been lying
concealed by reddish-brown camouflage designed to blend
with the ruins) to repeat the attempt. Their starting-point
was the Retour cross-roads, south of Poelcapelle. The
main road itself, that tragic thoroughfare, was now in a
condition baffling description. It was shelled without
ceasing day and night, and its shattered surface, swimming
in liquid mud after thirty hours' rain, was littered with a
frightful welter of dismembered men and animals and
broken limbers. Before the cross-roads were reached, one
tank slipped over the edge and was submerged instantly in
several feet of water. The remainder arrived at Retour,
and thence crawled on into Poelcapelle. The night was
as black as the Pit: it was raining in torrents; and upon
the destroyed village was crashing a more terrible rain of
shells. At the point beyond the cemetery where two roads
converge upon the main street, one from Langemarck and
one from the railway station on the Ypres-Staden line, the
leading tank became bellied in the mud and rubble, tried
to free herself with her unditching beam, broke that, and
remained immovable. Just behind her the second tank was
hit almost simultaneously by a shell and disabled. These
two completely blocked the road, and as there was no way
round, the others decided to return. But in the meantime
the last tank had fouled D 44, the machine abandoned on
the road two nights earlier, and in the collision became
ditched herself, thus closing the way home. The four tanks
in the middle were trapped. One or two attempted to find
a way round, but were bogged the instant they left the
pavé. Those left on the road were hit again and again,
and most of their people were killed or wounded.

In itself this was a lamentable disaster, and its results
were peculiarly unfortunate; for the six or seven burnt
and ruined tanks blocked completely the Poelcapelle road,
an artery upon which the troops in front depended for all
supplies, and which was essential to any further operations.

It rested with the Tank Corps to remove these obstructions.
A party under the Chief Engineer of the 1st Brigade began
the work at once. It had to be done at night, and then
under conditions of extreme danger, for the Germans knew
perfectly well what was happening, and shelled the village
and the road ferociously. One by one the tanks, filled not
only with their own dead but with the bodies of wounded
infantrymen who had crawled in from that tormented street
to die, were blown up by heavy charges of gun-cotton.
Within a week the ghastly road was clear again, except
for the human debris which accumulated always there.
And in the noise and flame of these explosions the active
work of the Tank Corps in the Salient came also to an end.
Only the salvage branch returned after a season to gather
in that which remained.

III.

G Battalion, having borne the brunt in the early days,
was so fortunate as to escape the horrors of this later
period. It did not go into action again after the Cockcroft,
although at the end of October every preparation was made,
and the approach-march actually was begun for what
promised to be a grisly undertaking at Spriet, between
Poelcapelle and Westroosebeke. To the profound relief
of every one concerned, this affair was cancelled at the last
minute. I was away at the time at the Wormhoudt rest-
camp (actually a very pleasant house in the village), where
I had been sent after becoming a victim to a sort of mild
dysentery which swept through our unhealthy quarters at
Lovie. As I was supposed to be suffering also from a
slightly strained heart, due theoretically to exertions undergone at a special course on tank repairs, I returned to camp
about 20th October with instructions to do only light duty
for a fortnight.

I had been away nearly three weeks. Everything was

very much as I had left it. The bustle and worry aroused
by the Spriet episode had subsided, and it was common
knowledge that tanks would not be used again in the
Salient. There was the usual talk of our withdrawing to
Blangy, or some other village in the Erin neighbourhood,
for winter training. As a battalion we were rather scattered
at this time. 20 and 21 Companies still lived in the camp
at Lovie, but 19 Company, always exclusive, had chosen
for some obscure reason to bury itself in Oosthoek Wood.
An assortment of tanks belonging to all three companies
still lived in the wood, and about as many more were at
Ghent Cottages. I do not think we had more than fifteen
machines altogether that were fit: the remainder were
under repair, or were still lying derelict between Admirals
Road and the Cockcroft. Nor, when it came to a pinch,
had we too many men available, notwithstanding our very
moderate casualties. It was the curse of all tank units
under the latest establishment that, with more extra duties
than any branch of the service, they had virtually no extra
duty men. Battalions now came out with the bare total
sufficient for the fighting crews and a few essential fatigues
and guards, and a proportion of this total might be written
off permanently for brigade duties and instructional courses
at Erin or elsewhere. At this time, for example, with our
strength reduced by these causes, and also by casualties
and illness, we had to find guards for the camp at Lovie,
the camp and tanks at Oosthoek, and the tanks at Ghent
Cottages; also for a brigade petrol and ammunition dump
at Vlamertinghe (whose *raison d'être* no one ever had discovered), and for one of our own at Dirty Bucket Corner;
while for a time there was a dump also at St Julien, now
become comparatively a peaceful spot. A guard can always
be calculated at three times its actual strength, for in addition to the men on duty there are those who are just
going on duty, and those who have just come off. Whenever one wanted an N.C.O. or man in those days, he was
certain to fall within one of these three categories, and in

consequence to be unavailable. The old headquarters sections, which had existed for a time at Wool, would have been invaluable in the field, to leave the fighting crews free for their proper work. The result of this multiplication of small duties with our inadequate personnel was that when we received the usual sudden orders to leave the Salient, bag and baggage, and the camp had to be struck and the tanks prepared for entrainment on the same day, these simultaneous tasks, four miles apart, had to be performed in theory by the same men—which was absurd. In my own case, I found I had not a single member of my crew at liberty to help me with my tank. Half were on guard somewhere, and half were striking tents and packing up at Lovie. I was obliged to borrow a couple of workshops men to drive the machine on to the train.

Alden having reclaimed G 47 after the Cockcroft, I had been given my third tank, by name " Goliath "—a very proper translation from the variety stage to the Scriptures. She had been recovered from the swamp where she had been left on 31st July, and after being furbished up she was as good, or better, than new, for she possessed the best-running engine in the company, and was notoriously a fast machine. She never left Oosthoek Wood, however, after her return there, until we finally departed; and as it fell out I had only one opportunity of seeing what she could do.

After the middle of October our advanced tanks were moved back to Oosthoek from Ghent Cottages, preparatory to what we supposed would be a withdrawal to refit, following the example of the 2nd and 3rd Brigades. E and D Battalions were also collected once more in the wood, with what machines remained to them. Reinforcements, however, began to arrive from Central Workshops, and as quite a number of salved tanks were under repair, our nominal establishments once more grew toward completion. This seemed to point to the fact that the 1st Brigade would not be withdrawn to refit, but was to be employed again before

very long. No whisper escaped, so far as I am aware, of
what actually was intended. It was realised that no further
work was expected of tanks in the Salient, where operations
had dwindled down to a final struggle for Passchendaele
village, all attempt to reach Westroosebeke, on the highest
part of the ridge, having been abandoned; but beyond that
we knew nothing. Nor, in our hand-to-mouth existence,
did we waste much time on speculation. I believe there
was some talk of a surprise attack in the Lens area, but
what interested us most was the question of leave, which
was scandalously overdue.

Late in October came preliminary orders for a move to
our old driving-ground at Wailly, near Arras, for instructional purposes and training with infantry — this last so
obviously called for and so long demanded that it served
as an excellent camouflage for the real object, and persuaded
most of us who thought at all about the matter that nothing
further was intended. We were in the penultimate month
of the year, and judging, as we naturally were inclined to
do, by the weather and ground at Ypres, training seemed
all that was left for tanks until the following spring. I have
forgotten the exact date when our final movement orders
arrived, but it must have been about the 1st or 2nd of
November. We were to move at once, but there was
nothing surprising in this, as all orders in the Army are
delivered on principle at the last moment, and sometimes
after it. There ensued, of course, a frightful scramble.
The Tank Corps, being a sedentary organisation which
requires huge facilities in transport and rolling-stock for
any serious removal, wherever it settles down gathers an
immense amount of stores, public and private. We had
been four months in the Salient; and apart altogether from
the spare tank equipment to which we were legitimately
entitled, and could not part from if we wished, the personal baggage of G Battalion alone was little short of a
scandal. We were going to train for the winter in an
inhospitable region of chalk trenches and barbed-wire, and

very naturally we took what comforts we could. Huts, furniture, souvenirs, duckboards, and other rubbish had to be carried by our long-suffering transport down to Oosthoek and shipped on board tanks and trucks. 21 Company had just erected an elaborate mess, beautifully made by our carpenters of timber, wire-netting, and tarred felt, with linen windows and a canvas lining. This also must be pulled down and carried with us. It was little wonder, in short, that there were few men available to look after such trifles as the tanks themselves. Final orders had come through on the morning of a pouring wet day. All three companies were to leave from the Oosthoek ramp thirty-six hours later. After a frenzied evening spent in packing and jettisoning my personal belongings, I went down next morning to the wood to prepare the tank for the move. The weather was now fine, but by this time the interior of Oosthoek was filthy beyond words. The continual coming and going of tanks during the past months, and the immense downfall of rain, aggravated by the dripping trees, had reduced the ground to a swamp excelled only in the heavily bombarded areas. On one occasion an entire engine, weighing a ton or two, having been removed from a tank, sank completely in the slough and was lost and forgotten, being discovered weeks later by some one stubbing his toe against it. All unnecessary movement of tanks eventually was forbidden in the wood, as they actually became ditched there. On three sides of "Goliath," as it happened, there was now a deep pool. Having no men to help me, for reasons already given, I spent the morning splashing about in this water, struggling single-handed to fold and stow away huge and sodden tarpaulin-sheets and camouflage-nets, unbolting the sponsons, and finally driving the latter inboard with a sledge-hammer. Happily "Goliath," in spite of its name, was a female tank. Male sponsons, even of the new type, required several men with crowbars and other implements to push them in. After lunch in a small mess which 20 Company had rigged up

in the wood, I collected two workshops' men, borrowed
Johnstone from a guard where I had discovered him, and
in this way got the tank driven on to the ramp, where
several others were waiting for the first train.

D and E Battalions had already left; and with our departure only a few broken-down machines, dedicated to
salvage, would remain in Oosthoek Wood. Before dark,
which fell early now, 20 and 21 Companies, with all their
paraphernalia, were on the first two trains. 19 Company
was following next day. And then ensued one of those
interminable waits to which, in the Army, one becomes
accustomed without becoming reconciled. The night was
intensely cold, with a wicked north-east wind and a moon
and stars frostily brilliant; and hour after hour we stamped
about the military road or gathered round the primus stoves
on which the mess staff brewed cocoa and hot rum at
frequent intervals. In theory I was still on light duty,
and did not in fact feel aggressively robust; and as I had
been soaked to the knees half a dozen times during the
day, these freezing hours of waiting induced a foreboding
that before long I should be down again with a chill. It
was two o'clock in the morning before the first train got
away. By a rare stroke of fortune it included a first-class
coach for officers, in which we were comfortable enough
and even moderately warm. The journey took about fifteen
hours, as we went at the usual tank-train pace round the
usual periphery of Hazebrouck, Lillers, St Pol, and Doullens,
and we drew into Beaumetz, the station for Wailly, some
time after dark that evening. Every one in the Tank Corps
knows Beaumetz, with its long street of half-ruined and
generally abandoned houses on the Arras-Doullens road,
its roofless railway station, and its single clean and reput-
able café, where a pig-tailed and precocious infant called
Émilie (or some such name) cheeked the patrons without
respect for rank or age. We had no time for the café that
night, however. The tanks had to be detrained and parked
near by, and then came the business of unloading all our

stores and lumber. The vast amount of the latter produced
a bitter and thoroughly justifiable outcry from the exhausted
R.T.O., who had been dealing with tank trains for the last
three or four nights and was heartily tired of the sight
of them. It was approaching midnight before we had
finished unloading this stuff and conveying most of it
across to the tanks, and then after a meal of hot stew
on the platform it became a question of finding somewhere to sleep. It was still fine, but colder than ever.
The men were sleeping in the tanks or under the tarpaulin
covers, and to the officers fell the spacious but otherwise
negligible accommodation of the station itself. Kessel and
some others burrowed into a big stack of fodder by the side
of the line. Chaddock and I, feeling like Scott or Shackle-
ton, unstrapped our valises, laid them out on the Arctic
platform, and tied ourselves up inside with Balaclava helmets over our heads. An icy hurricane whistled through
the station all night, and my expected chill, already developing, was not definitely improved by this rather foolish
arrangement.

The distance from Beaumetz to the training ground at
Wailly is about five miles. We moved off in the course
of the morning, and my new machine showed her capabilities by arriving three-quarters of an hour ahead of anybody
else. An advance party, travelling by lorry, had begun
already to erect a camp in the usual area, which actually
was just outside the village of Rivière. The whole countryside swarmed with tanks, all three brigades being concentrated here. H and I Battalions had followed E from
England, making a total of nine battalions, three to a
brigade. Altogether, with gun-carriers and supply-tanks,
upwards of 400 machines were gathered at Wailly during
those early November days. And, the moment one arrived,
one's eye was caught by a suggestive novelty. Lying
everywhere about the ground, or lifted high on the cabs
of tanks, were the immense brushwood fascines designed
for the Hindenburg line.

My own stay at Wailly, however, was brief, uncomfortable, and inglorious. On the second day after my arrival I was in bed in my tent with one of the innumerable maladies classed together by the Army under the symbol P.U.O. In other words, I had a high temperature and semi-crippled legs. As the temperature improved, the legs got worse; and after four or five days I was despatched under protest to the nearest field-ambulance at Ficheux.

Owing to this unfortunate illness (a mild sort of "trench leg" which crippled me for a month), I was not present at the battle of Cambrai. Most of the ground over which it was fought is unfamiliar to me, as, although I took part in the operations which led incidentally to the fall of Cambrai itself in the following autumn, our line of advance then lay to the north of the old battlefield. Only Bourlon and Bourlon Wood I know rather intimately. In any case, however, the battle has been described so often that its general outline should be familiar to most people; and I wish to fill in that outline from the point of view of the Tank Corps, and to correct the inaccuracies and wilful omissions which abound in most published narratives, rather than attempt in detail to relate the various phases of the battle. The actual story will be better left to open the second part of this book, because Cambrai stands for that great turn in the fortunes of the Tank Corps to which such an action as the Cockcroft gave only a small initial impulse; but we can consider very briefly here the means which brought about so startling an experiment.

Ever since its inception, the Tank Corps had been demanding a fair trial. It is one thing to demand, and another to receive. It so happened that tanks entered the field at a time when certain new tactical theories were being elaborated in practice. There was the theory of the limited objective, and the theory of the annihilating preliminary bombardment. Both of these broke down in the end: the first, because it often was the enemy, and not ourselves, who decided the limit of the objective; and the second, because the preliminary bombardment was found to defeat its own designs, as at Ypres. In an admirable and most interesting book on the Gallipoli campaign, recently published, General Callwell points out repeatedly that the most obvious means to some military end must be no less obvious to the enemy, unless the latter be afflicted by the Gods with judicial blindness, and upon this it is not safe to count. Given two armies of approximately equal strength and resources, facing one another from lines of trenches which cannot be turned, and excluding all miracles and other improbable contingencies, the normal expedients adopted by one side will have been foreseen by the other. We thought it astonishing on the Somme that the German machine-gun posts remained in action after the most terrific bombardment. But they had been designed to that end, with profound dug-outs that no bombardment could injure. The army, in short, that hopes to win speedily under these conditions, and does not count solely on that blessed but two-edged word "attrition," must have some abnormal factor up its sleeve. We possessed such a factor in the tanks. The initial surprise effected by tanks on the Somme was nothing. Their exceeding value lay in the fact that, properly used, they could always effect a surprise. They could take the place of all that preliminary bombardment which announced to the enemy the approaching attack days and weeks before it was to materialise. There are, of course, two sorts of surprises in war. There is the sort employed at Ypres, where your opponent knows you are going to attack him, but does not know when. There is the less common sort, when he does not expect you to attack at all, has made no preparations for an attack, and probably is asleep. Tanks were valuable enough in the first case, but tanks alone now could bring about the second. Wire and machine-guns had forbidden a genuine surprise to any combination of the other arms. The German use of poison-gas, designed originally to effect a surprise, was successful up to a point because it had not been foreseen, but it was countered at once by the gas-mask. There was no such thing possible, however, as a tank-mask. Provided tanks were used on suitable ground, in sufficient numbers, and with an infantry trained to support them, no dependable antidote to them existed. We had discovered — and this includes the French, whose *artillerie d'assaut* were invented independently of our tanks — a very powerful weapon which the Germans in their blindness had for some reason put aside. The idea must have occurred to them. Apparently, until it was too late, they pinned their faith to heavy howitzers, masses of men, and the excellence of their military machine. Afterwards they had neither the plant nor the labour to spare. They were building tanks before Cambrai, but these were obvious makeshifts — glorified tractors of great size and considerable speed, but clumsy and inconvenient to a degree.

The abnormal factor, then, was in our hands. For a year it had been wasted. Circumstances, presumably unavoidable, had led our series of offensives to incline always northward, where the conditions grew steadily worse; and when, after the Somme, Arras, and Messines, tanks found themselves at Ypres, it was felt that if the Army decided to wage a campaign on the Goodwin Sands the unfortunate machines would be called there too. And during all this time their peculiar attribute of affecting a genuine surprise, and, by so doing, revolutionising modern war, had hardly been tested.

On 17th September, while the Ypres battle was dragging out its weary programme, General Elles (as he now was) visited the commander of the Third Army, Sir Julian Byng. This army now held the southern extremity of the British line, opposite that part of the so-called Hindenburg system which covered the important railway centre of Cambrai. Following up the German retreat in the early spring, we had come to a halt in front of these fabulous earthworks, and had remained quiescent ever since. It was notoriously the most peaceful section of the line, a place where No Man's Land often was 1000 yards across, with the hostile trenches out of sight behind a hill, the Mecca of every wearied and decimated unit withdrawn from the Salient for a rest. Virtually untouched by war, except that the fields, long untended, grew nothing but coarse grass and weeds, it was an undulating, hedgeless, chalk country, dotted with frequent villages, a few small copses and one or two more pretentious woods, criss-crossed by sunken roads, and watered by several insignificant streams and two important canals. Athwart it, from north-west to south-east, ran the irregular trace of the Hindenburg Line, eight miles from Cambrai at the nearest point on the Bapaume road. This line was known to be weakly held. The immense belts of wire and the innumerable machine-guns were trusted, and justifiably, to fend off any orthodox attack by the very moderate forces under General Byng. The Tank Corps, however, alone among the various branches of the Service, had looked for months upon the Hindenburg Line as a lawful and easy prey. The wire was no obstacle at all, and the trenches, whispered of as though they were Charon's seven streams, were not worth even an obolus. They had been crossed at Bullecourt, and human ingenuity was equal to devising some means of bridging those which might exceed a tank's allotted span. The country was all that could be desired—firm, unbroken by shell-fire, and well drained. Every circumstance had long pointed to this region for an offensive carried out, as the Tank Corps maintained all offensives should be carried out—led and determined by tanks, and launched, without any overt preliminaries, as a genuine surprise. With these ideas General Elles had no difficulty in infecting the 3rd Army commander. A general plan of attack on this front had been worked out some time before. It was altered and trimmed to suit the particular conditions now in view, and the completed scheme was submitted to the Commander-in-Chief.

Three considerations, one may suppose, helped especially

FROM THE COCKCROFT TO CAMBRAI 253

to recommend it to Sir Douglas Haig. The Ypres offensive, however it might be disguised in public, was a lamentable failure, and needed some corrective; the Russian collapse was setting free the best German troops from the East; and within a few months it might be impossible to strike a blow anywhere with a reasonable hope of success. It is likely also that some rumours of the forthcoming stroke on the Italian front helped to quicken a decision. In any case, the scheme was approved on 20th October, and was fixed for a date exactly one month later. Unfortunately, G.H.Q. had not the courage of its convictions—or of the convictions of others. Probably in this case it had no convictions of its own. It did not believe that tanks, even when working under their own chosen conditions, could perform all that they claimed ability to perform. A highly interesting article by M. Paul Painlevé, French Minister of War in March 1917, contains an account of a visit to our G.H.Q. in that month, where, he records, the general opinion was in favour of "having a smack" at the enemy. This characteristic but rather primitive attitude undoubtedly governed the decision to carry out the Cambrai attack. Having lost upwards of a quarter of a million of men at Ypres, it was as well to have as cheap "a smack" at the enemy as possible. The conditions laid down manifested in every article the spirit of compromise. If the Tank Corps liked to sacrifice itself wholesale, well and good, but no additional infantry could be provided. The 3rd Army must make the most of its very slender resources in this respect. (It was stated officially that any additional concentration of troops would have betrayed the coming attack to the enemy. But it is difficult to accept this reasoning. On the 8th August 1918, to name only one instance, several army corps were gathered behind the line in perfect secrecy.) Finally, the whole operation was to be completed within forty-eight hours at the most, this being the time it was calculated the enemy would require to bring up reinforcements.

Restricted as it was, the opportunity was welcomed by all concerned—in especial by the Tank Corps, which saw at last a prospect of proving in the field those theories it had advocated in and out of season for the past twelve months. Preparations, already begun, were expedited, and the concentration of the three brigades at Wailly was put in hand.

PART II.

THE SECOND PHASE: CAMBRAI AND AFTER

CHAPTER XIII.

CAMBRAI.

I.

THE Tank Corps had to accomplish an immense amount of work in a very short time before the battle of Cambrai. This preparation consisted of five main features:—
1. The arrangements for secrecy.
2. The concentrating of three brigades of tanks at Wailly, and their subsequent dispersal to detraining centres behind the Cambrai front.
3. Rehearsals with the infantry of the plan of attack.
4. The construction of certain devices for crossing the wider trenches of the Hindenburg Line, for bringing up supplies, and for clearing the wire for the cavalry.
5. The establishment of petrol and ammunition dumps.

We will take these features in order.

The whole 3rd Army was involved in the question of secrecy. The bringing up of numerous additional batteries to positions close behind the front line, the assembling of several cavalry divisions, and all the thousand and one preparations for an advance on a wide front had to be completed without a suspicion reaching the enemy. This was accomplished successfully. The normal artillery activity was maintained, while dozens of new batteries were brought up and camouflaged. None of these were able to register before the battle opened. The Tank Corps, meanwhile, had its own especial difficulties. The withdrawal of one brigade from the Salient and another from the Lens front could not be wholly concealed, but the myth of winter training deceived the enemy, if he heard of it, as thoroughly as it deceived the troops concerned; and the activities of one or two wireless tanks, left at the front to send bogus messages, easily intercepted, to imaginary brigade headquarters, fostered the belief that the latter had not moved. The forward H.Q. established with the 3rd Army at Albert was disguised as the Tank Corps Training Office. In the beginning only four members of General Elles's staff knew of the forthcoming attack. The information was next revealed to battalion and company commanders and reconnaissance officers; and last of all, only two or three days before 20th November, zero day, section and tank commanders were admitted to the secret. Reconnaissance was carried out with every precaution, distinctive badges being hidden or removed, and senior officers visited the front disguised in steel helmets and trench-coats.

Thirty-six tank trains were needed for the almost simultaneous removal of the nine battalions. Our supply of K.T. trucks being insufficient, it was necessary to borrow a number of the smaller French type. A vast amount of work was thrown on the railway staff, all the entraining and detraining being carried out at night. In four or five nights upwards of 450 machines were entrained at Beaumetz. Twenty-seven train-loads were concentrated at Plateau Station, near Albert, by the 14th November, and dispersed to their final detraining points during the three following days, the remaining nine trains reaching Plateau on the 15th. Only the most careful management could have succeeded in disposing of these slow and heavy trains, amid all the normal traffic, in so short a time without a hitch. The 1st Brigade detrained finally at Bertincourt and Ruyaulcourt, behind Havrincourt Wood, the 2nd Brigade at Sorel and Ytres, to the south, and the 3rd Brigade at Heudicourt, near Epehy. At all these railheads new ramps had to be built or old ones repaired. With one or two minor accidents, 378 fighting tanks and 98 administrative machines were assembled at points from two to four miles behind the lines on zero minus two days—18th November.

The plan of attack and its rehearsal with the infantry at Wailly cannot be described more lucidly than in the account given in 'Weekly Tank Notes,' the official publication already referred to. I will quote this account entire.

"Before the infantry assembled for training a new tactics had to be devised, not only to meet the conditions which would be encountered, but to fit the limitations imposed upon the tank by it only being able to carry one tank fascine. Once this fascine was cast it could not be picked up again without considerable difficulty.

"Briefly the tactics decided on were worked out to meet the following requirements: 'To effect a penetration of four systems of trenches in a few hours without any type of artillery preparation.' They were as follows:—

"Each objective was divided up into tank section attack areas according to the number of tactical points in the objective, and a separate echelon, or line, of tanks was allotted to each objective. Each section was to consist of three machines—one advance-guard tank and two infantry tanks; this was agreed to on account of there not being sufficient tanks in France to bring sections up to four machines apiece.

"The duty of the advance-guard tank was to keep down the enemy's fire and to protect the infantry tanks as they led the infantry through the enemy's wire and over his trenches. The allotment of the infantry to tanks depended on the strength of the objective to be attacked and the nature of the approaches; their formation was that of sections in single file with a leader to each file. They were organised in three forces: trench clearers to operate with the tanks;

trench stops to block the trenches at various points; and trench supports to garrison the captured trench and form an advance-guard to the next echelon of tanks and infantry passing through.

"The whole operation was divided into three phases: the assembly, the approach, and the attack. The first was carried out at night-time and was a parade drill, the infantry falling in behind the tanks on tape lines, connected with their starting-points by taped routes. The approach was slow and orderly, the infantry holding themselves in readiness to act on their own initiative. The attack was regulated so as to economise tank fascines, and was carried out as follows:—

"The advance-guard tank went straight forward through the enemy's wire, and turning to the left, without crossing the trench in front of it, opened right sponson broadsides; the infantry tanks then made for the same spot, the left-hand one, crossing the wire, approached the trench and cast its fascine, then crossed over the fascine, turned to the left, and worked down the fire trench; the second infantry tank crossed over the fascine of the first and made for the enemy's support trench, cast its fascine, and crossing did likewise. Meanwhile the advance-guard tank had swung round, and crossing over the fascines of the two infantry tanks, moved forward with its own fascine still in position ready for the third trench line. When the two infantry tanks met they assembled behind the advance-guard tank and awaited orders. The leading wave of infantry planted a red flag at the gaps in the wire.

"In training the infantry the following exercises were carried out:—

(1) Assembly of infantry behind tanks.
(2) Advance to attack behind tanks.
(3) Passing through wire crushed down by tanks.
(4) Clearing up a trench sector under protection of tanks.

"To enable them to work quickly in section single files and to form these into section lines a simple platoon drill was issued, and it is interesting to note that this drill was based on a very similar one described by Xenophon in his 'Cyropædeia' and attributed to King Cyrus (*circa* 500 B.C.)."

The fascines above mentioned were designed to assist the tanks over the wider trenches of the Hindenburg system. Some of these were known to be 12 feet wide and of great depth, the actual width being increased by the inward slopes of a parapet and parados 2 feet 6 inches high. A Mark IV. tank could only cross a trench 10-11 feet wide, a fact of which the Germans were well aware. The real obstacle was the depth of the trench, as when the tank was half-way over, but not yet balanced on the parados, the tail left the parapet and dropped to the trench floor, shifting the centre of gravity and leaving the machine at an angle so near the vertical that the tracks could not grip against all the deadweight below. The object of the fascine, therefore, was not to fill the trench and form a bridge, as seems commonly to be supposed, for this was both impossible and unnecessary, but to keep the tail of the tank from dropping so far that the machine was unable to recover. These tank fascines were made by binding together with chains, under great pressure, seventy-five ordinary brushwood bundles 10 feet long. Each big fascine was 4 feet 6 inches in diameter and weighed a ton and three-quarters. This monstrosity was carried on the cab of the tank, and was dropped into a trench over the nose by means of a release mechanism from within. It was an abomination to man-handle, fifteen to twenty Chinamen being required to push each fascine through the mud at Erin; and during a train journey it had to be lowered on the truck and hoisted up again before detrainment. But in action the fascines fulfilled their purpose admirably. The widest and deepest Hindenburg trenches proved no obstacle at all.

Four hundred of these fascines were made at Central Workshops during the feverish three weeks before Cambrai. This involved the trimming to the correct length of 30,000 ordinary fascines, and the welding of 2000 fathoms of steel chain. Eighteen tanks, working in pairs, pulled on the chains in opposite directions after they had been wound several times round the huge bundles. In the same period were constructed 110 heavy timber sledges, to be towed by tanks with loads of petrol and ammunition. 127 tanks were repaired and issued, and a number were fitted with large grapnels for wire-clearing. Owing to the necessity of secrecy, the personnel at Erin were not informed of the extreme urgency of these tasks; yet during these three weeks the shops were working for 22½ hours out of every 24 without a break. Nor was this pressure confined to the workshops. Between the 10th and 25th November, 28 lorries covered between them 19,000 miles, or 744 miles per lorry, and some small box cars averaged 1200 miles apiece.

Three main supply dumps were established at the lying-up points of the three brigades — Havrincourt Wood, Dessart Wood, and Villers-Guislain and Gouzeaucourt. Among the stores collected here were 165,000 gallons of petrol, 55,000 lbs. of grease, 5,000,000 rounds of S.A.A., and 500,000 rounds of 6-pounder shell. The splendid system of light railways behind the 3rd Army front alone made this huge accumulation possible in so short a time. In the field, stores were to be carried from these dumps by supply tanks and gun-carrying tanks towing sledges.

This brief account will give some idea of the work required before a full-dress tank battle, and of the sudden problems with which the technical staff had to grapple at short notice. It must be remembered that there was no precedent whatever for this operation. Four times as many tanks as went in on the first day at Ypres were to be employed at Cambrai. There had been little time for preparation and less for reconnaissance. The Hindenburg trenches, until they were met and conquered, at least were impressive impostors; and there was a great weight of responsibility, as well as a sense of gratification, attached to the fact that for the first time in the career of the corps, tanks were to be the dominating factor in a big battle. Their method of use determined the whole tactical scheme. Confident though all ranks might be of gaining that triumph to which they had looked forward through a series of discouragements, lasting over many months, the importance of the occasion brought infinite anxiety and strain.

On the other hand, everything, at long last, had been done for them that could be done. They were to have their own way on ground of their own choosing. For over a week at Wailly tanks and infantry rehearsed over the old German trenches the exact tactics they were to employ over the new ones. To give the infantry additional confidence, they were asked to construct their own defences and wire entanglements, which the tanks then proceeded to obliterate. The deep German front line at Wailly, enlarged to a veritable gulf by the passage or ditching of innumerable tanks during previous months of training, was an admirable model on which to prove the efficiency of the fascines. The masses of rusty wire provided practice for the special machines whose grapnels were to clear the way for the cavalry. Short though the time was, nothing was left undone. Tank personnel and infantry practised together and talked together, and for the first time was reached an approximation to that mutual trust and understanding which these two arms had so long and so especially required.

II.

An examination of a layered map shows very clearly the conformation of the country between the Hindenburg Line and Cambrai. The 3rd Army, lying south-west of that town, was attacking north-east. The battlefield can be divided into two parts, north and south of a line drawn westward from Marcoing through Flesquières along the Flesquières-Havrincourt Ridge. The southern part is a triangle, bounded to the north by this ridge, to the east by the Canal de L'Escaut, which zigzags southward from Cambrai, and to the south-west by the Hindenburg Line, which almost touches the canal near Banteux. In this part of the field we should be fighting downhill to the canal valley. The northern part, beyond the Flesquières Ridge, is lowish ground dominated by one prominent landmark, Bourlon Hill and Wood, and delimited to the west by the Canal du Nord, which the Hindenburg trenches crossed immediately north of Havrincourt Wood, thence following its course northward to Moeuvres. The Flesquières Ridge itself is an important tactical feature, running from east to west against the general lie of the country and overlooking the whole northern part of the battlefield; and where it was crossed by the German line, west of Havrincourt, the latter made a pronounced salient, taking in a portion of Havrincourt Wood. This portion was held as an advanced position in front of the trench system, and farther south the hamlet of La Vacquerie and other posts were strongly occupied in a like manner. The Hindenburg Line itself, taking it correctly as the first line of trenches, was sited on reverse slopes, hidden from our observation, and covered in front by a dense belt of wire, nowhere less than 50 yards deep. The Hindenburg wire was, in fact, a remarkable sight. You saw it winding away over the ridges in three broad belts, clean cut and separated by narrower avenues of grass; miles upon miles of it, with great patches red with rust after any rain, and looking in the distance where it climbed some final crest to the horizon like zigzag stripes of plough or trimmed and level vegetation. Behind the front system of trenches were three others, the Hindenburg Reserve, wired almost as thickly as the first line, and two more. These last were not so formidable. The series varied in depth from three and a half to four and a half miles. The front line and reserve were pierced in every bay by the shafts of deep dug-outs, although some of these had not been finished. In places they were joined up to form considerable tunnels, forty feet underground. The chalk of which the higher land is formed, although hard to work, is admirable for such subterranean use. The shafts and dug-outs were timbered, walls and roof, and when, a year later, I lived in several of them, were always dry. The whole system was knitted together by a maze of communication trenches.

The third and fourth lines, which in fact formed one system called variously the Marquion, Masnières, or Beaurevoir Line, crossed the Canal de L'Escaut south of Cambrai and covered another important tactical feature, the Niergnies-Seranvillers Ridge, east of the canal. This ridge, like that of Flesquières, overlooked all the northern part of the battlefield as far as Bourlon, making any attack on that height from the south a matter of great difficulty. The Niergnies Ridge, therefore, was to be carried if possible as soon as the canal crossings had been seized, but this effort proved beyond our resources.

The infantry at the disposal of Sir Julien Byng for his main attack amounted only to six divisions, with two cavalry divisions, and upwards of 1000 guns, for a front of six miles from east of Gonnelieu to a point north of Havrincourt Wood. Subsidiary attacks to secure the flanks were to be carried as far as Bullecourt to the north, and from Gonnelieu southward to Vendhuile. The whole operation, as we have seen, was under a time limit of forty-eight hours, while the Commander-in-Chief intended to call a halt before that period had expired if sufficient progress was not made. The first twenty-four hours was expected to show, one way or another, how much might be expected. But one rather startling factor resulted from the inadequate means to be employed. Every tank and infantryman in the six divisions was to go forward at zero. There were no reserves other than local ones; nothing was left for the second day—except the cavalry. The Guards and one or two other divisions were within a few marches of the battlefield, but not near enough to come up in time; nor were they intended to be used. The plan, in fact, was stamped plainly with that spirit of compromise due to ignorance and consequent mistrust of the capabilities of tanks. It was not really believed that the latter could do all that they claimed. Six divisions, therefore, were enough to risk on the gamble. On the other hand, in case the unexpected should happen, a most ambitious programme was drawn up, for which six divisions were hopelessly inadequate. The last German positions, beyond the Canal de L'Escaut, were to be carried in the first phase of the attack, after which cavalry was to cross the canal, occupy Cambrai and villages to the north and east, and move forward with its right on Valenciennes. In the meantime, the 4th Corps, on the right, was to form a defensive flank until the cavalry had cut the Valenciennes-Douai line nine or ten miles north of Cambrai (an incredible supposition), when the corps was to continue its advance in a north-easterly direction. The second and third phases of the battle were in the hands of the 3rd Corps on the left, whose business it was to capture Bourlon and Inchy-en-Artois (on the Canal du Nord), and then, by crossing the Arras-Cambrai road toward the marshes of the Sensée, to cut off the enemy's troops in the angle which that river formed with the Canal du Nord. All this, with six divisions, reads like a dream, as in fact it was. Admitted that it represents the utmost possible and includes all that optimistic phase of "exploitation" which never throughout the war was reached in any battle, it remains an astonishing proposition. For if it was possible, three times six divisions would barely be enough to fill the enormously extended line we should have won; while as in the actual attack the infantry were found to be exhausted after an advance of four or five miles, it is difficult to see how, in the same time, they could be expected to cover ten or fifteen. Most extraordinary of all is the almost supernatural rôle allotted to the cavalry. It takes one back to the days of Marlborough and Prince Eugene, or to the triumphs of Murat. This venerable fallacy about cavalry would be pathetic if it were not so mischievous. For as an offensive weapon a man on a horse is an anachronism in any modern battle fought in an enclosed and cultivated country where everybody else is under cover. He cannot see his enemy, but can himself be seen a mile away, and, what is more pertinent, can be shot at that distance. He is tied to his horse, which he cannot hide. Even the pursuit of a routed enemy, supposed to be his especial *métier*, is governed now by conditions which render him useless. In every rout of a disciplined army some stout fellows will always be found as a rearguard, and two or three machine-guns can hold up a whole brigade of cavalry among villages and hedgerows. No ten feet high combination of man and beast, in short, has any chance whatever against modern small arms. It cannot be expected, however, that this ever will be admitted in an army controlled largely by influential cavalry soldiers; and as at Cambrai the mounted troops, with few exceptions, proved incapable even of arriving in time to attempt anything, the less said about them the better.

A further serious handicap to General Byng lay in the fact that most of his six divisions had come from the Salient, where they had been strained to the uttermost and had suffered heavy casualties. Their ranks were filled up with drafts who had no experience, while it had been impossible in the short time available for more than a small percentage to practice at Wailly with the tanks. But having enumerated these various adverse considerations, there remains much that was encouraging to be put against them. The divisions included some of the best in the army. The 29th had won an almost fabulous reputation in Gallipoli, although few of its original rank and file were left. The 6th was another formation with the traditions of regular service behind it. The 51st Highland Territorial Division (with which G Battalion had been associated in the Salient) had the distinction of coming second on a German list of those units most feared by the enemy. Among the troops taking part in the subsidiary attacks to the north, and likely to be involved in the main battle if all went well, were the 3rd Division, which headed the German list referred to, and the 40th London and 36th Ulster Divisions. On the right flank, where the 3rd Army linked up with the French, a strong force of French infantry and cavalry was put at our disposal. Then there was the known fact that the enemy's position, held by Von der Marwitz's 2nd Army, had been much depleted of troops, and especially of guns, while our own people must have gained confidence from the marked efficiency of our preliminary arrangements. Everything had gone well; every man, so far as was possible, knew what he had to do. Tanks and guns were in position; and the Germans in their deep trenches half a mile away, undisturbed by any breath of doubt or rumour, still performed mechanically the routine duties of a quiet sector, and reported that we were similarly employed.

The three Tank Brigades were disposed as follows: The 1st Brigade, of D, E, and G Battalions, with 42 tanks apiece, lay hidden in the western end of Havrincourt Wood, a large mass of timber of which the Germans actually held the eastern extremity, 3000 yards away. Colonel Hankey, of G Battalion, had under his command for the operation tanks from both the other units, giving him a total of 60 machines. The 2nd Brigade lay in Dessart Wood, two miles south of Havrincourt Wood. It consisted for the time of only two Battalions, B and H, A Battalion being attached to the 3rd Brigade. The tanks of the latter (A, C, F, and I Battalions), having no convenient wood in which

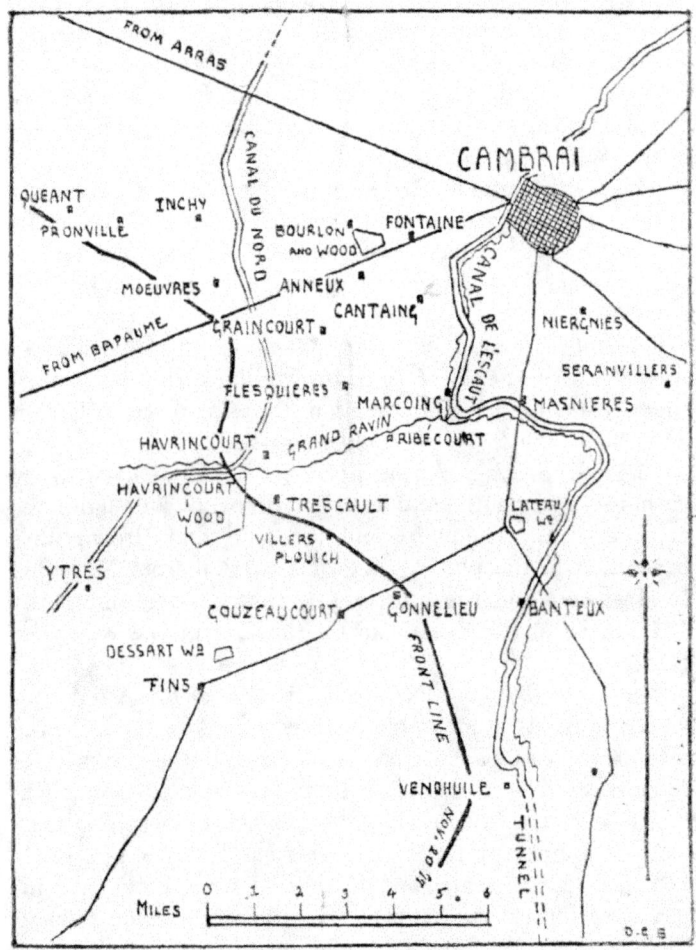

First Battle of Cambrai.

to hide, were concealed under brick-coloured camouflage netting in and about Gouzeaucourt and Villers-Guislain. The battalions of the 2nd and 3rd Brigades had also

42 tanks apiece. Each unit set aside a small number as a reserve to replace mechanical breakdowns. In addition to the whole total of 378 fighting machines, there were 32 wire-clearing tanks with grapnels to open passages for the guns and cavalry; 2 for carrying bridging material; 1 with a telephone cable for the 3rd Army signals; 54 supply tanks, some of them adapted gun-carriers; and 9 with wireless apparatus.

The 1st Brigade, on the left, was operating with the 62nd and 51st Divisions, its first objectives being Havrincourt village and Flesquières, with subsequent exploitation toward Graincourt, Anneux, Fontaine-Notre-Dame, and Bourlon.

The 2nd Brigade in the centre, leading the 6th Division, was to carry the Blue and Brown lines and Ribécourt, thence making for Marcoing on the Canal de L'Escaut and the Bois des Neufs further north.

The 3rd Brigade on the right, its 4 battalions working with the 29th, 20th, and 12th Divisions, had in hand the capture of La Vacquerie and the Blue and Brown lines beyond, then the bulging line of the canal from Marcoing to Masnières and the crossings at those places, and finally Crévecoeur on the east bank at the foot of the Niergnies ridge.

Zero was fixed for 6.20 A.M. on the 20th. After dusk on the previous evening tank routes would be taped to the assembly positions. Before 6 o'clock all the tanks were to be ready in one long line from Trescault to Gonnelieu, in front of our trenches and within 500-1000 yards of the German outposts; the "advance-guard" tanks 150 yards ahead, and the main body deployed at approximate intervals of 100 yards. At 6.10 the whole mass would begin to move forward, followed by infantry in section columns. At zero, ten minutes later, a barrage of shrapnel, H.E. and smoke shells from upwards of 1000 guns would fall on the enemy's outpost line, lifting after one minute, and moving forward in jumps of 250 yards, but remaining on certain objectives for stated periods. In addition, smoke screens were to fall on the Flesquières ridge and along the right flank of the 4th Corps, together with the usual counter-battery work and bombardment of roads and bridges.

The weather had been fine, but so misty that little aeroplane observation had been possible. This did not affect us, as motives of secrecy had kept our aerial reconnaissance within the normal routine, and it prevented awkward prying on the enemy's part. On the night of the 17th-18th November the Germans made a small raid near Havrincourt Wood and captured a few prisoners. These men were carried to Army Headquarters for investigation, a delay which had fortunate results for us, for some information about the forthcoming attack eventually was extracted from them. It came too late. A telegraphic warning reached the German front line only a few minutes before zero on the 20th, and was found half transcribed in a signaller's dug-out.

III.

General Elles, on the evening of 19th November, issued his "Special Order No. 6," in which he said: "To-morrow the Tank Corps will have the chance for which it has been waiting for many months—to operate on good going in the van of battle.... I propose leading the attack of the centre division." Enough has been said by others about the better-known newspaper version: "England expects every tank to do its damndest"—but I cannot refrain from pointing out once more that this impudent lie was only in accordance with all the traditions of modern journalism, which knows neither scruples, education, nor good taste. Herodotus was in the habit of putting imaginary speeches into the mouths of his historical characters; but we have indeed sunk low when some illiterate scavenger of Fleet Street is permitted, and even encouraged, to employ his own characteristic phraseology for the same purpose in the columns of a newspaper.

Before midnight that evening, from Havrincourt Wood and Dessart Wood, from Gouzeaucourt and Villers-Guislain, scores of tanks had uncamouflaged and moved out and were already on their way. It was such a gathering of these singular machines as never had been seen before, and was to be seen only once again—on 8th August of the following year. Section after section, company after company (twenty-seven companies were there, as against two on the Somme a year earlier), they crawled forward in long columns that split up after a while into smaller ones, and then again into twos and threes, until toward five o'clock the whole were deploying into a single line six miles long—a threatening, silent, curving line that faced and corresponded to the larger salients and re-entrants of the Hindenburg trenches. So silently had this approach been carried out that many of the infantry, assembling behind the gaps in our own wire, heard no tanks at all, and inquired with some anxiety if they had arrived. A few had broken down, and were replaced at once from the mechanical reserve. Upwards of 350 were in position. The night was very dark, with a dense ground mist, but so complete were all arrangements that this caused no inconvenience, while it helped to screen the massing of this unparalleled armada. A sudden burst of shelling and trench-mortar fire from the German lines about 4.30 startled every one and provoked suspicions of a premature discovery, but it died away in half an hour. From five o'clock until zero the whole front was quiet. At ten minutes past six tanks and infantry began to move; and at 6.20, with the sky lightening rapidly above the mist, the barrage exploded with a shattering crash of sound along the German outpost line, some 250 yards in front of the "advance-guard" machines. In the centre of the six-mile line, in a tank called the "Hilda" of H Battalion, General Elles was leading into the most revolutionary battle of the war the corps which had made it possible, and which he

had controlled almost from its infancy. It was not the
ordinary post for the commander of a large organisation,
but this was not an ordinary occasion. It was the consum-
mation of two years of struggle and disappointment. There
can have been little doubt in his mind, or in that of any
other man in the 350 tanks, as to what the result would be
now that the adventure was fairly launched.

The immediate onset of the tanks inevitably was over-
whelming. The German outposts, dazed or annihilated by
the sudden deluge of shells, were overrun in an instant.
The triple belts of wire were crossed as if they had been
beds of nettles, and 350 pathways were sheared through
them for the infantry. The defenders of the front trench,
scrambling out of dug-outs and shelters to meet the crash
and flame of the barrage, saw the leading tanks almost upon
them, their appearance made the more grotesque and terrifying by the huge black bundles they carried on their cabs.
As these tanks swung left-handed and fired down into the
trench, others, also surmounted by these appalling objects,
appeared in multitudes behind them out of the mist. It is
small wonder that the front Hindenburg Line, that fabulous
excavation which was to be the bulwark of Germany, gave
little trouble. The great fascines were loosed and rolled
over the parapet to the trench floor; and down the whole
line tanks were dipping and rearing up and clawing their
way across into the almost unravaged country beyond. The
defenders of the line were running panic-stricken, casting
away arms and equipment. The Hindenburg Reserve, with
its own massive entanglements, went the way of the first
trenches; and so far our following infantry had found little
to do beyond firing on the fugitives and rounding up gangs
of half-stupefied prisoners. It was now broad day, the mist
was thinning, and everywhere from Havrincourt to Banteux
on the canal was rout and consternation. The Grand Ravin,
a gully which runs from Havrincourt to Marcoing, was
choked with an unarmed mob streaming eastward. The
garrison of Havrincourt had put up a fight, but tanks closed

s

on it from the north, and it was cleared by the 62nd Division.¹ La Vacquerie had gone in the first onset; and now Ribécourt was carried, and tanks and infantry were approaching the vital canal bridges at Marcoing and Masnières. Over the whole southern half of the battlefield, the triangle I have described, the defence had collapsed; and this area was virtually cleared by midday. Only at one or two points had there been any serious resistance, the most notable being Lateau Wood, on a hill-top overlooking the canal, where a number of batteries were posted. Fighting continued here during most of the morning, and included an encounter between a tank and a 5.9 howitzer, in which the tank for once was the victor. The gun blew away the tank's right hand sponson, but failed to injure the engine, and was overrun before it could be reloaded. Eventually the wood was cleared and the guns captured. By two o'clock Marcoing was in our hands, and all but a portion of Masnières. At the former place a tank of A Battalion arrived in time to drive off the German engineers who were in the act of destroying the bridge, which was on the far side of the village. At Masnières, however, the bridge was partially wrecked, and a tank of F Battalion, endeavouring to cross, completed the destruction and fell with the wreckage into the canal. This accident helped to delay our advance at this point upon Rumilly and the Niergnies ridge. In the meantime a hitch had occurred in the northern portion of

¹ M'Elroy, of 19 Company, won the D.S.O. at Havrincourt in remarkable circumstances. The leading tanks and infantry had passed through the village, which was believed to be cleared of the enemy. M'Elroy's machine, following behind, caught fire just as about 100 Germans appeared round it from various hiding-places. Two of the crew, jumping out of one door to escape the flames, were killed instantly. The remainder, except the tank commander, scrambled out of the other door into a shell-hole. The Germans bombed them and killed one man, and then came and looked down into the shell-hole, where the survivors pretended also to be dead. M'Elroy, in the meantime, had remained in the tank and extinguished the fire. He then drove off the Germans with machine-gun fire and kept them at bay for nearly an hour until some infantry arrived. All this time other tank crews, a few hundred yards away, were walking about outside their machines, unconscious of the little battle going on behind them.

the field. The 51st Division, advancing against Flesquières, as soon as the fall of Havrincourt and Ribécourt secured its flanks, had adopted a formation of attack which does not seem to have combined successfully with the tanks. The latter entered the village, but the infantry were too far behind and were held up by machine-gun fire. Throughout the day tanks were in and out of Flesquières, driving the Germans into cellars from which they emerged again as the danger passed; but the 51st could do no more than obtain a grip on the outskirts of the place. The château, surrounded by a stout wall and impregnable to tanks, was the centre of resistance. Night fell with the village still untaken.

Largely on account of the inability of the 51st to give adequate support, the tanks had very serious losses in and about Flesquières. A number of batteries lay just over the ridge, and tank after tank was hit and disabled as it appeared on the crest, the easiest of targets at almost point-blank range. One gun in the west end of the village itself was believed to have knocked out no fewer than sixteen machines of D and E Battalions. This was the celebrated piece served single-handed by a very gallant German officer after all his men had abandoned him. He was killed beside his gun in the end by the infantry. Had the latter been able to support the tanks more closely, most of these mischievous batteries could have been silenced before they had a chance of doing any damage. A few riflemen pushed ahead would have driven off the gunners while the tanks remained hidden by the crest. It is no part of a tank's duty to make itself a helpless target for field-guns. As it was, while the wings of the army had swept on triumphantly to their third objectives and beyond, an unfortunate check had occurred in the centre. On the left of the 51st Division the 62nd, having cleared Havrincourt with the help of G Battalion's tanks, pushed on northward over the narrow neck of the Flesquières ridge up the line of the Canal du Nord. Some of our tanks were caught by the same batteries that were holding up D and E. Muirhead, of 20 Company, was killed here, and five or six machines were disabled. Chaddock, who had his section commander, Fearnley, on board, had an extraordinary escape. A shell came through the cab, took off the driver's head, and flung it on the knees of Fearnley at the brakes, killed or wounded the two right-hand gunners, and passed out at the stern without exploding. But the majority of the tanks were covered by a spur from the view of the batteries, and elsewhere there was no stopping this combination of G and the 62nd. Both the Hindenburg main and reserve lines were crossed in many places without the use of fascines, and tanks and infantry rolled swiftly down the slope to Graincourt, beyond which were the double row of trees along the Route Nationale No. 29, the Bapaume-Cambrai road, and the heavy mass of Bourlon Wood. Eight 6-pounder tanks advanced in line direct upon Graincourt, firing every gun they could bring to bear. Two German field-pieces concealed near the village were happily spotted by Charles Baker from the dust thrown up by the blast of their first discharge, and a few 6-pounder rounds drove away the gunners. By one o'clock Graincourt was captured. Still pushing on, tanks and infantry entered Anneux. This village was not wholly cleared that afternoon, for the 62nd were now exhausted. They had made the biggest advance of any division—4½ miles from their original front; but they would be the first to acknowledge that the tanks alone had made this possible, and had led them throughout. Some of G Battalion even had not finished yet. They crossed the Bapaume-Cambrai road and entered Bourlon Wood. There was little or no opposition: the great wood, which was to be the centre of such desperate fighting during the next week, appeared to be empty of defenders. It is certain that with a brigade of fresh infantry it could have been occupied and consolidated that evening. "The possession of Bourlon Ridge"—to quote Sir Douglas Haig's despatch—"would enable our

Battle of Cambrai. Bourlon Wood and Village, with Bapaume-Cambrai road in front.

troops to obtain observation over the ground to the north, which sloped gently down to the Sensée river. The enemy's defensive lines south of the Scarpe and Sensée rivers would thereby be turned, his communications exposed to the observed fire of our artillery, and his positions in this section jeopardised. In short, so great was the importance of the ridge to the enemy that its loss would probably cause the abandonment by the Germans of their carefully-prepared defence systems for a considerable distance to the north of it." Bourlon Wood itself, at the southern end of the ridge, was also on the highest part, and dominated the remainder. We could have captured it with ease on the evening of the 20th, and continued the advance next day, but there was no infantry capable of this final effort. The tanks unsupported could not penetrate far into the gloomy wood, still less attempt to hold it; and after a while they withdrew.

The first day's battle, in fact, was now at an end. It was after four o'clock, and the November twilight was falling. In the eastern outskirts of Anneux and Masnières, our furthest points of penetration, street-fighting was still in progress; and at Flesquières, far behind, the stubborn garrison continued to resist, although almost completely surrounded; but all around this isolated conflict the routine tasks of consolidation and clearance and preparation for the morrow were already in full swing. The meagre infantry reserves—some three or four brigades,—masses of belated cavalry and endless columns of guns, were pushing forward through the dusk; and everywhere the tanks were rolling home to their rallying-points. Except for the unfortunate check at Flesquières, the day had been one series of startling triumphs. In ten hours three defence systems, believed to be all but impregnable, had fallen like things of buckram: an area of ground as large as the whole Ypres salient, containing a dozen villages and hamlets, had been overrun; and 7000 or 8000 prisoners, with upwards of 100 guns, already were in our hands. Great masses of material had been captured; quartermasters' stores, field post-offices, canteens, cinema theatres, hospitals—all these were among the miscellaneous acquisitions of that day. The surprise had been overwhelmingly complete, and the German infantry, with few exceptions, had been routed with an ease that had no precedent in the war, because the correct use of the determining factor had no precedent either. The panic spread far to the rear, for in Cambrai and beyond all was confusion and dismay.

These great results had been gained at a relatively trifling cost to ourselves; and it is impossible to reflect upon this beginning without deploring the inadequate resources which caused it, in the end, to remain no more than a brilliant but disappointing fragment. There is no need, however, to go into this subject again. We have seen already that there were no fresh reserves available, or none to speak of. Sir Julien Byng had in hand a few brigades of infantry, tired but hitherto not engaged, a couple of hundred tanks, whose stipulated work was more than accomplished, and whose crews and supplies alike were exhausted, and an entire cavalry corps which practically had done nothing at all. There should also perhaps be included the French troops on his right, and the divisions engaged in the subsidiary attack at Bullecourt, which had been highly successful; but none of these were in a position to reinforce him to a degree comparable to his opportunities. With another three or four divisions, instead of three or four brigades, behind his main battle front, there would have been some chance even of the optimistic schemes of exploitation being realised without any miracles by the cavalry. There were still thirty-six hours before the enemy could hope to collect his own reinforcements.

What, in the meantime, of the cavalry, who were to be galloping for the Sensée? The great proportion of these troops, whose talk (in Amiens or Boulogne) was always of speed and dash and initiative, and for whose benefit, that these qualities might be utilised, the special tanks had cleared wide passages in the wire, had arrived upon the field four hours late. Any one who has seen cavalry on the march trying to find their way anywhere by the use of a map will understand readily how this occurred; and it is probable that these laggards, even in such a *débâcle*, would very soon have ceased to be of use as mounted troops; but they could have fought very usefully on foot, as they were forced to do when they did arrive. One small unit, a squadron of the Canadian Fort Garry Horse, less pedantic or more skilled in map-reading than its regular colleagues, pushed early to the front, managed to cross the Canal de L'Escaut by an extemporised bridge, rushed the half-finished Beaurevoir-Masnières line on the slope beyond, and dispersed some infantry and captured a battery behind it. This quite exceptional feat may be held to prove that cavalry are still the great winners of battles that they were in the time of Turenne. It remains, however, an isolated performance; and the Canadians in the end met their inevitable fate. All their horses were killed or wounded, and they were reduced to fighting, like any infantrymen, behind the bank of a sunken road. Their gallantry, skill, and good fortune only served to emphasise the case of the numerous regular regiments who were unable to achieve anything at all.

It is necessary to descend now from the sublime to the ridiculous, and to consider briefly the condition of the nine tank battalions at the end of this first day's fighting, to the success of which they had mainly contributed. " By 4 P.M. on the 20th November," to quote 'Weekly Tank Notes,' "one of the most astonishing battles in all history had been won, and as far as the Tank Corps was concerned, tactically finished, for no reserves existing, it was not possible to do more than rally the now very weary and exhausted crews, select the fittest, and patch up composite companies to continue the attack on the morrow." I have pointed out before the actual physical exhaustion, due to extreme heat, cramped quarters, jolting, and other causes, entailed in any prolonged operation in a tank. Of the machines which rallied on the evening of November 20th nearly all had been running for at least sixteen hours. Some had covered distances undreamt of in any previous tank action. All were out of petrol, water, and ammunition, and many had mechanical troubles that needed attention. The crews to a man were dog-tired, but before they could think of rest every remediable want had to be satisfied. Petrol and water tanks must be refilled, expended ammunition replaced, and minor repairs effected. For the brigade and battalion staffs there was the task of calculating losses and effectives, and of arranging for the formation of composite companies for the continuation of the battle next day. There was not an additional man or tank to be had: all had been in action; and, as the quotation above points out, the battle of Cambrai tactically was at an end for the Tank Corps. It had done all and more than it had promised to do, but there remained the necessity of continuing to help the no less exhausted infantry to round off, if possible, the first day's victory. The losses in personnel had been considerable, and in tanks, from various causes, very serious. The 1st Brigade alone had nearly 40 tanks hit and disabled, mostly on the Flesquières ridge. It is doubtful if half of the original 378 fighting machines were now available, and for immediate use the proportion was far smaller. Nevertheless, early on the morning of the 21st, detachments from all three brigades were in action again. On the right, tanks of F Battalion moved out from Marcoing against the Beaurevoir-Masnières line, but the infantry, a fresh brigade unaccustomed to tanks, failed to co-operate, and the attack was a failure. Twenty-five tanks of B and H Battalions of the 2nd Brigade, with infantry of the 51st Division, rushed Cantaing, Noyelles, and Fontaine-Notre-Dame. Cantaing was carried by tanks alone, and handed over to the infantry by noon. Fontaine, which is virtually an outlying suburb of Cambrai, was occupied after severe fighting later in the day. In the meantime detachments from D and G completed the capture of Anneux, and carried a trench line to the north of it. Tanks once more pushed up the grass drives in Bourlon Wood, and once more had to return through lack of support. The wood was now occupied in force by the enemy, and was full of machine-guns. With the close of the day the original time limit of forty-eight hours expired; but the Commander-in-Chief, for reasons which he explains in his despatch, decided to allow the operation to continue. Great progress had been made, the enemy was badly shaken, and the situation in Italy, where the disaster of Caporetto had occurred, required further efforts to pin down the German reserves. Some additional divisions, including the Guards and two detailed for the Italian front, were at this late hour given to General Byng, and he was ordered to proceed with the attack. The 22nd, therefore, was spent mostly in reorganisation, and in preparing for a renewal of the battle. This involved a reshuffling of tank units among others. The centre of interest having shifted to Bourlon Ridge and its neighbourhood, the 3rd Tank Brigade was attached to the 3rd Corps, and proceeded to trek northward from Villers Plouich, where all available tanks had concentrated. Further evidence of the importance of the northern area was forthcoming in the afternoon, when the Germans, whose own reserves were coming up, drove the 51st Division out of Fontaine-Notre-Dame. Nearly 60 tanks of the 1st and 2nd Brigades were collected for the attack on the 23rd. A furious struggle took place in Fontaine, lasting throughout the day. Eight times the tanks of the 2nd Brigade pushed through the village under an intense hail of bullets and grenades from the upper stories of the houses. As soon as they withdrew, the infantry, who had followed, were driven out again, and at length were unable to give any support at all. Field-guns had been brought into the village, and 11 tanks were hit and left there when the assault finally was abandoned. The 1st Brigade, however, admirably followed by the 40th Division, succeeded at last in clearing Bourlon Wood and village, in spite of the fact that G Battalion's tanks were delayed till noon by bad traffic control holding up their supplies. There was very severe fighting in the wood and village, the tanks expending every round of 6-pdr. shell and most of their S.A.A. The village itself could not be held, but the great wood remained in our possession. Further to the west, about Moeuvres, on the Canal du Nord, progress was also made.

The Tank Corps was now fought virtually to a standstill. Rest and recuperation were imperative for officers, men, and machines, or for what was left. "On the 25th and 27th November further attacks were made by tanks and infantry on Bourlon and Fontaine-Notre-Dame with varying successes, but eventually both these villages remained in the hands of the enemy. During the attacks which had taken place since the 21st November, tank units had become terribly disorganised, and by the 27th had been reduced to such a state of exhaustion that it was determined to withdraw the 1st and 2nd Brigades. This withdrawal was nearing completion when the great German counter-attack was launched early on the morning of the 30th November. . . . It is an interesting point to remember that in this battle the attacking infantry were assisted by 690 officers and 3500 other ranks of the Tank Corps, a little over 4000 men or the strength of a strong brigade, and that these men replaced artillery wire-cutting, and rendered unnecessary the old preliminary bombardment. More than this, by keeping close to the infantry they effected a much higher co-operation than had ever before been attainable with artillery. When on the 21st November the bells of London pealed forth in celebration of the victory of Cambrai, consciously or unconsciously to their listeners they tolled out an old tactics and rang in a new—Cambrai had become the Valmy of a new epoch in war, the epoch of the mechanical engineer."[1]

[1] 'Weekly Tank Notes.'

Disabled Tank in Fontaine-Notre-Dame, November 1917.
(German Photo.)

G Battalion Tanks at the Shooting-Box, Bourlon Wood, November 1917.
(German Photo.)

IV.

On 30th November, as everybody knows, the Germans launched two tremendous attacks on the north and southeast flanks of the pronounced salient which we now held in front of Cambrai. On the north, from Bourlon to Moeuvres, where the main blow was delivered, it ended in a sanguinary repulse. Far away to the south at Gouzeaucourt, however, where the line was very attenuated in consequence of our preoccupation with the Bourlon area, a very serious breakdown occurred. Assisted by a great number of low-flying aeroplanes and preceded by a short but intense bombardment, the attack for a time carried everything before it. Villers-Guislain and Gonnelieu were carried at the first rush, and by 9 A.M. Gouzeaucourt itself, the Headquarters of the 29th Division, was captured. It was a repetition on a smaller scale of our surprise ten days before. Hospitals, stores, and dumps of every kind of material, together with a great number of guns, were lost in the first three or four hours, and the roads westward were choked with stragglers and escaping transport. The nearest Tank Brigade to the danger point was the 2nd, concentrated about Fins railhead. A Battalion had rejoined, and the whole brigade was preparing to entrain for Plateau station and the winter quarters at Bray. Rumours of the attack arrived early, but it was not until 9.55 that a telephone message came through from the 3rd Corps. Although all the machines were more or less dismantled and totally unfit for action, within three hours 36 from A and B Battalions were moving toward Gouzeaucourt, followed two hours later by a reserve of 20 from H Battalion. The Guards having recaptured Gouzeaucourt, the tanks patrolled beyond as a screen. On the following morning a composite detachment from A and B helped the dismounted troopers of the 5th Cavalry Division to clear Gauche Wood, but attempts on Villers-Guislain and Gonnelieu—the latter by the Guards and tanks from H

Battalion—were eventually held up. The tanks, however, did tremendous execution among the enemy, who was in great force, and this spirited rejoinder stopped effectively any further attempts by the Germans to advance. The rapidity with which these tank counter-attacks were organised and carried out with stripped and unready machines, and in circumstances of peculiar difficulty, was in itself highly creditable. It provided also decisive evidence on a point hitherto doubted by sceptics—the value of tanks in such an emergency.

As a result of the German surprise, the Cambrai Salient was contracted and Bourlon Wood abandoned. There was no further fighting for the Tank Corps. The 1st Brigade remained for a dreary fortnight in a defensive position at Dessart Wood, passing the nights in towing heavy guns back from Villers Plouich. The other two brigades had withdrawn to Bray, and the 1st followed to Meaulte in the latter half of December.

NOTE.—Two authoritative German comments on the battle of Cambrai show how fully the enemy realised that he had been saved from a great disaster by our lack of faith in tanks. Hindenburg, in his 'Memoirs,' writes as follows: "By neglecting to exploit a brilliant initial success they had let victory be snatched from them, and indeed by troops which were far inferior to their own both in numbers and quality. . . . Moreover, his High Command seemed to have failed to concentrate the resources required to secure the execution of their plans and their exploitation in case of success. Strong bodies of cavalry assembled behind the triumphant leading infantry divisions failed, even on this occasion, to overcome the last line of resistance, weak though it was, which barred the way to the flank and rear of their opponents. The English cavalry squadrons were not able to conquer the German defence, even with the help of their tanks, and proved unequal to decorating their standards with that victory for which they had striven so honourably and so often."

General Otto von Moser, commanding the 14th Reserve Corps during the battle, points out that the British "failed because they luckily had not the dozen or two dozen divisions at hand to exploit the undeniable success of the 20th November."

CHAPTER XIV.

MISCELLANEOUS. THE GERMANS AND THE TANK:
THE FRENCH ARTILLERIE D'ASSAUT.

I.

THE battle of Cambrai having converted not only ourselves but also the enemy to a belief in the tactical and moral value of the new arm, it will be convenient at this point to deal with the German attitude toward tanks and the measures adopted to cope with the latter.

It often is assumed that the German conversion was yet more grudging than our own; that until Cambrai they refused to admit that tanks had any value whatever; and that even after that battle they remained for some time very sceptical about the new doctrines. But I think these are only half-truths. I think the Germans realised far sooner than we did the moral influence of the attack by armour, while failing perhaps to appreciate until it was too late the complete tactical revolution it was bringing about. In the end they became more bigoted converts than any British soldier outside the Tank Corps itself. I spent six months with the Army of Occupation in Cologne, and I found everywhere the same bitter feelings about tanks. "Deutsches' Tod" they were called—the Death of Germany. In private conversation, as well as in public print, they were coupled with the blockade as one of the two chief factors in the downfall of the country. With that extraordinary but quite sincere inability to understand any point of view but their own, the authors of the Belgian atrocities, the inventors of chlorine gas, the first people to poison wells, one and all are inclined to regard the use of tanks as a brutal and unjustifiable measure, worthy only of savages. A nation so illogical should be capable, through sheer thick-headedness, of going very far.

The early appreciation by the Germans of the moral effect of tanks is manifest in their repeated efforts to belittle them. The brave Michael was always being assured in published orders that these machines were worse than useless. "The infantry must not let itself be frightened by tanks. The fighting capacity of the tank is small owing to the bad visibility, and the shooting powers of the machine-guns and guns cramped and inaccurate as the result of the motion. It has been proved that tank crews are nervous and are inclined to turn back or leave the tank. . . . The hostile infantry follows tanks only half-heartedly. . . ." (Order issued to the 7th Cavalry Division, 26th September 1917.) The Mark II. tanks captured at Arras, and the Mark IV.'s left behind after the Cambrai withdrawal, were used to demonstrate the inherent weaknesses of the invention and the extreme discomfort endured by the crews. It was found, however, that with all this the Higher Command was unable to infect the German soldier with its own lofty contempt for tanks. The brave Michael persisted in his delusions, and was so wrong-headed even as to ask why the enemy was allowed a monopoly of these engines of war. It must be remembered that by the autumn of 1917 the French St Chamond and Schneider machines had been used in some numbers and with considerable success in Champagne, so that the German infantryman saw himself threatened everywhere by the new weapon; and he knew perfectly well that as an individual he was entirely helpless against it, whatever might be the general outcome of a battle in which it was employed. He could not acquire the detached outlook of the Great General Staff at Spa. And it was in consequence of this feeling in the subordinate ranks that, before the battle of Cambrai, the Great General Staff stultified all its own published convictions by authorising the construction of German tanks. There can be no doubt that this measure, half-hearted as it was, arose out of some sort of pressure from below. The Higher Command was still unconvinced, but it was necessary for the encouragement of the less intelligent to make a pretence of conversion. A good deal of talk, a little work, and the eventual appearance of a few German tanks behind the line would counteract these mischievous apprehensions —or so it was hoped.

The German Tank Corps bore all the marks of an indifferent, if not inimical parentage. In the beginning it was quite a small affair, and any subsequent attempts to enlarge it to adequate proportions came too late or were hampered by lack of means. An official German document states that only 15 machines were ever completed. Ten more apparently were under order in the autumn of 1918, by which date 25 captured British Mark IV. tanks had also been included in the new unit. The total of effectives (40) was divided into eight sections—or, as the Germans happily named them, *Sturmpanzerkraftwagenabteilungen*. (One would think this mouthful alone sufficient to deter recruits.) There were three sections of German tanks and five of British, each section consisting of five machines. An M.T. Testing Company stationed near Berlin instructed the crews and tested all tanks before issue.

The original German *Panzerkraftwagen* was a clumsy machine, based, it is said, on stolen drawings of the French St Chamond type. It weighed approximately 40 tons, was 24 feet long, 11 feet high, and 10 feet 6 inches wide. On good ground it could travel for a short distance at a speed of 8-10 miles an hour. It was propelled by two 100-h.p. German Daimler engines, each driving a single track, which permitted of a one-man control, as in our Mark V.'s. The interior was divided into front and rear compartments joined by narrow gangways on either side of the central engine casing. In front were one 5.7-c.m. Q.F. gun (equivalent to our 6-pounder) and two heavy machine-guns, and in the rear four more machine-guns. The crew consisted of an officer and no fewer than fifteen or sixteen men, who must have crowded the narrow quarters intolerably; and as three branches of the service—artillery, infantry, and technical —were represented, each ignorant of the other's duties, there was much friction between them. The tank was heavily armoured, especially in front, where the plating was $1\frac{3}{16}$ inches in thickness, and would keep out common shell from a field-gun at a moderate range; but the roof was very thin, and the whole machine was so roughly put together that wide crevices around the gun-ports made it unpleasantly vulnerable to the splash from machine-gun bullets. There was room in places for the bullets themselves to enter. Being built on the ordinary tractor principle, with a very low clearance from the ground and a long flat tread, the tank could neither cross a considerable trench nor surmount any serious obstacle. There was no unditching apparatus. The only improvement on our design was the sprung track, which reduced wear and shock, and in so ponderous a machine was a notable innovation. Observation was exceptionally bad. The officer and driver sat above the engine, their heads and shoulders in a central cab which rose two feet above the roof, and as the latter projected forward for ten feet, it hid from them all the ground immediately in front.

In every respect, in fact, excepting the sprung tracks, the *Panzerkraftwagen* was clumsy and inefficient to a degree. Notwithstanding its one-man control, the officers of the new unit preferred to handle the British Mark IV.'s, even during trials on level ground; and for all practical purposes there was no comparison between the two in general utility and handiness. And while the machine itself was mistrusted, and with justice, another and unforeseen difficulty was soon apparent. The higher command had talked more cleverly than it knew. It had belittled all tanks so persistently, had made so strong an argument out of the perils and discomforts of all tank warfare, that the brave

German Tank, "Adalbert." (German Photo.)

French Heavy Schneider Tank, carrying .75 field-gun. (German Photo.)

Michael, now that he had his own engine of destruction, showed no enthusiasm for using it. The German tank crews, in fact, were thoroughly afraid of their Frankensteins; and their rare appearances in action were marked almost uniformly by that discretion which seemed naturally to them by far the better part of valour. In some cases they ditched their machines deliberately before any further harm could overtake them. Only at Villers-Brettonneux did the German-made tanks achieve any success—the counter-attack at Niergnies six months later was carried out by captured British Mark IV.'s.

II.

German anti-tank measures in the early days followed obvious lines, such as the use of armour-piercing bullets and direct field-artillery fire. There was also employed on a few occasions a 1-pounder automatic gun of the "Pom-pom" type. One of these weapons was found in Kitchener's Wood, in the Salient. It is possible that the wider Hindenburg trenches were constructed with a view to discomfiting tanks. The battle of Cambrai, however, besides demonstrating what tanks could accomplish in a general way, given good conditions, demolished also the Hindenburg fetish, and the shock of this discovery produced a crop of reports and suggestions on the subject. Units were asked for statements as to their experiences in the battle. One division (believed to be the 119th, holding the Fontaine-Notre-Dame sector from the 23rd November onwards) reported as follows:—

"The division came into the Cambrai battle on the 22nd November, and since that date has fought on several occasions, and always successfully, against British tanks. Its experiences are borne out by the statements of several British tank crews, including the captain of a company of tanks."

These prisoners, by the way, appear to have been unnecessarily communicative. The report, after describing the method of attack and the size and armament of tanks, continues:—

"German defence and defensive measures were weak. Losses on both sides scarcely worth mentioning. . . . Pace (of tanks) three or four miles per hour. They may surmount practically all obstacles. One tank in Fontaine climbed up a steep orchard, broke the trees, crossed two well-built 5-feet high garden-walls, and, in turning, knocked down the corner of a house. . . . Serious obstacles are constituted by trenches at least 13-16 feet wide and 10 feet deep. Also by marshy ground. Ploughed land is easily negotiated; also barricades. *The building of obstacles does not pay. It is better to attack tanks energetically.* . . . Tanks must be heavily fired at (by artillery) during their advance, even if there is no likelihood of hitting them. The main thing is to prevent the infantry from following the tanks. The infantry must be made to fear the area where the tanks are. In point of fact, the British infantry was soon one to two miles behind the tanks, and at Fontaine did not follow them at all."

This is an interesting confirmation of a point already referred to. The report goes on to remark that—

". . . as actual anti-tank defence, only special guns situated in the forward zone, which put the tanks out of action by fire over open sights, are suitable. Each direct hit kills part of the crew, and often sets the tank on fire. Detachments situated further to the rear have no knowledge of the situation, and often arrive too late.

"Such guns must, on principle, be situated well forward; then the enemy will not succeed in a surprise attack.

"The O. i/c Defence Troops must be made responsible for the siting of the anti-tank guns.

"Guns mounted on lorries do excellent work if the roads are good.

"*Infantry.* The front line must only make a gap to let through tanks not put out of action, and take cover; they must not retire. Tanks must be dealt with *behind* the front. The chief object is the *repulse of the enemy infantry.* The tank captain said, '*Tanks can gain ground, but can never hold it alone.*' This is a great point to remember when discussing them.

"Isolated commands in rear should be detailed for anti-tank defence.

"*Means of Defence.* The chief one is the armour-piercing bullet. It is feared by the tank crews because it goes clean through the armour-plating, causing a long flame, and often setting fire to the petrol-tank.

"The tank is best attacked from the rear. House-to-house fighting against tanks is very favourable to infantry. The men take cover in the houses, let the tank pass, and then fire at it from the rear at close range with rifles and M.G.'s.

"The 46th I.R. accounted for four tanks in Fontaine in this way.

"*Hand Grenades.* Are useless singly; they only have effect if several are tied together and thrown under the tank, but this is very difficult.

"*T.M.'s.* Light T.M.'s can be made effective with flat trajectory fire. Used singly they have good results.

"Anti-tank defence must be discussed and practised, when the tanks lose their terror. Men fought for four hours violently against eight tanks which penetrated into Fontaine, and of which only two were able to return (four were accounted for by infantry and two by artillery); moreover, eleven derelict tanks are lying just outside our lines.

"MULLER-LOEBNITZ, Maj.,
for C.G.S."[1]

[1] 'Tank Corps Intelligence Summary.'

It will be seen that the Germans continued to magnify the powers of the armour-piercing bullets—a curious error, as the captured tanks must have shown its comparative inefficacy against the plating on the Mark IV.'s. Probably the captured personnel exaggerated the effect of splinters and the ordinary bullet splash round the gun-ports. It is interesting also to note the remarks about the petrol tank. This was always considered by the enemy to be the tank's weak spot, although in fact no more vulnerable in itself than any other.

Soon after Cambrai the Germans were devoting their whole energies to preparations for their own great offensive, which was launched in the following spring, and defensive measures of all kinds were secondary considerations for the time being. But when the three successive blows on the Somme, the Lys, and the Aisne had come at length to an end, and were countered, with startling rapidity and effect, by the French and British attacks on 18th July and 8th August 1918, the enemy was aroused very roughly to a realisation of his peril and of the power of the weapon he had affected to despise. The 8th August, in particular, was entirely a tank victory—a greater and more brilliant Cambrai; and the astonishing collapse of the defence threw the Great General Staff into a panic from which it never was allowed to recover. From this date to the end a persistent refrain, rising at length to a frantic crescendo of warning and exhortation, runs through all the orders issued to the German armies, and the burden of it is tanks, tanks, and again tanks.

A few extracts, taken at random, from captured German orders, prisoners' statements, and similar channels of information, will show very clearly the disillusionment and alarm which spread through the armies after the rout of Von Hutier and Von der Marwitz in front of Amiens. During the Arras operations at the end of August, for example, documents were secured which showed that divisional anti-tank officers had been created. A similar regimental appointment was recommended. The divisional anti-tank officer was not to be employed for any other purpose, and was to be given the utmost assistance by all ranks and units. Further, a G.H.Q. Routine Order laid down that officers and other ranks who had done good work in repelling tanks were to be mentioned in Army Orders, and that specially meritorious acts were to be rewarded by decorations. About the same time an order was issued from the headquarters of the Crown Prince's group of armies which ran as follows:—

> "According to reports received from G.H.Q. during the recent fighting on the Second and Eighteenth Army fronts, large numbers of tanks broke through on narrow fronts, and, pushing straight forward, immediately attacked the battery positions and headquarters of divisions. In many places no defence could be made in time owing to the fact that batteries which had their guns dug in were insufficiently mobile and were only ready to open fire too late to defend themselves against the tanks, which attacked them from all sides. Anti-tank defence must be developed on the lines of those experiences." [1]

Among prisoners' statements, again, we find that various N.C.O.'s all agreed that "tanks always create a moral effect on infantry, however often they have seen tanks, or have been told by officers that they will be quite safe if they take cover and let the tanks pass on. *It is recognised that infantry can do nothing against tanks.*" [2] On 25th August the 38th German Division was adjured to pull itself together and show a better front to tank attacks. "The troops themselves will await a tank attack with calmness. The first essential for the infantry is that they should keep their heads." A month later we find General Von Wrisberg endeavouring to encourage the civilians at home. Speaking for the Minister of War in the Reichstag, he remarked, "the American armies also should not terrify us. We shall

[1] 'Tank Corps Intelligence Summary.'   [2] Ibid.

also settle with them. More momentous for us is the question of tanks. We are adequately armed against them. Anti-tank defence is nowadays more a question of nerves than of material." Soon after General Von Wrisberg had spoken, the second battle of Cambrai began. The tanks once more proved too much for the nerves of the German infantry, and prisoners provided the usual illuminating confirmation of this. It appeared that in spite of all exhortations "the German infantry still considers that as soon as the tanks have broken through their line, further resistance is useless. . . . The officers gave as their opinion that tanks were a 'brilliant invention,' and wished that the Germans had more of them. Lack of material, however, stood in the way. . . . A number of intelligent N.C.O.'s (Sergeant-Majors and Sergeants) . . . stated that tanks invariably had a considerable moral effect on infantry, however often they might be told that they had only to let them through and the artillery would deal with them."[1] In the same month a German Corps Order lays down that "*Messages concerning tanks have preference over all other telephone calls, including messages regarding aeroplanes.*"[2]

For some time past Ludendorff had been growing more and more concerned over this new warfare. In a report on the battle of 8th August, he gave as the first reason for the defeat, "the fact that the troops were surprised by the massed attack of tanks, and lost their heads when the tanks suddenly appeared behind them under cover of natural and artificial fog." This, of course, was no more than the truth; but it was a novel confession for the Great General Staff to make, and indicated the grave apprehensions which the disaster had aroused, for there could be no guarantee against the troops losing their heads a second time, or a third. "Nerves" play an increasing part in official German cajolings and extenuations from now to the end, but this obnoxious and unsoldier-like word was never used before the tanks caused it to become a normal feature in every

[1] 'Intelligence Summary.'   [2] Ibid.

apologia. Ludendorff, once awake to the new danger, took vigorous although quite useless steps to combat it by practical measures in the field. These we will consider next, but before concluding this sketchy selection of documentary evidence, one final and authoritative witness remains to be heard—the Great General Staff itself. A short time ago, Colonel Bauer, who had been head of the Artillery Department at headquarters, and who is credited by German public opinion with having been the special confidant and political inspirer of Ludendorff, issued a pamphlet professing to give the General Staff's version of the events which led up to the Armistice. Throughout September and October, it appears, Ludendorff made repeated demands for peace while the armies were still intact, pointing out that it was necessary to reckon on an increasing deterioration of the military situation. At the end of September Von Hindenburg agreed to lay before the new Government just formed under Prince Max of Baden a true statement of affairs. On 2nd October the representatives from General Headquarters met the party leaders of the Reichstag, and presented to them the report. It began with this striking passage:—

"The chief army command has been compelled to take a terribly grave decision, and declare that, according to human probabilities, there is no longer any prospect of forcing peace on the enemy. Above all, two facts have been decisive for this issue. First, the tanks. The enemy has employed them in unexpectedly large numbers. Where, after a very liberal clouding of our positions with artificial mist, they effected a surprise, our men's nerves were often unequal to them. Here they broke through our first line, opened a way for their infantry, appeared in the rear, created local panics, and threw the control of the fighting into confusion. When they had once been identified our tank defence weapons and our artillery quickly settled with them. Then, however, the misfortune had already happened, and solely the successes of the tanks explain the large numbers of prisoners which so painfully reduced our strengths, and brought about a more rapid consumption of reserves than we had hitherto been accustomed to.

" We were not in a position to oppose to the enemy equal masses of German tanks. Their construction would have exceeded the resources of our industry, which was strained to the uttermost, or other more important things would have had to be neglected."—'Daily Telegraph,' 21st July 1919.[1]

This confession, coming from such a quarter, needs little comment. It seems to justify all the arguments by which I have tried to show how tanks, when at length properly employed, determined not only the duration, but also to a large extent the actual result, of the war. Yet, as I write, there appears to be every probability that no tank corps will be included in the post-bellum army! The cavalry, useless and inefficient, is of course to remain at full strength; infantry and artillery are to be cut down to a minimum to provide money for ameliorating the lives of coal miners; and the Tank Corps, as an unnecessary extravagance, is in danger of total abolition. Truly we are a remarkable people.

III.

After the 8th August the Germans began feverishly to devise anti-tank measures of every kind. It is doubtful if the immense fronts which modern armies occupy can ever be protected satisfactorily by artificial means against whole-hearted tank attacks; and in any case the Germans were allowed no time to perfect such stationary defences. Field artillery remained to the end the best anti-tank weapon. Special guns were now brought forward near the front line, to remain silent until the moment of attack, when they

---

[1] Also quoted by General Maurice, 'The Last Four Months.'

were to concentrate on tanks. Our barrage, however, usually accounted for most of these advanced pieces before they could do much harm, while the remainder were overrun by the tanks in the first rush, which always took place at dawn. More dangerous were reserve guns which moved up to selected positions further back as soon as the attack started. "Finally, all German batteries, including howitzers, had general instructions to plan their positions in such a way that advancing tanks would be subject to a direct fire at about 500 or 600 yards' range. In the event of a tank attack the engagement of our machines was now to be the first call upon the artillery, to the exclusion of counter-battery or any other work."[1]

The only novel weapon of offence introduced was the anti-tank rifle. This was a huge affair, 5½ feet long, and provided with biped legs and an ordinary wooden stock. It fired armour-piercing bullets of .530 calibre and had no magazine. "It was obviously too conspicuous and too slow a weapon to be really effective against tanks, though the steel core could penetrate the armour of British tanks at several hundred yards' range. The chief disadvantage of the anti-tank rifle, however, was that the German soldier would not use it. He was untrained in its use, afraid of its kick, and still more afraid of the tanks themselves. It is doubtful if more than one per cent of the A.T. rifles captured in our tank attacks had ever been fired."[2]

A great variety of fixed obstructions were set up in village streets, on roads, and at other suitable points. None of these gave us any serious trouble. Usually they could be avoided. The road obstacles, in fact, comprising craters, barricades of carts filled with bricks, and concrete blocks, allowing only a narrow passage which could be closed with railway iron, seem primarily to have been intended to hold up whippets and armoured cars. Land mines, on the other hand, which were used rather extensively, while generally

---

[1] 'The Tank Corps' (Williams-Ellis).
[2] 'Weekly Tank Notes.'

ineffective, served to impose caution on any tank commander who knew of, or suspected, their existence. They generally took the form of high-explosive shells with light fuses, buried in rows a few inches below the surface of a road or across some other likely defile, and fitted with a simple wooden device which the weight of a tank pressed down upon the nose-cap, so detonating the fuse. One or two large mine-fields were laid, in which a more elaborate apparatus was used. Oddly enough, it was one of our own mine-fields, prepared before the March retreat and afterwards forgotten, which caused the only serious disaster tanks ever suffered from this form of defence.

Two more unusual types of obstacle came within my own experience. Along the valley which runs between the first and second Hindenburg Lines from Pronville to Inchy-en-Artois, on the Canal du Nord, was the dried-up bed of a stream called the Hirondelle. Its banks were lined with stout willows, and where the gaps between these were wide enough for a tank to pass through, the Germans had planted lengths of railway line, upright but inclining forward, the ends embedded in concrete blocks sunk in the ground. As this part of the line was taken in reverse by the capture of Quéant, tanks had no opportunity of testing this obstacle. I think the rails would have been pushed over with ease, but the process might have held up the tanks for a few dangerous minutes in full view of the second Hindenburg Line. In the main street of Inchy itself were two massive blocks of concrete 6 feet high, with the usual narrow passage between, and each furnished with half a dozen of these inclined iron rails, which rose to the house-tops. This barricade would have stopped any tank. More interesting than this defence scheme, however, was the elaborate but unfinished stockade at Achiet-le-Grand. The Arras-Bapaume railway curves across most of this region on a high embankment. This in itself was not generally unsurmountable, but tanks in the act of climbing over it would stand out as magnificent targets for the German batteries, which then were posted on the other side. At one point, just north of Achiet-le-Grand station, a rise of ground caused the embankment to fall away to nothing for two or three hundred yards, and attacking tanks, it was thought, naturally would make for this crossing. In front of it, therefore, parallel to the line, the Germans began a really formidable anti-tank stockade. It was made of lengths of railway line and stout telegraph poles, three rails or two poles being lashed together, fixed in cement bases, and buried in the ground, above which they rose to a height of 4 feet. Inclining forward, these stakes were planted 7 feet apart in several rows, each row covering the spaces of the one in front. It was found that tanks could force a passage through this *abattis* only by approaching it obliquely and crushing down one row of stakes at a time, a slow process which would have exposed them helplessly to the batteries close beyond. In the attack on this position on 21st August 1918, when a great number of tanks were knocked out along the railway, the stockade was not attempted. There was a similar form of obstacle on the Bapaume-Cambrai road, and there may have been others.

Taken as a whole, these various artificial impediments inevitably proved a failure. There was no time for the Germans to cover every vulnerable point in such a fashion, and isolated obstacles were useless against a tank attack on a wide front. In any case, the principle of passive defence was bound to be fatal in the end; and the Germans, realising this, were at work when the war finished upon an instrument which they hoped would replace all these makeshifts. This instrument was the "Tuf" or *Tank und Flieger* machine-gun, a huge Maxim firing armour-piercing bullets of 13 mm. diameter. This formidable weapon must have been deadly against our Mark IV.'s and V.'s, for its stream of heavy bullets would have gone clean through the armour. Profound importance was attached to its speedy production, in which sixty factories were engaged, and it was given priority over submarines and aeroplanes (another testimony to the German fear of tanks). Major Williams-Ellis, in 'The Tank Corps,' gives the following interesting details of the fate of this invention:—

"No less than 6000 of these guns were to be in the field by April 1919, and delivery was to begin early in the previous December—just a month too late. However, when the armistice was signed the firms were already in possession of the greater part of the stores and raw material for the manufacture of the guns, a quantity of which were by then well on the way to completion. Immediately after the signing of the armistice all the factories, without exception, were instructed by telephone to continue manufacturing the 'Tuf,' and about 20th November they received confirmation in writing of this order, and were instructed to keep on their workmen at all costs. Our occupation of the left bank of the Rhine proved a serious drawback to a continuation of the manufacture, as it completely interrupted communication between several of the factories. The Piaff Works of Kaiserslautern (Palatinate), and the great Becker Steel Works of Crefeld, which played an important part in the manufacture of the guns, had to close down, both being on the left bank of the Rhine.

"The Minister of War, throughout the period of its manufacture, asked for daily and minute reports as to the progress of the 'Tuf.' But once more, as ever in all that concerned tanks, the Germans were several months too late. We were never destined to face this particular weapon with the Mark V. The modern tank fears it not at all."

IV.

It may seem ill-mannered to relegate an account of the French Tank Corps to the tail-end of a discursive chapter devoted mainly to the Germans and their doings. But the subject of the *Artillerie d'Assaut*, if treated adequately, would require a book to itself, and is, in fact, outside the scope of this narrative. Considerations of space, already becoming urgent, would alone forbid any detailed history. I wish merely to outline very briefly here the inception and growth of the new arm in the French service.

The French tank was evolved independently of our own. Its author may be said to have been Colonel Estienne, of the Artillery. This officer, observing in 1915 the Holt tractors used by the British Army, was inspired by the same idea which Colonel Swinton and his colleagues already were perfecting in England. At the end of the year Colonel Estienne put his views before General Joffre. After an interview with the latter, he approached the Schneider Engineering Company on the subject, and drew up with them the design of the machine he had in mind. In February 1916, Schneiders received a definite order to construct 400 machines, and a little later a second firm was told to build another 400 of a heavier type. These last were the St Chamond tanks, driven by petrol-electric motors. An instructional ground was established at Marly-le-Roi, and Colonel Estienne was recalled from Verdun to command the new unit.

The design of these French tanks differed in an important feature from our own. It is better, perhaps, to say that they remained in a more primitive stage of evolution. The idea of the wheel, and the subsequent modification which produced the unique shape and capabilities of the British tank, does not seem to have occurred to the constructors of the Schneiders and St Chamonds. Both these types were modelled on the ordinary tractor, and in consequence worked under severe limitations. Obstacles that were negligible to a British tank they found impassable. On the other hand, they carried a far heavier gun than our machines, the 75 mm. field-piece of famous memory. In appearance they were small editions of the German copy, the *Panzerkraftwagens*. Their light weapon was the Hotchkiss automatic rifle, carried on our Whippets and Mark V.'s.

Ten companies, of 16 tanks each, were formed in April 1917, one company only consisting of St Chamonds. In various actions during the year, the Schneiders did excellent work, but the St Chamonds proved to be a failure. In the meantime, still working on very similar lines to our own, Colonel Estienne was evolving an idea for a light tank. The result was the remarkable little Rénault machine, of which no fewer than 3500 were ordered in June 1917. If we had designed the better heavy tank, the French made a leap ahead with the Rénault; and it is highly interesting to see how national habits of thought appear manifestly in this connection. Our bias, in any sort of constructional work, leans towards the heavy, durable, and expensive article. We have a horror of anything cheap and fragile. This inclination, together with the ingenious design of the large tank, worked for good in the case of the latter; but when we came to build what we called light machines, our limitations were very apparent. The Whippet was nearly as conspicuous and as costly as the Mark IV. or V., was far more vulnerable and intricate, was incapable of surmounting any serious obstacle, and possessed only one merit—superior speed. It was absurd to describe it as a light tank.[1] Colonel Estienne and his colleagues, on the other hand, determined to produce a

---

[1] The Whippet was nearly as long as the heavy tank. The engine was in front, under an armoured bonnet. A small cab perched in rear held three men and two Hotchkiss machine-guns. The speed of the Whippet was seven miles an hour.

little, simple, inconspicuous machine which could be
manufactured rapidly at a small cost, and which was to be
capable of performing, under modern conditions, the task
of the French *Fantassin*, or skirmisher. The Rénaults, in
fact, were to be used in clouds in front of the infantry, like
armoured light troops. If 20, or 50, or 100 were destroyed,
they could easily be replaced. They were not expected to
cross wide trenches or climb vertical obstacles; this was the
preliminary task of the heavy tank. While the Whippet
was a weak compromise between the two types, the
Rénault was definitely limited in its functions. It was
experimental in the sense that all tanks during the war
were experimental. There was no time in which to play
about with various designs, and in consequence the accepted model had many faults, but it was a strikingly
successful experiment on novel lines. In appearance, with
its hunched-up shoulders topped by a bell-shaped cupola,
and its curving iron tail introduced to prevent it from turning on its back, it looked like some fabulous cross between
a grasshopper and a scorpion. Compared with all previous
tanks it was ridiculously small—a mere toy, even, beside a
Whippet. It carried two men, a driver who sat on the
floor, and a gunner who swung half-upright behind him in
a sort of leather sling and fired a Hotchkiss from the cupola,
which revolved. It had a Rénault engine of only 17 h.p.,
narrow sprung tracks, passing over a big idle wheel in
front and a small driving sprocket behind, and could travel
on good ground at a speed of six to seven miles an hour.
It was extraordinarily handy, and by means of two levers
which threw the tracks out of gear it could be spun about
like a top. Owing, however, to its light weight and springy
motion, it must have been extremely awkward to aim from
while on the move.

    Astonishing rapidity of production was one of the chief
merits of the Rénault. After the victorious counter-stroke
against the Chateau-Thierry Salient, in which these little

machines played a decisive part, whole battalions, each of 75 tanks, became available at the rate of one a week! This permitted of tired units being replaced speedily by fresh ones. The French Tank Corps was established on the normal continental infantry basis, in regiments of three battalions; and it was proposed to form, in addition to the regiments of Schneider and St Chamond heavies, thirty battalions (ten regiments) of Rénaults. By August 1918 the personnel of the Corps numbered already 14,600 of all ranks. During 1918, 3988 individual tank engagements were fought, to which number the diminutive Rénaults contributed 3140.

It is impossible here to give details of any of these tank actions. What is called the Battle of Soissons—the brilliant series of operations from 18th July onward which inaugurated the combined allied offensive—was the Cambrai of the French Tank Corps. After that date tanks were employed wherever possible, not only on the main front, but at St Mihiel and even in Flanders, where the 6th French Army was sent to strengthen General Plumer and the Belgians; and a company of Rénaults went as far afield as Salonika. "Finally," to quote 'Weekly Tank Notes,' "it may be stated that as there can be no doubt that the 18th July was the second greatest turning-point in the war, the first being the Battle of the Marne in 1914, so can there be no doubt that the Battle of Soissons would never have been won had not the French possessed a powerful force of tanks whereby to initiate success. The German General Staff, which should be the best judge of this question, candidly admit that the French victory was due to the use of 'masses of tanks'; neither was the General Commanding-in-Chief of the French Armies reticent, for on the 30th July he issued the following special order of the day to the French Tank Corps—

'*Vouz avez bien merité de la Patrie,*'

whilst General Estienne, to whom so much was due, received the Cravat of the Legion d'Honneur and was promoted to the rank of General of Division for the great services he had rendered to his country."

In England, it seems, we do not know how to do these things—or at least to whom to do them.

CHAPTER XV.

THE GERMAN OFFENSIVE. MEAULTE, BOUVIGNY, AND BÉTHUNE.

I.

A FURTHER expansion of the Tank Corps, as indicated already, was the natural result of the Battle of Cambrai. The rejected proposal for an 18-battalion establishment was now almost obsequiously adopted. A little later, indeed, the War Office (dragging with it a reluctant Treasury) rushed recklessly in where it had feared to tread before, and sanctioned a still larger increase. Before all this had happened, however, an outward and visible sign had testified to the dawn of a new era. The tanks were formally manumitted from the paper control of the Machine Gun Corps, and became in name what they had always been in fact, a separate organisation. For reasons of simplicity and common-sense I have written throughout of the "Tank Corps," where a pedantic conscience would have impelled me to speak of the H.B.M.G.C., for this change of nomenclature, with all that it implied, was not in force until late in 1917.

Two new tank brigades, the 4th and 5th, were now to be formed immediately in France. Pending the completion of these arrangements, as well as of those for the disposal of the various units in the coming year, the three old brigades, or what was left of them, were concentrated for the winter between Albert and Bray, on the edge of the

Somme battlefield. There was much to be done before any of the battalions would be fit for another offensive battle, and it was suspected already that defensive rather than offensive measures would be our portion for the next few months. In the meantime, Tank Corps Headquarters, faced with the dazzling prospect of a great and possibly indefinite expansion, made a simple calculation and found that it was in danger of exhausting the resources of the alphabet. Eighteen battalions, denominated alphabetically, would leave only eight letters for future emergencies; while to continue the illogical practice of numbering the companies consecutively throughout a growing corps promised in the end a surfeit of figures as well. And so another revolutionary translation came about. Letters and figures changed places. Our old battalion designations, which had acquired a sentimental significance, were abolished at a stroke, so that A Battalion, Tank Corps, became the 1st Tank Battalion, and, what was more harrowing, G became the 7th. This reform, however necessary, was painful to the victims. It might mean nothing to the new battalions forming in England, but we, in France, felt that we had lost our individuality. It was as if the law, without obtaining my consent, had decreed that I was to be called Smith or Jones. The old names, however, are not dead. In any gathering of officers or men from the first three brigades, you will find the battalions still spoken of as A or B, F or G, and so on, as the case may be.

At the same time that this nominal change took place, the numerical order of companies was abolished also. The three companies of a battalion were known in future as A, B, and C.

I have explained how I came to be absent at Cambrai. Just before Christmas I was released from convalescent quarters (cynically so-called) at Barly, near Avesnes-le-Comte, where I had been living with other unfortunates in the coldest château in France—an outwardly imposing but actually gimcrack house like "Hardwick Hall, more glass than wall," and short of coal into the bargain. With some difficulty (for R.T.O.'s and other dignitaries whose business it was to know such things invariably were ignorant of the whereabouts of tank units) I ran the 1st Brigade to earth in a camp of huts outside Meaulte, two miles from Albert. I will not dilate upon the arctic winter we spent at this unholy spot, beyond remarking that the camp, like all similar military establishments, was built on the bleak northern slope of a hill. There was no intervening shelter, so far as I could judge, between us and the North Pole. We contrived, however, to exist cheerfully, and indeed for a fortnight after Christmas almost too cheerfully. The celebrations common to that season and to the New Year were involved with others consequent upon the announcement of the Cambrai honours, and the promotions and partings brought about by the expansion of the corps. These last affected the 7th Battalion—as I hate to call it—very materially. Colonel Hankey, to every one's profound regret (a feeling not so common as the conventional accounts of such departures might lead the unsophisticated to suppose), left us to take over the new 4th Brigade, carrying with him several others. Major Fernie became Battalion Commander, and was succeeded in A (late 19) Company by Winters. Major Broome left C Company to command another battalion. There were a number of minor promotions, due to these changes and to casualties; and Henriquez, of A Compaay, having become battalion reconnaissance officer, his vacant post as company R.O. was offered to me. The work had always appealed to me, and I was the more pleased with the opportunity at the time because I believed then that most of my old friends in C Company were leaving the battalion for more exalted posts elsewhere.

Few incidents worth recording marked our stay at Meaulte. Heavy snow fell, which added, in my opinion, to the general discomfort, and the road up to the camp remained for weeks a corrugated and painful slope of ice, down which one slid helplessly into the village. Fuel, in more senses than one, was always a burning question, and next in importance came that of leave, now six or seven months overdue. A driving school, supplied with the few fit tanks the three battalions could muster, was started at Bécordel, on the old front line near Mametz. Drafts of officers and men came from the depôt to replace casualties. And in January began the reshuffling of units necessitated by the formation of two new brigades. Of the old 1st Brigade the 7th Battalion only was left. The 4th and 5th (late D and E) went to join the 1st Battalion in the new 4th Brigade, under General Hankey, as he was now, and in their place we received, with hot rum-punch and such other amenities as the arctic conditions indicated, two fledglings from England—the 11th and 12th (K and L) Battalions. The former suffered from a surfeit of Rifle Brigade officers, was rent always in consequence by internal dissensions, and, thus handicapped, struggled rather obscurely through its short active career. The 12th Battalion, to which I was posted shortly before the Armistice, was more normal and human; and, after a series of successful actions, wound up in a blaze of glory as the only one of the five surviving tank units selected to represent the corps in Cologne itself.

In February, amid half-incredulous rejoicings, the first leave allotments reached the 7th Battalion. I came to England in the middle of the month, returning in the first days of March to find our huts stripped and deserted, a rear party packing up a residue of stores and kit, and the main body of the battalion, with all the tanks, already departed northward for the 1st Army area. I followed by lorry the same afternoon. This was the last I saw of Meaulte, which then was full of inhabitants and little injured by war. A month later it was in ruins and occupied by the Germans.

II.

It was known by now that a German offensive on a large scale was imminent, and might be directed at any one point, or at several simultaneously, on the long front from Béthune to the Aisne. The move northward of the 1st Tank Brigade was part of a defensive scheme for the protection of the Bruay coal-fields, should the enemy make a direct attack upon them from the Lens-La Bassée sector. The front allotted to the Brigade extended from the La Bassée Canal to the Scarpe, and was divided into three parts — one to each battalion. These battalion fronts overlapped, while each unit was supposed to have some knowledge of the whole brigade area. The 12th Battalion was responsible for that part lying between the La Bassée Canal and Loos, the 7th Battalion for that between Vermelles and Vimy, the 11th for the remainder of the sector to a point south of Arras, where the 2nd Tank Brigade carried on the defensive line. It was assumed from the first that if tanks were employed at all it would be in a counter-attack, the probable directions of the enemy's offensive being (1) against the Hill 70 sector, (2) a frontal attack against the Vimy Ridge, and (3) a flanking movement from the south. He occupied already so large a part of the coal district that the repulse of any further attempt was essential; and in the event of his capturing some vital point in the defence line (such as Hill 70 itself), the tanks would be employed at once to assist in driving him out. This being the general idea, little or no time was to be spent at first in collecting information about the ground beyond our front line. Reconnaissance was confined to the region between the tank-parks and the main zone of resistance, known as the Black Line. By the middle of the month this reconnaissance was in full swing. Taken as a whole, the country was not bad for tank operations; but the wide belt of shelled ground and crumbling trenches which marked

THE GERMAN OFFENSIVE 311

the old front line before Lens, the numerous large mining villages which radiated out from that town, and the Vimy Ridge itself, so convulsed by high explosive that only three possible tank crossings could be found, presented difficult and dissimilar problems. A tank counter-attack in this unique region must have been extremely interesting.

Had such an attack taken place, almost the whole battlefield would have been spread like a map below our camp. I do not think there can have been in France any point of view quite so remarkable, in the circumstances, as the everyday outlook from the 7th Battalion's huts above Bouvigny-Boyeffles. This camp — it was a single row of Nissens, occupied only by the officers — was situated halfway up the bold ridge which ends to the southward in the famous spur of Notre Dame de Lorette, overhanging the rubbish-heap that used to be Souchez. In front of us there was nothing but the immense flat plain of Lens and Douai. On a clear day we had only to step out of our huts and look over a hedge garnished with a screen of camouflage netting; and before us, across a stubble-field and the roofs of Boyeffles village, there rolled away to north and east and south-east the fruitless battlefields of three and a half years — Vimy and Liévin, Loos and Hulluch, La Bassée and Neuve Chapelle. And, for a background, this astonishing panorama took in Mont Rouge and Mont Noir and Kemmel Hill, thirty miles distant, near Ypres, the low ridge that covered Lille from view, the towns of Bailleul, Armentières, and Béthune, the score of wretched suburbs about Lens, with more rising ground ten miles behind, the numberless *crassiers* and towers of the coal-fields, the smoke of trains on the Lille-Douai railway, the huge bulk of Drocourt Fosse behind which Douai itself was hidden. With my glasses, on many fine evenings before sunset, while standing at the back of my own hut, I have distinguished the church and the individual houses of Mons-en-Pevèle, a little village on a hill twenty-three miles from where I stood, and at least

fifteen beyond the nearest point of the German lines.
Nearer at hand in this crowded scene were other familiar
landmarks — the churches of Harnes and Carvin, behind
Lens, the fallen "Tower Bridge" of Loos, the white water
towers of Fosse 21 and 22, the huge red-brick building with
its three steel spires which had been the works of the
Metallurgique Company. And everywhere, far and near,
rose the black *crassiers*—the slag-heaps—of the coal-mines.
Some of these were long and dwarfish, as you may see them
in Lancashire, but those which took the eye were pyramidal,
like colossal sable sugar-cones. Beside them were the
skeletons of iron buildings, each with its tower and wheels.
The foreground of all this was a jumble of white and red—
white where patches of incongruous chalk were turned up
along the miles of trenches, old and new, from Liévin to
Loos, and red with a million shattered houses in the
miners' *cités* which clustered about Lens — St Pierre, St
Auguste and St Laurent, Calonne and Maroc, Angres and
Avion. Lens itself, lying on low ground by the Souchez
river, was hidden from our camp.

The men of the 7th Battalion were billeted in Bouvigny
village, close to the officers' huts. Battalion H.Q. took
over the principal house in Boyeffles, a few hundred yards
away at the foot of the ridge. The tanks were elaborately
concealed on the very summit, amid the trees of the Bois
de Bouvigny, a straggling wood which ran along the crest
almost to the site of the demolished chapel of Notre Dame
de Lorette, where the French line had run in the early days
of the war, and where one still came across skeletons and
rusted rifles three years old. North of us, in the Bois
d'Olhain, were the 1st Brigade headquarters and the 12th
Battalion, both in huts. The 11th Battalion was at Mont
St Eloi, on our right. The troops holding this front were
the Canadian Corps. During the past year they had captured Hill 70, Liévin, and a number of other suburbs of
Lens, and their front line now ran through the outskirts
of that dreadful town, reeking of poison-gas and corrup-

tion. It was held only by German outposts, in many places occupying the half of a ruined house of which the other moiety was held by the Canadians; but it could not be taken permanently until Sallaumines, a suburb on a hillock immediately behind, was in our hands. The Canadians, always energetic, and especially anxious to round off their work by the capture of Lens, were full of schemes by which Sallaumines was to be carried with the help of tanks, but none of these materialised. While the German offensives burst upon us and drove past us to north and south, the Lens sector was privileged to remain the quietest part of the whole British front.

My new work as Reconnaissance Officer made me only too familiar with this region. For two months I did nothing but explore it. To begin with, I took part in a preliminary survey with Henriquez, Beale of B Company, and Jack Brown of C. (Gordon had left us to start a Reconnaissance School at Le Tréport.) This business presupposed ability to ride a motor-bicycle—all R.O.'s being provided with these abominable machines. I learnt eventually to ride mine with a certain amount of confidence and spirit; but to the end I knew nothing about its internal mechanism, and did not want to. I was so fortunate as to possess a draughtsman who understood petrol-engines, and I left the upkeep of my bicycle in his capable hands. Having with its help acquired a general knowledge of our area and of the routes we decided to follow if called upon to move, I proceeded to initiate the officers, N.C.O.'s, and drivers of A Company into these mysteries. In this work I had the aid, and, what was better, the congenial companionship, of Maelor Jones, who was the assistant R.O. of the company. Day after day he and I tramped about the melancholy region behind our line, exploring roads, examining bridges, selecting lying-up points, repeating every journey half a dozen times with our parties of learners, like a pair of Cook's couriers. "On your left you now see Fosse 16, *dit de Lens;* beyond is Fosse 7, *de Béthune.* That handsome edifice far in front—it is not advisable to try to reach it—is the Metallurgique factory at Wingles. . . ." I have never been so heartily wearied of any piece of country as I became of the Lens coal-fields. I came to know by name and to loathe at sight every pithead, every road, every clump of derelict red-brick houses. And yet, with all this repetition and monotony, the work and the place had unusual points of interest. It is the worst of a book on any set subject, that the writer cannot be as irrelevant as he would wish, for I should like to write now at some length about those two months. I should like to write of Bully-Grenay, where one could buy almost anything, and where children played about in streets that stank of poison-gas; of Les Alouettes, where a woman (apparently the sole remaining inhabitant) took in washing and kept a chicken-run amid a battery of 8-inch howitzers; of the family of Aix Noulette, in whose house (rebuilt largely of biscuit-tins and brown paper) I ate so many omelettes; and of that exposed portion of the Souchez road where Jack Brown and I were sniped by a 5.9 at a moment when my wretched bicycle refused to climb a gentle slope on anything higher than bottom speed. But as these various adventures led to nothing in the end, space does not permit of any further discursions. The tanks, for whom all tribulations were undergone, were never called upon in this sector, although, before we had finished, we had extended our reconnaissance southward until we knew Souchez and the whole Vimy Ridge, with its craters and its tunnels, as well as we knew Piccadilly or Hyde Park—in the case of some of us, a good deal better.

In the meantime, startling events were happening elsewhere, and from our sort of peninsula we watched with increasing bewilderment and anxiety the great tide of the German offensives sweeping past on both flanks. On the morning of March 21, every one heard the roar of a heavy bombardment. It was known next day that the enemy was making rapid progress south of the Somme.

THE GERMAN OFFENSIVE 315

For nearly a week the news became daily more disheartening. The four other Tank Brigades involved in the general debacle had lost nearly all their tanks, and were fighting as machine-gun units. And then, on the 29th, the Germans launched their expected attack against the Vimy Ridge and the northern part of the 3rd Army front. It was a costly failure—so costly north of the Scarpe that no further attempt was made against the ridge. But while the result was in doubt, detachments of the 7th and 12th Tank Battalions were hurried down to Roclincourt, in front of Arras, with Lewis guns, and took up a defensive position there. This party was known to us as the Oppy Expeditionary Force. Full of warlike zeal, but ignorant of the situation and even of its own whereabouts—for it arrived in the middle of the night, and was pushed immediately into holes and corners along the Roclincourt Ridge—it passed several anxious hours of darkness in the mistaken belief that a bloodthirsty and victorious enemy was close at hand. As a matter of fact, he was still four miles away, and never approached any nearer. The strain was broken with the dawn, amid shouts of laughter, by the appearance of a Decauville railway train which puffed deliberately across the front which the Lewis gunners were holding so tenaciously. The attack having definitely collapsed, the detachment returned on the 29th.

Throughout this exciting week, filled with appalling rumours, our reconnaissance continued more busily than ever. The activities of the 7th Battalion were now concentrated on the Vimy Ridge, which we explored from end to end. The 11th Battalion, some of whose tanks were now in Roclincourt, was extending its own reconnaissance far to the south of Arras. As the 3rd Army, conforming to the retreat of the 5th, withdrew its right and centre, there seemed an increased likelihood that the enemy would attempt the third alternative mentioned earlier in this chapter—a flanking attack through Arras against the rear of the Vimy Ridge. His reoccupation

of Monchy le Preux and Orange Hill, in consequence of
our withdrawal, enabled him once more to overlook the
reverse slope of the ridge. Arras was shelled daily, and
nearly all its inhabitants were removed; and villages far
behind suffered from the German artillery. On account
of this threat, and of the crippled state of the 2nd and
3rd Tank Brigades with General Byng, the 12th Battalion
was transferred early in April from Olhain Wood to
Simencourt, north of the Arras-Doullens road. The tanks
trekked the whole way, by roads and across country—
a distance of nearly twenty miles. Concentration at
Simencourt was completed by the 10th April. The 11th
Battalion, with its Headquarters and some tanks still at
Mont St Eloi, was now in the centre of our increased
brigade frontage. The 7th Battalion, having become the
most northerly tank unit, would be the first involved
in any developments in the La Bassée area; and such
developments, of a startling character, were at hand.

During the reconnaissance of the Vimy Ridge one had
been able to follow to some extent the progress of the
German advance north of the Somme. From points about
the southern end of the ridge, near where the road from
Arras to Lens passes the crest and drops abruptly toward
Vimy village, I watched through my glasses on successive
mornings the dappled clouds of smoke pushing westward
like the trail of some great conflagration. Viewed thus
from a flank, the new salient appeared even more pronounced and ominous than it was in reality, especially as
the Germans were shelling busily many places far in our
rear. And when one climbed to the summit of the ridge
and looked eastward over the wide flat plain south of Lens,
everything was normal; a few brown puffs of dust where
our occasional shells were bursting, the distant smoke of
German trains, the black company of slag-heaps, and, far
away but often very clear, the three spires of Douai. It
was a singular contrast, and one felt like a privileged spec-
tator watching, from a high gallery, the two halves of some

gigantic tableau representing the extremes of modern war. But, as it happened, the tableau was incomplete. There was a third scene about to open, and one which our unrivalled situation at Bouvigny allowed us to witness without stirring from our camp, until we were drawn into the fringe of it ourselves.

III.

In the first days of April we were busy with what was known in the Tank Corps, from a remark by General Elles, as the "Savage Rabbit" scheme. The military outlook was gloomy, and the communications from those in authority were unusually pessimistic; and among other omens was a secret précis of instructions to be followed in various possible emergencies, including a prolonged retreat, and even a rout. The "Savage Rabbit" act was an application of tank warfare to such unpleasant circumstances. Tanks, instead of being held in hand for counter-attacks or concerted rearguard actions, were to be scattered in a long line and hidden—remaining hidden, in the event of a disaster, until our infantry had retreated through them and the enemy was close at hand, when the machines would appear from their holes, like "savage rabbits," and sacrifice themselves to hold up the pursuit. This was a nice encouraging proposition; it was also a very faulty and wasteful method of using tanks, and could only be done once. I do not know who was responsible for it. Very fortunately there never was any need to carry it into practice, although the 12th Battalion and others actually took up their positions of concealment. In our case, it meant stringing our tanks out along the base of the Lorette Ridge, from Bouvigny to Souchez. Especial attention was to be paid to the latter place. A feature of the new tactics employed so successfully by the Germans in their offensive was the skilful use of valleys, or any sort of low ground, for the purpose of infiltration. It was thought now that if they advanced from the direction of Loos and Hill 70 (the first alternative previously mentioned), and succeeded in reaching the foot of the Lorette and Vimy Ridges, they would endeavour to turn both these obstacles by penetrating between them up the Souchez Valley. Souchez, where the French suffered so terribly in 1915, blocks the quite narrow gap that separates the Lorette spur from the northern and highest end of the Vimy Ridge; and through it ran several vital roads to Ablain St Nazaire, Carency, and Arras. Two sections of A Company (6 tanks) were therefore detailed to hold it at all costs. The tanks were to be hidden close to the roads, so that, in the event of the place being lost, they could swing across them and be blown up to form obstructions. For several days I was exploring the country behind the Lorette Ridge for routes by which the tanks could be taken into Souchez. Hiding-places were selected about the village (which had been destroyed with quite exceptional completeness), and also others for the remaining two sections along the road from Souchez to Aix Noulette, on the eastern face of the ridge. But on the day when these preparations were finished, and nothing remained but to move the tanks to their posts of sacrifice, another scene of our local tableau opened with a shattering crash; and our eyes and thoughts were diverted instantly in the opposite direction.

The 12th Battalion, as we have seen, moved south from the Bois d'Olhain about this time. Its last company trekked on the 8th April, and the following day came the new German blow along the Lys. The attack was expected, and seems to have been launched in moderate force, and with no very ambitious designs; but that fatality (or fatuity) which on several occasions during this period marked our dispositions, had dictated that a Portuguese division should still be holding our line in front of Estaires. The Portuguese infantry, utterly worthless troops, fled at once, casting away their arms—except a few who retained theirs long enough to shoot down some of our own people who tried to stop them. The artillery, on the other hand, behaved better, in some cases keeping their guns in action to the last. The Germans, in the meantime, found in front of them a wide gap, and pushed through it. One battalion penetrated—most of the way in column of route—for three or four miles without firing a shot, when its commanding officer, suspicious of this extraordinary luck, went on ahead to reconnoitre and was captured by the 51st Division, which was hurrying up from support. It was said that we had been so rash as to rely on the Portuguese holding out for an hour; but they did not hold out for five minutes. And from this period also dates the rumour that the famous Army Order about our "gallant allies" had been formally cancelled. In any case the mistake was made, and brought on its heels a most disastrous retribution. In ten hours Von Quast's 6th Army had punched a hole 12 miles wide and 5 deep in our defences; and in front of him consternation and chaos were rolling onward like a flood.

From our huts on the slope above Bouvigny this new battlefield lay visible in its entirety. It was twelve miles away, but from our elevated site it was easy with good binoculars to follow the course of the advance. The country north of the La Bassée Canal is utterly flat, drained by innumerable small streams and ditches, and covered with orchards and villages, then full of prosperous people and hardly touched by war. It had been a quiet front since Neuve Chapelle. Even Armentières, two miles behind the line, was an inhabited town, with shops and cafés open, until the Germans began to shell it in earnest shortly before 21st March. And now, evening after evening, we used to gather with our maps and field-glasses behind our row of huts and watch the great wedge of burning villages pushing farther and farther westward behind Béthune. Those evenings were exceptionally clear, so that far across the smoking plain the church tower of Bailleul was visible against the grey background of Mont Rouge. Bailleul was a charming little town, with a wonderful red-brick belfry to its Hotel de Ville, and one of the best officers' clubs in France. Within a fortnight it was in ruins.

Certain dates I cannot remember, and I have no diary or other aid to memory, but it must have been on the 11th or 12th that an urgent message came through demanding Lewis gun detachments. All the gunners in the battalion, with a proportion of officers and 70 Lewis guns, the whole under Major Norton, the second in command, with whom was Winters of A Company, left that same evening by lorry. By dawn next day they were in the line at Robecq, in front of St Venant. There were rumours that the rest of us, with the tanks, would be moving somewhere by train. On the evening of the 13th or 14th, those of us who were left in A Company held a sort of guest night, interrupted by a bombing raid—the last guest night I attended until the war was over; and the following morning we received orders to trek after dark to Hersin station, to entrain for the north. The tanks at this time were in Noulette Wood, at the foot of the ridge, having moved down from the Bois de Bouvigny on the crest in order to take part in various training schemes with the Canadians. All that afternoon Jack Brown and I were marking out with small metal flags, painted white, a route from Noulette Wood to Hersin. It was after six when we returned to camp, and already growing dark. I was met by the news that only B and C Companies were entraining—the former for Lillers and the latter for Aire. I had got to lead A Company by road to a wood near Vaudricourt, south of Béthune. A route was indicated roughly on the map, but none of us knew the country. We were, of course, very short-handed, having about half a dozen subalterns and our three drivers per tank; and all the tanks had their sponsons unbolted and pushed in, preparatory to entraining. The Major being away at Robecq with the Lewis gun detachment, the conduct of affairs fell to Moore, the second in command of the company, Rudd, the only remaining section commander, and myself.

I packed a few things in a haversack, ate a cold supper, filled a flask, and reached Noulette Wood in a box-car about nine o'clock. I knew there was no immediate hurry, as the depleted tank crews had to pull out and bolt all the sponsons again. As a matter of fact, it was after ten when we moved off. The night was clouded and pitchy dark, as it usually is on these occasions, and our supply of electric torches was miserably small. The distance to be covered —about nine miles—was not excessive; but I knew the difficulties that attend a company of twelve tanks moving along an unknown route on a black night, and I was prepared for a very tedious journey. And in fact no other trek that I can remember, except our mule fight on the St Julien road, left me so thoroughly exhausted and foot-weary. We made only one mistake, missing in the darkness a short-cut out of Sains-en-Gohelle, which cost us half a mile; but until dawn we could see practically nothing, all the electric torches gave out, and the leading tanks, as necessarily happens in a column of a dozen, had to be halted continually to let the rear ones close up. What with scouting ahead in inky blackness for cross-roads and turnings, imperfectly studied on the map by the light of a match or an expiring torch, and trotting up and down the column to give warning of misleading features or to find out the reason for some delay, I must have covered nearly double our nine miles that night; and as I had been all the day on my feet, the latter may be excused for giving unequivocal signs of wear. We did not, however, cover our full distance. Dawn broke while we had still some way to go, and at eight o'clock, when we came to an excellent sunken road near Houchin, a mile short of Vaudricourt, we decided to call a halt. The country was open, and we were getting rather too near the line by Béthune to make it advisable to move tanks about in daylight. We camouflaged the machines in the sunken road, took off our boots, and had some breakfast. Our ultimate destination we knew to be Fouquières, a village on the outskirts of Béthune, and it seemed the obvious thing now to make one bite of the remaining cherry that evening, and pass Vaudricourt without stopping there. It had been given us only as an approximate halting-place. After breakfast, therefore, Rudd and I walked—or staggered, to be correct—on to Fouquières, to find a lying-up point for the tanks, and if possible billets for ourselves. There were a number of small woods and plantations about the village, but all were occupied in force by transport and ammunition trains of the 1st Corps, which held this part of the line. Billets seemed unobtainable, for the whole neighbourhood was crowded with troops. We found a fair piece of cover for the tanks under the trees of a road which led down to a tributary of the Lawe river, and then we searched the village for food, coming to rest eventually in a cottage where they gave us omelettes and cheap champagne. We subsisted very largely upon this diet for the next three or four days.

The tanks moved on to Fouquières that evening, except one which broke down in the main street of Douvrin and remained there for some time, to the endless joy of the inhabitants, who had never seen these machines before. At the foot of the road where the others parked up was a large white house belonging to the *Maire* of Fouquières. It was full of officers, including the headquarters of a company of the 11th Tank Battalion which was in the line at Givenchy with Lewis guns. We managed to find floor-space here for the night in a sort of hall on the top floor, into which opened innumerable doors. These were opening and shutting all night, as the occupants of the rooms into which they led came and went (and trod heavily upon us in transit) on mysterious errands of their own. However, we slept, after a fashion, and, as it fell out, we remained in this house for a fortnight.

The Major turned up next day with our gunners from

THE GERMAN OFFENSIVE 323

Robecq. Thrust into an attenuated and almost solvent line, whose elements included every sort of man who could hold a rifle, with little artillery, no trenches, and the vaguest idea of the general situation, the detachment had passed a very unpleasant three days and nights, and had suffered a good many casualties, mostly in B and C Companies, who lost three or four officers killed or missing. The three companies were now concentrated again, but strung out on a very wide front, with C far away at Aire, B at Lillers, and ourselves at Béthune. Battalion headquarters, being very comfortable at Boyeffles, remained there, far from us all. The reason of our sudden move to these three towns was the celebrated "Delta" scheme, as, for purposes of concealment, it was called. I would not inflict upon any reader the details of this exasperating project, for they were never the same for two days together, and it came to nothing in the end. The general idea (if the words can be applied to so amorphous a conception) was to ease the communications of the troops in the Givenchy sector and relieve the pressure on Béthune, from which the Germans were distant only a few kilometres to the north and north-west. In the very beginning we got as far as Y-day: everything was ready: we had reconnoitred hurriedly that strange, almost untouched country beyond the La Bassée Canal, where a few stray cattle still wandered in orchards thick with blossom, where the empty houses still showed the litter and confusion of their owners' sudden flight, and where no one knew where the front line lay : tank routes were worked out, bridges examined, and conferences held with corps and divisional pundits who seemed to know nothing about anything; and then the whole thing was cancelled (perhaps very wisely), and, in all its subsequent fluctuations, was never so advanced again. For another month we wrestled with its kaleidoscopic changes. The proportion of tanks to be employed rose from one battalion to the whole brigade, and frontages and objectives were shuffled like counters. After a while we felt that the whole thing had become a sort of confused and academic dream, and we ceased to take any interest in it.

This period in many respects was very novel and interesting. It was our first experience of what, in fact, was a phase of open warfare, with all its alarms and hopes and general uncertainty. The Germans were busy farther north, about Kemmel and Bailleul, but at any moment some new blow might be struck at Béthune. A few days after we reached Fouquières, indeed, an attempt was made to cross the canal on rafts opposite Hinges, and was repulsed. Béthune by now, of course, was a dead town, its shops closed, its inhabitants fled, its houses crumbling daily under shell-fire. At Choques, the big railhead just behind, two tanks of the 12th Battalion, with three of the new Whippets, had been posted to hold the roads against a raid by armoured cars. Hinges, north of Béthune, on the only hill in that level country, in whose pleasant château the 11th Corps headquarters had rested somnolently for upwards of two years, was a mere collection of empty ruins on our front line by the canal. The corps had fled hurriedly to Roquetoire, behind Aire. Our own post, Fouquières, was left more or less at peace for a while. Only a few high-velocity shells fell about it at intervals. It swarmed with people, for scores of refugees from the lost area were still living with the inhabitants. And presently its turn came also. As the shelling grew more persistent, its people were evacuated; and these unfortunates, with their box-mattresses and other cherished goods piled on waggons or hand-carts, went to swell the great flood of fugitives that streamed westward.

Everything we wished to learn about this country we had to find out for ourselves. The maps were bad, and no one knew anything. I remember trying to obtain some information and some better maps from the 1st Corps Intelligence Officer. He could give me neither. He admitted quite frankly that while he had masses of data concerning the country between our old line and the German frontier, of the Béthune district, at his very door (the Corps headquarters had been at Hesdigneul, a mile and a half from Béthune itself for many months), he knew nothing at all. Another curious sidelight upon army methods, at least during this confused period, was thrown by some inquiry I made about the "Delta" scheme at the 1st Division headquarters at Gosnay. We were attached to the 1st Division for operations, and for a fortnight past had been drawing rations from it, yet the G.S.O. 1, whom I interviewed, did not even know that there were any tanks in the neighbourhood . . . ! I have noticed so often in France that while brigade staffs, who lived near the line, in considerable danger and in touch with the fighting, always seemed to have their wits about them, the staffs of divisions and corps, long accustomed (at a distance) to trench warfare, became atrophied and absorbed in mere details of routine. It used to be said that prolonged trench duties would render infantry unfit for the sudden emergencies of attack or open warfare; but I think in many cases it was the higher formations who were in danger of succumbing to the spell.

A feature of this time which impressed me very strongly was the magnificent behaviour of the French population. To many Englishmen the French are still incomprehensible, vain, greedy, untidy (that fatal sin!), and altogether rather absurd. We are, of course, ourselves very like our spiritual kinsfolk the Germans in some ways, and especially in our inability to understand, or wish to understand, any Latin race. A common complaint in France was the extortionate prices put on everything for our benefit. Apart from the fact that this largely was our own fault, it is true that the French, for centuries a very poor people, have learnt habits of thrift that sometimes merit an uglier name; but we should have stopped, before crying out about it, to ask what our own behaviour would have been toward a French army settled in England for upwards of four years. Can any one imagine our shopkeepers carrying gratitude so far, after the first altruistic burst of thankfulness, as to restrict their profits or even limit them to reasonable bounds? I cannot picture this myself. And, on the other hand, can any one imagine our people working as diligently and suffering as patiently as the French peasantry in the war zone? Again I, for one, cannot. And these peasants, or shopkeepers, in the country districts were almost all women. There were young boys with them, and a few old men; but men between eighteen and fifty years of age you never saw at all. There were none of those sturdy and indispensable farm hands who were exempted in droves in the English counties. And when some great disaster came, such as this German advance of which I am writing, you saw these homeless and ruined folk at their very best — patient, courageous, and courteous even in their despair. While in England prosperous tradesmen were selling goods at 100 per cent profit, saying only in extenuation, "It is the war," the same phrase was being uttered in an infinitely finer spirit by the refugees of France, long broken to such tragedies. You met some woman leaving her home, pushing before her a hand-barrow loaded with her poor possessions; and if you commiserated, there came the inevitable answer, accepting an inevitable occurrence with a resignation that was far removed from apathy—"C'est la guerre, monsieur. . . ." I remember a little incident of this time which illustrates, more clearly than pages of generalities, the spirit that one found in these people. When Fouquières was shelled and the inhabitants removed, our own quarters in the *Maire's* house became so unpleasant that we departed also, tanks and all, to Hesdigneul. A day or two later I rode over to the house to settle some business of a billeting certificate. It had been raining heavily, and the road where our tanks had been lying, churned up by their tracks, was deep in mud. As I was coming away, the mud clogged my rear wheel, between the tyre and the mud-guard, stopping the bicycle just as I passed a little party of women and children who were escaping from the *Maire's* farm with a few household treasures on their backs. (The *Maire* himself, by the way, unlike most of his admirable class, had abandoned his flock long before.) Of the women in this party one was very old, and all were tired, heavily laden, and in tears. But as soon as they saw me poking about under the mud-guard with a stick they dropped their bundles, seized each a piece of wood, and ran up to help. Even the old woman was brandishing a twig and instructing the rest with a torrent of words. Before the little job was finished, the tears were forgotten and we were all chattering and laughing; and when I thanked them and rode away, they were still smiling and crying out as they shouldered their pathetic bundles, as if there were no such things as war and ruined homes.

CHAPTER XVI.

THE GERMAN OFFENSIVE (*continued*).

ANNEQUIN: AND THE TANK CORPS IN RETREAT.

I.

HAVING left Fouquières for Hesdigneul, where our tanks were parked up against the wall of the churchyard, A Company headquarters now occupied part of an immense farm—a great quadrangle of barns, stables, and living-rooms, with an attractive garden and one of the most magnificent kitchens I have ever seen. Two old ladies, with their niece (who had been educated in England), managed the establishment, the men of the family being as a matter of course in the Army. One of them, in fact, had been killed. They were cousins of the people who owned our battalion headquarters at Boyeffles; and the niece was provoked to one of her rare speeches when some one, in the usual English manner, referred to her relatives' house as a "château." "Ce n'est pas un château!" she said indignantly. "C'est une maison seulement . . .!" Before we came these kind people had suffered the infliction of an R.A.F. mess, whose members as usual got drunk every night and broke the furniture; and it took us some days to persuade them that there were Englishmen who knew how to behave. After that we were very good friends.

During our stay here, which lasted for about three weeks, a variety of nebulous schemes ran through their brief careers. One, due to a sudden panic, involved the

defence of Béthune against some expected onslaught. The
tanks were to take up positions on the canal quay, guarding
the precious bridges. Our enthusiasm for this was a little
damped by the discovery one day that our proposed lying-
up point, a parade-ground on the outskirts of the town, had
been uprooted by a deluge of 8-inch shells. Behind these
projects, like some tiresome genie, there hung always the
egregious "Delta" operation, in one or another of its
endless shapes. And then, of all things, came a fresh scare
about the distant sector south of Arras, more than twenty
miles away; and I spent three days with Henriquez, Beale,
and Jack Brown on motor bicycles or in a box-car, hunting
for tank routes between our old Bouvigny area and such
remote places as Bailleulmont and Pas, beyond the Arras-
Doullens road. On one of these happy jaunts Henriquez
led us inadvertently in the Ford car to within a few hundred
yards of Hébuterne, where the front line then ran. The
road was pitted with large shell-holes, but I have never seen
any one perform such miracles with a Ford, or any other
car, as did our driver when he discovered our mistake. We
rushed into Monchy-au-Bois at about thirty miles an hour,
and having climbed out there to adjust our dislocated limbs,
were welcomed by a sudden deluge of high-velocity shells.
There were a number of French troops in this neighbourhood, and also the remains of the 2nd Tank Brigade, whose
few surviving machines were still scattered thinly behind
the left of the 3rd Army, in accordance with the "Savage
Rabbit" policy. Practically speaking, the 2nd, 3rd, 4th,
and 5th Brigades were now organised as Lewis gun units,
with a small backing of Whippets and worn-out Mark IV.'s,
for 200 of the latter had been lost in the retreat. It was
because the 1st Brigade, alone unaffected by the disaster,
and mustering nearly 100 tanks, was the only striking force
left to the Tanks Corps, that our reconnaissances covered
at this period an area extending from La Bassée to Auchon-
villers, near the Ancre. We might be needed anywhere at
any moment.

The first phase of the German offensive, however, had come virtually to an end. The battle of movement below Arras was solidifying, as it were, in front of Amiens. The third phase, about to open upon the *Chemin des Dames*, would affect the mass of the British forces only indirectly. But the second phase, begun on the Lys as a distraction and since exploited with vigour, was not (to our knowledge) definitely finished. It had extended northward to the Salient, where we had lost all the ground won at such a terrible cost in the previous autumn; the Germans were on Kemmel Hill, in the ruins of Bailleul, and along the outskirts of the great wood of Nieppe; and now developments were expected immediately south of the La Bassée Canal. At this time—about the middle of May—when the 7th Tank Battalion had been for five weeks extended from Aire to Béthune, the 12th Battalion was still in the neighbourhood of Simencourt, and the 11th, so far as I remember, in its old quarters at Roclincourt and Mont St Eloi. 'Weekly Tank Notes,' which erroneously places the 7th at Molinghem, makes out the 11th to have been between Busnes and Robecq, but I think only the Reconnaissance Officers, working on the "Delta" scheme, came up to this area.

The final stage of the Amiens battle had brought German tanks into the field for the first time. There were only three of them, but they did so much damage before they were driven off that a thorough tank scare ran through the Army, and imaginary machines were detected in scores at every point of danger. It was now believed that the Germans intended to use them in an attack along the La Bassée road with the idea of reaching Béthune by turning the obstinate point of Givenchy from the south. An increased shelling of our back areas seemed to indicate that something was in the air; and the 7th Battalion, already in the neighbourhood, was ordered suddenly to concentrate farther east, between Cambrin and Vermelles, in readiness to repel any attempt.

The day before these orders reached A Company at

THE GERMAN OFFENSIVE 331

Hesdigneul, the German artillery provided us with a new sensation. The village had not been shelled since our arrival; but it housed, in its enormous château, the 1st Corps Headquarters, and this, I think, must have been the attraction for the appropriately colossal gun which suddenly disturbed our rustic peace. We were having tea in the farm when the whole place was shaken by a shattering crash from outside. No one paid much attention at first, as it sounded like the detonation of one of our own heavy guns, of which there were two or three on railway mountings in the neighbourhood; but the excitement in the village soon brought us out to see what had happened. It was then apparent that we were being shelled, and by something of uncommon size. A great pall of black smoke was drifting away from a field close at hand, where an observation balloon had its quarters, and I found immediately afterwards a steel splinter, some eight inches long, in our courtyard. Several more of these alarming explosions followed during that evening, and the discovery of the complete base of a shell proved the offending weapon to be of 17-inch calibre— the heaviest long-range gun then in use by any army.

The following morning there came the orders for our move. We were to proceed that night to Sailly-Labourse, on the Béthune-Lens road, near Annequin. I hurried off on the bicycle, over the very worst cobbles I have ever encountered, to find the 3rd Infantry Brigade Headquarters at the Château des Prés, outside the village. This journey was notable for two incidents: the roads were so atrocious that my engine shook loose, causing the chain to fall off; and, as a consolation, I discovered some tins of Sullivan's cigarettes in a Church Army canteen in Verquigneul—corn in Egypt, indeed, with a vengeance. The brigade staff in the Château des Prés had heard nothing about any tanks, but this was only to be expected. There was a wide dry moat round the château garden, where the machines could be hidden during the night, and on my way there and back I mapped out the latter half of the approach route, which

Maelor Jones was reconnoitring from the Hesdigneul end. Before sunset the tanks were backing out from the churchyard wall, and having seen them started I pushed off once more for the château, to meet there some lorry loads of petrol and other stores. Rather than face again the medieval cobbles of the more direct route, I went round by Béthune and so through Beuvry on the Lens road. Béthune in those days was always rather eerie, with its deserted streets and ruinous shuttered houses and shops: it called to mind the empty town of Semur in that charming story of Mrs Oliphant's, 'A Beleaguered City'; and there were times—during a bombardment, for example—when it was worse than eerie. It was being bombarded spasmodically that evening, and I did not linger to sentimentalise. At the Château des Prés I found that the brigade had at length been formally notified of our coming. This château, until the month before, had been one of the most eligible headquarters, for its advanced position, in all France. It was never shelled, it had all its furniture, and even all its window glass. But now this Utopian age was no more; the grounds were pitted with shell-holes, the trees were lopped and splintered, and all the windows were broken. The cellars had been sand-bagged, and every other preparation made for an enforced reversion to underground life. And that evening I received an unpleasant reminder of these altered circumstances, for as I walked down the terrace steps about eight o'clock on my way to meet the tanks, a shell came whistling over the roof and burst half a dozen yards in front of me on the gravel path. Very fortunately for me it burst forward and away from me, scoring a sort of fan of smoking grooves in the grass border. It was, in fact, an incendiary shell, presumably intended for the village, for a second burst some distance away, and the third fell among the houses. As I ran for shelter out of the smoke of the first explosion, heads appeared at the château windows, and a voice inquired inevitably, " Where did that one go to ? "

This interruption was short-lived ; and after a precautionary wait I walked off through Sailly-Labourse to find the tanks. They were fairly well up to time, but to get the twelve of them into the château moat was a tedious process. The moat was lined thickly with trees and bushes, which gave admirable cover in the day-time, but added to the difficulties of introducing tanks on a dark night. No lights, of course, could be used. It was after one o'clock before everything was settled satisfactorily, and Maelor Jones and I could accompany the Major to the comparatively luxurious shelter of a cellar in the château lodge.

After five or six hours' sleep we were washing and shaving, with the usual inadequate resources, when the Colonel's car drew up outside. At the same time there arrived, in an evil hour for himself, poor fellow, a Reconnaissance Officer named Saul from the 12th Battalion. Having been familiar with the Annequin area as a private in the infantry, he had been sent to put his knowledge at our disposal. While I finished my perfunctory toilet in the lodge, Saul and Maelor Jones strolled on together to the garden at the back of the house, where the servants we had brought with us were preparing some sort of breakfast. As I followed a couple of minutes later, a shell burst in the garden, which was full of brigade details and our own people. We all ran like hares for cover, and I remember seeing a dozen pairs of heels flashing upwards as their owners, including the Colonel and other dignitaries, leaped into the moat. I was in time to slide down after them, on top of a kettle and a primus stove, just as the second shell arrived somewhere in the neglected flower-beds behind me. This visitation, like that of the previous evening, was intended for Sailly-Labourse, to which it passed on as soon as the German gunners had corrected their range ; but the initial miscalculation cost us both Maelor Jones and Saul, who were wounded by the first shell—the former in the hand, and the latter more seriously in the leg and arm. Poor Saul had not been in the place five minutes. Fortunately, as a brigade headquarters, the château contained a telephone and a doctor; and in a quarter of an hour the two victims were in an ambulance on their way to the nearest dressing station.

Sailly-Labourse was a little over three miles from the front line. A mile nearer to the latter, across an open stretch of untended fields, was Annequin village and fosse, the former a straggling collection of houses joining on to Cambrin on the La Bassée road. Annequin Fosse, beneath which the Major and I were to live like troglodytes for the next three weeks, resembled nothing so much as a chessboard and a disproportionately large pawn, side by side. The chessboard was a walled square filled with miners' cottages in symmetrical rows, the streets crossing at right angles. Beside it, on a flat base of slag, was the pawn—one of those pyramidal crassiers I have spoken of, perhaps 150 feet high. It was the nearest one of its type to our front trenches; and from the summit where signallers, flash-spotters, and other details lived in holes dug out of the black slag and reinforced with iron and sandbags, one obtained an admirable bird's-eye view, not only over the German lines directly in front, but also right across the rear of the new salient north of the canal. This exceptional observation point, so far forward, must have been invaluable to us and a serious hindrance to the enemy. At the base of the pyramid, practically invulnerable beneath twenty feet of ground, and another twenty of coal refuse, were the dug-outs which housed the brigade holding the line. The latter, for a breadth of two or three miles opposite Annequin, had not changed since it crystallised there at the end of 1914—the only sector of our whole front possessing this distinction; and both Annequin and Cambrin had been inhabited throughout, until the increased shelling before the German offensives drove the people away. As late as the middle of March, when our field-guns were firing (and drawing fire) from behind the wall which enclosed the miners' cottages, children were playing in the streets a few yards away.

The 1st Division, then holding this sector, had the 2nd

Infantry Brigade north of the canal at Givenchy-les-La
Bassée (not to be confused with the Givenchy south of Lens),
and the 1st Brigade south of the canal at Cambrin and
Annequin. The 3rd Brigade was in support about Sailly-
Labourse. Having seen Maelor Jones and Saul despatched
in the ambulance from the Château des Prés, the Major and
I walked over to the Fosse to arrange with the 1st Brigade
Staff the disposition of our tanks, two sections of which were
to move to their final points of concealment that night. We
found the brigade very sceptical about the suspected German tanks, and quite confident of repelling any ordinary attack. The 2nd Brigade had just dealt in an adequate
fashion with a renewed German attempt on Givenchy. It
was agreed, however, that one of our sections should be
hidden among the houses of Annequin, and the other
among those of Cambrin. Two sections remained in
reserve at the Château des Prés. On our right B and C
Companies, coming by train from Lillers and Aire to the
railhead near Fouquières, were to take up positions between
the Fosse and Vermelles. The Major and I were invited
to live with the Brigade Staff in the dug-out beneath the
slag-heap.

That night the two sections moved quietly into their
new positions. Of the three tanks in Cambrin, one was
screened elaborately with branches in the garden of the
house used as the Support Battalion headquarters, while
the other two lay up in the yard of the schoolhouse. All
were in a position to move out at a moment's notice and
block the La Bassée road, which ran straight through the
village. In Annequin, the other three tanks were hidden
behind the miners' cottages. A little later a third section
was brought up in front of Annequin, and camouflaged
against the embankment of a railway which served the
mine.

We remained here for three weeks, until the beginning
of June. Our life was very idle, not uncomfortable, and
in many ways unusually interesting. Every morning the

Major and I used to walk through Annequin to Cambrin to visit the tanks, and with that our duties usually were finished for the day. The brigade mess, in a baby Nissen hut, protected by layers of slag at the base of the crassier, was an uncommonly good one, and its members were charming. In similar huts lived some of the officers, including the Colonel commanding an artillery brigade; the General and the rest of the Staff, with ourselves, having our quarters underground, where the various offices also were situated. The weather turned exceptionally fine, with a blazing sun; and the shadeless neighbourhood of the great slag-heap, which radiated heat like the rocks of Aden, became so intolerable at times that we were driven below to the cramped dug-out, which was always cool. Lack of reading matter was a serious trial, as the nearest inhabited towns, such as Nœux-les-Mines and Barlin, were only squalid mining centres; and as a shopping resort Bruay was little better. The last time I rode into Bruay the Germans were shelling it, the shops were closing down, and harassed A.P.M.'s and military police were endeavouring to expedite the departure of some of the surplus inhabitants.

Our chief diversions at Annequin were climbing the slag-heap (on top of which two old 15-pounder guns had now been hoisted), visiting the tanks and billets of B and C Companies, running over occasionally to Hesdigneul, where we kept up a rear headquarters at the farm, and eating and sleeping a great deal. It was so unusually hot for May that we spent most of our time in shirt sleeves. A less attractive feature was the rather persistent shelling to which the neighbourhood was subjected. The expected attack never materialised; but the German artillery had frequent bursts of zeal. A field battery, in camouflaged pits in the open, a couple of hundred yards from the Fosse, came in for a great deal of attention, as did another battery in Annequin village; while the railway embankment beyond was shelled so heavily on one or two nights that some tanks of B Company, which were hidden there, were withdrawn. The

G.S.O. 1 of the Division had a narrow escape on this same railway one morning, a shell knocking him down and killing his orderly. Cambrin was gassed every night, and an obnoxious German balloon which looked straight down the La Bassée road was apt to turn the gunners on to the village if people walked too openly about the street. At this time the inhabitants used to come back to fetch some of their belongings. One man had the temerity to drive up in a cart, and I saw him afterwards careering back towards Beuvry at a gallop, pursued by angry puffs of smoke and dust. After we had been living in the Fosse for about ten days, the 1st Brigade was relieved by the 3rd, and on the following morning, as I was returning with the Major from the usual round of inspection, high-velocity shells began to fall thickly about Annequin. We hurried in considerable disorder to the dug-out in the Fosse, where we found every one in a state of consternation. The new Brigadier, also on his way back from his first tour of the trenches, had been caught in the bombardment and wounded, with one of his staff—the latter seriously.

During all this time the unfortunate town of Béthune, which was only three miles away and in full view from the Fosse, was being shelled persistently. I happened to be watching it through my glasses when the church tower, which had been hit many times, was finally demolished. A great cloud of white dust billowed up over the houses, and when it cleared away the familiar landmark was gone. After a while, the Germans began to use incendiary shells, and the half-ruined town caught fire. All day the smoke hung over it, and every night, until we left, there was the glare of burning.

Toward the end of our stay a minor disaster, averted only by a miracle from becoming very serious, befell B Company, always unfortunate. The battalion was visited one afternoon by General Elles, who accompanied our Brigadier and the Colonel round the tank positions. The day was brilliantly fine, and the three cars which brought

the cortège raised great clouds of dust along the roads.
One cannot help attributing what followed to this rather
characteristic neglect of precaution, for the whole country,
being absolutely flat, was under observation from hostile
balloons, which as usual were up. B Company's headquarters were established in a solitary and conspicuous
house on the main Béthune-Lens road, near Noyelles,
immediately opposite the buildings of a small pithead
called Puits No. 12, where two reserve sections of tanks
were concealed. The visitors' cars drew up at this house,
and when the inspection was over, drove off again at a
great speed, trailing behind them clouds of dust which must
have been visible for miles. One cannot have all one's
hostages to fortune returned intact—especially when one
has offered other people's. The august party left at 4.30;
and before five o'clock Puits No. 12, deluged suddenly with
8-inch howitzer shells, was blazing merrily. Two tanks
were hit at once, set on fire, and burnt out. The other
four, by a combination of extraordinary pluck and still
more extraordinary good fortune, were started up and
driven away from the flaming buildings and the rain of
shells without injury to a single officer or man. When the
affair started I was down in that apartment of our dug-out
which the Major and I shared with the Brigade Gas Officer.
Intercepting a frenzied telephone message from B Company, I ran up on deck (as one may call it) with my glasses,
and for the next half-hour watched the shelling and the
conflagration, which was only 1000 yards away. Within
an hour the pithead buildings were mere smoking cinders,
the iron wheel-gantry had collapsed, and I could distinguish
amid the glowing wreckage the blackened shapes of the
two burnt-out tanks.

The last incident worth noting of this interlude at Annequin was connected with the third German offensive, on the
Aisne, launched on 27th May. The following evening,
during dinner, we were startled by a sudden terrific racket
of machine-gun and rifle fire. Running out to see what

had happened, we found a German aeroplane circling
impudently round the peak of the crassier, like some eagle
round Ben Nevis, while its pilot, paying no attention
whatever to our bullets, was casting overboard sheafs of
pamphlets! These productions announced, in perfect
English, the capture of thousands of prisoners and hundreds
of guns on the Chemin des Dames, and were signed by
Ludendorff. Having delivered his load, the German waved
his hand, circled away, and drove swiftly upward across the
lines and out of our sight. He was a very plucky fellow,
and deserved our bad shooting.

We were now nearing the end of these rather humiliating
adventures. The first week in June marked for us the
beginning of that period of transition from constant alarms
and ever-changing schemes of defence to the opposite
tactics of attack, which were to end only with the war.
Summoned suddenly one evening to battalion headquarters,
still at Boyeffles, I was told to reconnoitre next day a route
by road to Enguinegatte, a village behind Aire, whither
it appeared A Company was to trek at once to commence
training with the Canadian Corps. I spent that night in
our old quarters at Hesdigneul, where the 17-inch gun, still
spasmodically active, did its best to speed a parting guest
by dropping one of its huge shells so near that the glass of
my window was shattered and fell upon me as I lay in bed.
When I left next morning, after an imperfect rest, the two
old ladies and their niece were also packing up. The
17-inch gun, and several gas-shells in their garden, had
persuaded them of the propriety of a temporary removal.

Enguinegatte, the scene (at a less complicated period of
warfare) of the famous battle of the Spurs, lies almost at the
end of the longest and straightest Roman road to be found
even in France. From Arras to Thérouanne, just beyond
our destination, there are nearly forty miles of this abominable highway, straight as a die, except for two modern and
insignificant detours to negotiate precipitous hills. By the
route the tanks had to travel from Annequin, striking this

road near Bruay, the distance was thirty miles, and this, entirely over roads, was ruinous to the machines. Somebody estimated that the journey cost £7000 in damaged tracks and rollers alone, for our one company. (B and C Companies were returning to Bouvigny to train with other Canadians there.) However, we arrived at Enguinegatte eventually, although not until I was heartily tired of the Roman road, up and down which I was riding, on my bicycle or in the Major's car, for the best part of three days and nights. The village itself was charming, unspoiled by troops, quiet and unsophisticated, and set amid a really beautiful country of rolling hills, woods, and corn-fields. I had the most comfortable billet I ever secured in France. The weather throughout was gorgeous; and if the rehearsals with successive battalions of Canadians became for us somewhat tedious in the end, we suffered in a wholly admirable cause, which bore good fruit two months later. We were far away from any interference, and could do very much as we pleased. A ten days' interlude at Le Tréport, camouflaged as a rest cure *cum* reconnaissance course under Gordon, where Jack Brown, Ritchie of B Company, and I sat about on the cliffs above Mirs and read trashy literature, was a sort of gilding to the lily. Le Tréport was rather amusing at this time, because the camp was full of "Bolos" dislodged at last from their limpet-like grip at Bovington, and now fighting tooth and nail to secure fresh posts as instructors at the depot and elsewhere. The rest of us, of course, were hoping to see them posted to fighting units, so long as the latter were not our own. This, indeed, was the whole object of the belated clearance at Bovington; but in most cases, I regret to say, it was not achieved. Only after the Armistice did the majority of these people rush valiantly forward, demanding to be sent to Cologne.

Altogether, in spite of a few slight internal dissensions in our company at Enguinegatte, I look back upon that June as the most restful and pleasant month I spent in France.

I returned from Le Tréport to find the tanks gone by road to Erin, a few details packing up at Enguinegatte, and the rest of the company already back in our old quarters at Bouvigny.

II.

Before we come to begin the last phase of the war, as it was influenced by the Tank Corps, something must be said as to the four southern brigades in the March retreat and after.

The 1st Brigade, as we have seen, worked with the 1st Army, covered Arras, and was so fortunate as to escape all direct implication in the disasters of March and April. Next to the south came the 2nd Brigade, in the neighbourhood of Bapaume. Farther south again was the new 4th Brigade, working with the 5th Army around Peronne. The 3rd Brigade was in G.H.Q. Reserve at Wailly and Bray, and was in process of equipment with Whippet machines, but only one battalion, the 3rd, had received these novelties. The 5th Brigade consisted as yet only of a nucleus, one company of the 13th Battalion, without tanks, also at Bray. The losses in tanks at Cambrai had not yet been made good, as no more Mark IV.'s were being built, and the new Mark V.'s were not available till later; and the three equipped brigades mustered between them only about 220 heavy tanks and 50 Whippets fit for action. A number of training machines were at Wailly, Bray, and Aveluy Wood, near Albert.

The cyclonic advance of the Germans on the 5th Army front resulted in the 4th Brigade being sacrificed wholesale on the first two or three days, at the end of which time it had virtually no tanks left. In the frightful confusion of the rout, tank battalions, companies, and sections were pushed in anyhow to do as best they could, lost touch with each other and with the brigade headquarters, and fought independently a series of actions, which it is all but impos-

sible now to disentangle from the general obscurity. The
5th Battalion, having fought at Hervilly Wood, Roisel, and
Epehy, among other places, on the 22nd March, rallied
seventeen tanks at Cartigny that night, and tried to withdraw
across the Somme by the bridge at Brie. The bridge was
destroyed prematurely, and fourteen machines, being almost
out of petrol and unable to escape, were blown up by their
crews. The remaining three got across at other points, and
were lost in action next day. The 5th Battalion, now
without tanks, was hastily reorganised into Lewis-gun
detachments. The 4th Battalion, after managing to retain
some tanks a little longer, was in the same state before the
end of the month, and the 1st Battalion was reduced to half
a dozen worn-out machines and some converted supply-
tenders. By the 28th the brigade had 185 crews (including
the 13th Battalion nucleus) fighting in the line with Lewis
guns. Everything else had been lost—tanks, stores, and
even the kit of the officers and men; and the casualties in
personnel had been heavy.

On the 3rd Army front the 2nd Tank Brigade was in
action on the afternoon of the 21st, when tanks from the
8th Battalion took part in a counter-attack which recaptured
Diognies, but failed to hold it. Twenty-four hours later,
farther to the left, twenty-five tanks of the 2nd Battalion
counter-attacked without infantry to check the German
advance on Beugny and the Bapaume-Cambrai road. The
tanks came under concentrated artillery fire as soon as they
crossed the road, and several were knocked out at once.
The remainder put a field-battery out of action, surprised
the German infantry massing for an assault, and drove
them back in confusion beyond Vaulx-Vraucourt and
Morchies, which our troops reoccupied. Only five tanks
rallied, however, and 128 officers and men were lost. The
rest of the battalion personnel was formed as Lewis-gun
detachments, and fell back upon Bray on the 24th. In the
meantime, the 8th Battalion, losing nearly all its tanks in
attempts to cover the infantry withdrawal about Bus and

THE GERMAN OFFENSIVE 343

Barastre, was also converted into a machine-gun unit. The remaining battalion, the 10th, fought a series of rearguard actions through Sapignies and Achiet-le-Grand to Bucquoy, sacrificing most of its tanks.

The 3rd Tank Brigade, in G.H.Q. Reserve at Bray and Wailly, was soon involved in the general mêlée. Out of the two battalions at Bray, the 3rd and the 9th, one composite battalion was formed and equipped with forty-eight Whippets, the remainder of the personnel becoming yet another Lewis-gun unit. The 6th Battalion at Wailly seems to have had an easier time than most of the others, and to have preserved a large proportion of its tanks, which may be explained by the fact that it remained behind the left wing of the 3rd Army, which was never seriously shaken, and retreated only so far as was necessary to conform with the centre and right. On the morning of 21st March the 6th Battalion's camp was shelled heavily, and the whole of its orderly-room staff was killed. The battalion withdrew to La Cauchie on the 25th, and was transferred to the 2nd Brigade a week later. The 3rd Battalion's Whippets, in the meantime, had made their first appearance in action on the 26th about Serre and Hébuterne, routing considerable numbers of the enemy without suffering any loss themselves; and they were fighting again at Bouzincourt on the 31st. They were found particularly useful for that kind of patrol work which the peculiarities of the situation had thrust upon such tanks as were left—closing temporary gaps in the line, holding up attacks, and gaining information,—doing, in fact, those duties which in the old days were performed by cavalry.

The result of ten days' continued fighting and retreat was that the Tank Corps practically was without tanks, always excepting, of course, the 1st Brigade. Of the personnel of the other brigades 75 per cent had been in the line as Lewis-gun detachments. About 200 tanks had been lost. The big camp at Bray had been destroyed before evacuation, and a number of Whippets lying there under repair had to be blown up. Brigades and battalions, like all other units in the Army, were in a state of complete disorganisation, and the casualties, especially those incurred in the Lewis-gun units, were an added source of anxiety to Tank Corps Headquarters, owing to the few reinforcements available. The first steps taken toward reorganisation were hampered by the German attack on the Lys, as the 4th Brigade, which had just been withdrawn to the Bermicourt area to refit, was sent north to the 2nd Army front with Lewis guns, and remained fighting about Meteren and Wytschaete until the end of April. Then came the startling news that owing to the difficulty of finding sufficient infantry drafts in England, the Tank Corps was to be cut down from six brigades to four, which would mean the disbanding of the incomplete 5th Brigade in France and of the 15th, 16th, 17th, and 18th Battalions at home. Happily, this disastrous proposal was never carried out in its entirety. Two battalions at Bovington were reduced for a time to cadres, and a third was equipped with armoured cars; but the successes in July and August once more converted the harassed weathercocks in authority. All was changed again. The six-brigade establishment was not only revived but augmented; and while the cadres were made up to strength and rushed out to France, another six battalions were authorised to be formed.

The immediate task of reorganisation after the retreat was further complicated by the uncertainty as to whether the retreat itself was finished. The force of the initial German blow, which had driven us thirty miles backward in a week, expended itself in the first days of April, but only from temporary exhaustion and difficulties of supply. With Amiens almost in his grasp, the enemy was certain to make another effort as soon as he had found his second wind. It was necessary, in consequence, to maintain as large a force of tanks as possible with our battered armies; and a hurried reshuffling of units left skeletons of the 2nd, 3rd, and 5th Brigades, re-equipped with old machines sent up from Erin, within call of the threatened point. The

THE GERMAN OFFENSIVE

expected blow fell on 23rd April, along the whole line south of the Somme, but was not very vigorously delivered, and was successful only at Villers-Bretonneux. Here the Germans employed for the first time their own tanks, and the latter's performance, limited and half-hearted as it was, proved what might have been done with more faith and perseverance. The appearance of the three clumsy machines was enough for most of the garrison of Villers-Bretonneux. Nearly the whole of the large village was carried, 2000 prisoners were taken, and tanks and infantry pushed on toward Cachy and the Bois de l'Abbé. In the latter place was lying a section of the 1st Tank Battalion. Moving out at 8.30 in the morning, to help some infantry in the trenches about Cachy, two female tanks of this section sighted a German tank about an hour later, and at once engaged it. Exposed to the enemy's 6-pounder guns, to which they could make no effective reply, they were both knocked out; but the third tank of the section, a male, now appeared, and there ensued the first genuine contest between these machines. The German seems to have been outmanœuvred, although his one-man control should have given him an advantage over the awkward secondary gears of the Mark IV. The latter attacked him on his blind side, so to speak, where his single gun would not bear, hit him three times with 6-pounder shells, and drove him into a sandpit, where the clumsy tank became ditched. The two other German machines were now coming up, but after a very perfunctory pretence of engaging our solitary male, turned about and escaped. The victor, while in pursuit, was hit and disabled by a chance shell from a field-gun. Villers-Bretonneux was brilliantly recaptured by the Australians the same night.

The same morning a composite company of Whippets started out at 10.30 to clear up the situation east of Cachy. "Whilst proceeding round the north-east of this village, they suddenly came upon two or three battalions of Germans massing in a hollow preparatory to making an attack. Without a moment's hesitation the seven Whippets formed line and charged down the slope right on to the closely-formed infantry. Indescribable confusion ensued as the Whippets tore through the German ranks. The enemy scattered in all directions. Some threw themselves on their knees before the machines, shrieking for mercy, only to be run over and crushed to death. In a few minutes no less than 400 Germans were killed or wounded. The Whippets having now completed their task — viz., "Clearing up the situation," returned, one machine being put out of action by artillery fire on the journey home. In all only five casualties amongst the crews were suffered during this action. The two most remarkable features of this little engagement are: firstly, the helplessness of some 1200 to 1500 infantry against 7 tanks manned by 7 officers and 14 other ranks; and, secondly, that the tanks left their starting-point, which was three and a half miles from the scene of action, at 10.30 A.M., covered ten miles of ground, fought a battle, and were back home again at 2.30 P.M.[1]

It was reported at the time that when the Whippets returned their sides and tracks were dripping with the blood of the Germans who had been run over—a pleasant touch, but not authenticated.

There were two other tank actions on this front on the 25th and 28th, the latter with the French Moroccan Division at Hangard Wood. This last was a failure, largely because the barrage came down *beyond* the German line instead of in front of it. A final minor engagement on May 2nd marked the end of this semi-defensive phase of the campaign. The Amiens front settled down more or less to what used to be described as "peace-time" warfare: the Germans turned their men and guns southward to the Aisne; and the Tank Corps was engaged in no further operations, with one exception, until July, when the whole spirit of our tactics was happily changed, and a series of small offensives preceded the great attack on 8th August.

[1] 'Weekly Tank Notes.'

CHAPTER XVII.

HAMEL, MOREUIL, AND THE THIRD BATTLE OF
THE SOMME.

I.

On the night of the 22nd-23rd June, a night raid of peculiar interest was carried out against the village of Bucquoy, north of the Ancre. Five platoons of infantry and five female tanks of the 10th Battalion were employed. The notable features were the use of tanks at night, and the remarkable skill and success with which they were hidden for a fortnight within a few hundred yards of the German outposts. One section of four tanks was camouflaged right in the open, the machines side by side and covered by their nets, in a slight depression not half a mile from the village. Another four tanks were driven into old gun-pits by the side of the Bucquoy-Hennescamp road, even nearer to the enemy. Here the two sections remained for nearly fourteen days, waiting for a favourable opportunity with the full moon. Various causes postponed the enterprise, but at length the conditions were considered propitious, and the five tanks required moved yet farther forward after dark into a sunken road skirting the eastern gardens of Bucquoy, of whose main street one side was held by our outposts and the other by those of the enemy. But now the moon failed, and again the raid was cancelled. Those responsible for it do not seem even to have thought of the danger of leaving tanks indefinitely on the edge of No Man's Land. For two more days and nights the five machines actually remained in this preposterous position without being discovered. Movement by day was almost impossible, and extreme care had to be exercised at night. Finally, on the night of the 22nd, the raid was carried out. The infantry, after all this hesitation and consulting of omens, were held up almost at once by trench-mortar and machine-gun fire, and although reinforced, got no farther; but the five tanks pushed on right through the village, passed their objectives, killed a number of the enemy and started a serious panic, and returned undamaged. The darkness gave them little trouble, and, on the other hand, afforded them valuable protection from the trench mortars. Their experience, and the careful preliminary work carried out by the Reconnaissance officers, were of great service to the 7th Battalion when we attacked over the same ground two months later.

A more important action was fought on 4th July on the old Villers-Bretonneux battle-ground. It was the first definite offensive on our part since the German blow in March, and it also introduced the Mark V. tank. This machine, identical in shape and armament with the Mark IV. (except that the Hotchkiss light gun replaced the Lewis), possessed great mechanical improvements, primarily in the adoption of epicyclic gears, which enabled one man to drive and steer the tank, and abolished the dilatory business of gearsmen and secondary levers. Three men, in fact, were released for other work, while the tank's power of manœuvre was greatly improved. Fitted with a 180 h.-p. Ricardo engine, in place of the Daimler, the Mark V. had increased speed, five to six miles an hour, and could be turned as easily as the Whippet. Other modifications included a second cab for observation on the roof, where the manhole was situated in the earlier types. The only serious fault was bad ventilation, which, with the more powerful engine, raised the heat inside to a pitch that at times became unbearable.

The object of the attack on 4th July was the recapture

THE THIRD BATTLE OF THE SOMME   349

"as a necessary preliminary to any operation to disengage Amiens,"[1] of the spur which runs northward from the Villers-Bretonneux plateau toward the junction of the Somme and the Ancre at Corbie. The objectives included Hamel village and wood and Vaire Wood, and were strictly limited. The infantry to be employed was the 4th Australian Division, and a subsidiary object of the operation was to restore the confidence of the Colonials in tanks—a confidence which had been quite unnecessarily shaken by the failure at Bullecourt in the early spring of 1917, when, as a matter of fact, it was the tanks that had a grievance. That there should be no failure through lack of means on this occasion, the whole of the 8th Tank Battalion and two companies of the 13th (sixty machines in all) were allotted to the Australians. As soon as the attack was decided upon, training with the infantry was put in hand at Vaux-en-Amienois, the 5th Tank Brigade Headquarters, and a good mutual understanding was cultivated. The Australians, clinging still to old prejudices, insisted on the tanks following the first wave of attack instead of preceding it; but this adherence to a bad system did not in effect matter at all, as the Mark V.'s took the lead almost at once on the day of action, and remained ahead of the infantry throughout.

Zero was at 3.10, just after dawn. The final rather intricate approach-marches of the five tank companies, from Hamelet and Fouilloy to the starting-points behind the infantry, were covered by the noise of low-flying aeroplanes. At eight minutes before zero the tanks moved forward again, crossed the remaining 1000 yards in twelve minutes, and at zero, plus four minutes, the barrage lifted and they advanced with the infantry. The attack was a complete success. In an hour and a half the whole affair was over: Hamel village and the woods were carried, an advance of 2500 yards on a front of 7000 had been made, and 1500 prisoners, with 2 field- and 171 machine-

[1] Sir Douglas Haig's Despatch.

guns, were in our hands. Our casualties were under 700, most of them walking wounded, and 5 tanks hit and disabled; 57 tanks reached their final objectives, and 55 had rallied by 11 A.M. All the disabled machines were salved during the two following nights, some of them being towed 9000 yards, so that the enemy was without any knowledge of the new type beyond what he had discovered in action; and this must have been the reverse of encouraging. The increased manœuvring powers of the Mark V. astonished the Germans as much as they delighted the Australians. A feature of the action was the number of machine-gun emplacements overrun and flattened out by tanks at the request of the infantry—an entirely satisfactory process of elimination. The German machine-gunners fought in many cases with extreme bravery, continuing to fire until the very moment before their guns—and perhaps themselves—were crushed into the earth by the tanks; but the unexpected rapidity of movement shown by the latter, as compared with the deliberate actions of the Mark IV., continually took them by surprise. The results of the attack, in short, were that the Australians were satisfied with the tanks, that the tank crews were satisfied with the Australians, which was quite as important, and that a sure foundation had been laid for the greater partnership of the 8th of August.

A fortnight later the 9th Tank Battalion, temporarily attached to the 5th Brigade for the purpose, took part at very short notice in an operation south of Amiens with the French 9th Corps. The third great German blow, between Soissons and Rheims, had in its turn exhausted its momentum; but to all the world it seemed still in the full tide of victory when, on 18th July, with a rapidity founded on exact calculation, Foch's counter-attack, led by hundreds of Rénault tanks, fell on the flank of the new Salient from the Aisne to Château Thierry, and the last phase of the war had begun. The second battle of the Marne, or the battle of Soissons, whichever it is called, was the first of that series of Allied offensives which for the next four months were to succeed one another without a pause up and down the whole immense front from the Woevre to the sea. Five days after it began, Debeney's 1st French Army carried out a small attack north of Montdidier, with the double object of occupying the German reserves in that region and of capturing the heights which overlook the river Avre at Aubvillers and Mailly-Raineval. It was for this operation that the 9th Tank Battalion was lent. It proved a complete success, although the casualties in tanks and personnel were rather heavy, and it was of interest chiefly on two accounts: firstly, the excellent way in which the French infantry combined with the tanks, although only two or three days of sketchy training, handicapped by difficulties of language, were possible beforehand; and secondly, for the speed with which the tanks' share in the battle was arranged and carried out. The project was discussed for the first time on 16th July at the 4th Army Headquarters. An hour and a half later, General Elles and General Courage (commanding the 5th Brigade) interviewed the French Army commander, General Debeney, and arranged with his Staff the general outlines of the move and the action. The next day the 9th Tank Battalion, far away near Bus-les-Artois, received orders to trek on the 18th to Rosel, a distance of nearly ten miles across country. Entraining at Rosel, it detrained at Contay on the 19th, and that evening trekked another two and a half miles. During the three following nights a farther distance of twelve miles was covered in stages, the final lap, on the night of the 22nd-23rd, bringing the battalion into action with thirty-five machines out of forty-two, most of the absentees being old Mark IV. supply-tanks. During this period troops of the 3rd French Division, which was to supply the infantry for the attack, underwent a brief course of training with tanks at Vaux-en-Amienois, while the Reconnaissance Officers of the 9th Battalion hurriedly surveyed the battlefield.

After the action, in which 15 tanks were disabled by artillery fire and 54 officers and men were killed or wounded, General Debeney visited the battalion and expressed in very warm terms his appreciation of its services. The 3rd French Division conferred upon it a rare distinction in the form of its own divisional badge, which every officer and man of the 9th Battalion now wears on the left sleeve.[1]

II.

Even before the French counterstroke of 18th July, the first plans for an attack by the restored 4th British Army south of the Somme were under discussion. Limited originally to the recapture of the old Amiens defence line, the scheme expanded until it assumed the dimensions of a full-dress battle—involving at least a dozen infantry divisions, a cavalry corps, and four brigades of tanks on our part, and, on our right, the 1st French Army and part of the 3rd. Our objective, roughly, was the important railway which ran southward from Peronne through Chaulnes and Roye, which meant an advance in places of from twelve to fifteen miles.

Notwithstanding the reinforcements which had been poured into France in the past two months, so ambitious a programme, to be completed within three or four days, could mean only one thing—another tank operation on a large scale, or, in other words, a second Cambrai. Tanks were the only arm which could hope to produce such a result in so short a time. And yet, if we hunt through the official account of the battle and its antecedents, we find the determining factor hardly mentioned. We read of "the brilliant and predominating part taken by the Canadian and Australian Corps in this battle. . . ." And again, of "the fine performance of the cavalry, . . .

---

[1] This action appears to be known officially by us as that of Moreuil. That village, however, was not even one of the objectives.

THE THIRD BATTLE OF THE SOMME 353

the dash and vigour of their action. . . ." Far away, at the very end of a despatch which takes us to the Armistice, we find this significant sentence, which seems to have slipped in by mistake: "*The whole scheme of the attack of the 8th August was dependent upon tanks.* . . ."[1]

The italics are my own, and I will not labour again, in face of this belated confession, over the old arguments and manifest facts which I have reiterated so often already. I will add only one remark, that the very fact of the omission by name of the Tank Corps in accounts of all the attacks which it led and determined from 8th August to the end of the war, is a tacit (and, I am sure, quite unintentional) admission of its influence. It had become, although no one would confess it openly, so essential a factor that its recognition was reserved for those concluding paragraphs in a despatch which praise conventionally every branch of the service, from the Artillery and Engineers to R.T.O.'s and Sanitary Squads.

Zero day, fixed in the first place for 10th August, was put forward two days at the end of July. The Canadian Corps, borrowed from the 1st Army, and in the best possible condition after the first genuine rest it had known since its original contingents landed in France, was on the right of our line, from a point opposite Moreuil to above Hangard. With it was the 4th Tank Brigade, consisting of the 1st, 4th, 5th, and 14th Battalions, the latter newly arrived from England. On the left of the Canadians, extending past Villers-Bretonneux to the Somme, was the Australian Corps, with its old friend the 5th Tank Brigade, now made up of the 2nd, 8th, 13th, and 15th Battalions, the last being also a new arrival. On the left of the Australians, again, was the 3rd Corps, to which was attached the 10th Tank Battalion by itself. The 9th Battalion was

---

[1] Sir D. Haig's Despatch. For a trustworthy estimate of the value of tanks in this and all subsequent attacks, and of their influence upon the course of the war, see 'The Last Four Months,' by General Sir Frederick Maurice, quoted in the last chapter of this book.

still refitting after its action with the French, and would not be available for several days. This made a total of nine tank battalions, with a tenth in reserve, all except two being equipped with Mark V. machines. The two exceptions, the 1st and 15th, had for their sins a still later novelty known as the Mark V. One Star. This was a thoroughly bad invention, being merely a Mark V. lengthened by about six feet, and designed to carry infantry or machine-gunners as well as its crew, these passengers being deposited at suitable points in the enemy's country. It offered an enormous target, and if its supernumeraries survived the journey, and were not shot in getting out, they were usually incapable, through sickness or coma brought on by their prolonged confinement inside, of doing any useful work.

In addition to this total, there remained the 3rd and 6th Battalions of the 3rd Tank Brigade. Both these units were now equipped with Whippets, and were attached to the Cavalry Corps, which was charged with the usual magnificent schemes of exploitation, as though machine-guns and magazine rifles had never been heard of. There was also the 17th Battalion of Armoured Cars, attached to the 5th Tank Brigade, but intended to work with the Whippets and cavalry.

It will be seen that for the purposes of this operation the 2nd Brigade had ceased temporarily to exist, its units being distributed among the others. The 1st Brigade was still absent from the main theatre of war. Its three battalions were at Merlimont, practising gunnery, hoping to draw Mark V.'s, and preparing for the next offensive between Arras and the Ancre, in which they were to have their fill of fighting.

The number of tanks to be employed on the 8th August was 435, including 96 Whippets, but excluding the armoured cars. Again, as at Cambrai, there was virtually no reserve of tanks. On the second and subsequent days composite detachments had to be organised in the field. The country immediately in front was good, and still covered in part with growing corn, but east of the line from Roye to Frise, on the Somme, if they ever got so far, was the old shelled area. This, however, was easily negotiable by heavy tanks

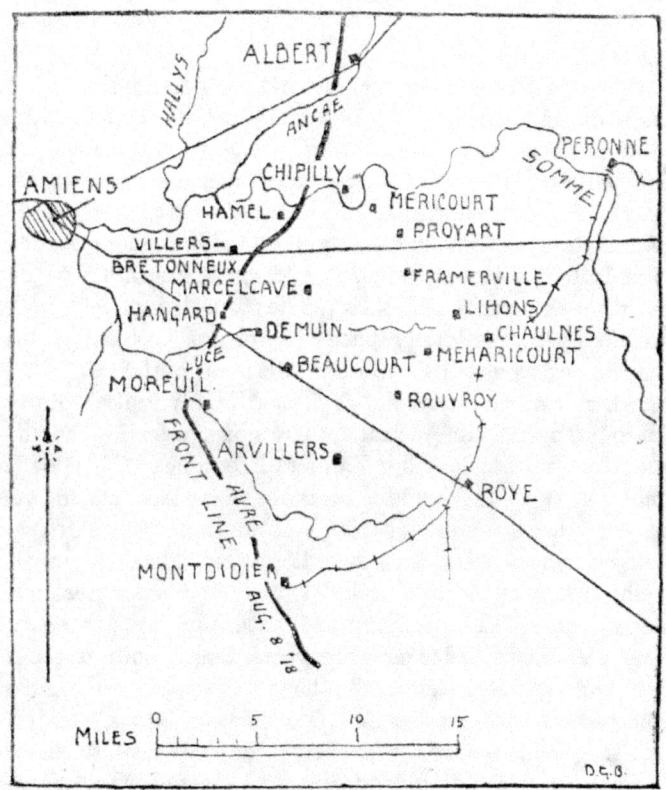

Third Battle of the Somme.

in dry weather. The preliminary arrangements were modelled on those of Cambrai—profound secrecy, reconnaissance carried out with every possible precaution, and no artillery preparation or activity beyond the normal until the barrage fell at zero. The Australians had been training with tanks at Vaux-en-Amienois, and the Canadians, after their work with the 1st Brigade at Bouvigny and Enguinegatte, at Cavillon with the 9th Battalion.

III.

Considerable anxiety was caused by the capture, on the night of 4th August, of an Australian outpost near the Roye road, as not only would this reveal to the enemy the extension of the Australian front over ground hitherto occupied by the French, but there also was a possibility of damaging information being extracted from the prisoners. The latter, however, refused to disclose anything beyond their names and units, their demeanour being held up as an example of soldierly behaviour in the German reports on their examinations. On the afternoon of the 7th, Y-day, another alarm occurred. Eighteen supply-tanks, allotted to the 4th and 5th Australian Divisions, were hidden in a small plantation north of Villers-Bretonneux. A chance shell burst in the middle of these machines, which were fully loaded with food, petrol, and ammunition; a fire was started, which drew upon the plantation a heavy bombardment; and 15 of the tanks, with all their stores, were destroyed. This calamity led naturally to a suspicion that the tanks had been discovered, but happily it proved unfounded. The Germans believed that only an ordinary dump had been exploded. The coming attack remained entirely unsuspected: the enemy, indeed was so misled by various artifices behind the 1st and 2nd Army fronts, including an early and conspicuous concentration of tanks near St Pol, that he made every preparation against a counter-offensive in Flanders and on the Lys.

During the night of the 7-8th, a heavy ground mist rose over the Somme battlefield, and became so dense by daybreak that tanks and infantry completed their assemblage and moved into action by compass. It aided the surprise,

however, and was attributed in part by the discomfited
Germans to a non-existent device which they described
as an "artificial fog." The only artificial element was the
usual smoke barrage included in the artillery programme,
which no doubt helped to increase the early obscurity and
confusion. When, at 4.20 A.M. on the 8th, there appeared
suddenly out of this veil more than 330 heavy tanks,
followed closely by lines of skirmishers and then by the
main waves of assault, the German front for twelve miles,
from the Somme to Moreuil, was rent like a cobweb. A four-
minute deluge of shells was the only warning, for, as the
barrage lifted, the tanks and infantry were close at its heels.
The advance went with a greater swing even than that
of Cambrai, for the two Colonial Corps were neither tired
nor weak in numbers, and the Mark V.'s were swifter and
more handy than the leaders in the earlier battle. Von
Hutier's 18th Army, composed in part of rather indifferent
troops, made no fight at all during the morning. So rapid
was the advance that within two or three hours the
majority of the German field batteries were overrun and
captured; the Albert-Montdidier road, beyond Marcelcave
and Demuin, was crossed before noon; officers and men
were made prisoners in their messes and billets; and one
entire divisional staff was taken. While the heavy tanks
were crushing such sporadic resistance as was offered during
this first phase by isolated posts and villages (Marcelcave,
it may be noted, was captured by a tank single-handed,
whose commander obtained a receipt for it from the
Australian infantry), the armoured cars had rushed ahead
down the two straight Roman roads which diverge from
Amiens upon Noyon and St Quentin. Mark V.'s hauled
the cars over No Man's Land and cleared away some trees
and other obstacles on the roads immediately beyond, after
which the machines had a clear run before them. As they
were a unit of the Tank Corps and manned by tank personnel, their exceptional opportunities and exploits deserve
notice. General Sir John Monash, commanding the Aus-

tralian Corps, gives the following account of the cars' experiences on the St Quentin road:—

"It has already been foreshadowed that the experiences on that day of the contingent of fifteen armoured motor-cars under Lieut.-Colonel Carter would form sensational reading, and the story of 8th August would not be complete without at least a brief reference to their exploits.

"It was nearly midnight when Carter, with a staff officer, got back to Corps headquarters to render their report. They were scarcely recognisable, covered as they were from head to foot with grime and grease. They had had a busy time. The substance of what they had to tell was taken down at the time almost verbatim, and reads as follows:—

"'Got armoured cars through to Warfusée-Abancourt. When we reached the other side of No Man's Land we found that the road was good, but a number of trees (large and small) had been shot down, and lay right across it in places. Obstacles removed by chopping up the smaller trees and hauling off the big ones by means of a tank. Pioneers helped us to clear the road all the way down. We did not come up to our advancing troops until they were almost near the Red Line.

"'When we got to Blue Line we detached three sections to run down to Framerville. When they got there they found all the Boche horse-transport and many lorries drawn up in the main road ready to move off. Head of column tried to bolt in one direction and other vehicles in another. Complete confusion. Our men killed the lot (using 3000 rounds), and left them there; four staff officers on horseback shot also. The cars then ran down to the east side of Harbonnières, on the S.E. road to Vauvillers, and met there a number of steam waggons; fired into their boilers, causing an impassable block. . . .

THE THIRD BATTLE OF THE SOMME 359

"'Two other cars went to Proyart and found a lot of troops billeted there, having lunch in the houses. Our cars shot through the windows into the houses, killing quite a lot of the enemy. Another section went towards Chuignolles and found it full of German soldiers. Our cars shot them. Found rest billets and old trenches, also with troops in them. Engaged them. Had quite a battle there. Extent of damage not known, but considerable. Cars then came back to main road. We were then well in advance of Blue Line.'

"The consternation and disorganisation caused by the sudden onslaught of these cars, at places fully ten miles behind the enemy's front line of that morning, may be left to the imagination. It was a feat of daring and resolute performance which deserves to be remembered."[1]

The Whippets were greatly handicapped by being attached to the Cavalry Corps. The latter, moving rapidly forward in the early morning toward the line, complained that the tanks could not keep up. As soon as it came to fighting, however, the situation was reversed: it was the cavalry that could not keep up with the Whippets, or indeed do anything at all. "By noon on the 8th August, great confusion was developing behind the enemy's lines, and by this time the Whippets should have been operating five to ten miles in advance of the infantry, accentuating this demoralisation. As it was, being tied down to support the cavalry, they were a long way behind the infantry advance, the reason being that, as cavalry cannot make themselves invisible on the battlefield by throwing themselves flat on the ground as infantry can, they had to retire either to a flank or to the rear to avoid being exterminated by machine-gun fire."[2] One sentence in this quotation sums up the whole case against cavalry. If the Whippets were idle

---
[1] Sir J. Monash, 'The Australian Victories in 1918.'
[2] 'Weekly Tank Notes.'

because "being tied down to support the cavalry they were a long way behind the infantry advance," what, in Heaven's name, was the use of the mounted arm? The latter in theory, and if it was to justify its existence at all, should have been a long way in front, instead of a long way behind. Cavalry behind an infantry attack are merely an annoying encumbrance, blocking up roads, losing their way, and behaving, at the same time, as if they alone are winning the battle. Colonel Buchan, tactful at the expense of accuracy, permits himself to say that "the whole British cavalry performed miracles, advancing twenty-three miles from their points of concentration." This is merely silly, for the points of concentration were far away to the west of Amiens. Sir John Monash, on the spot, and speaking from bitter experience of the uselessness and presumption of these archaic cohorts, tries to find excuses for them and writes with great moderation, but his conclusions tally with those of every other unprejudiced observer. He says:—

"The Cavalry Corps would appear in the battle area also, with all preparations made for a rapid exploitation of any success achieved. The utility of the cavalry in modern war, at any rate in a European theatre, has been the subject of endless controversy. It is one into which I do not propose to enter. There is no doubt that, given suitable ground and an absence of wire entanglements, cavalry can move rapidly, and undertake important turning or enveloping movements. Yet it has been argued that the rarity of such suitable conditions negatives any justification for superimposing so unwieldy a burden as a large body of cavalry, on the bare chance that it *might* be useful, upon already over-populated areas, billets, watering-places, and roads.

"I may, however, anticipate the event by saying that the First Cavalry Brigade was duly allotted to me, and did its best to prove its utility; but I am bound to say that the results achieved, in what proved to be very unsuitable country beyond the range of the

infantry advance, did not justify the effort expended,
either by this gallant brigade or by the other arms and
services upon whom the very presence of the cavalry
proved an added burden." [1]

The Whippets were peculiarly unfortunate in being so
shackled on this particular day. Such opportunities lay
before these machines as never fell to them again. Within
two or three hours of zero the enemy, on a wide front, was
thoroughly demoralised and in flight, with most of his field
batteries captured; and there lay ahead, occupied by his
headquarters, transport and stores, a great stretch of good
undulating country served by numerous roads in fair condition. It was the day of days for Whippets. The armoured
cars, few in number and confined to roads, did great things;
but for a light fast tank the opportunities were endless.
Colonel Buchan is in error when he says that the tanks
employed that day were " mostly of the Whippet type," for,
as we have seen, there were only ninety-six of the latter.
Yet if these had been let loose on roving commissions, the
haul of prisoners and guns, and the general demoralisation
of the enemy, would have been far greater even than was the
case. With extraordinary ineptitude, the two battalions
were dragged about at the heels of Cavalry Brigade headquarters, a position which alone shows an abysmal misunderstanding of their functions. Elaborate tactics for
their co-operation with horsemen had been drawn up, but
as the horsemen, when they attempted to advance in any
numbers, were checked almost at once by a few machine-guns, the bulk of the Whippets merely cruised about them
in exposed situations without being able to strike an effective
blow. A few, more fortunate, were set free for their proper
tasks, and showed what might have been accomplished had
all been handled in so bold a manner. Some came into hot
fighting about Cayeux Wood, Le Quesnel, Guilleaucourt,
and Harbonnières, along the Amiens-Chaulnes railway, and,
by cutting telegraph and telephone wires, increased the

[1] Sir J. Monash, 'The Australian Victories in 1918.'

enemy's confusion. One, "Musical Box," of the 6th Battalion, had an extraordinary career. Passing through the advanced infantry line and a few cavalry patrols two or three hours after zero, it engaged a field battery which had already knocked out two Mark V. tanks. Sweeping round behind the guns, it drove off the crews and pursued them, killing or wounding nearly all. Turning north toward the railway near Guilleaucourt, the tank then busied itself with various parties of fugitives, moved on again after a short halt, entered a German hutted camp where troops were hurriedly packing up their kits, and accounted for about sixty of these; continued in chase of fresh bodies of infantry retiring eastward, shot the drivers of several motor and horse vehicles, and finally got among some horse and transport lines near Rosières, where an immense amount of damage was done. The little tank, being entirely alone, far ahead of its fellows and of the infantry, was subjected to continual machine-gun fire, and petrol was pouring down the sides and into the interior from riddled tins carried on the roof. The petrol fumes, together with the intense heat, obliged the crew to breathe through the mouthpieces of their box-respirators. Eventually, about three o'clock in the afternoon—for the " Musical Box " was in action continuously for nine or ten hours—the tank was hit by a field-gun and set on fire on the eastern side of the Harbonnières-Rosières road, beyond our farthest objective for that day. The officer, Lieutenant Arnold, managed to drag out his two men, who were overcome with the smoke and fumes. The clothing of all three was on fire. Endeavouring to escape, after rolling in the grass to extinguish the flames, the driver was killed, and Arnold and the second man were captured and brutally ill-used. The full story of this remarkable exploit was only known after Arnold's release at the end of the war.

The heavy tanks had met with most trouble on the two wings. On the left the enemy's stubborn defence of the Chipilly Spur, overlooking a loop of the Somme, held up

THE THIRD BATTLE OF THE SOMME 363

the 3rd Corps until the next day, and the 5th Tank Brigade had forty machines knocked out, mostly by enfilade artillery fire from this flank. Those which passed this danger point, however, did remarkable work, which included the capture of the 51st German Corps headquarters, with most of the staff, near Framerville, where the armoured cars helped. The Mark V. Stars of the 15th Battalion in many cases delivered their unhappy loads of machine-gunners on the final objectives, but the great size of these machines made them such excellent targets that a disproportionate number were knocked out, their crews and passengers being too often burnt to death inside them. The survivors of the infantry who were carried in them were emphatic in their determination to have nothing further to do with this method of transport in action.

The 4th Tank Brigade, working with the Canadians on the right, also suffered considerable losses in the early part of the day, owing to Débeney's Frenchmen being held up for a time along the Avre valley. The little stream of the Luce, close behind our front line, had to be crossed without the enemy's knowledge, and had caused much anxiety, as on account of its position and the necessity for secrecy, adequate reconnaissance of it was impossible. All the tanks, except two, crossed in a dense mist without a hitch and undiscovered by the Germans. Everything went with a rush at first, and there were few casualties; but in the second phase of the attack, until the French broke through the resistance about Moreuil and were able to bring their left level with the Canadians, tanks and infantry had a hard time at Beaucourt and Le Quesnel, where the enemy brought field-guns into close action with great boldness and success. One company of the 1st Tank Battalion, caught by a battery in enfilade near Le Quesnel, lost in a few minutes nine out of eleven Mark V. Stars, all of which were burnt out with heavy casualties to their crews and to the hapless infantry volunteers on board. One tank commander swung his machine round and steered straight for the battery, but this desperate and gallant act was useless. He was killed, with most of his crew and passengers.

Such incidents, however, were only local set-backs in what, as a whole, was a victory without parallel. On a twelve-mile front we had advanced at one point to a depth of seven miles. Twenty-four hours after zero 16,000 prisoners and over 200 captured guns had been counted. Amiens and its railways were freed, and the enemy's chief means of lateral communication in this sector, the Chaulnes-Roye line, already was within range of our field-guns. Only at Chipilly, on the left, had there been any permanent check; and that flank was in its proper alignment the next day. The greatest result of all, however, coming as it did upon the battle of Soissons and Von Boehn's retreat, was the profound moral effect wrought upon the German soldier. In this respect the 8th August stands pre-eminent. Ludendorff himself testifies that " August 8th was the black day of the German Army in the history of the war. This was the worst experience I had to go through. . . ." And immediately, in public and secret documents, he proceeded to point the moral. The tanks alone had done this thing; and to combat tanks every nerve must be strained and every effort directed. On 11th August, while the battle was still in progress, he issued an urgent and secret order:—

> "Troops allowed themselves to be surprised by a mass attack of tanks, and lost all cohesion when the tanks suddenly appeared behind them, having broken through under cover of a mist, natural and artificial. The defensive organisation, both of the first line and in the rear, was insufficient to permit of a systematic defence. . . . As a weapon against tanks the prepared defence of the ground must play a larger part than ever, and the aversion of the men to the pick and shovel must be overcome at all hazards. . . . Especially, there must be defences against tanks. It was absolutely inadmissible that the tanks, having penetrated into our advance line without meeting with obstacles

or anything, should be able to push on along the roads or beside them for miles. . . . The principle that a body of troops, even when surrounded, must defend their ground, unless otherwise ordered, to the last man and the last cartridge, seems to have fallen into oblivion . . . a large proportion of our ranks fight unskilfully against tanks. A tank is an easy prey for artillery of all calibres. . . ."

Then followed a summary of the various anti-tank measures which I have already described. All this was too late, however; it was shutting the door after the steed —in this case the German soldier's nerve and heart— was irrevocably gone. And Ludendorff must have known, ever since Cambrai, that against a massed tank attack, supported by good infantry, no army in the world could stand.

Five days later, on 16th August, Sir Henry Rawlinson added his testimony in a Special Order to the Tank Corps.

"The success of the operations of 8th August and succeeding days was largely due to the conspicuous part played by the 3rd, 4th, and 5th Brigades of the Tank Corps, and I desire to place on record my sincere appreciation of the invaluable services rendered both by the Mark V. and the Mark V. Star and the Whippets.

"The task of secretly assembling so large a number of tanks entailed very hard and continuous work by all concerned for four or five nights previous to the battle.

"The tactical handling of the tanks in action made calls on the skill and physical endurance of the detachments which were met with by a gallantry and devotion beyond all praise.

"I desire to place on record my appreciation of the splendid success that they achieved, and heartily to congratulate the Tank Corps as a whole on the completeness of their arrangements, and the admirable prowess exhibited by all ranks actually engaged on this occasion.

"There are many vitally important lessons to be learned from their experiences. These will, I trust, be taken to heart by all concerned, and made full use of when next the Tank Corps is called upon to go into battle.

"The part played by the tanks and Whippets in the battle of 8th August was in all respects a very fine performance."

About 100 tanks had been knocked out or otherwise disabled in the first day's fighting. In the next day's advance 145 took part, mostly formed as composite companies, the evil effects of the absence of any reserves being felt once more. The 10th Battalion helped the 3rd Corps to clear the Chipilly Spur and the difficult gullies which abounded in that region, while the 4th and 5th Brigades fought in Framerville and Rosières and Bouchoir. A few Whippets cut loose from their leading-strings and penetrated as far as the devastated area of the old Somme battlefield; but most of these machines remained tied to the ineffective wanderings of the cavalry, who displayed their usual *penchant* for collecting in valleys where they were certain to be shelled. Another 39 tanks were hit on this day. In the meantime Humbert's 3rd French Army had attacked south of Montdidier. On the 10th Montdidier fell, and we were on the edge of Lihons and within 3000 yards of the railway station of Chaulnes. Sixty-seven tanks were engaged in this fighting, of which 30 were disabled by shell-fire. Another 40 machines were in again on the 11th, when Lihons was captured in part and Humbert was on the edge of the much-talked-of Lassigny *massif*, familiar to Mr Belloc's numerous readers; and with this the share of the Tank Corps in the battle of Amiens came to an end. The battle itself was virtually over. The old tactical ideas of hammering for weeks at one point had vanished with the acceptance of the new doctrines of tank warfare. The devastated area had now been reached: the objectives aimed at had been won; and with the

THE THIRD BATTLE OF THE SOMME

enemy thoroughly awakened and obsessed with the danger south of the Somme, the time had come for another blow in the new style in a different quarter.

Some idea of the wastage in tanks involved in a battle of this description, and of the infinite advantages we might have gained if we had possessed an adequate supply of these machines, may be gathered from the following figures and dates. In the four days' fighting, a total of 688 tanks had been engaged. No fewer than 480, including supply tanks, had been handed over to salvage. The few remaining fighting machines needed a thorough overhaul before they would be fit for another battle. There were left the 9th Battalion, with 27 tanks, which had rejoined the 4th Brigade; the 11th Battalion, with 42, which had been rushed down from the 1st Brigade to the Somme area, but had not been used; the 7th and 12th Battalions, still with Mark IV.'s (42 apiece), and the 16th Battalion, with another 42 Mark V.'s, just out from England. With the 9th Battalion brought up to strength, this would give 210 tanks as an untired reserve on 12th August. The next offensive, for which three whole brigades were needed at the very start, was due for the 21st of the month, or in little more than a week!

CHAPTER XVIII.

THE GREAT ADVANCE: FROM BUCQUOY TO BAPAUME.

I.

I CAN now take up again my own thread in the story and follow it through to the end.

In the first week of July I returned from Le Tréport to Enguinegatte, where, as I have said, I found all the company but a few headquarters' details already gone back to our old camp and billets at Bouvigny. I followed the next day. Our tanks had trekked across country to Central Workshps at Erin to be handed in. B and C Companies, in Noulette Wood, were waiting to entrain for the same purpose; and then the whole personnel of the battalion was going to Merlimont for Hotchkiss and driving courses preparatory to drawing its quota of Mark V.'s. The 11th Battalion was already there, and the 12th, which was to follow, was to become a light battalion with Whippets. Such, at least, were the arrangements. In practice, however, things fell out very differently.

On 18th July I came home on leave. Returning on 1st August, I caught the influenza and a particularly unpleasant bombing raid at Boulogne, and from there proceeded to Merlimont, where I expected to find the battalion. I found however, only A Company. B and C had drawn their old tanks again, and returned to Noulette Wood, where they were engaged in some mysterious business which turned out to be part of a scheme to delude the enemy into the expectation of an attack on the Lens front. At Merlimont I went straight to bed in a hut where I was deluged with sand every time the door opened, and remaining there three days saw little or nothing of the place—in which I do not think I lost much. The day after I began to totter about again in that gentle melancholy which influenza induces, there came the usual twenty-four hours' notice to move. All our hopes, it appeared, had come to nothing. Owing to Labour troubles at home—the old story—and in view of the certain need of heavy replacements after the battle of Amiens (then just beginning), the supply of Mark V.'s and Whippets was insufficient to equip the whole Tank Corps. In our brigade, therefore, while the 11th Battalion was to draw its forty-two machines of the new type and be rushed forthwith to the Somme on the fruitless errand I have mentioned, the 12th Battalion and ourselves were to be re-equipped with our old Mark IV.'s before leaving for some unknown destination. The 12th, which had been training as a Whippet battalion, was particularly annoyed. In our case, I think we came in the end to regard this misfortune as at least a compliment. If any battalion could make the Mark IV. capable in the field of rivalling its more powerful and handy successor it was " G "; and in the end, both the 12th and ourselves, I think, not only rivalled but excelled the performances of most of the Mark V. battalions. The amount of work we got out of our obsolete machines was astonishing. Some of them, almost falling to pieces for want of repair, were still pressing on with the 4th Army, at the especial request of the Guards and other infantry, until just before the Armistice, when they had covered, including battles and all the gambits involved by treks and approach-marches during the greatest advance since 1914, well upwards of 100 miles.

We left Merlimont for the Bermicourt area by lorry on 7th August, and were billeted in Blangy, next door to Erin, on the Ternoise. The officers of the company occupied a couple of dormitories in the most depressing institution imaginable—a huge dilapidated religious hostel for the feeble-minded. Very mercifully there were only a few of these unfortunates left at the time, mostly old men and women, with two or three nuns who looked after the establishment; but I know of no place more chilling and uncomfortable as a residence. We were here for a week. While the Tank commanders and crews were away at Erin every day, receiving their Mark IV.'s and equipment, there was little for me to do. I took a few runners in map-reading classes, drew from the M.T. workshops at Auchy a new combination Douglas and side-car to replace my old one, which somebody had smashed up in my absence, and paid the usual visits to Hesdin, a charming little town temporarily spoilt by the British Army in general and the Tank Corps in particular. I also visited once or twice the field of Agincourt, which lies on the hills above the Ternoise. The country has changed very little, so far as one can judge, since Henry V.'s insignificant army crossed the river near Erin, climbed the steep ridge beyond, and stood at bay on the tiny battlefield. The villages of Azincourt (as it is spelt) and Tramecourt, between which the French knights were killed in thousands, and that of Maisoncelles, where Henry established his headquarters on the night before the battle, still lie invisible in their trees just as they were hidden 500 years ago. The few fields which separate them are tilled now as they were tilled then; and only a road, some iron palings, and a signpost need to be obliterated to re-endue that fragment of landscape with the air and spirit of the fifteenth century. It was an odd contrast (if one may acknowledge such obvious reflections) to the vast tormented battlefields to which we were returning.

The workshops at Erin (which would have startled Henry V.) were now working full blast in consequence of the Somme battle. Stray crews of almost every unit in the Tank Corps were there, drawing new or repaired machines. A party of the 15th Battalion, just blooded at Proyart and Framerville, and slightly above themselves in consequence, descended upon our effete heads in the madhouse

one evening. Our own orders to move, couched in the
usual cryptic form reminiscent of a dime novel, reached
us on the afternoon of 14th August. The message began
in words like these—" 14 crows entrain Birmingham 2
P.M. 15th detrain Dublin 10 P.M. . . ." Decoded into
sense, this meant that the company would leave Erin next
day for Saulty Station, on the Arras-Doullens road. I
had to find the 1st Brigade advanced headquarters at
Sarton, near Doullens, and learn there the destination of
the tanks. Having seen the latter on their trucks at Erin,
I pushed off on my bicycle on the afternoon of the 15th
with Lishman, the company equipment officer, in the side-
car. We ran the brigade to earth in a dilapidated house
at Sarton about five o'clock, discovered that the tanks
were to lie that night in Bazèque Wood, two miles from
Saulty, and went on immediately to survey the route
between the two places. We found the wood full of dug-
outs, which promised some shelter for the night, and found
also a branch of the invaluable 6th Corps Club in marquees
at Bavincourt, near by, where I ordered dinner. Owing
to various accidents, however, we were not free to attend
this very necessary function until 9.30, and with the tank
train due in at ten we did not dare to leave the station
for so long. The train, of course, chose to be abominably
late. We sat and dozed and hungered in the R.T.O.'s office
until long after midnight; and it was daylight before we had
all the tanks camouflaged in the wood and could begin to
think of sleep.

B and C Companies had already arrived at similar
hiding-places in the neighbourhood. The following night,
that of the 16th, the whole battalion, with 42 tanks, moved
on to Bienvillers-au-Bois, where there was a company of
the 3rd Battalion's Whippets. Battalion headquarters
joined us next day and took over our most comfortable
billets — which were very primitive at the best. Bienvillers was a half-ruined and wholly deserted village about
four miles from our front line at Bucquoy, with which place

it was connected by a direct road through Hannescamps
and Essarts. It was surrounded by orchards in full leaf,
in which the tanks were hidden, and where there were also
a number of 60-pounder guns installed for the coming
offensive. The country to the eastward was good, rolling,
chalk land, forming a series of low ridges between Bienvillers and Bapaume. Before the German withdrawal to
the Hindenburg Line in the spring of 1917, the front
trenches had run between Hannescamps and Essarts, both
of which were entirely ruined. The present front line, so
far as it concerned us, now ran from north to south as
follows: east of Ayette, west of Ablainzevelle, through
Bucquoy, east of Puisieux-au-Mont, and so to Miraumont
on the Ancre, the enemy having just abandoned (on 15th
August) the small salient he had held in front of Puisieux
and Serre. Viewed from the high ground at Essarts, the
landscape before us was divided with a curious exactness
into two kinds. North of a line drawn between Bucquoy
and Puisieux, although wasted, desert, and seamed with
trenches, it still bore some resemblance to a state of nature.
Fragmentary houses were erect in the villages, and the trees
which invariably surround the latter in north-east France
seemed at a distance to be in fair preservation. But south
of the line the track of a hurricane—the first battle of the
Somme—had sheared everything away. Trees, houses, the
very sites of villages and farms, had vanished in a wholesale
annihilation; and the country westward to Bapaume and
southward to the Somme was one vast nondescript expanse
of ruin, broken only by a few stumps or a cloud of dust.
This obliterated area determined, so far as tanks were concerned, the front of the new attack, interposing a wide gap
between the 1st, 2nd, and 3rd Tank Brigades, working with
the 3rd Army to the north, and the 4th and 5th Brigades
which were to come into action again with the 4th Army a
day or two later. The time was past when tanks were
thrust in, willy-nilly, over any kind of *terrain*.

The 3rd Army's attack, to be launched on 21st August,

was to extend from Moyenneville to the Ancre—a frontage
of 17,000 yards. The first objective was the line of the
Arras-Albert railway, which ran from Moyenneville through
Achiet-le-Grand to Miraumont. On the 22nd the left of the
4th Army was to come into line between the Ancre and
the Somme, while on the 23rd, south of the latter, the
Australians would renew their advance, so that the offensive
would become continuous from Boyelles to the Amiens-St
Quentin road. The battle of Bapaume, as it is convenient
to call the northern part of the combined operation, was of
particular interest in that it brought us against a new
system of defence adopted by the Germans—or rather an
old system, tried with success at Ypres, now revived in
greatly altered circumstances. The idea was defence in
depth, the enemy's front positions as far back as the Arras-
Albert railway being held very thinly, chiefly by machine-
gunners with a number of scattered and camouflaged field-
guns for anti-tank purposes. Behind the railway were his
battery positions and his main line of resistance. The
main object of this arrangement was to hamper the tank
attack, the first phase of which would be delivered as it
were in the air, while the German batteries, instead of
being overrun at the start, as happened on the 8th August,
would be waiting 5000 yards in rear to deal with the second
phase, which must always be less coherent owing to loss of
tanks, accidents to infantry, and the general confusion that
ensues once a battle has begun. On 21st August this
defence in depth caused us undoubtedly a good deal of
anxiety and loss; but such a method can never be popular
with that minority of the defending troops which has to be
sacrificed as a matter of course in the advanced positions,
and this disadvantage in the end outweighed its merits. It
was found before long that the German soldier, whose
moral was deteriorating week by week, surrendered so
freely when left without artillery support far in front of the
main defence line that the whole purpose of the scheme was
vitiated.

The Tank Brigades had been thoroughly reshuffled before the battle. The 2nd Brigade, on the left of the 3rd Army, consisted now of the 12th and 15th Heavy Battalions and the 6th Light Battalion (Whippets). The 3rd Brigade, in reserve, had the 9th, 11th, and 14th Heavy Battalions. The 1st Brigade in the centre was made up of the 7th and 10th Heavy Battalions, the 3rd Light Battalion, and the 17th Armoured Car Battalion. " In consequence of the enemy's new system of defence and the varying powers of the three marks of machines used by the 1st and 2nd Tank Brigades, tanks were disposed in echelons as follows:—

1. Two battalions of Mark IV. tanks (7th and 12th) to operate as far as the second objective.
2. One battalion of Mark V. and one of Mark V. Star machines (10th and 15th) to operate against the second objective and proceed as far as the Albert-Arras railways.
3. Two battalions of Whippets and one of armoured cars to operate beyond the railway."[1]

As no such advance as that of 8th August was contemplated, the railway being the final objective for the first day, this employment of the Whippets and armoured cars seems to have been a mistake. There was little point in their disorganising the enemy's forces in an area over which we had no intention of advancing until the 23rd; and, on the other hand, their appearance, unsupported, beyond the railway, would put them at the mercy of the German batteries, by that time fully prepared. And, in fact, a company of the 3rd Battalion lost most of its tanks around Achiet-le-Petit (together with a number of armoured cars) before even the railway was reached.

There was very little time for reconnaissance before the attack. It was, of course, to be another surprise, based on tanks, but the battalion commanders of the latter were only informed of the details on the 18th. The 6th Corps

[1] 'Weekly Tank Notes.'

on the left, with the 2nd Tank Brigade, was to capture Moyenneville and Courcelles and the line of the railway beyond. The 4th Corps, in the centre, with the 1st Tank Brigade, had to carry first the villages of Ablainzevelle and Bucquoy, then Logeast Wood and the German second line to Achiet-le-Petit, and thirdly, Achiet-le-Grand and the railway. The 5th Corps, on the right, was advancing without tanks along the edge of the obliterated area against the Dove Cot at Beauregard and the village of Beaucourt. The 7th Battalion was primarily interested in Bucquoy and Ablainzevelle. B and C Companies were to capture the former, A Company the latter, after which one section from each company was to push on with the Mark V.'s of the 10th Battalion as far as Logeast Wood and Achiet-le-Petit. Bucquoy was a large village shaped like a badly drawn cross, one stroke of which ran up the Ayette road, parallel to our front, while the other crossed it at right angles along the road from Bienvillers and Hannescamps to Achiet-le-Petit. The opposing outposts were both in the village. Ablainzevelle, a more compact and much smaller place, lay 1000 yards to the north-east, just beyond the Ayette road. The infantry with whom we were co-operating in this first phase were two brigades of the 37th Division, in which I had served in the ranks in the early days of the war. By a coincidence, my old unit, the 10th Royal Fusiliers, which I had not seen since June 1915, was to take Ablainzevelle with A Company's tanks. In spite of the fact that the new German tactics of defence in depth presupposed the holding of both these villages very lightly, the infantry were extremely nervous about them. The 111th Brigade would have it that Ablainzevelle was a warren of dug-outs and tunnels and full of men. Personally, I do not believe there were fifty Germans in the place. In case, however, it proved to be a second Flesquières, six tanks (all we could get into it comfortably) were to rush it from three sides, the other eight machines of the company devoting themselves to the trenches and alleged strong points to the north and south. I spent a part of the 18th and 19th reconnoitring Ablainzevelle from our forward lines along the Ayette road, and on the first day the Major and I, having passed in front of our outposts by mistake, found ourselves in the ditch beside the road which led into the village from Bucquoy, and within 100 yards of the nearest house. We could see straight up the road into the middle of the village, which appeared to be as deserted and peaceful as any one could wish. There were Germans hidden somewhere in the ruins, but I am sure that if it had been desirable our people could have walked over any time after dark and taken the place with very little trouble. The same applied to Bucquoy and all similar advanced posts under the new German scheme of defence.

During the days before the attack the weather held gloriously fine with hot sunny days and moonlit nights, and the front was very quiet indeed. On the evening of the 19th, about dusk, we began to get the tanks of A Company out of their orchard. By midnight all were well on their way to the lying-up points we had selected. These were in the shallow valley which runs north and south between Bucquoy and the high ground about Essarts, and on the average were less than 2000 yards behind the front line. Wright's section, the farthest forward of all, was to lie up in a sunken road which ran into the northern end of Bucquoy, M'Chlery's behind a bank alongside the road from Essarts to Ayette, and Custance's under a row of trees near Quesnoy Farm, behind M'Chlery. Except for Custance's row of trees there was no real cover whatever in this neighbourhood beyond a few banks and sunken roads. From Essarts to Bucquoy the ground was a trough of grass-land where once fields had been. Besides our company, B and C were also to collect in the valley, so that forty-two tanks would be lying in the open a mile from the German outposts throughout Y-day. Behind us, over the Essarts Ridge, was the 10th Battalion, whose

Ablainzevelle, Logeast Wood, and Achiet-le-Grand.

Mark V.'s would move up at zero. The 12th and 15th Battalions on our left had the extensive shade of Adinfer Wood for concealment. Tanks, however, if hidden from direct observation and properly camouflaged, are as safe, or safer, in the open than in some conspicuous mass of timber. They are invisible from the air and extraordinarily difficult to locate even from close quarters on the ground, as was proved when the brigade Intelligence Officer, who knew the approximate positions of all our sections, could only find eight tanks out of the forty-two. By 2 A.M. our three sections were disposed of in their hiding-places without any disturbance from the enemy or trouble from the tanks. Having seen them camouflaged and the crews preparing to turn in for the rest of the night, the Major and I walked back to his car, which was waiting behind Essarts, and returned to Bienvillers for our own few hours' sleep. The rest of that day, the 20th, we were busy about many things. We went out to the tanks again after breakfast, and found everything well and the German artillery as quiet as before. The section and tank commanders were going out for a final reconnaissance that afternoon. I spent it in studying maps and photographs in the R.O.'s office at Bienvillers, drawing up operation orders with the Major, and making a few preparations for my personal comfort during the battle. After an early dinner we set off again about 7.30 for Essarts. As darkness fell, the whole countryside, which had been so empty of life the night before, became filled with quiet noises—the tramp of hoofs, the rattle of wheels, the voices of men passing orders or warnings. Dozens of field batteries were moving forward to take up their positions in front of Hannescamps for the opening barrage, and the assaulting infantry were on the way to their assembly trenches. The moon, which was almost full, rose intensely bright—too bright for my liking.

Zero was at 4.55 A.M., and before midnight all the tanks of the battalion were uncamouflaged and ready to move. The three sections of A Company were to be formed up in line beyond our front trench—Very Trench—at 4.40. To be on the safe side the route of each section was to be taped to this point, a task which normally falls to the Reconnaissance Officer; but as I could not be in three places at once, it was decided that the taping should be left to the section commanders and to Jukes, my assistant R.O., who had taken Maelor-Jones's place. I wandered round with the Major, visiting each section in turn. One startling incident disturbed these preliminaries. We were with Wright's section in the sunken road about midnight. He had no more than 1500 yards to cover, and there was no point in his starting at that hour; but some limbers appeared in the road with ammunition which had to be taken farther forward, and as the tanks blocked the way we started to get them up the bank to one side. The first tank reached the top, with some difficulty, for there was no room to swing in the road, and the bank was 12 feet high and very steep. The moon was now blazing like an arc-light upon everything, and the tank was silhouetted on a rise half a mile from Bucquoy, the trees of which village, as well as those along the Ayette road, were clearly visible. Everything was so brilliant, in fact, that we ordered men to hold up the canvas horn covers to hide the flashing of the tracks in the moonlight as the machine moved along above the cutting. I was down the road again watching the second tank endeavouring to climb out, when there came the whistle of a shell, and the leading one on top was hidden in smoke. Several more shells followed, all of which burst round the tank, and the crew came flying out and down into the road. The shooting was so extraordinarily close that we felt certain that the tank had been seen. Yet, after about a dozen rounds, none of which actually hit her, the gun or guns stopped firing. Apparently the shelling was meant for the road, which the Germans must have known to be used for transport at night, for after this a machine-gun opened on it at long range, and bullets came zip-zipping into the grass of the bank. With this epilogue,

however, the incident closed, and the night resumed its
normal quietude. We backed the leading tank behind the
crest, and got the rest out of the way of the limbers by
reversing them to the end of the sunken road. We were
taking no more risks in full view. As it happened, a mist
began to rise soon after and thickened so fast that all fear
of our being seen was at an end. Before morning it was
a veritable fog, which, lasting until ten o'clock, was to
hamper seriously the first phase of the attack. I spent an
hour on an errand to C Company later on, and as I was
returning saw the Mark V.'s of the 10th Battalion drawn
up in the valley our tanks had just left. The mist was very
dense when I rejoined the Major at the 111th Brigade
headquarters in a dug-out in Top Trench, the support line.
I remember getting some sleep here. Shortly before zero
runners came in from all three sections to report the tanks
lined up in No Man's Land. We climbed up into the
trench, to find we could not see a hundred yards in front
of us; and a few minutes later the massed batteries behind
broke the silence with an appalling crash of sound, a torrent
of shells whined overhead, and the attack had begun.

II.

For all we could see, we might have remained in the
dug-out. The fiendish uproar of the guns seemed to
increase, if that were possible—a modern barrage is one
continuous throbbing blast of noise beyond description—
but, looking back, there was not even a flicker of light
to be seen from all those smoking muzzles. Dawn had
broken, and we could see one another, but that was all.
Even Misty Trench (appropriately named), only two or
three hundred yards in front, was invisible. No hostile
shells seemed to be coming our way, but it was true they
might have been bursting quite near without our knowing
it. I cannot recall anything outside a London fog as dense

as that capricious mist which covered the whole battlefield
during the early morning of the 21st. The road in which
Wright's tanks had been concealed cut through Top
Trench close to where we were standing, and presently
the last section of C Company, detailed for the second
objective, came rolling along it out of the gloom. It was
now full day, and we could see perhaps a quarter of a
mile at the most. Bucquoy was still entirely hidden. A
brigade staff of the 63rd Naval Division, which was to
pass through the 37th to attack the railway, had come
up to the neighbourhood of Top Trench, and its members
were standing about flapping maps, sending and receiving
telephone messages, and cursing the fog. Runners and
despatch-riders were coming and going busily in our vague
radius of vision. There was a constant bustle about the
mouth of the dug-out, where the 111th Brigade was
receiving reports every minute by telephone from the
headquarters of its battalions; and inquiries here confirmed the impression that the first objectives had been
carried with ease, in spite of the mist. The latter was
at last thinning as the sun rose, and at length the trees
of Bucquoy, 1000 yards away, became faintly visible, like
ghostly and tattered scarecrows. It was now, I suppose,
about seven o'clock, and the Major and I began to make
our way toward Ablainzevelle. A few walking wounded
were straggling rearwards, and the endless torrent of
shells was wailing overhead; but there was nothing else
to be seen or heard of the battle. The northern end of
Bucquoy, through which we passed, reeked of gases and
corruption, but the one or two dead bodies visible had
only too palpably been lying there for days. The Ayette
road was more forlorn than ever, and littered with a new
layer of bricks and branches. The appearance behind us
of some cavalry, who rode into the village with a great
clatter and parade, indicated that the attack so far had
progressed satisfactorily. A little way up the Ablainzevelle road we met the first tank returning, followed by

several more. As I had suspected would be the case, there had been little or no fighting in the village. The fog had caused far more trouble than the Germans, of whom hardly any had been seen. One machine-gun had kept firing from a ruined house until a tank drove over it, one or two others had loosed a few bursts before their crews fled, and then proceedings had degenerated into a hunt for souvenirs. There were plenty of these, for the attack had come as a complete surprise.

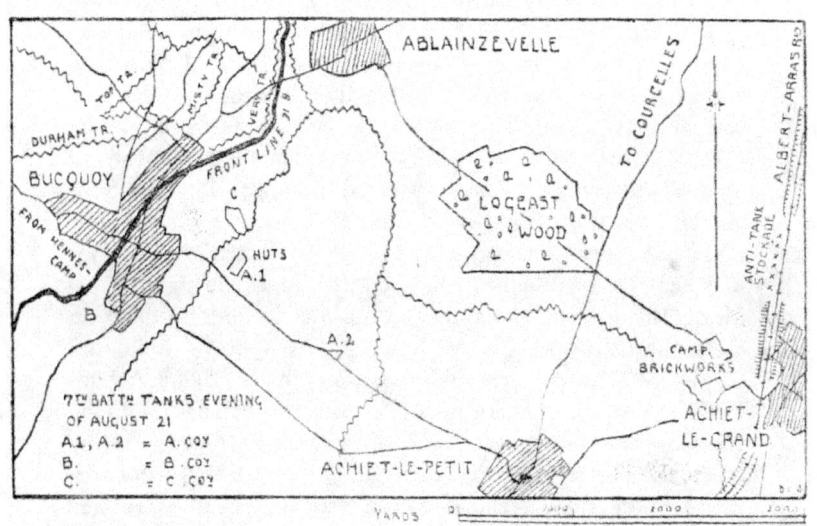

Attack on August 21, 1918.

We returned with these tanks to the rallying-point near Durham Trench, behind the northern gardens of Bucquoy. All the machines detailed for Ablainzevelle were accounted for. One had broken a track near the village, and its commander, slightly wounded in an unromantic part of his person by a stray bullet, was the only casualty to date. During the morning all the remaining tanks rolled in except the three of Wright's section, which had pushed on to Achiet-le-Petit. No one, so far, had met with any serious opposition, but all had difficulties on account of the mist. One tank commander, at the request of the Naval Division, had entered Logeast Wood and demolished some machine-gun posts there.

There was a little shelling of our neighbourhood, and of Bucquoy in general, toward midday, and Jukes and I very nearly had our promising careers cut short by a large projectile which landed in a road along which we were walking in search of news or food—I forget which. Jukes's water-bottle was the only victim. After a scrappy lunch, having learnt that Wright's section had returned from Achiet-le-Petit and rallied in a small copse between that place and Bucquoy, I set out to find Battalion headquarters, which was to have established itself by this hour in a trench east of the latter village. The mist had now cleared, at an awkward moment as it turned out, for the 10th Battalion and the Whippets. The day was brilliantly fine and even uncomfortably hot, and as I reached the far side of Bucquoy, I could see very plainly the battle in progress along the line of the railway. Achiet-le-Petit, hidden in trees, had been taken by tanks and was firmly held, but to the left smoke was billowing in clouds about Achiet-le-Grand and the eastern end of Logeast Wood. I found the Colonel, Henriquez, and Smith, the Adjutant, sheltering from the sun under some corrugated iron at the appointed spot, where their trench—which was in fact the German front line, there having been only advanced posts in Bucquoy — was cut by the road from that village to Achiet-le-Petit. I got a little news from them. B and C Companies, it appeared, had taken Bucquoy as easily as we had taken Ablainzevelle; but the second German line, and in particular Logeast Wood and Achiet-le-Petit, had given more trouble. The Mark V.'s and Whippets, passing through our tanks, had been caught bunched together near the railway as the fog lifted at ten o'clock, and had been knocked about badly by the German guns. The Naval Division, losing its direction, had wandered too far to the

Bucquoy and Achiet-le-Petit.

right, even across the Achiet-le-Petit road, with the result that Achiet-le-Grand, which it should have carried, was still holding out. Apart from this accident, everything so far had gone well. I was told now to bring A Company's tanks through Bucquoy to some point east of the village. One of our old camps of Nissen huts, mostly in ruins, lay immediately in front, and having noted this as a suitable place to camouflage the machines, I returned to lead them to it.

Before three o'clock we had the two sections hidden in the huts, which we knocked down and then built up again over the tanks. We established ourselves in the trench behind. The accompanying photograph, taken five days before the attack, shows very clearly this region behind Bucquoy. Our trench ran from the five-sided enclosure on the left to the first elbow in the main road, where the trees are. Beyond are the Nissen huts. Beyond them again is a small copse, beside the road, where Wright's section had rallied after taking Achiet-le-Petit. The latter village is seen at the end of the road, having on its left the line of trees along the road to Achiet-le-Grand. In the foreground is Bucquoy, the distance between the two villages being about a mile and a half. C Company had concentrated their tanks in the five-sided enclosure on our left, while those of B Company were under some trees at the south end of the village.

We were left here in peace during the rest of the day, only a few heavy shells whining overhead at intervals into Bucquoy. Battalion headquarters had returned to Bienvillers. It was blazing hot, and we were plagued by innumerable flies. Our only protection from the sun was a few small shelters in the trench wall—the dug-outs, of which there were a good number, being filled to suffocation by the infantry of the 37th Division, now holding this line as a support to the general advance. When we were not trying to sleep, our chief occupation was watching the struggle still raging in front of Achiet-le-Grand. We looked straight up a shallow depression to Achiet Junction, which stood on rising ground, so that, although it was two miles distant, we witnessed the whole attack like spectators at a play. The infantry had carried the line of the railway to north and south, but the Germans still held out tenaciously in a little salient that jutted out westward around the station, the brickworks, and a number of huts erected there. Throughout the afternoon I saw at intervals with my glasses lines of minute figures pressing forward up the slope into the smoke-clouds that rose and eddied over Achiet; but they always came back, and in smaller numbers. The station was still uncaptured at nightfall.

It was extremely cold that night for August. Jukes and I were huddled together in a bay of the trench when the Major roused us at 3 A.M. He had become anxious about Wright's forward section in the copse beside the road, and wished Jukes to walk across and bring the tanks in to the Nissen huts, with the others, before dawn. As I was too cold to sleep, I accompanied Jukes across to the copse. It was brilliant moonlight again, with none of the mist of the previous night. There was very little artillery fire in progress, and only the occasional mutter of a machine-gun along the railway. The copse, when we got to it, proved to be no more than a triangle of tattered hedge enclosing half a dozen small trees. There were now in it six tanks: three of A Company's (Wadeson's, Clegg's, and another), one each from B and C, and a supply tender. We found B and C's machines already under orders to withdraw, and in the act of uncamouflaging; and having woken up our own people, we hurried them on with the same business, for the eastern sky was brightening, and it takes some time to uncamouflage a tank, stow everything away, and start up a cold engine. The crews were sleepy and chilled, and half an hour had passed before the first tank was under way. This was C Company's machine. Then two of ours, Clegg's, and one commanded by an N.C.O., went off with Jukes, followed by Borrisow of B Company. The tender was remaining behind, and our last tank (Wadeson's) refused at first to start up. While I was standing beside it, looking toward the railway, where the trees along the road between the two Achiets were now visible in the rapidly growing light of a clear morning, a close line of black shell-bursts sprang up about 500 yards away—apparently a very well-spaced barrage along what had been the German second line. The tank was just moving, to my sincere gratification; but before even it was clear of the copse the barrage had jumped forward and was falling all round us. The two tanks which Jukes was leading vanished in a cloud of smoke, and I was certain that one at least had been hit. I saw Borrisow crossing the road and making at full speed for the shelter of Bucquoy. I led Wadeson after him, as the shells at the moment were falling only on our side of the highway; but as soon as we were across, with that malignity which so often seems to inspire indirect artillery fire, the infernal things began to fly up in front of us. In the twilight one could see the flash in the heart of each black plume of earth and smoke. One shell cleared the cab of our tank by inches and burst twelve yards ahead of us. Wadeson and I were walking in front to direct the driver, and in the perturbation of the moment it never occurred to either of us to get inside the tank, which we might safely have done, there being enough light for us to pick out our way through the flaps. We swung back presently on to the road, as the ground to the left became obstructed with large craters and other excavations of some sort, which reduced seriously our very moderate rate of progress. The tank, in fact, from some mechanical fault, would only crawl along on second speed. From the copse to our huts was no more than a thousand yards, but this distance seems interminable when one is condemned to walk at about one mile an hour through a heavy deluge of 5.9's. The shells followed us with the same uncanny accuracy, and were crashing among the huts when we reached the latter. As we turned in from the road I met Wright, the section commander, stumbling about, half-blinded by blood from a wound in his head. I took his arm and ran him down the road to the trench, and judged from the brisk way he stepped out that he was not very badly hurt. Hurrying back, I called in the crews. It was not the moment to keep them out in the open camouflaging the tanks, which could be done later. As it was, I was too late. Poor Clegg, having after all come safely through the journey, was the first in, and was standing behind his tank helping his crew to cover it with corrugated iron from a hut, when a shell burst at his feet and killed him instantly.

The whole thing was a striking example of bad luck. The tanks could not have been seen in that half-light, and the bombardment was a mere speculation, aimed, I imagine, at the trenches we occupied east of Bucquoy. It cost the 7th Battalion a heavier casualty list in officers than any action it ever fought. For while in A Company Clegg was killed and Wright wounded, almost at the same time a shell landed among B Company's tanks in Bucquoy itself, killing a tank commander, M'Lean, and a gunner, and wounding another officer and several men. M'Lean, a Canadian, was one of the best fellows I have ever met, and one who hated war almost as much as I did. Throughout the series of operations which began at Bucquoy and ended beyond Cambrai, the 7th Battalion, always comparatively fortunate in casualties to personnel, had four officers killed, of whom two lost their lives in this brief and purposeless shelling on the morning of 22nd August.

III.

A Company's trench was not actually hit during the bombardment, but all who were in it were much perturbed by our predicament as well as by their own. As the three returning tanks were hidden entirely for a while by the smoke, most of us were given up for lost. The shelling died down after about half an hour, when parties went out to bring in Clegg's body and to complete the concealment of the tanks.

The rest of the day passed quietly enough, so far as we were concerned, until the evening. The 3rd Army was pausing, while the 4th Army came into line between the Ancre and the Somme. On our front Achiet-le-Grand was carried in the course of the morning, and the infantry was then established along the whole line of the railway. A little information reached us concerning the previous day's events on our left. The 12th Tank Battalion in their first battle had done all and more than was asked of them, capturing Moyenneville and pushing on to the railway. The Mark V. Stars of the 15th Battalion, which should have passed through the 12th, lost all direction in the mist, and for the most part wandered aimlessly about north of Logeast Wood without achieving anything. As, however, the battalion (by one of those dispensations peculiar to the Army) collected something like a dozen military crosses for an ineffective performance which did not merit one, it had every reason to be satisfied with its day's work. It was fortunate, perhaps, in that its tanks did not contrive to get very far forward, for the 10th Battalion, which played the same rôle on the right, passing through our Mark IV.'s to attack the railway about Achiet-le-Grand, met with wholesale disaster. Of the company which went in, every tank except one, I believe, was knocked out on or near the railway by the German batteries beyond, eleven out of twelve officers being killed or wounded. The 3rd Battalion's Whippets, endeavouring to pass through the Mark V.'s, were caught in line ahead on the Achiet-le-Petit road when the mist lifted suddenly about ten o'clock in the morning, and most of them suffered the same fate. Two got through Achiet-le-Petit and were hit and burnt out beyond. The armoured cars had also paid the penalty of other people's convictions in the same neighbourhood. An area a mile square around the two Achiets and the curve of railway between them was in fact littered with derelict Mark V.'s, Whippets, and armoured cars; and the result of this, as the 10th Battalion was very short of tanks to begin with, was that the 7th now remained the only heavy unit approximately up to strength in the 1st Brigade.

Some of our machines, however, were in need of an overhaul, and as it was impossible to work on those of A Company in their exposed position east of Bucquoy, we were ordered to withdraw after dark to our original rallying-point near Durham Trench, west of the village. These orders had just come through, at about seven o'clock in the evening of the 22nd, when the enemy chose to repeat his display of the early morning by bombarding our trench with 5.9's. He was very accurate on this occasion, the first shell landing full in the trench, and all the others being unpleasantly near. As the dug-outs were full of infantrymen, we had to sit hopefully on the trench floor and trust to luck. For a quarter of an hour this shelling was very heavy, and caused a number of casualties among those of the infantry who were crowded out of the dug-outs, and also in C Company in their hedged enclosure to our left. The trench was beaten flat in several places. After a while, as this infliction might herald a counter-attack, the Major and I sprinted vigorously up the trench to a dug-out where a brigade headquarters of the Naval Division was established, hoping to get some news there. We were met on the way by a panic-stricken rabble of signallers and other oddments, who declared, with what little breath they had left, that the Germans were in fact advancing and had recaptured Logeast Wood. This did not sound probable; and on penetrating at length to the brigade headquarters, wrapped in ideal calm and silence twenty feet below the ground, we found the General having dinner amid an assortment of telephones, and every one perfectly happy. Guy and Chaddock, of C Company, were also there on the same errand of inquiry as ourselves. We sat on the dug-out stairs for some time, drinking whiskies and sodas, while telephone reports came through from the battalions in the front line to the effect that everything there was normal; and being thus assured that our tanks would not be needed to repair any disaster, we climbed out again to find the shelling ceased and a blazing moon rising once more above Bucquoy. Something else was blazing also—the unfortunate supply-tank we had left in the copse that morning, which had been hit and set on fire during the bombardment. Without any further delay we got our tanks out of their shells of corrugated iron, and in an hour or two were back near Durham Trench, where we made bivouacs out of tarpaulin sheets for the night. C Company, having received similar orders to withdraw to the west of Bucquoy, were also concentrated at their old rallying-point.

While we were sleeping, the resumption of the general offensive, due for the morning of the 23rd, was initiated by a brilliant night attack made by the 12th Tank Battalion, with the 3rd Division and the Guards, on Gomiecourt and Hamelincourt, north of Achiet-le-Grand. The two operations were quite distinct affairs, the villages, which lay 1000 yards beyond the railway, being nearly two miles apart. Both were captured, with a number of prisoners and guns, the tanks doing extraordinarily good work in the darkness. Three Military Crosses, one D.C.M., and three Military Medals were gained by the 12th Battalion in these actions, in which thirteen tanks were actually engaged. With this successful prelude, the whole battle awoke again at dawn along a front of thirty-three miles from Lihons, in the south, to Mercatel, beyond the Cojuel; and while in a sunken road near Durham Trench we shaved and washed in a leisurely manner beside our tanks, the guns were roaring once more, and strings of German prisoners were already passing by on their way to the cages. On this morning, in our sector, the remaining tanks of the 10th Battalion helped the 37th Division to clear Bihucourt, beyond Achiet-le-Grand: the 9th and 11th Battalions of the 3rd Brigade co-operated in a successful attack toward Heninel; and about midday fifteen

Whippets of the 6th Battalion were engaged in very severe fighting around Sapignies, Behagnies, and Ervillers on the Arras-Bapaume road. Ervillers was carried, but the two other villages held out until the 25th, when the 7th Battalion assisted at their capture.

About five o'clock in the afternoon orders arrived at Durham Trench for a move by the whole battalion at dusk to the railway embankment east of Achiet-le-Petit. A Company led, C following on behind as we passed again through Bucquoy. B Company took their own route from the south end of the village. Owing to various breakdowns, due to the age and general disrepair of some of our Mark IV.'s, the battalion now mustered little more than thirty tanks. It proceeded along the east side of the Achiet-le-Petit road. The Major and I went on ahead in the car to a conference at the headquarters of a New Zealand Brigade near Achiet, which we reached just before dark. The New Zealanders were attacking Biefvillers, Grévillers, and Loupart Wood the next morning, and wanted two sections of heavy tanks and some Whippets. Custance's section of A Company, with one from B, were detailed from our battalion, the whole being under the orders of Rossi-Ashton, commanding B Company, for the operation. As there was nothing for the Major and myself to do, we were ordered to return to Bienvillers to get a good night's rest while we had the chance; and having seen the tanks on their way round the north side of Achiet-le-Petit, we returned to the car and drove away. We passed the Whippets coming up, and, behind Bucquoy, along the road which two days before had been deserted, ran into masses of transport, finally ditching the car in a shell-hole near Hannescamps, so that it was after midnight when we reached Bienvillers.

A night in a camp-bed, followed by a bath and a comfortable breakfast in our tarpaulin-covered mess, worked wonders, and we were on our way back by eleven o'clock next morning. One could see very plainly by day the

THE GREAT ADVANCE 391

changes wrought in these back areas by our advance. The
Bucquoy road was choked with cars, lorries, ambulances,
and horse-transport, moving under a cloud of dust. There
was a Y.M.C.A. canteen established in the ruins of Essart,
and we saw actually an A.P.M. endeavouring to control
the traffic in that place. We were able to take the car
through Achiet - le - Petit itself, over indescribable roads,
and so down into the valley beyond, where our tanks

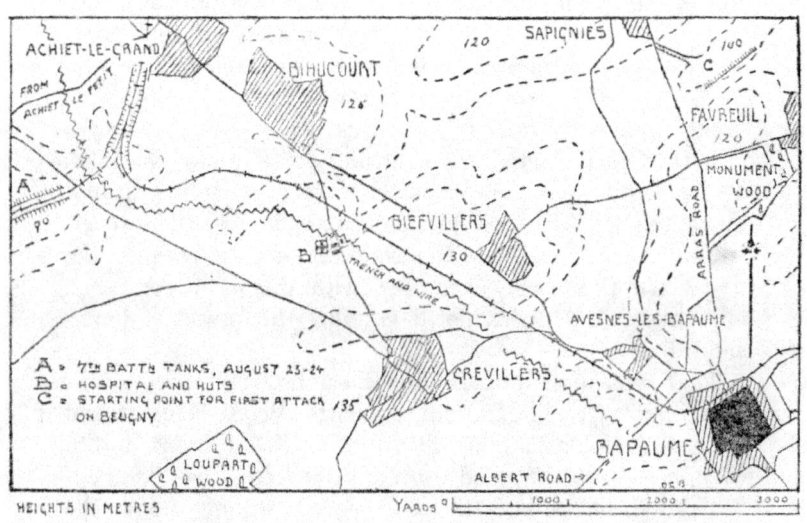

The Advance beyond the Arras-Albert Railway, August 23-29.

were lying alongside the railway embankment. Around
Achiet were many relics of the tank attack of the 21st, in
the shape of burnt-out Whippets, armoured cars, and
Mark V.'s. South-east of the village the ground falls very
steeply and then rises to the railway, while the embankment over which the latter runs is at this point quite thirty
feet high and clothed with bushes; and in the regular
gulley thus formed there was now accumulated an astonishing mass of men, animals, and material. Against the
bushes of the embankment were camouflaged the thirty-

odd tanks of our battalion, a few Mark V.'s from the 10th, and several Whippets. A battery of 4.5 howitzers was firing with an intolerable noise straight over our machines from a distance of twenty yards, while on the slope behind, which rose like a *glacis* up to Achiet, were three or four field batteries in action. Long lines of limbers and horses filled the lower end of the valley, and the men of an infantry battalion in reserve were lying in the grass higher up beside our tanks. Two infantry brigade headquarters were established in the open here, so that there was a great coming and going of despatch-riders and orderlies. All this activity was crowded into a hollow 1000 yards long by 200 or 300 yards wide — a magnificent opportunity for the German artillery. The day was fine, and a hostile aeroplane could have seen everything from a great height. The possibilities of the place seem, however, to have been overlooked during the earlier part of the day, when the enemy was busy with the level crossing a mile higher up at Achiet-le-Grand, which was violently shelled.

That morning's attack had been entirely successful— Biefvillers, Grévillers, and Loupart Wood being taken after severe fighting, in which three of our tanks and a Whippet were knocked out. Armoured cars had endeavoured to exploit the success by pushing along the road from Biefvillers into Bapaume, but had found the shell-fire too heavy. Our casualties had been slight, and Custance and most of his people were back again with the company, covered with dirt and glory. The battalion was supplying another three sections (twelve tanks) the following morning—the 25th—for two separate operations. M'Chlery's section of A Company was to help the 37th Division complete its unfinished task at Sapignies and Behagnies; while two sections of C, with seven Mark V.'s (all that the 10th Battalion had left), were working with the 63rd Division immediately to the south against Favreuil, Avesnes-les-Bapaume, and Ligny-Thilloy. Avesnes was a

suburb of Bapaume, and Thilloy was south of that town, on
which we were now closing on three sides. M'Chlery's
section came under the orders of C Company for these operations. The battalion being no longer at full strength,
sections were borrowed in this way to make up composite
companies with the normal number of tanks, and the three
company commanders took it in turn to direct successive attacks. A Company having two tanks at Durham
Trench which should now be ready again for action, I
was sent off after lunch to order them up. My combination Douglas had broken in half during our move
from Saulty to Bienvillers—the combined weight of the
Major and myself, coupled with the corrugations of a
ploughed field which we were crossing, proving too much
for a war-time framework; and for this journey I borrowed
Henriquez's 4-h.p. machine, from which the side-car had
been detached. Ridden as a solo, it was unfamiliar,
powerful, and rather alarming; but after the usual anxious
moments in the dense traffic that now, beneath a fog of
dust, congested the Achiet-le-Petit road, I reached our old
rallying-point behind Bucquoy, delivered my message, and
returned. It was shortly after this, there being at the
moment nothing for me to do, that I climbed the railway
embankment and strolled up to the crest of the hill beyond,
and so came to witness a singular little comedy. From the
crest one looked down a gradual slope of grass, broken by
a few trenches and gun-pits, to Loupart Wood, 1000 yards
away, with Grévillers just beyond to the left on a farther
ridge which hid Bapaume. The Wood, as I have told,
had been captured that morning by B Company and the
New Zealanders. Subsequently the Germans counter-
attacked and retook the eastern part, whereupon two tanks
of C Company had been hurriedly summoned to drive
them out again. This was accomplished; but both tanks
were then put temporarily *hors de combat* while still in the
Wood—one with a broken track and the other with engine
trouble. At the time, about 5 P.M., when I walked up

from the railway, these machines were still there, with their crews working on them. Nevertheless, for reasons which I never discovered, the New Zealanders had withdrawn again from the entire Wood, and were calling for yet more tanks to deal with some alleged (and I believe wholly imaginary) German machine-guns re-established there. Standing on the crest of the hill above the railway, I looked down at this juncture upon all the dispositions for a pitched battle — with nobody. Loupart Wood lay dark and quiet on the Grévillers spur, while within it our two tank crews worked on quite peacefully, entirely ignorant of their desertion and of all this pother. In front of the Wood, in extended order on the ground, were some New Zealand infantry and a battalion of the K.O.S.B.'s, borrowed from the 5th Division to help in this crisis. Behind the infantry a field battery had come into position, its limbers in rear, and a squadron of dismounted cavalry were standing by their horses in a hollow close by, while from a crossing over the railway to my left two more tanks of C Company were advancing to the rescue. It was a very pretty and gallant sight, and reminded one, in its formality and completeness, of those mimic battles one used to enjoy at the Military Tournament. Only the stock pontoon bridge was missing. Not a shot was being fired, except by one rifle which cracked occasionally far away to the right of the Wood. This belonged, I heard afterwards, to a solitary German sniper who seems to have represented in his own person the entire enemy against which this force of all arms was arrayed. What made the whole affair even more absurd and unreal was the fact that, 1000 yards to the left, infantry were marching in fours along the road into Grévillers . . .! As I looked on, in some astonishment, developments ensued along the orthodox lines laid down at Olympia and the Agricultural Hall. A cavalry patrol of about a dozen men, greatly daring, mounted their horses and trotted off toward the Wood. A few hundred yards from it the men dismounted

THE GREAT ADVANCE 395

again, left two or three in charge of the animals, and
walked forward in extended order. Every other individual
present (I hope) held his breath as these gallant fellows disappeared among the trees. Even on my hill-top I seemed
to feel the atmosphere of suspense which emanated from
that silent battlefield, disturbed only by the single shots of
the indefatigable sniper in the distance. . . . In the Wood,
of course, nothing happened, for there was nothing to
happen. But I should like to have witnessed the meeting between the anxious patrol, scouting warily among the
trees, and our two perspiring and irritable tank crews toiling at their tracks and engines. After a while the infantry,
reassured, got upon their feet, and in their turn began
cautiously to advance: the Wood was reoccupied; and the
bloodless battle was handsomely won.

My study of its concluding phase was disturbed by the
appearance of a squadron of German aeroplanes. There
were about a dozen of them, and they drove down suddenly from a great height upon the valley behind me,
coming so low as they cleared the crest on which I
was standing that the nearest machine was not 200
feet overhead. I saw quite clearly its observer stand
up in his cockpit and begin to fiddle about with his
machine-gun; and realising suddenly that I was a solitary
and fairly conspicuous figure on the hill-top, I ran rather
hurriedly to a trench close at hand. From here I saw the
aeroplanes swoop down across the railway and rise steeply
beyond, and heard the rattle of their machine-guns. The
bullets, as I heard afterwards, flew all round our tanks,
although no one was hit. The Germans must have
realised what a magnificent target the crowded little
valley offered to their heavy guns, and all of us expected
the place to be shelled furiously within half an hour; but
nothing of the sort happened, as the enemy's artillery
was already in the act of withdrawing to positions farther
back.

While I was in the trench I was joined by a doctor

belonging to the 5th Division. The latter was just back from Italy, and the M.O. was very caustic on the subject of the Italian Army. After talking to him for a while I walked down to our valley again by way of the nearer railway crossing, and there overtook the two tanks of C Company on their way home from the 3rd battle of Loupart Wood. Coutts and Chaddock were with them, both very angry at having been called out on such a fool's errand. It was seven o'clock when I rejoined the company by the embankment, and our servants there were preparing some dinner, the *menu* including three tinned chickens which I had brought from Bienvillers that morning. I had to eat my share cold, however, on a hunk of bread, for as I arrived the company received orders to move after dark to a point indicated on the map as a German camp and hospital at G 23, b 56; and Jukes and I had to set off at once to investigate the place. It was 3000 yards away, on the high ground near Bihucourt. We found it to consist of a couple of immense sheds, presumably the hospital wards, a neat double row of Nissens, either sunk in the ground or protected by breastworks against aeroplane bombing, and a scattered collection of other huts all round, the whole extending on either side of the Bihucourt-Grévillers road. Immediately to the north of the camp ran the third German trench line, thickly wired; 300 yards beyond that was the railway from Achiet-le-Grand Junction to Bapaume; and across the railway were Bihucourt and Biefvillers, a mile apart, and almost equidistant from the huts. Bapaume itself, less than two miles away, was still hidden by the final ridge, on top of which a derelict Whippet made a conspicuous landmark. The whole of this country was elevated and rolling grass-land, very little shelled, and covered with old camps which we had lost in the March retreat.

As we returned to the valley there were ominous signs of a change in the weather. Clouds were rolling up, and a premature twilight was fading rapidly. We found the

tanks pulling out from the embankment, with the exception
of M'Chlery's section, which was moving later with C Company for the attack next morning. Before we were halfway to our new quarters it began to rain heavily, and the
night fell as black as pitch. The Major and I had eventually to find a New Zealand Brigade whose whereabouts
was very vaguely indicated, there being some talk of a
couple more tanks going into action near Bapaume in the
morning; and having accompanied our machines as far as
the camp, we left them to settle themselves in, and plunged
off into the darkness on our own voyage of discovery. I
cannot imagine a more appalling night for such an expedition. The blackness was extraordinary, and the rain
fell in torrents. We had only the haziest idea of the loca-
tion of this brigade headquarters, and for nearly two hours
we stumbled about in long grass and mud, tripping over
invisible wire, dead bodies, and other debris, falling into
shell-holes and sunken roads, and getting always more
drenched and exasperated. The few people we met were
either lost themselves, or else gave us contradictory directions involving the recognition of landmarks which we
could not possibly see. After a while a thunderstorm burst,
and the lightning afforded occasional eerie visions of a
black and sodden world. One of these flashes found us
slithering down into a road filled with large dark objects,
which turned out to be the guns, men, and horses of a
German battery which had evidently been caught by shell
or machine-gun fire while limbering up.[1] Over this welter
of bodies there came crashing and rocking several of our
own field-guns, which nearly rode us down. This incident,
brief and startling in the lightning flashes, filled me with
a profound respect for our artillery. The guns went rattling
by in the pitchy dark over all these grisly obstructions on
the road with as much apparent ease and surety as if it
had been broad day. Very soon after this, near a cross-

[1] This may have been the battery which a Whippet caught and destroyed on the 23rd.

roads, we were cheered by the discovery of some lights that seemed to be shining out of the ground, and found that, more by luck than judgment, we had very literally stumbled upon our destination. The brigade headquarters was established in some huts sunk in what appeared to be a quarry, and practically invisible even in daytime until one fell over the edge. Having groped our way into the Brigade Major's office and introduced ourselves, the Brigadier presently appeared from some subterranean quarters and explained what he wanted us to do. He proposed to capture some huts and railway sidings between Bapaume and Favreuil in the course of the following morning, and wished for two tanks to mop up after his infantry. The time of the operation had not been fixed, but it would take place in daylight, as a subsidiary development of the main attack which the 63rd Division with C Company's tanks was carrying out at dawn from Favreuil to Thilloy. The scheme did not commend itself to us in the very least. It showed the common misapprehension of the correct use of tanks, and violated all our tactical principles, based on bitter experience. There were only two tanks to be used, which left no margin for accidents; they were to be employed wrongly to mop up after the infantry, instead of preceding the latter; the attack was to begin in broad daylight; and the approach-march necessarily led over the bare and prominent ridge in front of Bapaume, where the machines would certainly be detected before they got into action at all. It was this last consideration which impressed the Brigadier most forcibly. I do not think he cared over much about what happened to the tanks, but he was very anxious that his attack should not be discovered prematurely. In the end, nothing was settled definitely. We agreed to have the two tanks ready to move if required. The brigade headquarters itself was moving forward in the early morning to some dug-outs in the German trenches in front of our huts, and we were to report there at nine o'clock for further orders.

THE GREAT ADVANCE

This proposed attack, which came to nothing so far as we were concerned, illustrates one of the difficulties tank units continually met with during this final stage of the war. The infantry naturally wanted tanks whenever they could get them, and brigade and divisional commanders were always demanding two here or three there for use in some wasteful and impracticable manner in minor operations. Apart from the faulty tactics (from the point of view of tank warfare) which these hurried little schemes usually involved, tanks were getting very scarce in France, and such as were available needed to be conserved as much as possible for attacks on a large scale.

Having left things in this nebulous state, the Major and I plunged once more into the darkness and rain, and contrived to find our way back to our new camp, where we settled down in a hut about 2 A.M.

CHAPTER XIX.

THE FIGHTING FOR BEUGNY, AND THE ADVANCE TO THE CANAL DU NORD.

I.

The storm blew itself out in the night, and the morning of 25th August was again sunny and clear, with that bracing freshness that follows after heavy summer rain. At nine o'clock I walked over with the Major to see the New Zealanders. We found them now immured in an uncomfortable and, as I thought, highly dangerous dug-out near the crest of the ridge where the derelict Whippet was standing. The dug-out was merely a cramped, unfinished, and untimbered gallery cut in a crumbling soil which appeared to be in imminent peril of falling in. One entrance, indeed, was half-choked with detritus shaken down by concussion. Our interview settled the question about the tanks. After some discussion, the Brigadier decided against their use, to our considerable relief, and I was no less pleased to get out of that untrustworthy tunnel into the fresh air.

I walked down to the railway embankment after this to hear how M'Chlery's section and C Company had prospered in that morning's attack. A Company's four tanks, it appeared, had led the infantry into Sapignies and Behagnies, but these villages were only cleared after severe fighting. One tank was knocked out by shell-fire in Behagnies, its commander, Charnock, being wounded.

THE FIGHTING FOR BEUGNY

C Company and the Mark V.'s, attacking Favreuil, Avesnes-les-Bapaume, and Thilloy with the 63rd Division, met with an even more tenacious resistance and suffered heavily. Neither Thilloy nor Avesnes could be held, although both were partially cleared. Favreuil was captured; but the section of C Company which took the village met with disaster later on. The tanks were returning south of Favreuil, between Monument Wood and Bapaume, when a field-gun in the outskirts of the town knocked out three of them. Brassington and his driver, O'Mahony, in the first tank, were killed together by a shell which came through the side of the cab and set the machine ablaze. A gunner was killed while getting out, and there were several other fatal casualties among the N.C.O.'s and men in the two disabled tanks behind. Poor Brassington's death came as a great shock to me. We had been in the same hut as cadets at Bisley and in the same section in G Battalion, had shared quarters at Bovington, and had been much together in France. Before joining the Tank Corps, Brassington had been a sergeant in the Duke of Wellington's. Like so many North-country men, he was genuinely musical, with a good voice and a knowledge of how to use it; and he shared another local characteristic —that sort of independence (as it is called) which, often aggressive and unpleasing, in his case took only the form of a determination to go his own way. He would never bother to cultivate friendly relations with influential people if he did not like them, an attitude fatal to progress in the Army. A really capable soldier, with long experience in the war, he always said he would end as a tank commander.

After these actions on the 25th, the 7th Battalion enjoyed a rest for three days, being taken into Corps Reserve. B Company's tanks moved up to a little valley behind our huts. We made ourselves fairly comfortable in the latter, and were disturbed very little by shelling, although a battery of our 60-pounders, posted a few hundred yards in rear, rendered the nights hideous. We had driven some of our tanks into one of the big hospital sheds, and camouflaged the others behind it, there being now eight fit machines left in the company. A certain amount of reorganisation was necessary throughout the battalion; but everything was turned upside down by a most extraordinary development on the 28th. It had been known for some time that a proportion of the officers and men of the Tank Corps in France were to be sent home to provide an experienced nucleus for new units forming at Bovington, the establishment of the corps having been raised again from eighteen to twenty-five battalions. Now that we were involved in a general offensive, however, it naturally was supposed that these changes would be postponed for a time. That the offensive would end only with the war was not then suspected, of course, by any one, least of all by Tank Corps H.Q. in London, which now took an entirely unexpected step. The personnel selected for England was called for at a few hours' notice. In the middle of a battle, some units, including the 7th Battalion, found themselves deprived at a blow of 30 per cent of their already reduced complements. The first intimation we of A Company received at Bihucourt was a message which arrived during the afternoon of the 28th ordering all officers and men detailed for Bovington to prepare to leave that evening. This sudden and wholesale removal affected our company more seriously than either B or C, for the party to go included the Major, the second in command, two section commanders out of three, Jukes, the Assistant R.O., several tank commanders, the orderly-room corporal, and a number of our best N.C.O.'s and men. The company, in fact, lost all its senior officers. M'Chlery, the junior section commander, as the only remaining Captain, found himself in charge pending the arrival of a new O.C. to be posted to us from the 11th Battalion. B and C Companies, while less hard hit, sent away two section commanders apiece (Merchant being among them), with a proportion of subalterns and men. As for battalion headquarters, it virtually disappeared. The Colonel left, to command a new unit, and took with him the Adjutant, Henriquez the R.O., and most of the orderly-room staff, who, rumour had it, were all promoted sergeants in the train. All this happened, as I say, in two or three hours. Lorries arrived at Bihucourt to take away our contingent immediately after we received the order. The Colonel rushed up in his car to say good-bye and to introduce his successor, Major Thorp, to the bewildered residue of A Company; and then M'Chlery, M'Elroy, and I, the only survivors present of the original officers, and in consequence responsible between us for the immediate prosecution of the Great War, retired in a dazed condition to our hut to have a much-needed drink before grappling with the new situation.

II.

In the meantime, while the 3rd Army paused in front of Bapaume, the general offensive was extended northward, where the 1st Army struck out from Arras. The 3rd Tank Brigade, some of whose units trekked twenty miles during the 24th and 25th August, advanced with the Canadians against Wancourt, Guémappe, and Monchy-le-Preux, on the 26th. These places were taken, and on the 27th Roeux and Gavrelle, north of the Scarpe, fell also. Far to the south the 4th Army and the French were advancing again, and on our front the Germans evacuated Bapaume on the 28th. Our line in the 3rd Army sector now ran, from north to south, east of St Leger, east of Mory, east of Beugnâtre (beyond Favreuil), across the Cambrai road between Bapaume and Fremicourt, and east of Thilloy.

The German armies, bewildered by this series of blows, were preparing to retreat to the Siegfried Line and the Canal du Nord. But to give time for their heavy guns and supplies to escape, they held out stiffly during the last days of the month along the whole front. The 3rd Army, attempting to advance from Bapaume up the Cambrai road, was checked before Fremicourt and Beugny; and a series of assaults on the latter village ended in sanguinary failures. In two of these the 7th Tank Battalion took part.

On the morning of the 29th, while the battalion was in the throes of reorganisation after the startling disappearance of a third of its officers, it was ordered to provide eight tanks for an attack with the 5th Division on Beugny the following morning. One section of A Company and one of B were detailed accordingly, Major Rossi-Ashton of B Company being in command. M'Elroy and I were now running affairs in the camp near Bihucourt, M'Chlery having left us to wrestle with returns and other horrible matters at Bienvillers, where our rear headquarters was still situated. Early in the afternoon we received instructions to move four tanks to the valley beyond Biefvillers. This valley was a wide and shallow depression running north and south between the village and the Arras-Bapaume road. We got our tanks here by about four o'clock, parking them up under a bank beside a battery of 4.5 howitzers, whose people were very annoyed at our arrival. Behind us the whole of C Company's tanks appeared from the railway at Achiet-le-Petit and hid themselves among some huts on the west side of the valley. An hour later we moved again, following the valley northward and then north-east across the Arras-Bapaume road to a point almost north of Favreuil, where, under another high bank, we joined the four tanks of B Company which were to co-operate with ours in the attack. I will try to make clear the features of the country that now lay before us. Bapaume, 3000 yards due south of our lying-up point, stands on a moderate elevation about 450 feet above sea-level. The ground falls away from it in a series of spurs to the north and north-east. There radiate out from the town, like the fingers of a hand and alternately along the spurs and in the valleys between, four roads, the most westerly the main highway to Arras, running west of north;

Bapaume burning. End of August 1918.

next a road through Favreuil, running north; next again one through Beugnâtre, running north-east; and finally, the highway through Fremicourt and Beugny to Cambrai, running north of east. All these diverging roads except the last-named were now behind our front, which had reached a point two or three hundred yards east of Beugnâtre, whence it trended a little west of south, crossed the Cambrai road between Bapaume and Fremicourt, and then continued east of Thilloy. The whole of this country was bare rolling grass-land, of a uniform appearance, all traces of cultivation and even of the boundaries of fields having vanished. It was dotted with a large number of hutted camps, mostly old ones of our own, and the only cover, apart from these, was to be found in the trees around the various villages. The roads were sunken in places, and there was a general resemblance to parts of Salisbury Plain, except that the undulations were less pronounced.

Our two sections of tanks were to lead the 13th Infantry Brigade into Beugny. This village lay on the Bapaume-Cambrai road a mile east of Fremicourt. It was surrounded by wire and entrenchments, and was further protected by one of our old defence systems converted by the Germans, two lines of trenches and entanglements running obliquely into our front north of Beugnâtre. On our left the 2nd Tank Brigade, with infantry of the 3rd Division, was to carry Ecoust, Longatte, and the Noreuil Switch, while on our right the New Zealanders, with a few Mark V.'s, were to move straight forward from Bapaume upon Fremicourt and Bancourt. Zero was at 5 A.M. on the 30th.

The valley in which we were lying preparatory to the attack was a thoroughly unpleasant place. It curled round to the north of the spur on which stood Favreuil and Monument Wood. There had been a good deal of fighting here, and a number of dead men and horses, in varying degrees of decomposition, were lying about. Our tanks were drawn up under a high bank topped by a row of trees on the south side of the valley. On the north side a little gully, lined with rough hutments that were full of old straw, dirt, smells, and flies, led up to the main Arras road at Sapignies. Eastward, at the foot of the valley, field batteries were in action; and beyond them one could see the line of trees along the road from Beugnâtre to Ecoust-St Mein, which marked approximately our front. Having found Beale, the Reconnaissance Officer of B Company, with his tanks, I walked forward with him past Favreuil to some rising ground near Beugnâtre. We wished to see something of the country before us while the light held, but although the evening was fine a mist had risen, and the smoke of shells bursting around the village helped further to hide the landscape beyond. We sat for some time in a trench, memorising as much as we could verify on the map. Camps of Nissen huts were clustered about Beugnâtre, and others seemed to extend far over the monotonous plain behind toward Beugny. It was agreed between us that our sections should move together by the track we had just followed to within a few hundred yards of Beugnâtre, when Beale would lead his tanks south of the village while I took mine round by the north. Once over the front line, where our duties would end, the two sections would have each an unmistakable guide to direct them on to Beugny. M'Elroy's tanks would strike sooner or later the old converted trench system of which I have spoken, and which it was their first task to clear. It would lead them down to the village from the north. B Company's tanks, on the right, had for a guide the Bapaume-Cambrai railway, running north of the main Cambrai road and roughly parallel to the latter until it crossed it between Fremicourt and Beugny. In an attack over such monotonous country, shrouded in smoke and the mists of early morning, it is very easy to lose one's direction in a tank, and as even a temporary delay may provoke serious trouble, any obvious means of guidance is an inestimable boon. In this case we were very fortunate. The trenches and the railway, like two hand-rails, converged together and crossed immediately in front of Beugny; and the tanks, moving up this angle, could not possibly lose their way. The chief feature of the country they had to fear was a gentle rounded spur behind which the village itself was hidden, and on whose

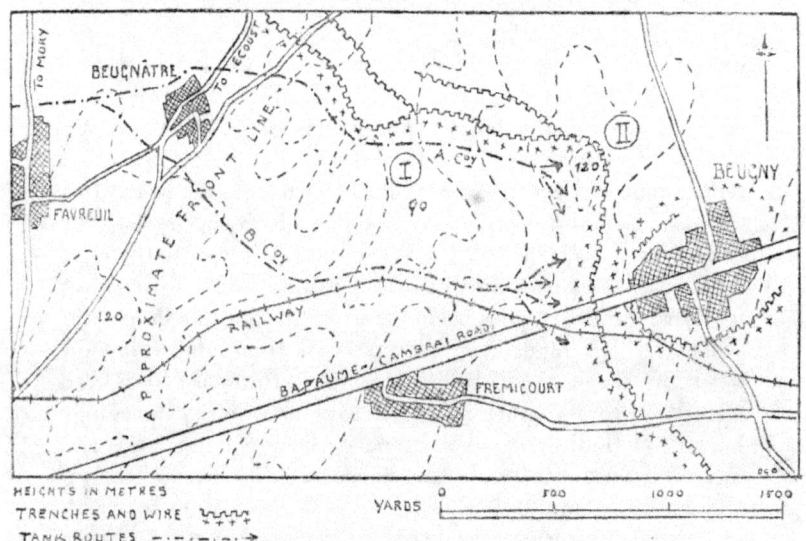

Beugny.

absolutely bare crest they would stand out as admirable targets as they approached.

I had some dinner that night with B Company's people beside their tanks, and then went for a few hours' rest in one of the wooden shacks in the gully opposite, which had been cleared of litter. At midnight the tanks were unsheeted and the engines started up. By one o'clock seven of them were in line above the bank, ready to move. The eighth, one of A Company's, developed engine trouble at the last moment and had to be left behind. There was no moon now, and the night was very dark, with a slight mist. The distance to our front line beyond Beugnâtre was only 3000 yards, but part of the route was unknown to us, and we had to move at the slowest speed to prevent noise. The two sections separated at the point Beale and I had chosen, and he led his four tanks away to the south of Beugnâtre, while M'Elroy and I held straight on to pass the north end of the village. So far there had been no hitch; but now I could not find the track I had noted earlier in the evening, and was forced to feel my way without this slight help. There was no danger of our losing our way here, for the trees of Beugnâtre and the huts about it were quite visible, but there was always the chance of coming upon some obstacle which the track naturally would have avoided. We ploughed forward through long grass, M'Elroy and I in front feeling about with sticks for wire or holes, and were passing to the north of the village, which made a vague mass of trees and ruins on our right, when shells began to burst in front of us. There ensued a very disturbing quarter of an hour. A regular barrage fell directly in our path, between us and the Beugnâtre-Ecoust road, the flashes of the shells coming and going in rapid succession. We had no time to waste in halting until this was over, and indeed we were almost in it at the start; and having ordered our runners and every one else who was walking to get into the tanks, we moved on through the barrage. M'Elroy and I continued to walk in front, as it was necessary for me to act as a guide, and he insisted on staying with me. For a few minutes we were hopping nimbly about to take shelter on one side or the other of the leading tank, as the shells were crashing and sparkling unpleasantly near. With that good fortune which always seems so extraordinary in the retrospect, we passed through without damage to the tanks or ourselves. The barrage was still falling behind us when the trees along the Beugnâtre road appeared out of the darkness. We were now among the huts of a camp, and having missed the

track I had aimed for, we struck the road at a point
where it was deeply sunken. The first tank crossed without
difficulty, but the other two experienced some trouble in
mounting the farther bank. I pushed on with the leader,
leaving M'Elroy to bring on the others. We had come so
slowly that the few minutes' delay caused by the barrage
and our wanderings among the huts threatened to make
us late. Beyond the Ecoust road, a second one runs out
of Beugnâtre to the north, leading to Vaulx-Vraucourt, and
immediately beyond this was our front line. The tank I was
leading, commanded by Sergeant Duddridge (we were so
short of officers that two out of the three machines were
in charge of N.C.O.'s), was now several hundred yards
ahead of the others. The sky was already brightening in
the east, zero was due in a few minutes, and as soon as
we crossed the second road I began to peer about for the
front line. So far I had not seen a single infantryman
since we started. In the semi-open warfare in which we
were engaged, front lines were always indeterminate features
difficult to recognise and liable to frequent fluctuations; and
on this occasion all I ever discovered was a group of three
men crouching in a shell-hole, who told me they were in
support. A hundred yards farther on a blaze and a crash
behind me signified the opening of our barrage at zero.
I hauled myself up on to the front of the tank, yelled to
Sergeant Duddridge to get into fourth speed and push ahead,
and then ran back to look for the others. I remember
nothing more until I found myself sitting on the ground,
with my head spinning like the proverbial top and a general
feeling of having been hit all over with some violence,
watching the two rear tanks going by. As they were a
long way behind the leader, several minutes must have
elapsed. There was a hideous noise everywhere, and heavy
shells were thudding all round. The Germans, expecting
an attack, had dropped their barrage a few seconds after
ours along our front line, and I must have been knocked
over (and temporarily out) by the explosion of a shell close

astern of Duddridge's tank. I got on to my feet with some difficulty, and looked for M'Elroy, but he was nowhere to be seen. The two tanks were already past me, and rolling on in great style, and as my head still appeared to be doing several hundred revolutions a minute, I decided to get out of this inferno for a while, if I could find some sheltered spot in which to recuperate. It was growing light, although the mist and smoke were very thick, and just behind me was a row of old Nissen huts, protected by earthen banks against bombing raids. There were no trenches in sight, and I ran, therefore, rather unsteadily, into one of these huts and found at the end of it a sort of miniature dug-out, where I sat for some time trying to induce my head to behave in a normal manner. It was perfectly evident that the German counter-barrage was uncommonly heavy as well as very prompt, for the whole gimcrack place shook continuously with concussions close outside.

I must have remained here for half an hour, for it was quite light when I came out again. Nothing could be seen for smoke, and the shells were falling as thickly as ever. I had now to make my way back to the headquarters of the 13th Infantry Brigade, near Beugnâtre, to report that the tanks had started at zero. Still somewhat fogged, as I suppose, I pushed off in the wrong direction altogether, toward the battle instead of away from it. I met a wounded infantryman looking for a dressing station, and with the best intentions took him with me. After wandering about for some time among huts, dodging shells, I realised that we were going wrong by the lie of the ground, which was steadily downhill, and we turned about and groped our way back again through the smoke. The brigade headquarters, where I guessed there would also be a dressing station, occupied some dug-outs in our part of the old defence trenches, just west of the Ecoust road. We reached it at length, after various vicissitudes, to find every one driven underground by the shelling. The latter, in fact, was something quite out of the ordinary. The enemy,

THE FIGHTING FOR BEUGNY 411

determined to cling for another few days to his last position west of the Canal du Nord, had put down, not a normal barrage, but a heavy bombardment by 5.9's over a large area. I have never, before or since, seen such consistently severe shell-fire so widely spread. It extended for a mile back from our front line. At the brigade headquarters, where ordinarily one would have found most of the staff and details standing about as interested spectators with maps and field-glasses, there was not a soul above the surface; and shells were falling as far back as Favreuil.

I got very little news from the staff, as nearly all the telephone wires had been cut, and after waiting in the dug-out, in a temperature of about 190 degrees, for half an hour or so, I decided to try to make my way to the rallying-place chosen for the tanks. This was a valley which ran northward from Fremicourt. It was now about eight o'clock, and another brilliant day, but the shelling was as fierce as ever, and smoke and dust hung thickly over the country between Beugnâtre and Beugny. I made my way down the trench, as the only sort of covered approach, past our original front line, over a number of bodies, British and German, to the point where it crossed the valley from Fremicourt. But I could not see the rallying-point for smoke. The place was being shelled mercilessly, and it was obvious that no tanks could stay there. If they had rallied by this time, they must have come farther back. I tramped back up the hill to the brigade headquarters, seeing on the way a party of prisoners and their escort blown to pieces by a shell, and having several narrow escapes myself. Obtaining no information from the brigade beyond the fact that things were not going at all well, I walked down the Beugnâtre road to see if the tanks had rallied somewhere near the village, found no sign of them, nor indeed of any infantry or anybody else, and then made a second attempt to get to the original rallying-point in the Fremicourt Valley. But things there were as bad as before. A number of huts were on fire, and the whole place was smoking like a furnace. It was impossible to see anything, and it would have been suicidal to have gone groping about in the murk for problematical tanks. It was quite possible that all had been knocked out long before this. The whole battlefield was extraordinarily deserted. In my two journeys I had met only a couple of artillery officers reconnoitring for battery positions, two or three walking wounded, and the prisoners whom I saw destroyed. Every one who could find some cover from the ferocious shelling had taken it.

After a final hunt about Beugnâtre, I decided to walk back to our starting-point behind Favreuil. And there, about midday, I found some of the officers and men of the two sections, who had been in an hour or two already. Close, of B Company, was having a number of small wounds attended to. Beale, hit slightly in the leg by the same shell, was there also. Two out of the three tanks of A Company, it appeared, had been knocked out, and two out of the four from B, all on the dangerous ridge looking down into Beugny. The surviving tanks, returning to the rallying-point after it was plain that the infantry could not get near the village, had found the Fremicourt Valley, as I suspected, too hot to hold them—so hot, indeed, that it was considered inadvisable even to attempt to get them back through it into safety. They were driven against the railway embankment at the head of the valley, which afforded some slight protection, and there temporarily abandoned until the unprecedented shelling should have slackened. The crews had taken refuge in culverts and other holes and corners, where they still remained.

Almost everywhere the attack had been a failure. A slight advance had been made, and the New Zealanders and Mark V.'s on the right had captured Fremicourt and Bancourt; but the backbone of the position was untouched. On our left, four tanks of the 12th Battalion, misled by an infantry guide, arrived late, and the 3rd Division, attacking Ecoust and Longatte without them, could make no progress. Two other tanks which advanced against the trenches called the Noreuil Switch became ditched before they could effect anything. The assault on Beugny itself, as I have indicated, was hardly more successful. Of M'Elroy's three tanks, which had cleared without much trouble the old trench line as far as the spur in front of the village, two were knocked out by gun-fire the moment they appeared over the high ground. The third tank reached Beugny, but found that the infantry could not follow. B Company's section, moving along the railway, had a similar experience—two tanks disabled and the others unable to make any permanent impression on the village for lack of infantry support. In addition to Close, whose injuries sent him to hospital, we had two officers wounded. Sergeant Duddridge, whose tank was one of those hit on the ridge, performed extraordinarily fine work. Getting out his Lewis guns, he took his crew forward to join the infantry, and rallied parties of the latter who had lost their officers and were retiring. Having used all the ammunition of his own gun, he returned alone to his tank for more, and remained inside for some time firing 6-pounder shells into Beugny. He sent his crew back eventually, but stayed in the firing line himself throughout the day, turning up at Favreuil, as placid and cheerful as ever, late in the evening. He won the D.C.M. for this performance.

The 3rd and 5th Divisions seemed badly shaken by this affair, in which they suffered heavily from the terrific shelling. The latter continued on into the afternoon, so that it was two o'clock before the crews of our three surviving tanks (which, by a miracle, were untouched) could issue from their hiding-places and drive the machines back to Favreuil. A semi-humorous element in an otherwise nerve-wracking morning was provided by an officer of the American Tank Corps, one of three attached to us for a few days' experience. He had only been in France a week, and had hardly seen a gun fired until he rashly volunteered to go forward with Beale and the Major to the rallying-

point, where he found himself in the middle of as ferocious
a bombardment as any one there had ever experienced. I
met him afterwards, when I returned to Favreuil from my
wanderings in search of the tanks. He was an extremely
nice fellow, and quite ingenuous in his obvious delight and
surprise at finding himself still alive. I think his ideas of
modern war had been drawn from the surprising journals
of his native land, on which our own newspapers are so
successfully modelled; and undoubtedly that morning's
ordeal had been one of the shocks of his life. He was
burning to use his new-found knowledge in confuting some
of his fire-eating colleagues, who had been proclaiming
(from a distance) their fondness for battles and gore.

III.

The fighting on the 3rd Army front from 30th August
to 3rd September was practically a rearguard action on a
very large scale. Von Below's 17th German Army, its right
threatened by the advance from Arras, still clung desperately to its position from Ecoust southward. Our first
attempt to hustle it into a premature retreat having failed,
the attack was renewed the next morning, 31st August.
The hard-hit and somewhat shaken 3rd Division was reinforced by units from the 56th and 62nd Divisions, and nine
tanks of the 12th Battalion led this infantry in another
attack on Ecoust, Longatte, and the Noreuil Switch, which
were carried in spite of a very stubborn defence. The pair
of tanks responsible for the switch and other trenches
between Longatte and Vaulx-Vraucourt provided two of
the most notable incidents of the morning, described as
follows in the '12th Battalion History':—

"'Lorraine' (Lieut. Staub), after working down
Vraucourt trench to within a thousand yards of Vraucourt itself, turned north again at the request of the
infantry to deal with some machine-guns near Vrau-

court Copse. While heading to take these guns in the rear, the tank was disabled by a bullet from an anti-tank rifle hitting the magneto. Intense machine-gun fire was now concentrated on the tank, and four of the crew were wounded by A.P. bullets. Our nearest infantry were in a trench 150 yards away, and unable to advance, so Lieut. Staub, with great gallantry, got his badly-wounded men out of the tank and pulled or carried them under a severe fire to the trench. For this action he was recommended by the infantry for a decoration, and received the Military Cross. Meanwhile 'Lupin,' the other tank, had disappeared into the blue. Its commander, Lieut. Acroyd, was the only officer to cross the front line the previous morning, and on this occasion he seems to have carried on until well in front of our foremost infantry, when his tank stopped through magneto trouble. While in this situation some of the enemy managed to climb unseen on to the roof, and having from there shot the N.C.O., either through the manhole being unbolted or by means of an open revolver port, compelled the rest of the crew to surrender. The N.C.O., who was shot through the stomach, was left behind in a cellar when the enemy retreated, and *after three days* was able to make his way out and summon assistance."

The 7th Battalion was not engaged on the 31st. The 5th Division was licking its wounds in front of Beugny, and no further attempt was made upon that place until the general offensive was resumed on the 2nd. By the evening of the 30th, M'Elroy and I, with most of the crews that were in action that morning, had been conveyed in cars and lorries back to Bienvillers, where we indulged in hot baths and clean clothes, and met our new company commander, Merriam, just arrived from the 11th Battalion. Inhabitants were already returning to Bienvillers, and we were threatened with eviction from our fly-blown and dilapidated billets. The 6th Corps Club, an institution which followed up the army on the heels of the heavy guns, had now moved its branch from Bavincourt to our village, and one was able to enjoy some of the sweets of civilisation in the form of comfortable chairs and passable wine. Within a day or two this enterprising club had opened another branch at Gomiecourt, and a third actually in Behagnies, while the latter was still odorous with dead horses and other uncleared refuse of the battle.

Returning to Bihucourt on the afternoon of the 31st, we heard the first rumours of a possible German counter-attack with tanks. Two of A Company's few remaining machines were ordered to stand by to assist the New Zealanders in the event of these rumours materialising into facts. No one believed in them; but on the following day the enemy did counter-attack at Thilloy with a couple of his massive *Panzerkraftwagen*, and six tanks from our three companies moved toward Bapaume to be at hand if wanted. They were not wanted, although the right-hand pair, from B Company, did a little voluntary work among some huts south of the town. The counter-attack was a failure, and the German tanks did not get into action at all. Their half-hearted crews drove them (apparently on purpose) into a sunken road and abandoned them there. They were afterwards towed into Bapaume, where they lay in the station yard for many weeks.

Preparations were in hand for a heavy blow to be struck by both the 1st and 3rd Armies on 2nd September. The Canadians of the 1st Army astride the Arras-Cambrai road, and in touch, north of Ecoust, with the left of our 17th Corps, were now in front of the famous Drocourt-Quéant switch-line, supposed to be stronger than the main Hindenburg system. All the available tanks of the 3rd Brigade (9th, 11th, and 14th Battalions) were to lead the 4th Division and the 1st and 4th Canadians against these formidable trenches. To the remnants of the 2nd Tank Brigade, the 12th and 6th (Light) Battalions, was allotted the capture of Lagnicourt and Morchies, north-east of

THE FIGHTING FOR BEUGNY

Beugny, with the infantry of the 6th Corps. For our part, we were to supply twelve tanks for a renewed attempt with the 5th Division on Beugny, and for a further operation south of Bapaume against Villers-au-Flos, beyond Thilloy. Four tanks of C Company were detailed for each of these objectives, a section of B Company following up in reserve.

As everybody knows, the attack of the 1st Army on the Drocourt-Quéant Switch was a brilliant success. To quote Colonel Buchan, " It went clean through all the line of one of the strongest positions in the West, and took six miles of the switch, the villages of Etaing, Dury (with the important Hill of Dury), Villers-les-Cagnicourt and Noreuil, and 8000 prisoners." The Switch, in effect, had fallen as the Hindenburg Line fell at Cambrai, instantly, and this time irrevocably. But Colonel Buchan does not explain how it was carried so swiftly and easily. He does not mention tanks, and leaves it to be assumed that the infantry unaided fought their way in an hour or so through triple trenches and belts of wire. It will be well, therefore, to point out that once more the assault was led by tanks, of which fifty-seven (all the 3rd Brigade could muster) were employed. Fifty-three got into action. Only the most strenuous exertions got the depleted and disorganised tank units ready and in position for the battle. The 11th Battalion, which had recaptured the debris of Monchy-le-Preux on the 25th, had to trek across the whole front of the Canadian Corps, often within 1000 yards of the line, to reach the 4th Division, with which it was attacking Etaing, in the marshes of the Sensée. It is possible that the enemy heard this approach, as he sent up S.O.S. signals three minutes before zero. The tanks carried the massive trenches of the Switch, but had to make so wide a detour farther on to avoid the marshes that they could not reach Etaing with the infantry. In the centre, twenty-three out of twenty-four machines of the 9th Battalion reached their final objectives, which included Dury, where the Town Major was taken prisoner. The 14th Battalion, on the right, was no less successful, but had seven tanks knocked out beyond the Switch. "It is estimated that in this attack one company of tanks alone destroyed over seventy hostile machine-guns, the German gunners surrendering to the tanks as they approached."[1] South of the Canadians, the 17th Corps of the 3rd Army closed on the great knuckle of fortifications about Quéant, where the Switch joined the main Hindenburg Line. Quéant was almost surrounded by nightfall. The 6th Corps, in the meantime, had not fared so well; and two companies of the 12th Tank Battalion were sacrificed by the failure of the infantry to arrive at the time they themselves had arranged, and by their inability to get forward when at length they did reach the point of attack. Zero, for some reason, was fixed for 5.30, half an hour later than was the case with the corps on the left, so that the enemy's retaliation there, overlapping the 6th Corps' front, fell about the tanks of one company of the 12th, and they were moved forward into No Man's Land to escape it. Our barrage came down at 5.30, but the assaulting infantry had not arrived; and it being considered equally dangerous to keep the tanks stationary or to attempt to withdraw them, they were sent forward alone, in the hope that they could keep down the German machine-gun fire while the belated infantry got into position and advanced. The latter were forty minutes late, and then made no advance at all. The tanks cruised about, destroying machine-gun posts around Noreuil until they came under the fire of field batteries, when most of them were knocked out. Only two out of nine returned. The company on the right, with eight tanks, received little better support in its attack on Vaulx Wood and Morchies, and suffered almost as heavily. The battalion left twelve machines out of seventeen on the field, and lost eight officers and fifty-six other ranks. The 3rd Division, which was responsible for the disastrous fiasco on the left, had shown a progressive deterioration in quality

[1] 'Weekly Tank Notes.'

since the attack on 30th August, and its staff work had gone
from bad to worse. Such cases are not uncommon; but it
is unjust that the sacrifices of one arm should remain hidden
in order that the blunders of another may be hushed up.
There was very little reticence in the old days, when tanks
were uncertain and untrusted novelties, if they did not
perform some impossibility expected of them. Now that
the boot was on the other foot, a discreet silence shrouded
every small misadventure. From the first capture of
Monchy-le-Preux in 1917 to the end of the war there was a
multiplication of cases where inefficient staff work on the
part of infantry brigades and divisions caused tanks to be
sacrificed unnecessarily. In the strain and hurry of the last
advance these incidents became very frequent. The new
tactics, in which every attack was led by tank units, made
the latter absolutely dependent upon proper co-operation by
the infantry staffs concerned. Tanks are large objects
which cannot easily be hidden, and any misdirection, any
omission to notify changes of plan, any hitch in the
assembly of the assaulting troops (all common faults), meant
in nine cases out of ten that the particular tanks involved
would find themselves sooner or later caught in the open
without support in face of an enemy who could devote his
whole attention to destroying them. I will give chapter and
verse later on for an instance within my own experience;
but what I wish to point out now is that the general ignorance of the part played by tanks in the last year of the war
is due to an official reticence based very often simply on a
determination to avoid unpleasant disclosures. The tanks
were not the only victims of this tendency. Their case
happens to be peculiar, but every arm suffered in turn for
the susceptibilities of the others.

While the 12th Battalion, through no fault of its own,
was losing tanks in vain about Morchies and Noreuil, we
were suffering again at Beugny and winning a welcome
success at Villers-au-Flos. The latter village was carried
by the 42nd Division with the help of one section from C

Company, three of whose tanks subsequently broke down east of the village while on their way home, and had temporarily to be abandoned. The fighting was severe, the German machine-gunners holding out to the last with that conspicuous bravery which they displayed in almost all these actions; and the fourth tank, commanded by Sergeant Penny, having done splendid work in the village, returned plastered grey with lead and stuck all over with armour-piercing bullets. The other section, in the meantime, working again with the 5th Division, had again found Beugny unconquerable. The place was a veritable fortress, entrenched and wired and held by a large garrison with field-guns; and although our infantry, as a result of the first attack, were close to the outskirts, they were checked at the start by intense machine-gun fire, and failed to make any progress beyond a slight advance to the north of the village. The tanks could do nothing alone, and the affair was another expensive failure. It cost us the life, among others, of Adney, a boy who joined the battalion before Cambrai, where he got the Military Cross, and who was now killed in rather extraordinary and still obscure circumstances. He had with him two of my old crew, Corporal Mitchell and Taylor. His tank, having pushed on alone in default of infantry support, cruised along the north side of Beugny, firing into it, and then started to return. It was hit, apparently, somewhere in front, by a shell which wounded Taylor (who was driving) and filled the inside with smoke. Adney and the rest of the crew, believing the machine to be disabled, as it had stopped, scrambled out, but finding themselves isolated among groups of Germans, ran back and got inside again, with the exception of Corporal Mitchell, who was captured. The tank, on examination, proved to be still in running order. She was therefore started up and driven toward our lines. She was now hit a second time, in the petrol tank, and finally disabled, and simultaneously, it appears, Adney was killed by a bullet which came through his open flap. Presumably it was

THE FIGHTING FOR BEUGNY

fired by one of our own infantry. The latter making a slight advance at this point, the rest of the crew escaped, carrying Taylor with them, and shortly after Corporal Mitchell was rescued from a dug-out where his captors had left him. I happened to be in C Company's huts in the Favreuil Valley, talking to Coutts and Alden, who had just returned from the action, when Mitchell, who was supposed to be killed, made a dramatic reappearance. He had lost his watch and everything else in his pockets, but otherwise was none the worse for his fifteen-minutes' captivity.

IV.

We had not yet finished with Beugny. Toward dusk on 2nd September I was waiting about in our camp at Bihucourt for the Major, who was taking me back to Bienvillers in his car. Word had come through that the 1st Tank Brigade was to be withdrawn into Army Reserve to refit, and those of us who had nothing particular to do were returning to our old headquarters that night. I was especially glad of this release, as the symptoms of another attack of influenza (or some kindred variant of P.U.O.) were beginning to affect me, and I was longing for bed. At this time battalion headquarters had established an advanced base at Bihucourt in one of the huts, and the Major was now conferring there with the Colonel, who had just arrived. Unconscious of my doom, like one of the infants in the poem, I was standing about outside when the Major appeared to summon me, as I supposed, to the car. His first words dissipated this natural delusion.

"There's another dog-fight on to-night," he said. "They want two of our tanks for Beugny again. . . ."

Beugny was becoming a perfect curse to the battalion, a sort of King Charles's head, or Old Man of the Sea. This was the third time in five days that we had been called upon to tackle it, and it was A Company's second turn in the pleasant round. We were, I think, inclined to feel that the 5th Division might have done their own work on this occasion without dragging us into it again, as we had given them two opportunities which they had failed to seize. However, the thing had to be done. We were working once more with our old acquaintances the 13th Infantry Brigade, who had attacked the place with us on the 30th. Our only fit tanks, three or four, and none of them in good condition, were still in the valley by Favreuil. We had no officers available as tank commanders, and two sergeants were sent off to prepare the most likely machines for action. M'Elroy, who was once more to share with me the responsibilities of office, was already away at Bienvillers, no doubt luxuriating in a bath and the prospect of several days of peace; and a car was despatched to bring him back to these unpleasant realities. After a hurried meal with the Colonel, the Major and I departed in his Vauxhall for the 13th Brigade Headquarters, still in the dug-out near Beugnâtre. As it was now quite dark, we were able to drive most of the way to the village. We found the Brigadier and his Brigade Major in the dug-out, and obtained from them the plan of attack and the *rôle* the two tanks were expected to play. Beugny, it appeared, was to be dealt with faithfully at last. Six field batteries and one battery of 6-inch howitzers were to pound it for half an hour before the infantry advanced. The tanks were required only to clear a trench which ran immediately behind the village. It appeared rather obvious that if the latter was carried, the fall of the trench would be only a matter of time, and that if the artillery preparation was sufficiently thorough and accurate, both village and trench (together a small and compact target) would be rendered so untenable that tanks would not be needed for their capture. One cannot argue with brigadiers, however. We promised that the tanks should arrive, if we could get them there. I remember this interview, held in a candle-lit compartment of the dug-out, with peculiar clearness. I had seen the

THE FIGHTING FOR BEUGNY

Brigadier and his Brigade Major before, and was to meet them again some weeks later when I was with the 12th Battalion at Solesmes, and I was struck by the marked contrast between them. The General, whose name I forget, was a powerful bulky man, with an odd resemblance to a boar. Stewart, the Brigade Major, was very young, very fair, slim, and rather exquisite. He seemed to find speech an exhausting process, and wore a permanent expression of boredom and fatigue, neither of which, I dare say, was an affectation at that time.

When we returned to the tanks at Favreuil, the two machines detailed for the attack were filled up and ready to move, and M'Elroy had arrived from Bienvillers. I spent half an hour explaining the details to the crews and plotting out compass-bearings on the map. We should be approaching Beugny in the dark over ground that was unknown to me except for the few glimpses I had obtained through the smoke on the 30th, and I determined to strike the railway, of which I have spoken, as soon as possible, and use it as a guide to the village. Soon after midnight we started, following the road north of Monument Wood, through Favreuil, and so through the deserted camps south of Beugnâtre. The two tanks, although the best we could provide at this stage, were in great need of an overhaul, and we soon began to have trouble with them. One stuck in the sunken road beyond Beugnâtre. After waiting for some time, M'Elroy and I went on with the remaining machine, as we had still a long way to go. We were now launched upon the open grass-land, devoid of landmarks, and I began to use the compass. Far ahead of us, in a direct line with the bearing I had taken to the railway, a fire was burning behind the German front, and this served us as a useful guide. I supposed it to be a village or a dump set alight by our shells, but presently a second fire was visible, and then a third, and I began to wonder if these conflagrations did not signify that the enemy was burning his stores before retreating. Our guns were very quiet, as they had been throughout the evening, and it was difficult to account otherwise for these sudden glares on the horizon. In the meantime, the tank we had left in the sunken road had not overtaken us, and our remaining machine was giving trouble. One or two delays, due to engine defects, wasted a lot of valuable time. Zero was at 5.40, and it was four o'clock before at length we struck the railway at a point marked by two stacks of fodder and an overturned Whippet. This machine, incidentally, had been the cause of a very gallant action a few days before. One of a section of the 3rd Battalion sent in to "clear up the situation" (whatever that euphemistic phrase may mean) on 29th August, the Whippet had turned completely over in a shell-hole, catching fire at the same time. The door of the cab was jammed in the earth, and the crew of three was imprisoned upside down in burning oil. The commander of another Whippet, Lieutenant Sewell, got out under intense machine-gun fire at close range, and with a shovel dug out and forced open the door of the inverted tank. He liberated the crew, but was shot in several places and killed, together with his driver, while endeavouring to return to his own machine. A posthumous V.C. was awarded him.

Having found the railway, we pushed along beside it at a good speed. The fires in the east were growing brighter, and the extreme quietness of the night confirmed me in my belief that the expected retreat of the enemy actually was begun. When we reached the head of the valley which had been our inauspicious selection as a rallying-point for the 30th, the tank developed further eccentricities, and eventually refused to move at all. The engine stopped, and no coaxing would start it up again. There was no sign of the second tank. At a quarter past five, as we were still 1000 yards from our front line, M'Elroy and I decided that nothing more could be done. We told the crew to take refuge in a culvert, which ran through the railway embankment close at hand, if the tank was discovered and shelled at dawn, and then we began to make our way back to the

13th Brigade Headquarters to report our failure. We were nearing the Beugnâtre road as the barrage fell upon Beugny at zero. Dawn was breaking, and as, deafened by the throbbing clamour of the batteries all round us, we looked back eastward from the rising ground, we saw fresh fires blazing and clouds of white smoke rolling away from a dozen points far beyond the range of our shells. There could be hardly any doubt about it now: the German retreat had begun. At the brigade headquarters we found nobody but a few signal officers and other details staring at these distant conflagrations, and they had no news to give us; but tramping on to Biefvillers we met the Major in his car, and learnt from him that the enemy had indeed vanished in the night. Beugny, pulverised for half an hour by high explosives, was empty of all living things. Only a few machine-gunners were left amid the debris of the retreat between us and the Canal du Nord.

V.

On 4th September the whole Tank Corps was withdrawn into G.H.Q. Reserve to refit and reorganise. Since the 21st August, 511 tanks had been in action, and had been largely responsible for a succession of victories in which we had captured 53,000 prisoners and 470 guns. The 1st, 2nd, and 3rd Tank Brigades were now so crippled that they could not have mustered fifty fit machines between them. The 4th and 5th Brigades, having suffered heavily on 8th August and after, had less work to do in the course of the 4th Army's subsequent advance south of the Somme, for which reason I have not attempted, amid so much other matter, to follow their actions during this fortnight; but they were hardly less reduced and in need of rest than the three northern brigades.

Strikes, and the vacillating policy of the authorities in respect of tanks, had left the corps with no reserve from which casualties and worn-out machines could be replaced. The ratio of wastage in any series of tank actions, from mechanical causes alone, was very large, increasing proportionately as machines were used again and again with no opportunity between times for a thorough overhaul. On the other hand, the majority of repairs needed were only of a minor character; and after a week's rest a battalion which had been reduced perhaps to half a dozen serviceable tanks could put twenty or thirty into the field again. Cases of disablement by gun-fire, of course, fell into a different category. Such machines as could be salved on the spot and were worth repairing were despatched to Central Workshops, whose personnel at this time was working day and night, but the replacement of shattered armour-plate was a longer job than a change of track-plates or rollers. In any case, nothing could make up for the lack of an adequate reserve of new tanks. The batches of Mark V.'s which came out from England replaced only a small portion of the casualties in the dozen battalions which used that type, and the 12th Battalion and ourselves carried on to the end with Mark IV.'s, most of which were nearly two years old.

The period of reorganisation after 4th September included the inevitable reshuffling of battalions among the five brigades. It will be enough to state here that the 1st Brigade was made up once more of its old units, the 7th, 11th, and 12th Battalions. The 301st American Tank Battalion was attached for a short time and came with some Mark V.'s to Bihucourt, where the 7th remained.

The fever, which I had felt to be impending before our last abortive attempt to reach Beugny, took a good grip of me immediately afterwards, and I spent three or four days in bed at Bienvillers, at first in my tumble-down billet, in a room that swarmed with flies and reeked of chloride of lime, and then, when I could stand this no longer, under a tarpaulin in an orchard. When I visited the camp at Bihucourt again, after a lapse of a week, it was a scene of violent activity, due largely to the Americans. Why these

people called themselves the 301st Tank Battalion I never
understood, as they were in fact the 1st, but it was of a
piece with their other eccentric customs. They took over
all the huts in the camp which A Company did not occupy,
and they provided us for days with interest and amusement.
They seemed to spend most of their time pulling their tanks
to pieces. There was usually a Mark V. in some stage of
disintegration in the space between the two main rows of
huts, where it had no business to be, and over it and around
it swarmed crowds of Americans filled with what (to us) was
incomprehensible zeal. Perhaps by this time we were somewhat satiated with tanks and with the war in general. Our
Allies were inspired with all the enthusiasm of belated
proselytes. They were like children with a new toy, and
very like children, too, in other ways. Some of their
methods were stupefying even to casual persons like myself, who am no stickler for pedantic ritual in anything.
One did not expect to find an American tank unit (or any
other) behaving like the Guards; but mere intelligent order
and discipline, which common-sense should indicate as
essential to any military body, seemed to be unknown to
these people. Their orderly-room they themselves described very aptly as "the mad-house." The junior officers,
a set of excellent fellows, lived in a state of wholly unnecessary discomfort, partly from obscure notions of democratic
behaviour, and partly (I imagine) because they had obtained
from books some odd conviction that warriors should at all
times be Spartans. They appeared to have no batmen
(presumably the free-born American citizen would not
serve openly in that capacity), and they certainly had no
mess, as we understand the term. Those of them who
visited our headquarters at Bienvillers were quite over-
whelmed by the primitive luxuries of A Company's tarpaulin
shelter, with its rickety forms, dirty table-cloths, and imperfect crockery. An American officer drew his meals in
his tin pannikin from the men's cook-house, sometimes
fetching the food himself, and sometimes being obliged in

this little matter by a condescending and casual-mannered N.C.O. or private, full of familiar talk and audibly chewing gum. The meal was then consumed, from the pannikin, wherever the officer happened to be. This was not in some trench before an attack, but in camp at Bihucourt, now eight or ten miles behind the line. The whole American Army, of course, was "dry" in theory, and seemed to subsist largely on beans and bacon. Poor Jack Brown, who was attached to the 301st for a few days when that battalion left us for the Havrincourt region, complained bitterly that he was half starved while he was with them, as the officers, dependent upon the men's cook-house, had no meal after tea, and nothing alcoholic to drink at any time. These peculiarities, trifling in themselves, were symptomatic of that puerile element in the American character which seems so incongruous in an otherwise preternaturally acute people. The whole force was a strange compound of zeal, intelligence, fads, and conceit. The men fought well enough, as did every one else except the Portuguese. Being the first contingents drawn from a vast population, they were physically and mentally of the best type. They were keen to a degree, and honestly anxious, in their own peculiar way, to learn everything. But they had learnt no more than the rudiments of their job when the war ended. Their staff work broke down hopelessly under any strain. The army, in short, wanted another year or so of hard experience. After the Armistice, in America, I understand, people wore in their button-holes little discs, on which were inscribed the words, "We went to do it, and we've done it." In the same spirit the Prussians and the Belgians claimed to have won the battle of Waterloo.

This peaceful interlude at Bihucourt lasted for a fortnight. The battalion was busy overhauling tanks, resting, washing, and re-equipping personnel, and preparing in general for the forthcoming attack on the reputably formidable position to which the Germans had retired. The

weather, changing with the fortunes of the war, after a
few rain-storms in the beginning of the month, had settled
down to another spell of sunny days, which made even
the obliterated landscape around Bapaume seem comparatively attractive. For amusements, we had a veritable
museum of battle relics at Achiet-le-Grand, where, in addition to a host of disabled tanks awaiting trains for Erin,
there was the anti-tank stockade and a miscellaneous
assortment of captured German guns, which a week or
two earlier had made our lives a burden; while we were
surrounded by a congeries of officers' clubs that reminded
one of St James's Street after a social upheaval and an
earthquake. The E.F.C., after many months' enforced
absence from the Promised Land, had erected once more
its huge marquees at Achiet-le-Grand itself, the 6th Corps
had its clubs at Gomiecourt and Behagnies, and in Bihucourt there was a New Zealand Officers' Club with a first-
rate library — manna from heaven in such a wilderness.
For one who lives on books it is difficult to speak with
calmness of the spirit and enterprise which inspired this
literary mission. No British club or institution that I
ever discovered in France troubled about books at all, if
we except the dog's-eared cheap editions in the Y.M.C.A.
canteens. The Canadians had a small library of instructional works (horrible things) which followed them about;
but it was left to the New Zealand Division to establish,
in a ruined house in Bihucourt, among other places, a
genuine library of volumes in good editions—shelves of
verse, history, geography, books of reference, fiction, and
so on, labelled and well kept, and obviously in demand.
Among the many miracles of this war, I count this discovery among the most noteworthy. Unfortunately for
me, I came upon it too late, although it was at my very
door. One does not look for pearls among the refuse of
a battle, and I only heard of the library by accident. Two
days later we had left the place, and did not meet the New
Zealand Division again. But if any one from that Dominion

should read this book, I hope he will accept the thanks of one (I have no doubt among many) who received benefits from this exceptional enterprise.

On the morning of 18th September the battalion received orders to trek to Morchies, north-east of Beugny, of evil memory. The Colonel and the company commanders went ahead in cars to prospect for a camp, and returned enthusiastic about some mysteriously empty huts (another German hospital) which they had discovered. Early in the afternoon, in brilliant sunshine, the eight tanks that A Company had now got fit again for action were trekking across the rolling grass-land of our old battlefield; B Company, from the valley behind us, and C, from Favreuil, had joined in the procession; and before dusk we were unpacking and settling ourselves down in our new quarters.

CHAPTER XX.

THE CANAL DU NORD AND BOURLON.

I.

THE ruins of Morchies lay a mile and a half north-east of Beugny, at the head of a valley which descended past Lagnicourt to Quéant. On the summit of the high ground to the east of the village stood a conspicuous group of large hospital huts containing a number of beds and some rough furniture. Our men were accommodated in these, while the officers occupied a group of smaller huts a quarter of a mile away at the edge of the village. The tanks of the battalion (now twenty-four in number) were camouflaged in the ruins. About this time battalion headquarters moved to Bullecourt, to be in touch with the H.Q. of the Canadian Corps, with whom we were to work in the next advance.

The valleys around Morchies were filled with horse lines and transport, and there were many troops living in the village itself; and it struck me at once as singular that we should have found this capacious hospital empty, and not even ear-marked for any newcomers, especially as it was the only camp of huts in the neighbourhood. When one sees a cheap and otherwise desirable house untenanted in a popular district one suspects bad drains: a solitary and empty camp in an area four miles behind the line and crowded with troops made one think of shells. Soon after our arrival I was looking round the country with my glasses, and I discovered that we were overlooked, from a distance of seven miles, by the trees of Bourlon Wood. I began to feel sure that these apparently eligible quarters had their disadvantages, which had proved too much for previous tenants; and in fact on the following morning, just after the crews had marched away to their tanks, heavy shells began to fall among the huts. A cook and a water-cart driver were killed, and several other men badly wounded, and it became painfully obvious that the hospital was no place for us. Bivouacs were formed at once in the valley, and the men transferred to them that night. The officers remained for another day in their own huts nearer the village, but eventually were driven out by persistent shelling, and only one large building was retained as a Reconnaissance Office. Beale (who was now Battalion R.O. in place of Henriquez), Jack Brown, and I were fortunate in discovering the only empty dug-out in the neighbourhood—a cosy little place of two rooms partly excavated from the side of a sunken road, where we lived in great comfort for the remainder of our stay. Every one else moved into tents in the valley. Intermittent shelling of the high ground continued every day.

We were very busy during this time with preliminaries for the forthcoming renewal of the general offensive. The Germans had fallen back to their last prepared position in the West, and this was to be attacked by the 1st, 3rd, and 4th Armies on a front of over thirty miles from the Sensée to St Quentin. The 1st and 3rd Armies were to deliver the initial blow toward Bourlon and Cambrai on 27th September. Operations in this sector were complicated, and to some extent awkwardly cramped by a water obstacle which completely protected Cambrai to the north and north-west. The marshes of the Sensée, running from east to west, cross the line of the Agache and the Canal du Nord, running from north to south, near Ecourt St Quentin, the two systems forming an impassable angle of water and marsh which limited the share of the 1st Army in the attack to its right wing, the Canadian Corps, south of the Arras-Cambrai road. In addition to the marshes of the Agache, the Canal du Nord, although unfinished, was full of water as far as Sains-les-Marquion, five miles south of its crossing of the Sensée. For another four miles to a point south of the Bapaume-Cambrai road, where we were now east of the canal at Havrincourt Wood, it was dry, forming an immense ditch 50 feet wide and 15 feet deep, with steep banks of brick. At the village of Mœuvres, 3000 yards below Sains-les-Marquion, it was crossed by the original Hindenburg or Siegfried Line, which trended away to the southeast until it reached the Canal de L'Escaut at Bantouzelle. West of Mœuvres this line was in our possession; and operations since the German withdrawal, and known as the battles of Havrincourt and Epehy, had carried the 3rd and 4th Armies across the canal south of Mœuvres to within striking distance of the eastern or German section of the famous trenches. Tanks of the 4th and 5th Brigades had helped the 4th Army in these operations on the 18th, 21st, and 24th September. From north to south our line on the 26th ran from Ecourt St Quentin near the Sensée, west of the Canal du Nord to below Mœuvres, thence across the canal and through Havrincourt, Gouzeaucourt, and Epehy in face of the Siegfried Line. The main battle was to open on the 27th, when the Canadians and the 3rd Army were to carry the line of the canal and the Hindenburg trenches [1] as far as Gouzeaucourt, the 4th Army carrying on the offensive to the south on the 29th.

The impossibility of crossing the Canal du Nord above Marquion had led to a redistribution of the 1st Tank Brigade. The 7th Battalion having become well acquainted with the Canadians in the course of several weeks' training, was attached to them for their attack between Marquion and Mœuvres. The 15th Battalion, with Mark V.'s, was borrowed from the 2nd Brigade to help the 17th Corps of

---

[1] The Hindenburg Line, it may be noted, was a generic term used by us to cover the whole series of defence systems called by the Germans the Siegfried, Hunding, Wotan Lines, &c.

the 3rd Army south of Mœuvres. The 11th Battalion, also with Mark V.'s, having moved down from our left, was allotted to the 4th Corps for the front between Trescault and Gouzeaucourt. The 12th Battalion remained in reserve.

It is necessary to give here a more detailed description of the canal and the country on either side of it. I have spoken of a valley trending north-eastward from Morchies to Quéant. If one walked along the high ground from our camp to the right of this valley one came presently to another depression which fell away to Pronville, a mile east of Quéant. From Pronville a third valley led at an obtuse angle due east to Inchy-en-Artois and the canal. Down its centre curled the dry bed of the Hirondelle stream, lined by willows, poplars, and the anti-tank *abattis* of railway iron; and along the ridges which enclosed it to north and south were sited the deep trenches and triple belts of wire of those portions of the Hindenburg Front and Support Lines already in our possession. The southern ridge rose to a considerable height—some 350 feet—and on approaching the canal inclined northward in a final spur which sank to the levels of the Agache near Sains-le-Marquion. The village of Inchy stood on the tip of this spur, raised slightly above the levels and within 1000 yards of the canal. Mœuvres, a mile to the south and almost on the canal bank, was at the foot of the higher end of the spur. The eastern slope of the latter fell gently like a *glacis* to our front line, and through scattered trees beyond one could see the white chalk embankment of the canal about Lock 4. Our line took in both the villages, but there was fighting in Mœuvres a day or two before the big attack, and the front here was rather vague and was given incorrectly on our maps. On one occasion, when Jack Brown had driven me almost into Inchy in his side-car, we walked casually along behind the village until we found ourselves in a ditch full of Stokes guns and people crawling about in furtive attitudes, and learnt to our astonishment that we were in our outpost line. Our subsequent attempts to see something from the outer houses of Inchy itself,

where not a soul was moving, were marked by extreme
caution. We could see little in any case, for the canal was
masked from this direction by intervening trees. From the
hill above Mœuvres, however, one looked over the whole
area behind the German front as far back as Bourlon Wood;
and one particular point in the Hindenburg trenches near
Tadpole Copse (where there had been severe fighting during
the first Cambrai battle) gave us a bird's-eye view of the

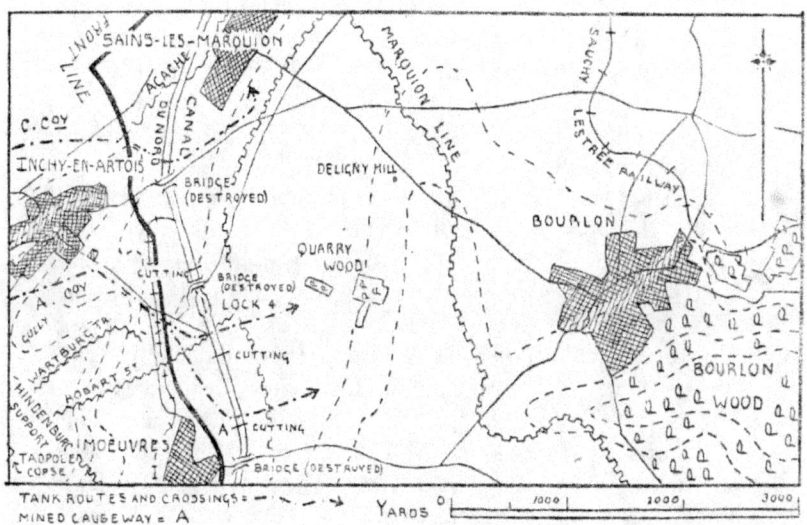

The Canal du Nord and Bourlon.

whole section of the canal which especially interested A
Company—the section about Lock 4. C Company was to
cross north of Inchy, where a fairly close reconnaissance
was possible. Our chief perplexity over this celebrated
obstacle was caused by our lack of reliable knowledge concerning it. Fragmentary information was obtained from
civilians engaged on its construction before the war, and
was supplemented by engineers' drawings of various sections; but there were intermediate patches about which we
could find out nothing definite. The sections were found

to differ considerably in detail, and the drawings themselves were of uncertain value. Time and shell-fire had changed the profile of the canal banks in many places, while the Germans were reported to have been at work on the unfinished portions for some purpose of their own.[1] A number of indications pointed to the fact that they considered the canal to be an insuperable obstacle to tanks, except at the causeways they had cut through its banks. These it was almost certain would be mined. The sum of our discoveries, obtained from these sources and from aeroplane photographs and more or less distant observation through binoculars, can be set out as follows. It refers only to that portion which the 7th Tank Battalion had to negotiate.

North-east of Inchy was a broken iron girder bridge. From this point to another bridge, also destroyed, at Mœuvres, the canal ran in a dead straight line pointing a little to the east of south. The embankments on their outer sides were 6 to 10 feet in height. They were 20 feet broad. The inner faces fell to the canal bed in two stages: first, there was an almost sheer drop, partially bricked, of about 9 feet, then a step or platform 8 feet wide, and finally a slope of 1 in 2 which descended for another 5 feet to the canal bed. The latter was 36 feet across. Midway between Inchy and Mœuvres there was an unfinished concrete lock, numbered 4. Immediately south of the Inchy bridge the banks had been cut and a causeway constructed out of the debris across the canal bed. Two similar causeways existed between Lock 4 and Mœuvres. All these were required for our artillery. It was suspected that they were mined; and as they would be completely blocked by any tanks which happened to be disabled while crossing, we were allowed to use only one, that nearest to Mœuvres.

---

[1] It was found that, for several hundred yards between Mœuvres and Inchy, the Germans had cut in the eastern bank a vertical wall nine feet deep, evidently as an anti-tank obstacle. Tanks of the 15th Battalion succeeded in climbing this.

A and C Companies, each with eight tanks in two sections, were detailed for the operation, B Company remaining in reserve. C, crossing near the Inchy bridge, had a comparatively easy task. The canal at this point was only half-finished, and the banks were low and dilapidated. A Company on the right was faced by a far more serious problem. We had, it is true, the use of a causeway, but this was a doubtful privilege. If, as every one believed (and as the event proved) it was mined, the leading tank probably would be disabled and would block the passage. One section, however, was detailed to attempt this hazard. It remained to find some crossing-place for the other section over the embankment itself. The latter was known to be almost finished in this portion, and appeared to be little damaged; and while it might prove easy enough for tanks to slide down on to the canal bed (although the first drop of 9 feet was not an attractive feature), to climb the other side was a very different matter. As the brickwork was incomplete we could only hope that the earth on top, after four years' exposure to rain and a recent pounding by shell-fire, had crumbled and fallen over the steep upper lip to form a possible slope. The difficulties were thought to be so great, however, that a very wild expedient to overcome them was proposed and actually adopted. Three unfit Mark IV. tanks were to be brought up, driven into the canal at zero, and there manœuvred into position side by side across the bed to form a bridge for the others. This was all very characteristic of theoretical staff officers who had never driven a tank themselves and had no conception of the difficulties involved in such a scheme. With unfit Mark IV.'s, at least half an hour would have been taken in getting them into position, if everything else went well. If one was hit by the barrage which was almost certain to fall on the canal, the whole enterprise would be ruined at the start. Finally, assuming the bridge to be made, it is very doubtful if it would have stood the weight of the fighting machines as they crossed over. Tanks are not constructed to support thirty tons in movement on their roofs.[1] In the end, however, the experiment never reached the point of test. The only machines available were some of the 7th Battalion's derelicts, still lying under repair far behind at Bucquoy in the hands of salvage crews. Three were put more or less in order and started on their long trek several days before the battle, but the effort was too much for them. They broke down repeatedly, and on the evening of the 26th were still some miles from Pronville. The only result of this fantastic scheme was to put an added strain upon already overworked salvage personnel.

In the meantime we had not troubled much about it. We continued to work on more normal and practical lines, seeking some point on the canal bank where tanks might cross unaided. From the Hindenburg trenches near Tadpole Copse, after a careful scrutiny through my glasses, I discovered what seemed to be a likely place immediately south of Lock 4. Both banks were somewhat dilapidated and fallen in through shell-fire at this point, and the nearer one was pierced by a communication trench called Hobart Street, which ran down from the front lines. Here, if anywhere, a tank could climb out from the bed. It was decided that the left-hand section (M'Elroy's) should follow Hobart Street and attempt this crossing. The right-hand section (Paul's) was to use the causeway 700 yards to the south.

Beyond the canal the ground rose gently again to Bourlon Ridge. A trench system, heavily wired, known as the Canal du Nord Line, ran parallel to the farther bank. Behind this, 1200 yards from Lock 4, was Quarry Wood, a T-shaped enclosure of meagre timber. From the Canal du Nord Line communication trenches zigzagged up the slope on either side of the wood to the Marquion Line, the last defensive work in front of Bourlon. This line was still unfinished, and, as we found when we reached it, was very

[1] Trials at Erin and elsewhere had proved that a tank will support another on its roof: but these experiments were made in conditions differing greatly from those which obtain in action.

Canal du Nord at Lock 4. A Company, 7th Battalion, crossed where the lettering is, by end of Hobart Street. Quarry Wood beyond.

THE CANAL DU NORD AND BOURLON 439

imperfectly wired, there being wide gaps where only the stakes had been planted. Bourlon village and wood, upwards of 3000 yards east of the canal, were protected by a final series of trenches and entanglements, nowhere very formidable. The Canadians' ultimate objectives for the first day included Bourlon and Haynecourt to the north, with the usual arrangements for further exploitation if circumstances permitted.

A Company's eight tanks were to leave the front line at zero with the infantry in the normal manner. The 4th Canadian Division, however, with whom we were working, expected the tanks to be delayed considerably by the canal, and framed its plan of attack on the supposition that they would not overtake the infantry again until the latter was approaching its second objective, the Marquion Line. This supposition, as it happened, proved erroneous. As soon as the Marquion Line was carried and the barrage lifted again, the two sections were to converge on Bourlon village. The great wood was reserved for a novel treatment. We had proved by bitter experience in the first Cambrai battle that gas hung sluggishly about its hollows and undergrowth. On this occasion it was to be deluged with gas-shells for two days and nights before the attack. No frontal assault against it was to be made on the 27th, but such of its defenders as survived the poison were to be captured or driven out by envelopment from the north and south.

C Company, working on our left with the 1st Canadian Division, had in hand the capture of Sains-les-Marquion, with a subsequent advance against the northern part of the Marquion Line. The Divisional Staff was unnecessarily anxious about the tanks being heard if they approached the front line before zero, and accordingly insisted on their starting 1000 yards behind the infantry. The attack on this flank was cramped in its early stage by the water obstacle of the Agache and the canal, the latter being flooded as far south as Lock 3, above Inchy. Sains-les-Marquion and Marquion itself would therefore have to be carried by a pivotal movement from the south and east, after the canal had been crossed lower down; and this swing to the left on the part of the tanks and infantry produced, among other things, a highly complicated barrage table, the barrage turning back upon itself through half a circle. In practice this difficult evolution was performed without a hitch, as indeed were all the other arrangements made by the Canadians, whose preliminary work was thorough and intelligent to a degree which, unfortunately, was none too common. It was a pleasure to be associated with most of the divisional and brigade staffs. They were anxious to do all they could for us, they understood our difficulties, and they appreciated our help. The Canadian infantry was at this time in the best of condition. The whole corps had been withdrawn for the first prolonged rest it had known some time before the general offensive began; and by the breaking up of the new 5th Division in England the four old ones in France were brought up to a strength which no British unit could ever approach. The brigades we trained with at Enguinegatte had forty-five officers and eleven hundred men per battalion. Having broken triumphantly through the Drocourt-Quéant Line in the first days of September, the corps was still fresh and but little reduced in numbers. I never met the South Africans, whom many people declare to have been the best of the Colonial troops; but of the others, speaking from my own experience and on general grounds, I should put the New Zealand Division first and the Canadians a close second. The Australians, gifted with one essential military quality—an aptitude for fighting—were in many other respects an unmitigated nuisance.

II.

On the evening of the 25th we moved all three companies of tanks from Morchies to the neighbourhood of Pronville. Each tank was now provided with the latest

THE CANAL DU NORD AND BOURLON 441

development of the old Cambrai fascine — an immense hexagonal crate of timber and steel, carried as before on top of the cab. These things were intended for the Hindenburg trenches, but as the 7th Battalion worked to the north of that line, we never had occasion to use them. Most of our tanks shed them at the first opportunity after zero. I do not know that they were any improvement on the primitive fascine bundle. They were little, if at all, lighter, and required a lorry apiece to bring them on their fruitless journey to Morchies. On one or two occasions when they were used by other battalions, I believe they buckled up under the tank's weight—an accident which could not happen with the fascine. When carried into action they undoubtedly terrified the enemy, who took them for some new engine of destruction. Some of ours were riddled by machine-gun bullets.

The fine weather had held throughout our stay at Morchies, and the night of the 25th was brilliant with a full moon. The trek to Pronville, a distance of three miles, was accomplished in peace and with only one or two slight breakdowns, which were soon rectified. The little valley leading down to the village was full of 6-inch howitzers, which fired intermittently with a blaze of flame and a shattering noise. Across the mouth of the valley, where it widened and became one with the larger depression leading eastward to Inchy, extended the black barrier of the Hindenburg wire, looking in the moonlight like a vast bed of some evil weed; and just in front of this, on the hillside to the right, were two long banks, against which the tanks of A and C Companies were parked up and camouflaged. The prodigious cribs which they carried rose high above the top of the banks, and we stretched camouflage nets outward from them to the slope of the hill beyond. B Company's machines had pushed on by the road which led through the wire and trenches, to lie up under the willows lining the bed of the Hirondelle in the bigger valley. We had found previously and marked as our own (for what this

was worth) a few small unoccupied dug-outs in the front
Hindenburg trench. They were still empty, and in one of
them, an L-shaped untimbered excavation about the size
of a large cupboard, accessible by the usual breakneck
flight of steps, the Major, M'Chlery, M'Elroy, and I settled
ourselves down about 1 A.M., ate a little food, drank a little
whisky and chlorinated water, and composed ourselves for
a little folding of the hands in sleep.

The following morning (the 26th or Y-day) was again
brilliantly fine. I walked out once more to the high ground
above Mœuvres and made a final examination of the distant
canal and the bare slope toward Bourlon. In the afternoon
I intended to take M'Elroy and Paul, the two section commanders, over the route to Inchy and as far beyond as
seemed advisable. It was very simple going for tanks along
the floor of the valley, however dark the night might be, for
the trees of the Hirondelle formed a guide which it was
impossible to miss; but no one except myself had walked
over this final stretch, and in case of accidents it was
advisable for the section commanders to know it. Un
pleasant developments, however, supervened to spoil our
excursion. As we were having lunch the German guns
became active, and we could hear and see the shells crashing
in the valley toward Inchy. When we set out, about two
o'clock, we were obliged to keep to the high ground along
the front Hindenburg trench, so as to have a shelter
to jump into in emergency. We could follow the route
of our approach-march almost equally well from here, but
when we got to the spur between Inchy and Tadpole
Copse, with the intention of seeing what we could of the
forward slope down to the canal, it began to rain shells.
We spent an anxious hour dodging among half-finished
trenches and sheltering in dug-outs about the head of
Hobart Street, already mentioned, where there was a nasty
little gulley which for no apparent reason was receiving
marked attention. A small dump of 18-pounder shells was
hit and exploded, and the camouflage net which covered

it having caught fire, the smoke drew a heavier burst of
shelling; and as the very indifferent trenches in this neighbourhood were packed with infantry and gunners, now
tumbling over one another to get away from the dangerous
area, there were a good many casualties. When we managed to get clear and return to Pronville about five o'clock,
we were exceedingly hot and thirsty, and very little wiser
for our pains.

The Pronville valley was now filling up, in a discreet
way, with troops and guns. The Hindenburg trenches
were crowded with men of the 63rd (Naval) Division, which
was attacking on the right of the 4th Canadians. In every
little gulley which offered concealment there were heavy
howitzers, four huge 9-inch weapons being packed together
by a cemetery close to B Company's tanks. Zero was at
5.20 A.M. the next morning, and we decided to pull out our
tanks half an hour after midnight. As luck would have it,
heavy clouds drove up after dusk, and the night fell extraordinarily black until the moon rose. I had some difficulty
in this intense darkness in finding even the road through
the Hindenburg wire, only 200 yards from where our tanks
were parked up. By one o'clock, however, we had them
in line at the head of the Inchy valley, with the useful
trees of the Hirondelle on our left. C company was ahead
of us. The only untoward incident in this early stage was
the fall of one of the huge cribs from the cab of a tank,
which crushed a man's leg. Soon after we started a drizzle
of rain set in, increasing after a while to a heavy downpour; but the full moon having risen, enough light filtered
through the clouds to enable us to see our way. A few
shells whistled over and burst in the valley, but on the
whole the German artillery, after its activity earlier in the
day, was commendably quiet.

Crawling along at a snail's pace, it was three o'clock
when we reached Inchy. C Company had already turned
off to the left across the Hirondelle to follow the valley
round the back of the village. We had still so much time

to spare, being now within 1500 yards of the front line, that we halted the tanks for nearly an hour, on a sort of terrace cut out of the spur within a stone's-throw of the ruined wall and trees of Inchy Château. Before we moved on again the Major left us to return to the 10th Canadian Brigade H.Q. in the Hindenburg Support Line across the valley. The Colonel had insisted on this very sensible arrangement, whereby company and section commanders, instead of wandering rather aimlessly about after their tanks had gone into action, were under definite orders to attach themselves respectively to the headquarters of the infantry brigades and battalions concerned, where they were better able to keep in touch with events, and where they could easily be found.

Shortly before four o'clock, while M'Elroy and Paul got the tanks started up again, I went ahead with a runner, one Corporal Deucars, to examine the forward slope of the spur, it having been impossible to reconnoitre this thoroughly in daylight. A road, lined by tattered trees, ran from Inchy up the spur and over the main ridge to the Bapaume-Cambrai highway near Doignies. The trees, and a conspicuous ruined factory by the roadside, a quarter of a mile from the village, stood up very prominently on the crest, and it was inadvisable to show one's self on this road in the daytime, as it was in full view from the German lines. A second road, or rather lane, left the eastern side of Inchy, descended the slope, and split in two almost on our front line, one fork leading southward to Mœuvres and the other holding straight on to the canal bank by Lock 4. It was my intention to lead the tanks round the village until we struck this lane, which would take the left-hand section direct to its crossing-place. The right-hand section would have to head south-east after zero to make the causeway, but there were several small landmarks, including a ditch lined by willows, to serve as guides. Dawn, moreover, would be breaking as the tanks moved off. Our front line for once was clearly defined between Mœuvres and

THE CANAL DU NORD AND BOURLON 445

Inchy, where it ran along a light railway which would make an excellent jumping-off point for the two sections.

I had taken some rolls of tape with me, as I knew that there were several wired machine-gun posts on the forward slope, which it might be necessary to avoid, while the ground here had been badly shelled at one time and another. I found, however, that the Canadians themselves, thorough in everything, had laid down that evening a number of tapes to guide their infantry and field batteries to the front line; and, following up one of these, it led me straight across the angle of the village to the lane I wished to reach. On leaving the main street of Inchy, this lane was lined for a short distance by houses and gardens. As these were now being shelled, I did not push my investigations right up to them, but having satisfied myself that the tape would serve us, I returned with Deucars to meet the tanks. They had climbed up out of the terrace by a limber track, and were approaching the road on the crest when I found them, and found also that there were only seven. One of Paul's section had broken down—the trouble, I think, was a twisted extension-shaft—and was left behind under the trees of Inchy. I led the others across the road between the village and the factory, and then along the tape. The rain had now ceased, but the night was still very dark. Once on the forward slope we moved with extreme care. At five o'clock, twenty minutes before zero, we were close to the side of the lane and within 300 yards of the front line. A few shells were still crashing and sparkling in the gardens behind us. Halting the tanks for a few minutes, I collected the tank commanders in a shell-hole and reviewed rapidly for the last time the various points that they had to bear in mind in approaching the canal. I have forgotten to mention that owing to our extraordinary shortage of officers at this period, due to casualties, leave, and the departures to England, six out of our remaining seven tanks were commanded by N.C.O.'s. These, however, were all extremely capable men—the pick of the admirable personnel we had brought originally from Bovington. During the past week, in addition to reconnaissance, I had coached them as thoroughly as possible on the map, helped by some of the best aeroplane photographs I have ever seen; and I had little doubt of their ability, if they were able to cross the canal without undue delay, to accomplish all that was expected of them.

After five minutes' talk they returned to their tanks, and we watched the line of dark machines file very slowly down the slope beside the trees of the lane. There was nothing more that M'Elroy, Paul, or I could do. The tanks would follow the lane until they came to the light railway, where they would wait during the few final minutes before zero. Having watched them disappear in the shadows, we turned back accordingly to a communication trench called Wartburg, which led uphill to the main Hindenburg Line near Tadpole Copse, as we had now to find the battle headquarters of the two Canadian battalions forming the first infantry wave in this sector of the attack. The morning was still very dark, its utter quietness broken only by the rare whine and crash of a German shell. There is something very impressive and eerie in this silent hour before an attack at dawn. Troops and guns are crowded everywhere, in trenches and pits and hollows, behind the front line, but one can see and hear nothing; and one wonders how much the enemy, listening nervously (as he has listened perhaps for a week or more) only a few hundred yards away, fears or suspects. As we stumbled uphill along the convolutions of the trench, picking our way among the waiting infantry whose equipment rattled faintly as they moved, the east began to lighten rather suddenly. The clouds which had blackened the night were clearing away. And ten minutes, perhaps, after we had left the tanks, the whole crest of the spur behind us blazed instantaneously with stabbing flames, and we were deafened and stunned by the intolerable crash of the opening barrage. . . .

THE CANAL DU NORD AND BOURLON 447

III.

Wartburg trench curled up through the little gulley where we had been caught by the German bombardment the previous afternoon. This gulley was now a nest of field batteries, all firing furiously. Scores of other batteries were in action higher up the slope and along the crest, and from the Pronville valley came a howling torrent of shells from the heavier howitzers. In the cup of ground up which we were climbing the noise was abominable, and my whole head throbbed and ached with it. It is always worse to hear concentrated gun-fire from close in front than from close behind. The Canadians had brought their field-guns very far forward in the night, and as the light increased I witnessed a spectacle which spoke both for their supreme confidence and for the altered aspect of the war. One or two batteries in the hollow did not fire at all, but limbered up at zero, and went rolling and jolting down the slope after the advancing infantry. I heard afterwards of an artillery Major who rode forward on his horse with the first wave of the attack to select new gun positions under the canal bank.

After much climbing about tortuous and misleading trenches on the big hill, we found the headquarters of one of our infantry battalions. From here we pushed on to the second headquarters. These were established in a fairly capacious dug-out on the summit, 100 feet above Mœuvres. It was now about six o'clock; but the whole country below was so shrouded in mist and smoke that we could see nothing. Having informed the battalion commander that the tanks had started, we sat about in the welcome peace of the dug-out for some time, listening to reports as they came through on the telephone, and having a comforting breakfast of bacon and tea. (Incidentally, at whatever hour of the day or night you interviewed Canadians, they were always drinking tea — without prejudice to the ordinary alcoholic beverages which, of course, were there as well.) From the fragmentary news which reached us the attack seemed to be going like clockwork, but we could get no information about the tanks. The bogey of the canal was always in our minds, and I began to be afraid that they had failed to cross it. At seven o'clock we scrambled to the surface again, to find the morning bright and sunny and the trenches on the hill-top lined with interested spectators of the battle. Groups of signallers were working heliographs from the parapets, and a few heavy German shells thudded on the slope below; but when I joined the audience I found that there was still little or nothing to be seen. Sheets of white vapour, out of which rose the dark trees of Bourlon Wood, covered the whole battlefield. M'Elroy and Paul decided to remain here until it was time for them to go forward to the sunken road, between the canal and Quarry Wood, which had been selected as a rallying-point for the tanks; and I left them soon after to make my own way back to the Major at the infantry brigade headquarters on the opposite ridge above Inchy.

By the time I had got down into the valley, now full of roaring guns and moving infantry and transport, and had climbed the farther slope to the Hindenburg Support trenches, the sun was growing powerful and I was becoming uncomfortably hot. I was wearing a trench-coat and other warm garments which had been welcome enough in the cold and rain of the night, and I was of course hung all over with the ghastly impedimenta that civilised officers are impelled to carry with them into battle (or near it)—glasses, water-bottle, box-respirator, revolver, map-case, compasses, and so on, all depending from an infuriating harness of separate little straps. I cannot imagine why officers are not provided with a uniform combination equipment for these articles. It would be easy to design one. The Sam Browne belt is a useless anachronism in action, and the private soldier's webbing or leather equipment, while excellent for his own requirements, was worthless for ours.

We were compelled to walk about like badly-arranged Christmas-trees suffocated by straps. . . .

All this, however, is rather by the way. To return to our text, I found at the infantry headquarters the Brigadier and staff of the 1st Tank Brigade peering through their glasses at the battle, and also the Major, full of good news. Plenty of information had been coming through on the telephone, and all our apprehensions were proved needless. Our tanks, indeed, had won a really notable little triumph by crossing the problematical canal as easily as if it had been an ordinary trench, and actually leading the Canadians the whole way from start to finish, through the Canal du Nord Line, Quarry Wood, and the Marquion Line into Bourlon. The left-hand section apparently (for, of course, no details were to hand) had climbed in and out of the canal without a pause. The first tank of Paul's section on the right had been disabled by a mine in the causeway, whereupon the other two had found their way over the walls with equal agility. The Canadians, who had not counted on any help from the machines short of the Marquion Line, were as astonished as they were pleased by this performance, and were generously flattering in their commendations.

From this crest by the brigade dug-outs one obtained an excellent view, over the roofs of Inchy, of the whole undulating escarpment which rose to Bourlon, and also of the country to the south around Anneux and Graincourt, other old acquaintances of the first Cambrai battle. Much of the smoke and mist had lifted, for already the tide of advance was through Bourlon and Anneux and beyond the Wood. Graincourt, just visible behind the spur above Mœuvres, was still holding out, and continued to resist, like a second Flesquières, until late in the day. I sat for some time watching this scene through my glasses. Columns of thick white smoke were rising out of Bourlon Wood, where the enveloping attack was clearing out the defenders under a screen of smoke grenades. To the right, between Anneux and Graincourt, the bare upland was diversified by the forms of four or five disabled tanks, presumably Mark V.'s of the 15th Battalion. One of them was on fire, and a second was emitting volumes of white smoke from a patent contrivance fitted for this purpose on the roof. (A tank in M'Elroy's section was equipped with this novelty, and used it very effectively in front of Bourlon.) And presently, out of the thin haze which still hung in drifts over the slope beyond the canal, appeared one of our own machines homeward bound; and at that the Major and I began to walk down into the valley on our way to the rallying-point. The time must have been about ten o'clock in the morning, five hours since the battle opened. We followed the route the tanks had taken, round the southern gardens of Inchy, and so on to the lane which led to Lock 4. There is always a peculiar interest attached to one's first entry into ground occupied only a few hours previously by the enemy. It is like a journey into a foreign country—which, after all, is exactly what it is. A hundred little contrasts, even amid the levelling conditions of modern war, differentiate one side of the line from the other. Either combatant betrays his personality in such common tasks as digging trenches or building cook-houses, and there seems to supervene a different atmosphere, a sort of alien local colour, as one passes from No Man's Land into newly-captured territory. This may be largely my personal fancy: certainly the grass is the same colour and the shell-holes are very similar; and it is true that superficially there was little to show which side of the light railway at Inchy-en-Artois had been British and which German ground. Between the rusty metals and the canal bank were a few groups of our dead—mostly, I think, casualties suffered by the later waves of infantry under the counter-barrage. I did not see any Germans among them, and it was evident that this first stage had been carried at a rush with little or no trouble. Probably the scattered outposts had surrendered on the spot. The canal itself, the first solid obstacle capable of defence, did not appear to have been

THE CANAL DU NORD AND BOURLON 451

held with any approach to determination. One German infantryman, lying dead on his back and already stripped of every article that would make a portable souvenir, was the only piece of jetsam in the wake of the attack near Lock 4. Yet, as a singular example of the contrasts and uncertainties of war, at the very time I was scrambling down into the canal-bed with the Major, six hours after the opening of the battle, a group of plucky German machine-gunners was still holding out near Mœuvres, three miles behind our new front.

The canal, which we examined with the keenest interest, bore very little resemblance to the engineers' drawings. The sides were far steeper than represented, and the "step," where it existed, was higher up. The photograph reproduced in this book will show more clearly than any description what sort of an obstacle it was that our worn-out and obsolete Mark IV. tanks had surmounted with such ease and speed. The farther wall near Lock 4, where M'Elroy's four machines had crossed, was so nearly vertical that only the layer of fallen earth, combined with exceptionally skilful driving, made its ascension possible. The two surviving tanks of Paul's section, baulked at the causeway, scrambled in some miraculous manner over the brickwork close by. His leading tank, as we have seen, was disabled by a mine on the causeway itself. The explosion broke the tracks, blew in the floor, and shattered a man's legs. The N.C.O. in command very sensibly ran at once down the canal to Mœuvres, where some of the 15th Battalion's tanks were crossing, and managed to induce one of them to turn back and tow the derelict off the causeway, where it was holding up our artillery. The first drivers of all the six tanks which crossed were very properly recommended for the Military Medal for this feat alone, and one or two of them received it.

As we walked on from the canal we met our first tanks returning to it. They had been shelled persistently on their way back from Bourlon to the rallying-point, the German guns apparently being kept on to the moving targets by an observation-balloon which still hung insolently behind the wood, unmolested by our aeroplanes. (It was an instructive fact that when we ran up a balloon the next day from a similar position on our side of the wood, a German aeroplane had it down within an hour.) The ground at the rallying-point being entirely open, it was no place for the tanks under this malignant scrutiny, and they were returning accordingly to the canal itself for shelter. We led them through the middle causeway and parked them up against the eastern wall. The photograph shows the first three immediately after their arrival. The figure in the trench-coat fluttering a map is, I believe, myself.

In almost every case the tasks allotted to the tanks had been easily and rapidly accomplished. They were out of the canal as soon as the infantry, and in consequence were able to lend the latter unexpected help at the Canal du Nord Line and Quarry Wood, where they led the attack, crushed the wire, and disposed of numerous machine-gun posts. Still leading, the whole six charged the Marquion Lion, which was carried very quickly. One tank broke down here and was not ready to move again until the others were returning for good. These, in the meantime, patrolled beyond the Marquion Line while it was being consolidated under cover of a stationary barrage, and as soon as the latter lifted once more, pushed on for Bourlon. Two entered by the main street and a third from the north, the remaining pair working along the trenches round the village. The resistance was spasmodic, and as soon as the tanks had crushed down the barricades in the streets and silenced a few machine-guns which held out in the houses, the place was rapidly overrun and cleared by the following infantry. One tank, fired on by field-guns in the outskirts, screened itself very skilfully in smoke from the experimental apparatus fixed on the roof, and passed into the village unhurt behind this curtain. Another machine, after Bourlon had been carried, pushed on at the request of the Canadians

Tanks of A Company 17th Battalion, parked in Canal du Nord after capturing Bourlon Village, September 27, 1918.
(Official Photo.)

to the railway which ran past the eastern end of Bourlon
Wood to Sauchy-Lestrée, silenced some machine-guns on
the embankment, and enabled the infantry to seize and
consolidate the latter. In four or five hours the whole
action was over, so far as the tanks were concerned.
There were no casualties to personnel or machines, except
in the case of the mined tank on the causeway. All the
other six rallied. The attack had been a model of completeness and efficiency, and was backed up throughout
in the most intelligent and whole-hearted manner by the
infantry.

C Company had been equally successful, although it had
not escaped so lightly. Sains-les-Marquion was carried
with very little effort, and the tanks spent the rest of the
morning cruising about beyond the Marquion Line, mopping
up machine-gun nests and enjoying some good shooting at
parties of fugitive Germans. Two tanks, however, were hit
and burnt out by field-guns near Deligny Mill, on the spur
north of Quarry Wood. After the action the Company
rallied behind the canal in the gulley below Tadpole
Copse.

IV.

While our tanks were parking up in the canal bed I met
the brigade commander and the Colonel with Beale and one
or two other people, and after a little talk was sent back to
Pronville to arrange for some lorries to be in readiness to
carry all the tank crews of both companies, less the necessary guards, to Bullecourt, where a camp had been erected.
On my way I met the tanks of B Company moving up to
the canal. At Pronville, where I arrived very hot and dusty
and incredibly thirsty, about one o'clock, I was stopped
within 100 yards of our headquarters in the trench by a
bucolic and extremely unintelligent private of the Battle
Police, who poked his bayonet at me and demanded to
know where I was going. As it never occurred to me that

I could be mistaken for a deserter, I thought the man was drunk, and was on the point of putting him under arrest. Realising in time that he was only densely stupid and performing what he conceived to be his duty, I burst out laughing at his absurd face and manner, and left him there gaping after me, and wondering, possibly, if he should have fallen upon me or run me through.

By four o'clock that afternoon the tired crews had marched back to Pronville and were packing themselves in lorries, while M'Elroy, Paul, and I, glowing with a sense of virtue rewarded, were bumping over the vile roads to Bullecourt in the car. Every road and track was roaring with a flood of transport rolling eastward. All the guns about Pronville had gone forward except the 9.2 howitzers, and Holt tractors were standing by these unwieldy weapons in readiness to tow them also away. A long naval gun had come up on the railway near Quéant, and was firing from its truck. There was always something fresh and exhilarating to me in this universal surge onward which came in the wake of any big advance—perhaps because we were not yet habituated to big advances. The tide had now set in with a vengeance, and we were to become well accustomed to this healthy symptom of its progress before the end.

At Bullecourt, where our tents had been set up amid the annihilation of one of the most murderous and contested battlefields of the war, we spent that night and most of the next day. We were, I suppose, very fortunate to possess the transport which alone made these brief interludes of rest and recuperation possible. They were certainly well worth the trouble they involved. After twenty-four hours spent in moderate comfort, with rational meals, baths of a sort, and a change of clothes, officers and men returned to the forward area refreshed and ready for another spell of work that, in our case, became increasingly arduous the longer our old machines were denied their own turn of renovation.

M'Elroy left us in the morning to go on leave. He had

THE CANAL DU NORD AND BOURLON 455

been due to go a week before, but had stayed on to take part in the attack. When he returned a fortnight later, the battalion had finished its work, and was waiting to be withdrawn to refit. I was about to leave it to join the 12th Battalion. And a short time after I had gone, he was dead—killed, when the war virtually was over, by an epidemic of influenza and pneumonia which swept through the unhealthy camp in the Ternoise valley, and cost the battalion in addition the lives of some of its best N.C.O.'s and men, who also had come through all its battles, from Ypres to the second Cambrai, only to meet this miserable end. M'Elroy and I had been much together in the later stages, having been largely responsible between us for the company's work in most of the final actions, and I had come to know him very well. He was a tall, dark Irishman, usually quiet and casual, but with that rare combination of a level head and careless courage which earns so many of the decorations that are worth anything, and which gained him his D.S.O. as a subaltern at Cambrai. One has always a grudge against Providence for the waste of such lives when all need for sacrifice is past.

During the interlude at Bullecourt we gathered some information about the progress of the attack in general, and in particular about the fortunes of the 15th and 11th Tank Battalions which had been in action on our right. Both of these units had suffered heavily in a rather desperate morning's fighting. The tanks of the 15th, having negotiated the canal at Mœuvres with some difficulty, reached their final objectives beyond Anneux and Flesquières, but lost eleven machines out of twenty-six, many of them around Graincourt. The 11th Battalion, usually unfortunate, fared very badly. A dozen tanks were sent in between Trescault and Gouzeaucourt, of which eight received direct hits and two were ditched. Their casualties were heavy, and the attack in this sector was only partially successful. Elsewhere, however, everything had gone extraordinarily well. Ten thousand prisoners and 200 guns had been captured by the two armies; and on the evening of the 27th our line, from north to south, had been advanced to east of Oisy-le-Verger (in the angle between the Sensée and the canal), east of Epinoy, Haynecourt, and Bourlon Wood, through Fontaine-Notre-Dame, and east of Ribécourt and Beaucamp. Another five miles of the Siegfried Line, from Mœuvres to Ribécourt, had been carried; and from Bourlon Ridge we looked down upon the roofs and spires of Cambrai, less than three miles away.

On the morning of the 28th, eight tanks of B Company, which we saw moving up to the canal, led the infantry of the 3rd Canadian Division in an attack on Raillencourt and St Olle, on the Arras-Cambrai road. Both these villages were carried after severe fighting, several of the German machine-gun crews continuing to resist until they were crushed to death by the tanks. All the latter rallied. St Olle was a suburb of Cambrai, and the Canadians were now on the outskirts of that town, but still faced by the formidable obstacle of the Canal de L'Escaut.

That evening the personnel of A and C Companies, having spent exactly twenty-four hours at Bullecourt, returned by lorry to their tanks in or near the Canal du Nord. Both companies were to trek forward that night to the neighbourhood of Bourlon, and the Major and I went straight to that village in the car to decide where we would put our machines. As we passed through Inchy we found that the indefatigable Y.M.C.A. had already established a canteen there, and were using one of our abandoned cribs as a background for their triangular sign. The day had been fine and hot, and the country everywhere was full of pungent smells. The Canadians had a bad habit of leaving their dead horses and mules for weeks without burial, even alongside the roads, and some of these carcases had by now attained an appalling stage of decomposition. At Bourlon we fixed on the huge chateau wall, riddled with immense holes but still erect, as a good shelter for the

tanks; and having sent the car off, walked back across
country to the canal to survey an approximate route. The
Major then left to interview the 4th Canadian Division. I
waited about for two or three hours while a number of
small irritating defects were put to rights; and toward
ten o'clock, the night being starlit but very dark, we
managed to get away. We had now six tanks left out
of the fourteen with which we had started from Bienvillers
five weeks before. Wadeson, just back from leave, was in
charge in M'Elroy's absence.

The beginning of the journey was unpropitious. Our
exit from the canal bed, by way of the middle causeway,
coincided with the arrival immediately above us of a
bombing squadron of German aeroplanes, which proceeded to drop their cargoes liberally all round. I
pushed everybody inside the tanks and walked on hopefully in front. The bombs were thudding and flashing in
large numbers in the direction of Mœuvres, and some fell
much nearer than was pleasant; and presently one of the
raiders released a magnesium flare attached to a small
parachute or balloon, which hung for a long time a few
hundred feet overhead, and seemed to light up the whole
country for miles. The illumination was so bright that I
thought of halting the tanks until it expired, but reflected
that these lights are always much less efficient, from the
point of view of the observer up above, than they appear
from the ground. The flare dwindled out after a while,
the humming of the aeroplane engines and the crash of
the bombs receded behind us as the raiders swept over
the canal, and we pursued our journey without further
interruption.

On arriving, after some struggles in trenches and wire,
at Bourlon Château, we found that our wall bounded a
narrow lane in which was situated an artillery brigade
headquarters. As our tanks would have blocked the lane
and interfered with traffic that might include the cars of
infuriated Generals, we decided to push the machines

through the holes in the wall into the tangled garden
beyond. The fact that this was possible will convey some
idea of the size of the holes (which did not reach even to
the top of the wall in most cases), and of the immense
height and solidity of the structure. After much backing
and swinging and dislodging of bricks, the manœuvre
was accomplished, and all six tanks were safely inserted
under the trees inside. It was now midnight, or after,
and we proceeded to make ourselves comfortable under
a couple of tarpaulins stretched over a trench, where,
packed like sardines, we had some sort of a meal and
went to sleep.

CHAPTER XXI.

THE FIGHTING ROUND CAMBRAI: SANCOURT.

I.

WHEN the 1st and 3rd Armies attacked on 27th September, the general bombardment was extended southward to the extremity of the British Line, although only preliminary operations were undertaken by the 4th Army on that day and the next. The 28th was notable for two simultaneous blows delivered upwards of 100 miles apart—by the 2nd British and 3rd French Armies and the Belgians from the coast to Ypres, and by the 5th and 10th French Armies on the Aisne. On the 29th, after two days' continuous shelling, the 4th Army and the right wing of the 3rd took up the attack against the last and strongest remnant of the enemy's final organised position in the West, the Canal de L'Escaut and the Siegfried Line from Marcoing to Bellenglise. This reversion to something like the old type of offensive, with a preliminary bombardment, was necessitated by the obstacle of the Canal de St Quentin (a continuation of the Canal de L'Escaut), which could be crossed by tanks only at the gap, 6000 yards wide, where it passed under the famous tunnel between Vendhuile and Bellicourt. The 3rd, 4th, and 5th Tank Brigades with about 170 machines took part on the first day of this decisive battle, and had some desperate fighting, losing a great number of tanks and men. The 301st Americans in their first action met with tragic disaster, apparently through no fault of their own. Moving forward from Ronsoy, they ran into a mine-field which we had laid down before the March retreat. It consisted of rows of buried trench-mortar bombs, each loaded with 50 lb. of ammonal. In a few minutes ten tanks were blown up, their bottoms being torn out and most of their crews killed by the terrific explosions. The remainder of the battalion, shaken though it must have been by this appalling stroke of misfortune, got into action and suffered heavily there, only 11 tanks rallying out of 34. On subsequent days units of all three brigades were helping to widen the initial penetration of the Siegfried trenches at various points, as many as 40 tanks going in on 3rd October, when we broke through the northern part of the Beaurevoir - Fonsomme Line five miles beyond the canal tunnel, and saw in front of us at last open and cultivated country. These events led up to the final phase of the battle, which began on 8th October.

In the meantime, the Canadians, with the 22nd and 17th Corps respectively on their left and right, had a week of very severe and costly fighting around Cambrai, in the course of which the 7th Tank Battalion fought its last action. After the surprise and collapse on 27th September, the German resistance stiffened appreciably every day as it had stiffened a month earlier at Bapaume; and Sancourt, Abancourt, and other villages played the same *rôle* which had fallen before to Ecoust and Beugny. Our advance was still hampered by the obstacle of the Sensée Marshes and the floods to the north of them. This vast area of water cut across our front at right angles, with the result that as we penetrated eastward toward Cambrai we developed a long flank facing due north; and the German guns south of Douai, enfilading this salient, caused much annoyance. The re-formed and very weak 5th Army facing Lens and Douai was unable to help actively until the operations on its flanks were further advanced.

The morning of 29th September found the three Companies of the 7th Tank Battalion disposed as follows:

A Company, as we have seen, was at Bourlon. C Company had moved overnight from its rallying-point near Tadpole Copse to the top of Bourlon Ridge north of the village, where its tanks were camouflaged in the open in a shallow basin of ground. B Company, after its fighting in Raillencourt and St Olle, had rallied at the former village and still remained there, its machines hidden under the trees of the Arras-Cambrai road within 3000 yards of the front line. Early in the morning a despatch-rider reached us at Bourlon with orders for the company to join C on the ridge; and after breakfast we backed the tanks out of the chateau garden through the holes in the wall and trekked northward round the village. We made a considerable gambit to avoid appearing on the crest, where a few shells were falling as we approached, and climbed eventually to our destination under a bridge, still intact, which carried the railway from Cambrai to Sauchy-Lestrée. We camouflaged our tanks in the open a few hundred yards from those of C Company, one of whose officers had just been wounded by the shelling. We were screened here from direct observation by the final rise, the ground ascending very gradually from our basin to the Arras-Cambrai road, only 500 yards away. The double line of trees along the road ran obliquely across our front and dropped down the ridge behind us to Marquion and the Agache flats. Standing on the highway, one saw straight ahead the cluster of villages on the spurs which fell to the Sensée north and north-west of Cambrai—Haynecourt and Epinoy, west of the Douai road, and now in our possession, and, beyond, the trees about Sancourt, Blécourt, Abancourt, and others still held by the Germans. To the north extended the long hostile flank beyond the Sensée, with such places as Bugnicourt and Fressain easily distinguishable. The morning being misty, although brilliantly fine, visibility was limited, but it was easy to see how vitally important was this ridge, and how on a clear day one could have overlooked Douai and all the enemy's communications across the plain. Cambrai, three

miles to the south-east, and lying low, was hidden from this
point by the trees of Raillencourt and Sailly. The shallow
depression in which we lay, like all the rest of the country
around, was bare grass-land, crossed by a multitude of dusty
tracks, a lane leading from Bourlon to the main road, and a
line or two of half-finished trench. There was a big dug-
out, an old German headquarters of some kind, close to the
railway bridge at our back. To our right stood a solitary
half-ruined building called Pilgrim's Rest, which poked
a blackened gable above some shrubs; and a few small
copses beyond led the eye up to Bourlon Wood, towering
above a sudden little hill which was superimposed, as it
were, on top of the ridge itself. It was this steep acclivity
which caused the wood to be visible from so great a distance
(from the towers of Mont St Eloi, behind Arras, for
example), and to dominate so effectively all the valleys
leading toward it from the west. During our reconnaissances before the 27th this sinister mass of trees seemed to
overlook every movement. But now its ladders and its
lofty observation platforms had had their final day, and
curious wanderers were peering and poking among the
glades and thickets bleached with gas and scarred by shells,
where some of its later victims still lay rotting in the undergrowth, and where there rested, smashed and stripped and
rust-eaten, the shells of tanks we had lost there nearly a
year before. Two-faced, like Janus, the wood had now
turned a menacing visage eastward, and lowered over
Cambrai. A new activity flowed beneath its shadow.
Khaki had replaced field-grey in the dismembered village;
and over the dusty plain to the canal, along the reverse
slope of the ridge, and even in the little hollow by Pilgrim's
Rest, were scattered infantry bivouacs and endless horse
lines and the massed limbers of ammunition trains. The
countryside was alive with movement, and near Bourlon a
Canadian band was playing, its instruments glittering in
the sun. . . .

When we had camouflaged the tanks in pairs, we set

about finding some shelter for company headquarters, and
the few other officers we had with us. A half-finished
trench ran across the basin, and over a part of this we
rigged up a tarpaulin roof. C Company, the first in the
field, had found a large excavation in a bank near the railway, where they made themselves moderately comfortable.
It was always well to take these precautions, for one might
be stranded in such a place for a week. As it happened,
this little gutter of ours was in use as a base for several
days. Close to us here, curiously enough, were some odd
by-products of the tank idea, a number of open lorries
carrying Vickers guns and Stokes mortars, part of a singular
unit which included motor machine-guns and armoured
cars, and was known as Brutinel's Brigade. It had been
organised by the Canadians for the battle on 8th August,
with a view to rapid exploitation in company with our
Whippets and cars along the Amiens-Roye road. I believe
it met with a certain measure of success on that exceptional
occasion, but its subsequent opportunities were few. All
Canadian operation orders at this time ended with an
optimistic paragraph asserting that "Brutinel's Brigade
will seize every opening for a vigorous exploitation and
pursuit of the enemy," and the heterogeneous medley of
vehicles did its best to find such openings; but with the
Germans very wide awake, and fighting for every inch of
ground, nothing on wheels had any prospect of penetrating
far. The brigade was badly cut up more than once, and
the armed lorries, in particular, were described by their
unfortunate crews as death-traps.

After lunch Wadeson and I walked to the high ground
by Bourlon Wood, where there were a number of abandoned
German guns and many dead of both armies, and looked
down upon the roofs and spires of Cambrai. The canal
and all the approaches to the town were hidden in trees,
and there was nothing to be seen but an ambulance or two
passing below us into St Olle. It was more interesting to
turn our glasses to the south-west and follow the imma-

culate line of the Le Cateau road, its double row of trees in full leaf rising and dipping over a succession of ridges increasing in height as they receded, and topped by villages and small towns untouched by actual hostilities since the first month of the war—Awoingt, just outside Cambrai, Beauvois, Caudry, Bethencourt, and yet another Inchy. I had no suspicion then that I was to know all these places well enough a few weeks later. Le Cateau itself, lying in a deep valley, was hidden from us; but we could follow many of the roads leading eastward from the main highway, and these were black with German transport pouring to the rear before the blast of the 4th Army's attack along the Canal de St Quentin that morning. Another cheering portent was the fact that the enemy's line of observation balloons was withdrawn well to the east of the Le Cateau road. It was while we were standing here that one of our balloons, run up an hour before by the side of Bourlon Wood, was shot down by a German aeroplane which escaped with the usual ease. Neither at this time nor before nor after during the whole advance did I see a German balloon brought down.

A very disgusting feature of this neighbourhood was the number of ghoulish pilferers of the dead who infested it. These noxious creatures are common enough in the wake of any battle: indeed the ordinary decent soldier is callous to a degree in the way he will handle some mangled body in his search for what he calls souvenirs; but the Colonial troops always supplied an excessive proportion of the deliberate looters. A case which filled me with peculiar horror, because I had known and liked the man whose corpse was so mercilessly stripped and rifled, had occurred in the Canadian Corps a short time before this. An officer in our battalion who joined it as a Captain in the Salient, and afterwards shared a cubicle with me at Meaulte, went to the 11th Battalion as a company commander. He was killed by a shell during an approach-march in the course of the attack on the Drocourt-Quéant Line. His body was left for a quarter of an hour while two men ran to a dressing station close at hand for a stretcher. When they returned they found that the Canadians, in this short interval, had stripped the body of everything worth taking—tunic, belt, glasses, and even field-boots. I do not know if I am peculiar, but this practice, which was reduced to a science, filled me with loathing. And around Bourlon Wood, where in places the dead lay thickly, there were a number of men prowling furtively about, turning over bodies, peering into holes and trenches, carrying out systematically their search for money or such pitiful small valuables as a man will carry even into action. These scoundrels sheered off when any officer approached, and if summoned and interrogated, explained of course that they were looking for the body of a friend. . . .

II.

At five o'clock that evening (the 29th) the usual harbinger of evil arrived at our trench in the shape of a despatch-rider, with an urgent message to the Major to report at once to the headquarters of the 12th Canadian Infantry Brigade. This headquarters was quite near us, in some dug-outs just off the Arras-Bapaume road, by a building called Lilac Farm. I accompanied the Major in his car, which we took to save time. As we arrived on the highroad several heavy shells crashed about Lilac Farm, and we left it for the dug-outs with some haste. We had a brief interview with the Canadian Brigadier, in which he propounded a rather ambitious scheme for the next morning, and asked for three tanks. C Company was working on our right with another brigade. The situation on the front of the 12th Brigade was as follows:—

Beyond the Arras-Cambrai road was the road to Douai, which trended a little to the west of north toward Aubencheul-au-Bac, where it crossed the Sensée. On a line drawn north-east from the Pilgrim's Rest these roads were about 4000 yards apart, and midway between them was the village of Haynecourt. Beyond the Douai road, again, was the main Cambrai-Douai railway. Road and railway ran side by side out of Cambrai for two miles, when the line curved eastward before returning to a parallel crossing at Aubencheul-au-Bac. Where it turned away from the road it passed between the villages of Sancourt and Blécourt, the former being half a mile east of the road and a few hundred yards short of the railway, on which at this point there was a *halte* or small station. A road from Sancourt crossed the railway in a north-easterly direction, and descended a narrow and steepish valley called the *Ravin de Bantigny*, through Blécourt and Bantigny itself, 800 and 2500 yards respectively from the level-crossing. A mile and a half south of Blécourt, just beyond the railway, was Tilloy.

The Canadian line, as given to us, ran almost due north from the Arras road at St Olle, crossed the Douai road 3000 yards out of Cambrai, and continued just to the west of the railway, passing between Sancourt and the *halte*. The railway was a serious obstacle, and already had held up the advance for two days. It ran alternately over embankments and through deep cuttings, which were lined thickly with machine-guns; and the Germans were fighting desperately to retain it, and so prevent Cambrai being outflanked from the north. There is no need to go at length into the plan of attack proposed by the Canadians for the 30th, because half of it was a signal failure. It will be enough to say that one brigade on the right, with three tanks of C Company, was to carry the railway west of Tilloy and then seize that village, while the 12th Brigade, with our three tanks, on the left, was to cross the line on either side of the Sancourt *halte*, capture the high ground enclosing the *Ravin de Bantigny*, and then perform a complicated swing to the left, which was intended to cut off the German forces holding the curve of the railway northward.

THE FIGHTING ROUND CAMBRAI: SANCOURT

Our tanks, having assisted to clear and consolidate the railway at Sancourt, were to move along to north and south of the *Ravin*, avoiding Blécourt and Bantigny in its depths, as these villages were to be smothered and isolated by artillery fire and occupied at leisure.

The General explained this plan of attack in a dashing and confident sort of manner, which seemed to take a good deal for granted. It took more for granted than we guessed

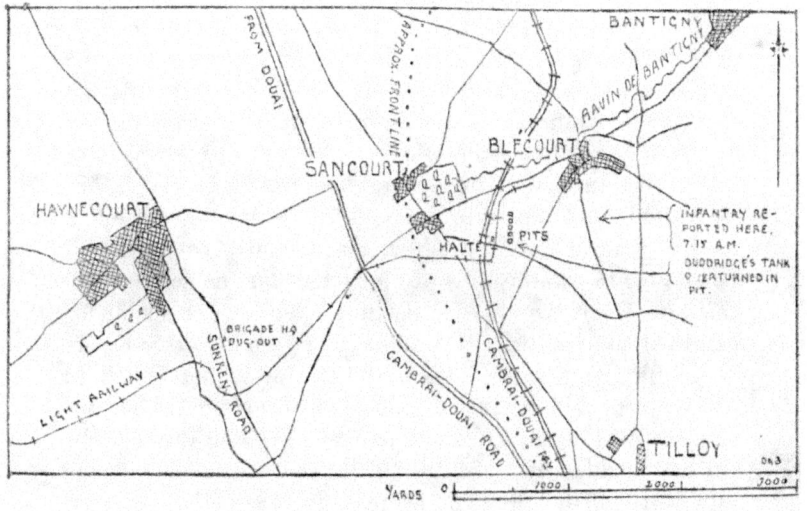

Sancourt.

at the time; but one could not help reflecting even then upon the speculative qualities of the scheme. The Canadians had been fighting now for three days, during the last two of which they had battered their heads against the Douai road and railway, and had lost very heavily in the process, without making any material advance. The task set for the 12th Brigade was highly ambitious, in face of the very obstinate resistance which the enemy, as usual reacting strongly against the consequences of his initial defeat, was offering along the whole Cambrai front. Fresh divisions had come into the German line, fresh batteries had accumulated behind it, and machine-guns were sown everywhere like dragon's teeth. The situation was similar to that which had developed around Bapaume at the end of August, with the additional incentive to the enemy that he was now fighting in his last organised position; and Sancourt, as it turned out, was to prove for A Company a second and more tragic Beugny. The Major and I came away from the brigade headquarters feeling already rather dubious about the whole affair. We did not suspect, however, after our recent experience of the usual efficiency of Canadian methods, that the attack was to be doomed to failure before it began through inexcusable blunders by the brigade staff. Zero hour had not been fixed at this conference. We were to return later for detailed orders. The General had stated, however, that he wished our tanks to be lined up before dawn in a sunken road which ran southward from Haynecourt, where he proposed also to establish his headquarters for the action. By this time we had only four machines out of our six fit for action at short notice. C Company was even worse off. It could supply only two tanks, and borrowed our fourth to make up the deficiency. It was about six o'clock when we returned to Pilgrim's Rest, and already growing dusk, as the sky had clouded over. While the tanks were uncamouflaged and overhauled, I studied the map and took compass bearings to help us in the approach march. Toward seven, the Major and I started off to walk over this route, and on our way called at the brigade headquarters for our further orders; but there were none forthcoming. Zero, we were told, probably would be at 10 A.M. The General and his staff would be at the sunken road at five, when everything was to be arranged and the belated orders issued to us. In the meantime we were to get our tanks there. We set off accordingly on our walk, feeling more dubious than ever. The daylight attack alone was against all our instincts and precepts, and was the more puzzling because Jack Brown had told me that the zero hour for C Company and its infantry was six o'clock, just after dawn. There might be method, however, in this apparent madness: attacks were sometimes carried out in this fashion, in echelon, at different hours. In any case, we were definitely under the orders of the 12th Brigade, and had to do as we were told. The trouble was that so far we had been told so little.

We found the sunken road without much difficulty, although it was now very dark indeed. A perfect maze of light railways, radiating out from Cambrai and linking up a number of big dumps with the original German positions behind the Canal du Nord, covered all this country, and being marked on our excellent maps, were invaluable guides at night. The road, midway between the diverging Arras and Douai highways, connected Haynecourt with the outskirts of Raillencourt and St Olle to the south. It ran parallel to the Douai road at an average distance of 1200 yards. Toward its northern end at Haynecourt its banks were 10 to 12 feet high, forming perfect cover for the tanks, and we selected a hiding-place for the latter 1000 yards from the village, near where the road was crossed by one of the light railways which would lead us directly to it. In the western bank were the black shafts of several dugouts in which the brigade headquarters was to take up its abode. A few dead lay in the roadway, and infantry in support were moving about in the shelter of the banks. The front was very quiet at this time, but Very lights were rising and flaring from the outpost line. It struck me at once that they were much nearer to us than they should have been if that line coincided with the one given us by the brigade staff. They seemed to rise from the Douai road itself, whose mangled avenue of trees was visible intermittently in the cold illumination. According to the brigade (whose information I had set down at the time on a map that lies before me now) our line at Sancourt, toward which we were looking, took in the village and ran close to the railway, nearly 1000 yards beyond the road. It was impossible to decide this point either way with certainty, and some infantrymen whom I questioned were characteristically vague. An outpost line in semi-open warfare is always nebulous and variable, but if appearances were correct and our information wrong, it might make a serious difference, as it would mean that Sancourt was not, as stated, in our possession. I never understood the real facts of the case. As late as eight o'clock next morning Sancourt undoubtedly was full of German machine-guns, but whether this was due to a temporary fluctuation of the line, or whether we had never really held it, I do not know. Our original information proved in all respects so erroneous that I incline to the latter opinion. The Canadians gained it definitely in the course of this attack, but, as we shall see, this was all they were able to accomplish on the 12th Brigade front.

The Major and I were a little careless on our return journey, and overrunning the particular branch of the light railway which we should have followed, wandered for some time around Haynecourt. It was nearly midnight when we reached the Arras road again, both of us rather leg-weary, as we had been stumbling about in the dark for five hours; but there was no rest for us yet. We found the three tanks, with Wadeson, who was in command, waiting at the side of the road by a farm called Mont Neuve, westward from Lilac Farm. All three were commanded by N.C.O.'s, among them Sergeant Duddridge, whom we have met at Beugny, and who was to be one of the victims of the deplorable muddle the 12th Canadian Brigade made of this attack. We started off again at once, leading the tanks past Mont Neuve to the little railway line which led straight to our sunken road. The distance, following this railway, was just two miles, but we had ample time, and took it very slowly. Soon after we started I saw C Company's tanks, three black shapes outlined momentarily against a distant glare, crawling away to our right. The journey was accomplished without incident, except that toward the end I became seriously alarmed by the noises proceeding from our worn-out machines. They were on their last legs, or, to be literally accurate, their last rollers. These had not been replaced since we drew the tanks from Erin two months before, and now, ground down and misshapen by overwork, they began suddenly to complain only too audibly. It seemed impossible at times that this shrill squeaking should not be heard by the enemy, especially if his outposts were as near as the pistol lights still indicated that they were. We struck our road at a point where the banks had fallen away to nothing, so that only a level field stretched before us to the trees along the Douai highway. The occasional flares which soared and died above them silhouetted every branch, and once a yellow glow appeared at the ground-level and grew swiftly to a bright tall flame which seemed to lick the trunks before it dwindled and expired. A few shells whined and burst far to our right, but apparently no one heard the noise of the tanks, for nothing more urgent happened to disturb us. By 2.30 we had the three machines under cover of the bank and the crews busy with the camouflage nets. I felt the usual intense relief that comes after the strain of conducting any approach march, however short or simple. The responsibility (which I loathe in any form) and the sense of being tied to the tanks if anything went wrong or if we were discovered, always made these journeys my especial bugbear. Time could not stale nor custom wither their infinite anxiety. Or so I always found it. To go into action in a tank was, in a way, a lesser evil.

Having seen the machines camouflaged and the crews settled down for as long a rest as Providence, the Germans, or the Canadian Corps permitted, I accompanied the Major and Wadeson to the Brigade dug-out, a couple of hundred yards up the road. We found there, representing for the moment the staff, the brigade Intelligence Officer. He appeared to be the reverse of intelligent, and had no orders for us and no news. He had heard nothing about tanks until we arrived. We made ourselves as comfortable as possible among the feet of the innumerable orderlies, signallers, and other vagrants of no apparent occupation who always infest headquarter dug-outs, and endeavoured to sleep. It was very cold outside, and the warmth below, if a trifle poisonous, was comforting. Wadeson found it excessive after a while, and climbed upstairs again. The Major and I dozed off during the intervals when no one was treading on us. I was aroused finally by a great deal of trampling and excitement, and heard at once, muffled by twenty feet of earth, the unmistakable throbbing of concentrated gun-fire overhead. It was six o'clock; and although I thought for a moment that this might be merely covering-fire for the attack on the right, we soon discovered that our own infantry had gone forward—or attempted to do so. There were no orders for us, and no signs of the General and his staff, who should have arrived an hour before. The Intelligence Officer remained the sole representative of the brigade headquarters. He was hanging on to the telephone, receiving messages from the battalions in the line, and seemed very harassed by his responsibilities; and he could give us no satisfactory advice. Our position was extraordinary and very unpleasant. We had been told by the Brigadier himself that zero would be at ten o'clock or thereabout, and that we should receive our orders from him on the spot. Beyond this, and an incomplete outline of the proposed attack, we had been given no instructions, verbal or otherwise. The attack had now started *four hours before the specified time.* Our tanks, camouflaged and unready for immediate action, were still in the sunken road, some 1500 yards behind the original front; and the infantry, if successful, must already be on the railway or beyond. The Major and I scrambled up the stairs of the dug-out, now packed to suffocation with earnest helpers who very naturally preferred life below ground to life above at this juncture; and when we had fought our way through them and emerged again in the road, we found a dreary dawn just breaking. Close behind us massed batteries of 18-pounders were bellowing. The Germans were

THE FIGHTING ROUND CAMBRAI: SANCOURT 473

replying with vigour and with heavier metal. The inevitable 5.9's were bursting freely on both sides of the road, in which there was now a crowd of infantry, all packed against the farther bank, digging themselves holes in it with entrenching tools. Wadeson and his crews were standing by their tanks, as perplexed as ourselves by the situation arisen out of this precipitate muddle. It was still too dark to see much when we climbed the bank and looked over the top. The mournful trees along the Douai road stood up like spectres out of the smoke and mist, the dark shape of the little wood at Sancourt was just visible beyond, and here and there in the level foreground the heavy shell-bursts sprayed upward their fountains of black soil. One shell missed our tanks by a few feet and exploded in the opposite bank of the road.

We got the machines uncamouflaged as a preliminary measure, and, after waiting by them for a little while, descended again to the dug-out to attempt to communicate with the Brigadier by telephone. Nothing came of this: the cable, I believe, was cut. Telegraphic messages, however, were still coming through from the headquarters of the battalions in front, and these provided another inexplicable instance of that morning's confusion. I was standing by the instrument with the Major and the Intelligence Officer, and I followed on the map the apparent progress of the attack as the signaller at the board decoded the irregular bursts of Morse. The hostile machine-gun fire was very heavy. . . . Colonel So-and-so had been killed . . . Major So-and-so was wounded . . . Many casualties . . . Advance held up in places, but elsewhere progressing. And then came a quite definite statement from one of the battalions. Our infantry had reached the road in Square S 9 c. Now S 9 c was on the high ground south of Blécourt, and the road indicated was 1000 yards beyond the Sancourt *halte*. This meant good progress. Some little time had passed while we had been listening to these messages, but it was not yet seven; and after a further fruitless attempt to get in touch with the brigade, the Major decided to send the tanks forward. They might have to cover anything from one to two miles before they overtook the infantry, assuming this recent information to be correct; but there was a chance of their being useful, if only for mopping-up purposes. It was about 7.15 when they climbed the bank and headed across the level field toward Sancourt. Wadeson walked with them, intending to see them as far as the Douai road. The morning was dull, and beyond the trees of Sancourt itself one could see nothing for smoke. Shells were still crashing fast on both sides of the sunken road, but it was never actually hit—a fortunate circumstance, as by now it was crowded with the best part of a battalion of infantry, the R.A.M.C. personnel of two dressing stations, a number of walking wounded and a few stretcher cases, and an assortment of machine-gunners, engineers, and other people. A shell or two square between the banks would have made a fearful shambles of it. At its northern end, in a lane which ran across to the Douai road from Haynecourt, I saw some of the armed lorries of Brutinel's Brigade waiting "to seize an opening for vigorous exploitation." They did not wait long. A German aeroplane came over, flying low, circled above the batteries behind us, machine-gunning them, and discovered the lorries. Soon afterwards the Haynecourt lane was plastered with shells, and Brutinel's Brigade withdrew in a hurry. Of our own aeroplanes, two squadrons of which (the 8th and 73rd) were supposed to be co-operating in the attack, I did not see a single one throughout the morning. They may have been somewhere on the scene doing good by stealth; or, as is quite probable, the breakdown of the Canadian staff work may have affected their movements as it affected ours.

We waited for nearly two hours before any news of our tanks reached us. In our ignorance we pictured them striving to overtake the advancing infantry. Wadeson came back, having seen them across the Douai road, which he found covered with fallen trees and dead Canadians, and we divided our time between the dug-out and the surface, watching the shells fall above and trying occasionally to get a little rest below. It was at nine o'clock that I came up into the road after an attempt at sleep and saw two tanks returning. It was a very fragmentary story that we got from their crews, but one at absolute variance with everything we had been led to believe. They had encountered machine-gun fire from Sancourt itself, at the very start, when they had supposed themselves still to be a long way behind the infantry. (They should have been at least a mile behind, according to the telegraphic message we had heard.) Crossing the railway at the *halte*, where a road led down through a gap in the walls of a cutting, they had been simply plastered with bullets. So fierce was the fire that they had to close all flaps and resort to periscopes. There was not a sign of our infantry, and indeed this reception made it clear that if the latter had ever crossed the railway at all, they had gone back very soon. The tank commanders, however, decided to carry out their orders, at least in part, and headed north-east toward Blécourt, always under intense machine-gun fire. Two of the machines reached the neighbourhood of the village. One was pulling so badly that it would not take some small obstacle in the front, and the N.C.O. in charge had no choice but to enter Blécourt and risk the bombardment which that place was supposed to be undergoing. This bombardment proved to be another myth: hardly a shell was falling in the village, which was, however, full of Germans. As it was now manifest that the infantry attack had failed, the half-crippled tank started to return, still pelted with bullets. Near the railway it was met by Sergeant Duddridge, who was in command of the third tank. This, it appeared, had fallen on its side in a large pit just east of the *halte*, neither the sergeant nor his driver being able to see the obstacle through their periscopes. Duddridge, having scrambled out of the only sponson door which could be used, found himself under machine-gun fire at close range, and dropped into the pit for shelter. Two men who tried to follow him were shot instantly, and the others remained inside the overturned tank. After crouching in the pit beside it for a while, Duddridge saw the other tank returning from Blécourt, and contrived to crawl on his stomach through a heavy fire until he could hail it, when he was taken on board. He wished to divert this tank to the rescue of his crew, but it was in no condition for any extra work, being in fact on the verge of a complete breakdown, and only induced to move by continued hand-feeding with petrol. Every man inside was injured about the face and hands by splinters and bullet-splash. It contrived to crawl back across the railway to the sunken road, pursued by the hail of bullets to the last. Duddridge's crew was left imprisoned in the pit. In the meantime, the second of the surviving tanks had pushed up on to the ridge south of Blécourt, meeting everywhere the same terrific fire; and having established the fact that there were no Canadians east of the railway, still less in Square S 9 c, where they had reported themselves to be an hour before, it turned back also and arrived at the sunken road close behind the others. The N.C.O. and several of the crew were injured by bullet-splash. Both tanks were simply coated in places with a deposit of lead as a memento of the ordeal they had been through.

The urgent need remaining was to rescue the men imprisoned in the overturned tank, if it were possible. Duddridge, who was desperately concerned for them, begged to be allowed to go back himself to see what he could do. But we had still one tank capable of moving, and its crew, wounded and exhausted as they were, at once volunteered to return in it to the *halte*. It seemed possible that by now the infantry would at least have got a hold on the railway, from where they could command the level ground around the pit (which was only 300 yards farther on), and,

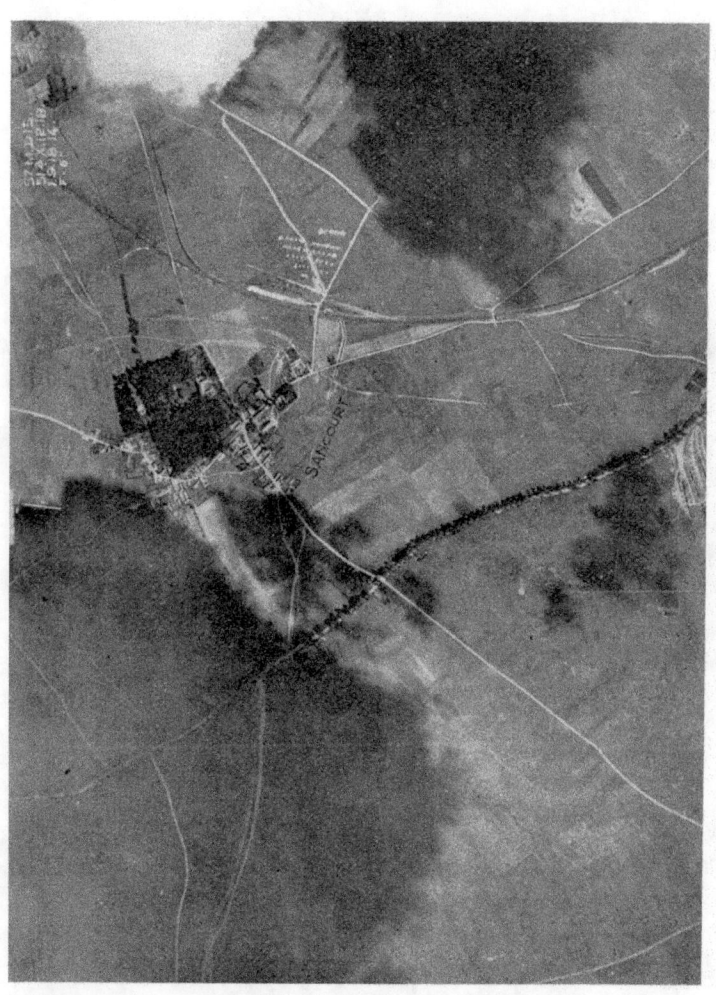

Sancourt, with Cambrai-Douai Road and Railway. The line of pits, in one of which Sergeant Duddridge's tank was overturned, are the last row of white dots beyond the railway.

by keeping down the hostile machine-gun fire, facilitate the rescue. Our remaining tank, accordingly, was sent forward again, accompanied by Wadeson, Duddridge, and a runner, Hilton. The little expedition disappeared among the smoke of shells bursting between us and the Douai road, and we settled ourselves to wait.

It was not long, however, before the tank returned, at a crawl. It had developed engine trouble almost at once, and Wadeson had sent it back. He had gone on himself with Duddridge and Hilton to try to reach the capsized tank on foot. The story of this conspicuously gallant attempt makes a tragic footnote to the chronicle of that morning's misfortunes.

It was, I suppose, nearly an hour later, and the Major and I were below in the dug-out, when Wadeson reappeared, the only survivor of the little party. He looked frightfully ill, and was in fact hysterical and on the verge of a collapse, having been badly gassed. Afterwards, while I was trying to get him to rest near one of the dressing stations in the road, where a Canadian doctor had attended to him, I heard his account of the forlorn hope.

Having sent back the tank, the three rescuers crossed the Douai road and cautiously approached the railway. They passed the level crossing without incident, although they could see nothing of our infantry and had no idea of where the front line ran. Having come so far in safety, they assumed that it must now be beyond the railway. Creeping forward, they were allowed to reach the tank. It lay completely on its side (I saw it a few days later) in the end one of a row of four or five large pits, each about 30 feet by 12 and 5 feet deep. One track had slipped over the edge, and the machine (a female) had then fallen on its left sponson, filling the pit. Whatever these excavations were, they were not deliberate tank traps, as alleged. Some had steps cut in the walls, and probably they were dug out to accommodate sunk huts in connection with a large engineers' dump of timber, wire, &c., which was formed at the *halte*. The rescuers found Lewis guns lying outside

the tank, and its right sponson doors wide open to the sky.
They had just looked inside, and realised that the crew was
gone, when a number of machine-guns opened on them at
close range. Except for the pit itself, in which they would
merely have been trapped, the nearest sort of cover was a
small mound of earth fifty yards away toward the railway,
the ground everywhere else in this neighbourhood being
absolutely flat. They ran for the mound, pursued by con-
verging streams of bullets. Hilton was killed almost at
once. Duddridge was shot, apparently through the body,
within a few yards of the exiguous shelter. Wadeson alone
reached the latter unhurt and flung himself down behind it.
He made repeated attempts to crawl out again to Duddridge,
who was dying before his eyes and almost within reach,
but every time he showed his head the bullets whipped up
the earth all round it. He must have lain here for some
time. At length, seeing that poor Duddridge was dead, he
began the hazardous task of creeping back to the railway.
He accomplished this successfully, although under heavy
fire; but on the way a gas-shell burst immediately in front
of him, and he inhaled the fumes before he realised what
had happened.

III.

So ended, as far as the 7th Tank Battalion was concerned, not only this miserable and inexcusable fiasco at
Sancourt, but also all direct participation in the war. The
battalion was not again employed in action, although we
sent a few tanks to Escadœuvres a week later; for, excepting one or two in B Company, it no longer had any
machines fit to fight. While we had been suffering for
other people's blunders on the morning of the 30th, C Company had met with better fortune, but had lost two-thirds
of their little section. The tank borrowed from us broke
its tracks while crossing the railway between Sancourt and
Tilloy. The crew of a second machine had a positively

THE FIGHTING ROUND CAMBRAI: SANCOURT 479

miraculous escape. A 5.9 came through the roof and burst inside, and yet no one was touched except the tank commander, Collins, who sustained a scratched finger. The third tank reached Tilloy, helped the Canadians to establish themselves there, and then rallied.

I have said enough, perhaps, about the staff work of the 12th Canadian Brigade. As, however, the Canadian Corps took up the cudgels on behalf of their unit, and complained of our alleged misdeeds, I will recapitulate the evidence. Apart from the circumstances that we received no definite operation orders whatever, verbal or written, and that zero was fixed (and put forward four hours) without any notification being sent to us, the Brigadier, having told us to meet him in the sunken road at 5 A.M., did not in fact arrive there until 11. Nor did any responsible member of his staff: during this period, with the action already in progress, the only brigade representative at advanced headquarters was the Intelligence Officer, a subaltern, who did not even know that tanks were co-operating. The initial error about the position of the front line (which was never more than a few yards beyond the Douai road, and almost certainly did not include Sancourt) may have been excusable in the uncertain conditions of semi-open warfare; but the fables which came through on the field-telegraph after the action had begun are more than I can explain. Bad map-reading may have had something to do with them. Even the artillery was afflicted by the general malady, to judge from the fact that Blécourt was found by our tank to be almost untouched, at a time when it was supposed to be smothered by concentrated shell-fire. This accumulation of blunders convicts the 12th Brigade of mismanagement, not, unfortunately, too uncommon in our huge army as a whole, but quite exceptional in the Canadian Corps. Before this date tanks had often suffered, from other quarters, in a similar manner. The attack on Monchy-le-Preux, on 11th April 1917, is a case in point.

The general situation at the end of the morning, in so far

as it was susceptible of definition, appears to have been that the 12th Brigade had at length a permanent grip of Sancourt and a more uncertain one of the railway beyond. Nothing more had been accomplished. The ambitious plan of exploitation on the left never, of course, got so far as a beginning. The brigade suffered very heavy casualties. The other brigade on the right seems to have made adequate arrangements, and in consequence carried most of its objectives, including Tilloy, an important outwork of Cambrai, although only a single tank was in at the finish. Before Cambrai itself fell, however, the Canadians were to have several hard days of fighting in front of them.

In this, our final action, one officer (Wadeson) and twenty-five N.C.O.'s and men of A Company were engaged. Of this little total, two at least were killed, seven were captured, of whom two were known to be seriously wounded, and twelve were slightly injured in various ways—twenty-one in all. On the following day we received notification of the award of a D.C.M. to poor Duddridge for his exploit at Beugny. For his two attempts to rescue his crew at Sancourt a recommendation for a posthumous V.C. was sent in, but I do not think anything more was heard of it. Wadeson received the Military Cross.

IV.

The affair at Sancourt, besides closing the active career of the 7th Tank Battalion, happens to provide also an appropriate peg on which to hang a few general remarks which I have been storing up against such an opportunity. They may not appear to be essential to the subject of this book, but they will be all the better for an airing.

Local operations of the Sancourt type, recurring daily, naturally attracted little attention amid the larger features of the general offensive. They were insignificant episodes in the whole, even when they employed as many troops

THE FIGHTING ROUND CAMBRAI: SANCOURT 481

and cost as many lives as ever fought and died at Talavera or Inkerman. On the other hand, a modern battle, after the set programme of the first day, becomes merely a series of these episodes. They react upon one another, and by their success or failure influence in a varying degree the main strategy. They form, in short, the greater part of an offensive, which the public conceives only as a succession of spectacular, full-dress attacks on well-defined positions. And to those who take part in them they assume inevitably a dimension out of all ratio to their true scale. The modern army commander sits in a house many miles behind the line, and is able to take a detached view of all that happens: perhaps he goes fishing, like Kuroki or the General of the story in the 'Green Curve'; but the platoon or company commander who sees his men slaughtered in front of some trench or village, and can yet reflect philosophically that they are only inconsiderable atoms in a huge and complex mechanism, will never, happily for mankind, be discovered. It is partly for this reason that contemporary newspaper accounts of battles are now so diluted as scarcely to make even sense, all individual impressions of the fighting, if unfavourable in tone, being suppressed. For these impressions, while perfectly honest, may together give a totally false idea of the situation as a whole. A case in point is that of the informants who supplied the data for the famous Sunday telegram describing the retreat from Mons. They told the truth so far as they knew it, and an unscrupulous or very gullible journalist, feeling himself a second Russell, did the rest. In any case, there is no excuse for the opposite extreme of ignorant optimism and buffoonery to which our newspapers became wedded, and in which, presumably, they were encouraged. The point I am approaching laboriously in this digression, however, is that a similar state of things seems to obtain, with no justification whatever, now that we are getting professedly sober and accurate histories of the war. Instead of a faithful picture, made up like all things of good and bad, we find the details keyed up to a universal and artificial tone, and so altered beyond recognition, to suit the blazing colours of the general design. All is for the best in the best of all possible armies. Unmerited misfortune occasionally intrudes, but it is never admitted that any one has made a mistake. All Generals are infallible and all soldiers heroic. I am not speaking, of course, of that class of history which deals only with large strategical and tactical features, and from which the personal equation and the small undercurrents of battle, pulling this way and that, necessarily are omitted. Histories of this kind usually are written by soldiers, and the general public does not read them: it likes stronger and simpler fare; and we have in consequence volumes which attempt to give a detailed picture of events as they affected units and even individuals. These, apparently, are to be written by novelists. The ordinary novelist is at his worst when he tries to keep to facts. He mistakes a profuse harvest of names and numbers for an accurate statement. He depends for the most part on official documents which are sure to be more or less unconscious perversions of the truth. And so it is that we are threatened with elaborate histories which are not histories at all, books in which an appearance of almost pedantic veracity is built up out of a mass of inaccurate and misleading details.

I have been provoked especially to this discursion by an accident. While I was writing my account of the action at Sancourt, as I saw it, I found in a library the final volume of Sir Arthur Conan Doyle's 'British Campaigns in France and Flanders.' With some difficulty, owing to the peculiar arrangement of the narrative, I discovered his brief reference to the fiasco on 30th September. It is a typical example of the facile journalistic style which conceals while it affects candour. "By 9.45 in the morning," he writes, "the 12th Canadian Brigade had taken Sancourt and had entered Blécourt, where some fierce bludgeon work was going on. . . . For a moment the 12th Canadian

Brigade was staggered by a heavy counter which broke upon it, but the ranks soon rallied and the ground was regained." There appears to be no particular point here to which one can take exception, apart from that characteristic touch about "bludgeon work" at Blécourt; and yet the general impression deliberately given to the reader is entirely opposed to the facts. There lies the mischief of this ill-informed type of narrative, especially when it is inspired by a determination to find no fault with any one. Even as a statement of events, the account is typically vague. Ground, we are told, "was regained." What ground? No place is specified. The reader very wisely is left in doubt as to what happened in Blécourt after the "bludgeon work," but he is at liberty to assume, on his own responsibility, that it was that village which was "regained." Nothing, of course, is said about any breakdown in the arrangements, because Sir Arthur, having depended upon official Canadian sources of information, probably was quite ignorant that such a breakdown ever occurred. These incidents are not mentioned in official documents. He seems to realise, however, that everything had not gone according to plan, and, true to his brief, conceals the suspicion in vague phraseology. It must never be admitted that things go wrong if it can possibly be avoided. My chief contention is that in the circumstances it would have been far better if he had left the matter (and the book) altogether alone.

This will seem an impertinent fuss about nothing, and in any case an unfair method of criticism. An isolated and trivial instance of inaccuracy is no proof that the disease is chronic. But, unfortunately, we have a multitude of proofs that it is. I could quote a dozen or a score of similar instances, within my own experience, out of this one volume, to say nothing of the earlier ones which I have read and forgotten. Now this book probably has a very large circulation. It was trumpeted everywhere as the first authentic history of our share in the war. Yet, as a history, while desperately conscientious in its own way, it is thoroughly bad. Some unhappy person or persons must have spent months, which might have been far better employed, in collecting and verifying the names of battalions and individuals which clog its pages. Not only is it impossible to see the wood for the trees; one cannot see even the trees because of the undergrowth. Verisimilitude, which is infinitely more important than literal accuracy, is not to be obtained by reciting a string of nouns and numerals, still less by concealing every fact which does not agree with the thesis of perfection conquering adversity. There is no attempt at any broad treatment of events, nor any comprehensible explanation of the sudden reversal of fortune which ensued after the three great German offensives had shot their bolt in 1918. The most revolutionary feature of the war (to reintroduce our King Charles's head) is hardly noticed. The author seems to be unaware of the complete change of tactics initiated at Cambrai and determining every subsequent operation we undertook; or, at least, if he is aware of it, he has not troubled to convey it intelligibly to his readers. It is enough to point out that in a volume dealing with the whole of our final offensive, from Hamel and the great tank victory on 8th August up to the Armistice, and professing especially to deal with the fortunes of every division, brigade, and battalion, the word "tank" does not even appear in the index! From the few cursory references to tanks in the text, the reader might imagine that these machines controlled themselves, rather indifferently and in a comic manner, and fired automatically their own guns. He is left to discover, by the light of nature, that there existed such an organisation as the Tank Corps, with six brigades, vast workshops, a numerous personnel distributed in eighteen battalions, novel tactics and problems of its own, and a predominant influence upon the fate of the war. We read of "dour" Yorkshiremen, of "hatchet-faced" Colonials, of the inevitable "grim, determined" faces of every one, of "iron" divisions, and even of infantry who

go " blithely " into battle (which no sane creature ever did);
but in this last volume I can remember only one perfunctory
reference to the men who fought and stifled and were burnt
alive in tanks while leading these others to the ultimate
victory. . . .

It is a great pity (if one may say so without further offence)
that the creator of Sherlock Holmes did not stick to his
very excellent last, instead of creating a bad precedent. One
devil does not make a hell ; but the trouble of it is, we shall
get more of these books, more tactful omissions, more
clichés and claptrap and crown octavo journalese. The
average Englishman would far sooner read a history of the
war by, let us say, Mr Hall Caine or Miss Ethel M. Dell,
especially if published in cheap parts with cheaper illustrations, than one by a competent authority. He is built that
way, unfortunately, and he will get what he wants and
deserves. There is no statute of limitations for literature ;
and, what is at the heart of the mischief, there seems to be
no longer such a thing as a literary or artistic conscience,
call it which you will.

CHAPTER XXII.

FROM NIERGNIES TO THE ARMISTICE: CONCLUSION.

I.

IN his recent book, 'The Last Four Months, the End of the War in the West,' General Sir Frederick Maurice describes how Marshal Foch, when asked by the statesmen at Versailles for his plan of countering the final German offensive, "answered by striking out three rapid blows with his right, with his left, and again with his right, following these by launching out a vigorous kick."

The preliminary punches, begun on 18th July on the Ourcq, and ending with the American capture of the St Mihiel Salient in mid-September, were uniformly successful—successful, indeed, to a degree which even the Marshal himself can hardly have anticipated. The British armies, having lost 300,000 men and 1000 guns, with immense accumulations of material, within four or five weeks, accomplished the most extraordinary recovery in history, and played the leading *rôle* in this counter-offensive. I do not know what effect the tremendous disasters of March and April had upon opinion in England, but I know that they abated in no way the illogical conviction of the ordinary Englishman in France, that we were bound to win the war in the long-run; and this self-confidence, based neither on reason nor on knowledge, innate, matter-of-fact, and often very irritating in prosperity, was an unrecognised inspiration of our resistance and reaction. It took extraordinary form at times. I remember how, when three British armies out of four were in full retreat or fighting for their lives, and when people in Calais and Boulogne were packing up for flight, one rushed to the newspapers to follow, not the progress of the war, but the case of Mr Pemberton Billing and the 47,000. Our belief in ourselves is so unconscious and irrational that it must always be incomprehensible to such a people as the Germans, who hate the casual and have a conscious sort of arrogance which is a very different thing; and no doubt it has its dangers. But it served its purpose once more in 1918. We went forward again, as a matter of course, when the tide turned, without any particular exaltation or parade, still less any surprise at our own powers, and with hardly a thought (so far as the great mass of us was concerned) of the genius which was directing all our movements, as well as those of three other national armies. But I think that toward the end of the preliminary stage, when Foch's successive punches, carried just so far as was necessary and no farther, had exhausted and demoralised the enemy and driven him once more to the fallacious shelter of the Hindenburg Line, we began to understand that something more than luck and confidence lay behind this transformation. For the first time since the war began every man in the Army felt an interest and a pride in the combined strategy in which so obviously he was playing a part. The peculiarly English analogy of the skilled boxer was patent, and appealed to all. And from now to the end, in spite of losses and exhaustion, a new spirit of enthusiasm urged us on, and was manifest in many ways.

With its growth, not only in our ranks but in those of the French, Belgians, and Americans, coincided a notable decline in the German *moral*. The resistance to our advance became spasmodic and liable to sudden collapses. And before the end of September—far earlier than at one time any one can have hoped—the hour was ripe for the big kick. This was launched on a scale, and on broad principles of calculated opportunism, beside which the isolated German blows earlier in the year seemed mechanical and clumsy. On 26th September the American 1st and French 4th Armies opened the ball on a front of forty miles astride the Argonne: on the 27th came our assault on the Canal du Nord: on the 28th, Belgians, French, and British were sweeping over the lost desolation of Flanders, and the 5th and 10th French Armies were climbing once more the slopes beyond the Aisne; and on the 29th the remaining fraction of the battered German front, the Siegfried Line from Vendhuile to St Quentin, began to slide into ruin before General Rawlinson's 4th Army. A compound operation of this magnitude, reaching its climax in four days, extending over 250 miles of country and involving twenty-four separate armies, or from four to five million men, with 30,000 guns, is almost beyond the capacity of the human brain to imagine as a whole. It is like contemplating infinity. Some one has called it, I believe, the Battle of Europe, and this seems indeed the only name by which it can be described.

Everywhere along this immense front tanks were helping to complete the overthrow they had done so much to bring about. The French used their light Rénaults in clouds before every attack. Our own Tank Corps, with no reserves, had lost in two months' continuous offensive action three-fourths of its machines and a third of its personnel, but it played a conspicuous part, as I have tried to show, on 27th September and after. Sixty-six tanks were in action on the first day, and another 170 on the 29th. Everlasting reorganisation and reshuffling of units was one of the trials of this period, and indeed the manner in which battalions were shifted from one brigade to another before almost every attack caused more worry and labour than the attacks themselves. "The rapidity with which these changes were made would have bewildered both the Tank Corps Headquarters Staff and the brigade and battalion commanders themselves a few months back: now the knack of rapid movement had been mastered, and though great energy had to be exerted during such reorganisations, they were generally accomplished in time and efficiently."[1] The necessity for some of them, it must be said, was not apparent. The 1st Brigade was very fortunate in this respect, as, except for the battle of Bapaume, it retained throughout at least its three original battalions; but some of the others suffered such constant permutations that their staffs must have been driven almost crazy. The 3rd Brigade, consisting on 8th August of the two Whippet battalions, the 3rd and 6th, was completely reconstituted on the 18th, when it was made up of the 9th, 11th, and 14th Heavy Battalions, while early in September its units were the 3rd, 6th, and 9th. The 4th Brigade, which started its career in December 1917, with the 1st, 4th, and 5th Battalions, found itself with the 4th, 5th, and 13th in May, the 5th and 10th in June, the 1st, 4th, 5th, and 14th early in August (the 9th being added a little later), dropped back to its original constituents before September, received the 301st Americans on the 19th of that month, the 16th Battalion on 5th October, and the 10th a day after, and fought its last battle with the 1st, 6th, 10th, 16th, and 301st. The 5th Brigade, which had no corporate existence until April, had the following battalions at one time or another on its strength: 1st, 2nd, 3rd, 6th, 8th, 9th, 10th, 11th, 13th, 15th, 16th, 17th, and 301st! These bewildering transfers were not always on paper only. They involved very often long additional treks for various units immediately before an action, and they were complicated by the wide dispersion which each individual battalion suffered in the course of an advance, disabled tanks, dumps, and rear-headquarters being scattered for miles behind the line. When, for example, we moved from Bihucourt to Morchies in the middle of September, the battalion and companies' rear-headquarters, with a mass of stores, were still at Bienvillers, at least twelve miles away, while there were three or four tanks under repair at Bucquoy and a couple left at Bihucourt itself. This was quite a normal situation; and when it is remembered that every one of the

[1] 'Weekly Tank Notes.'

seventeen battalions with the armies had left a similar trail behind, swallowing up men for guards and other duties, it will be realised that the co-ordination of these scattered fragments in the event of any reshuffling, and the ordinary routine of keeping in touch with them and feeding them, were complicated problems which entailed an immense amount of work for the staff and the transport. Nor was this all. There were in the field as well seven tank supply companies (two of which worked with infantry and artillery), each with twenty-four machines, a number of field (or salvage) companies, and an advanced stores attached to each brigade. All these various units, whether combatant or administrative, moved forward with the armies, and all drew their maintenance supplies in the last resort from the Central Workshops at Erin. It was a tremendous organisation that had sprung from the two companies which fought on the Somme in 1916; and not the least of its achievements was the adaptability and energy displayed in keeping the battalions supplied with their manifold requirements during the final rapid advance. The deplorable shortage of tanks themselves was the fault of no one in the Tank Corps. In the fighting units during these days perhaps the busiest men were the battalion and company engineers and equipment officers, who toiled like slaves to keep the dwindling residue of machines fit for service.

II.

I have carried the story of the 7th Battalion up to its last fight on 30th September. I will run very briefly through the remainder of its history, and through that of the Corps as a whole up to the Armistice.

On the day after Sancourt I returned from Pilgrim's Rest to Pronville, where battalion headquarters had arrived from Bullecourt and where our tents were now erected. Our few remaining tanks (there were no more than six fit for action in the three companies) were still at Pilgrim's

Rest and Raillencourt. For over a week we were left in
peace. On our front the Canadians were pushing slowly
forward, in the teeth of a most determined resistance by
fresh German divisions, toward the line of the Canal de
L'Escaut north of Cambrai, being hampered by that town
on their right and by the Sensée marshes on their left.
But farther south the Germans were being pressed back
upon the Beaurevoir-Fonsomme Line, and the big kick,
with more room for its swing, was preparing to demolish
these last defences. St Quentin had fallen, and everywhere south of Cambrai we were across the canal by 6th
October, while the Canadians were approaching Ramillies
and Eswars. On 8th October the storm burst. The
Beaurevoir-Fonsomme Line, Malincourt, Esnes, and Niergnies, with all the high ground south of Cambrai, were in our
hands by the evening. Cambrai was entered that night, and
the Germans were retreating to the Selle in great confusion,
having lost 10,000 prisoners, 200 guns, and much *matériel*.[1]

The 1st, 3rd, and 4th Tank Brigades had a conspicuous
share in this victory, although the six battalions engaged
mustered between them only 82 tanks. Of these, 20 were
furnished by the 12th Battalion, which had not been in
action since 3rd September. It signalised its re-entry by
becoming involved in the second tank *v.* tank battle of the
war. It was working single-handed with the left and centre
of the 3rd Army, its companies being attached to the
4th, 6th, and 17th Corps. B Company, on the right, with
seven tanks, having helped our old friends the New Zealanders and the 37th Division about Lesdain and Esnes,
rallied without further incident. One machine had been
disabled by a shell which killed four of the crew. C and A
Companies, attacking Seranvillers and Niergnies with the
infantry of the 6th and 17th Corps, saw the latter established on the high ground east of the villages, and were
returning to the rallying-point, when the Germans made a

---

[1] On the whole, however, the German retreat was conducted with great skill
to the very end. There was no general demoralisation, and one saw very few
prisoners except after set attacks on a large scale.

counter-attack led by seven captured Mark IV. tanks. The Germans had fitted their own 5.7 cm. guns, with very clumsy mountings, into the male machines, but retained the Lewis guns in the others. For the interesting episode which ensued, I will quote the 12th Battalion 'History,' beginning with A Company's experiences:—

"Owing to the smoke and imperfect light, these [the German tanks] were at first taken to be some of our own, both by our infantry and tank crews, the latter supposing the strangers to belong to C Company. L 16, Captain Roe, was near the farm of Mont Neuve, east of Niergnies, when these tanks appeared in sight, and the foremost was within fifty yards before that officer realised that it was an enemy. One 6-pounder round was then fired at it, apparently disabling it, but almost simultaneously L 16 received two direct hits, one of which came through the cab, wounded Captain Roe, and killed his driver. Roe, believing his tank to be disabled, as the engine had stopped, got his crew out, went to L 9, which was near at hand, and led it back toward the German tanks. L 9 had already had five men wounded, had been on fire, and, having no gunners left, could not use its 6 pounders; but its commander, 2nd Lieut. Warsap, engaged the enemy with his Lewis gun until his tank received a direct hit, setting it on fire a second time. He was now forced to evacuate it, and as the counter-attack appeared to be successful, he blew the machine up to prevent it falling into the enemy's hands. L 12, another 6-pounder tank, was hit twice and disabled before its commander had discovered that the strange tanks did not belong to C Company. There remained L 8, 2nd Lieut. A. R. Martell, but this tank had a leaking radiator and was almost out of water. Lieut. Martell therefore sent his crew back and went himself with an artillery officer to a captured German field-gun, which the two turned round and used against the enemy's tanks, knocking one out. The tank which L 16 had engaged was crippled, either by the 6-pounder shell or by a captured anti-tank rifle, and the remaining two having been driven away by a female tank from C Company, the situation was restored."

So much for A Company. C Company, in the meantime, had fared better. It started with seven tanks, of which one was hit and set on fire. "The others, having seen the infantry consolidated on the final objective across the Cambrai-Esnes road, were returning to the rallying-point when the German counter-attack began. On the extreme left, L 54, a female tank commanded by 2nd Lieut. T. B. Walters, encountered the enemy's tanks which already had been engaged with A Company's section. Lieut. Walters at once attacked two female tanks, fired several thousand rounds at them, silenced their guns, and drove them off the field. One was subsequently knocked out by shell-fire. While this brisk little battle was in progress, a couple of male tanks, L 45 (2nd Lieut. Clark) and L 49 (2nd Lieut. Sherratt), had the good fortune to meet, near a sunken road east of Seranvillers, two hostile female tanks firing on our infantry, who had been driven back from the second objective. The 6-pounders made short work of this pair, hitting them repeatedly and setting them on fire. As the survivors of their crews scrambled out, the Lewis guns were turned on them. . . ."

These hostile tanks formed the backbone of the counter-attack, being very badly supported by their infantry. Nevertheless, only the presence of our own machines averted a serious local disaster, for the men of the 63rd Division had broken completely and were running back, until the tank battle gave them time to rally; while the Germans had reoccupied the high ground beyond Niergnies, and were pushing on into that village. After the repulse of their tanks they were easily driven off. A Company, owing to the natural misunderstanding when the German machines appeared out of the smoke, lost three tanks out of four; but after the action, General Blacklock, commanding the 63rd Division, expressed to all ranks his appreciation of their services, which had saved his infantry heavy losses. The intense gratitude of the infantry themselves (for what, but for the smoke, would have been a simple business, as we had several more male tanks than the Germans) was an earnest of the severe fright they had suffered, and should have brought home to their superiors in a trenchant fashion the moral value of the weapon which they were so fortunate as to have almost exclusively at their disposal. A few hundred German tanks, instead of a dozen or so, would have made our progress, even at this late hour, a much slower and more difficult matter. So far as the Tank Corps was concerned, the only lesson to be drawn from the encounter at Niergnies was one already learnt at Villers-Bretonneux—namely, the advisability, in view of further similar meetings, of fitting every tank with a 6-pounder gun. It was as a result of these two actions that a number of Mark V. and V. Star females were converted into composite or "hermaphrodite" machines, with a 6-pounder sponson on one side. The occasion for which they were designed, however, did not recur. Although the Germans used one or two tanks in subsequent counter-attacks, our machines did not meet them again.

III.

On October 10th, when the Canadian line was several miles beyond Cambrai, the 7th Battalion sent a composite detachment of four fighting tanks and a wireless machine, which I accompanied, to Escadœuvres, a suburb of the town to the north-east, on the road to Iwuy. This involved crossing the Canal de L'Escaut and two parallel streams by a series of narrow bridges (two of them temporary structures) between Morenchies and Ramillies. Escadœuvres was a working-class suburb, and its small houses, many of which were shattered, were littered with the poor belongings of its inhabitants, who had not been evacuated many days. The Germans, before they left, had

flung everything about in a final hunt for loot, or in sheer
destructiveness, and, thorough to the last in small details,
had put a bullet through every mirror, clock, and piano
which was not already broken. The tanks were here for
two days and nights, the officers occupying a tiny house
of one room and a cellar which had been used by the
German *Ortz-Kommandant*. As the enemy was still holding on to the Douai front, the 1st Army now had a left
flank twelve or fifteen miles long, extending from Thun-
Levêque on the canal to somewhere near Etaing, at a
right angle to the rest of the line; and in Escadœuvres
we were shelled persistently by a high-velocity gun which
fired from a point well behind us across the Sensée. This
was an annoyance, but a greater tragedy to me was the loss
of my valise, which was cut off from the back of the Major's
car as he was bringing it at night through the packed traffic
in Cambrai. My servant had of course filled it with things
I did not want at Escadœuvres and could not replace—old
cherished garments and other oddments such as one feels a
positive affection for.

The detachment was withdrawn from Escadœuvres on the
12th, as the country in front, seamed with small rivers, was
unsuitable for serious tank operations, and a few days later
the battalion was placed in G.H.Q. Reserve and concentrated
at Fontaine-Notre-Dame. This was preparatory to a return,
when railway exigencies permitted, to the Bermicourt area,
for a complete refit with Mark V.'s. Another party of
officers and men had left to stiffen the new battalions in
England, and I was expecting to follow in a few days. On
16th October, however, I learnt that I had been posted as
Battalion Reconnaissance Officer to the 12th Battalion. The
next day I said good-bye to the 7th, with which I had worked
and fought for two years, and joined my new unit at Cattenières, south of the Cambrai-Le Cateau road.

On this front the enemy had fallen back everywhere to
the Selle river. Douai at last had been abandoned, and
the 5th Army was approaching Lille. We had now entered

a new type of country, which to those accustomed to four years of fighting backwards and forwards over the devastated area seemed almost unnatural. During one's visits to England on leave, the first sight from the train of the Kentish orchards and hop-fields always left a strange illusion, as of something lacking, which was caused in fact by the absence of shell-holes; and the country beyond Cambrai affected one at first in a similar manner. It was so unlike war as we had known it. Every inch of the land was under cultivation. Immense fields of cabbage and beet, unbroken by any hedgerows, rolled onward for miles; the villages and farms were of great size and often untouched, and, with the little towns, such as Caudry, Le Cateau, and Solesmes, completed a picture that proclaimed in every article a previous state of comfort and prosperity. Before the war this region must have been one of the most flourishing in France. And, except that for the moment it was deserted, it was flourishing still. The Germans had seen to that, and had taken the profits. It was indeed a novelty to enter house after house where roofs, windows, and furniture remained untouched, and where, only a day or two before, civilians had been living. A little later, and we had moved forward again to places where half-starved women, dressed tidily in black, who had lived without meat for upwards of four years and without hope for almost as long, still cowered in cellars while the fighting passed by overhead, and who, when they were rescued and moved out of the gas and shelling to safer quarters, could yet find time (as I saw myself) to lay flowers on those of our dead that were lying in their streets. This was in St Python, a little suburb of Solesmes; and Solesmes itself, by way of contrast, provided a stupefying sidelight upon the minds of the most extraordinary people that ever inhabited this earth, for it was gay with new tricolour flags, manufactured, imported, and sold to the inhabitants by the Germans themselves in readiness for their defeat. . . .

In many respects these last weeks were the most in-

FROM NIERGNIES TO THE ARMISTICE 497

teresting of all, but I will not attempt to describe them
here. There is a limit to the irrelevant matter permissible
in any book, and I have more than a suspicion that I have
exceeded it already. So far as tank operations are concerned, there is very little more to be said. When I joined
the 12th Battalion at Cattenieres, it was still working with
three corps of the 3rd Army, its companies being at
Avesnes-les-Aubert, Quiévy, and Viesly, all to the north
of the Le Cateau road; and preparations were in hand
for the forcing of the Selle river on 20th October. By this
time the battalion, in spite of a reinforcement of 4 old
Mark IV.'s from Erin, had only 12 tanks fit for action;
and as 78 officers and men had just left for England, it
was no less short of personnel, particularly of experienced
drivers. As it happened, there was little chance of tanks
being used in this region. A succession of rivers, running
northward into the Scheldt—the Selle, the Harpies, the St
Georges, the Ecaillon, and the Rhonelle—lay parallel to our
front, and (except the St Georges, a mere brook) could only
be crossed by tanks when the engineers had built bridges
to replace those which the enemy was certain to destroy.
Farther up these streams, where the 11th and other tank
battalions were co-operating with the right of the 3rd Army
and the whole of the 4th, they ceased to be insuperable
obstacles; and on 17th October, tanks of the 4th Brigade
crossed the Selle with the help of cribs. In the big attack
of the 20th, four machines of the 11th Battalion got over near
Neuvilly by means of an ingenious bridge made of sleepers,
which was sunk in the river by the engineers the night
before. Being under water, this bridge was not discovered
by the Germans during the day, although the Selle approxi-
mated to No Man's Land. But for our part, being faced
by these various waterways where they were broader and
deeper, we had a cheerless prospect of endless trekking
with very little probability of arriving anywhere in time
for action. Only once, in fact, were our tanks engaged.
The attack on the 20th was entirely successful, except at

Beaurain, a small village on very high ground a couple of miles due east of Solesmes, where the Germans continued to hold out for two days after the rest of their line had been forced back to the Harpies. Our tanks having been got across the Selle at St Python and Briastre, B Company was detailed to assist the 5th Division in the capture of Beaurain on the 23rd. Owing to accidents, only two tanks were available, and neither of these was mechanically fit. One had a cracked sleeve, and could only travel at low speed. The little action which ensued possesses one or two points of interest.

From the Selle Valley at Briastre the ground rose steeply in a series of ridges, each slightly higher than the last, to Beaurain, which was on the summit. Our outpost line was just east of the farm and road-junction at Marou, 2000 yards in front of the village. Between the two places was a spur of ground called the Grand Champ Ridge, where the Germans had a great number of machine-guns in pits. The two tanks were to clear this ridge, which was the enemy's main line of resistance, and then proceed to mop up in Beaurain if required. They reached the valley in front of Marou at 10 P.M. on the 22nd, zero being at 3.20 in the morning. At 1 o'clock the enemy put down a heavy barrage along our front line, and the assaulting infantry suffered several hundred casualties and were thrown into great confusion. Expecting an attack, they sent up S.O.S. signals, while the tanks prepared for action. Nothing came of this bombardment, however, and it died down after half an hour to the normal intermittent shelling; but the infantry was so shaken that only the presence of the tanks induced them to go forward at zero. The Germans fought with desperate courage on the Grand Champ Ridge, where the machine-gunners fired until they were run over, and where the engine of L 13 (the tank with the cracked sleeve) stopped and could not be restarted for forty-five minutes. Our infantry being some way behind, the enemy swarmed round the tank, one officer bringing a machine-gun into the road within a few yards of it. The other tank, L 23, was having an equally hard task on the ridge, finding it very difficult in the mist and twilight to locate the hostile machine-guns; and the two were fighting alone for a quarter of an hour before the infantry at length came up, having collected on the way some fifty prisoners who had surrendered to the tanks. The latter had broken the back of the enemy's resistance on the ridge, and the advance now went forward rapidly. Beaurain was cleared with little trouble, neither of the tanks being required, which was just as well, as one was broken down and the second pulling very badly. The officer and one man in L 23 were wounded, and the crew of L 13 was badly gassed, so that the company commander, walking forward from the rallying-point to meet the machines, found it crawling homeward out of control, the tank commander and driver being unconscious. Considering that both tanks went into action labouring under mechanical defects, their performance would have been highly creditable in any circumstances; and it fell out that in addition they alone carried the operation through, as the infantry concerned fully recognised. The latter, disorganised and badly shaken by the barrage which caught them before zero, and by a second which fell among them in the first minutes of the advance, would have made no progress against the nests of machine-guns on the Grand Champ Ridge if the tanks had not been there to take the lead and draw the enemy's attention to themselves.

B Company was now left without any tanks fit to move. A Company, with four machines, was at Haussy, on the Selle north of Solesmes, and remained there. C Company alone, with three tanks, continued for two or three days to follow the Guards Division in its advance. It had been pointed out that the decrepit condition of these tanks, added to the series of obstructions formed by the rivers, made their chances of affording practical help very remote; but the Guards insisted on their following up as far as possible, on account of the great moral effect the mere knowledge of their presence had on the men! On the 24th, therefore, C Company had reached Capelle, at the junction of the Ecaillon and St Georges, our line being then within a mile of Le Quesnoy. On the following day orders came through from Tank Corps Headquarters for the withdrawal of the battalion. All companies, having patched up their machines, began the long trek back to the entraining railhead at Marcoing on the Canal de L'Escaut, a tedious process, as some of the tanks had to be towed most of the way. On 1st November I went on ahead to take over our winter quarters, a hutted camp in the devastated area at Ecurie, near Arras. Here we remained for six months, in extreme discomfort; and then, made up to strength from disbanded units of the corps, and provided with 24 Mark V.'s, entrained for Cologne.

The last tank battles of the war were fought on the 4th, 5th, 6th, and 7th November, just before the Armistice, around the Forest of Mormal. An idea of the lamentable state to which the corps was reduced will be gathered from the number of tanks and units employed on the first day. The 6th, 9th, 10th, and 14th Battalions were engaged. At full strength they would have mustered between them 168 tanks, they could now raise only 37. An interesting feature of the day's fighting was that three supply-tanks, armed with one Hotchkiss gun apiece and carrying bridging material for the 25th Division, came into action near Landrecies. Our infantry was held up on the west bank of the Sambre Canal, and the officer in charge of the supply tenders decided to see what he could do to help them. One tank was knocked out. The other two, followed by the infantry as if they had been fighting tanks, forced the German machine-gunners to surrender. During the next day eight Whippets of the 6th Battalion helped the 3rd Guards Brigade in the difficult enclosed country north of the Forest; and with two further actions on the Maroilles-Avesnes road, the Tank Corps' active share in the war came to an end.

Captured English Tanks being used during the Revolution in Berlin.

Mark V. Tanks of the 12th Battalion at Cologne.

"Ninety-six days of almost continuous battle had now taken place since the great tank attack at Amiens was launched by the 4th Army on the 8th August, since when many officers and men of the Tank Corps had been in action as many as 15 and 16 times. During this period no less than 1993 tanks and tank armoured-cars had been engaged on 39 days in all, 887 machines had been handed over to salvage, 313 of these being sent to the Central Workshops, and 204 having been repaired and reissued to battalions. Of the above 887 tanks, only 15 had been struck off the strength as unsalvable. Casualties against establishment had been heavy, 598 officers and 2826 other ranks being counted amongst killed, wounded, missing, and prisoners; but when it is considered that the total strength of the Tank Corps on the 7th August (9500 of all ranks in France) was considerably under that of an infantry division, and that in the old days of the artillery battles, such as the first battle of the Somme, an infantry division frequently sustained 4000 casualties in twelve hours' fighting, the tank casualties were extraordinarily light. From this we may deduce our final and outstanding lesson from all these battles—namely, that iron mechanically moved is an economiser of blood, that the tank is an economiser of life. . . ."[1]

IV.

In the first days of November, when the Tank Corps was endeavouring to withdraw all its crippled battalions for a reorganisation and refit, pressure was put upon it to maintain some units in the field. The Army, in fact, discovered that it could not go on without tanks, in spite of the demoralisation which plainly was spreading among the enemy. The cavalry, provided at last with all the conditions most favourable to their use, were as helpless as ever, and the

[1] 'Weekly Tank Notes.'

infantry still needed the moral support which the presence of tanks afforded, even if the latter were hardly ever used. It was decided, therefore, that each tank brigade should send forward one composite battalion. Orders to this effect had just reached us at Ecurie (the whole of the 1st Brigade being now concentrated in this area), when the Armistice was signed.

For some time after 11th November, however, the Tank Corps, in common with every other branch of the service, was still busy preparing for further eventualities. The composite battalions were no longer immediately required, and only the armoured-cars went forward into Germany; but at Bermicourt and Erin there was no relaxation of effort until the occupation of the Rhine bridge-heads, and the enemy's surrender of his fleet and artillery rendered any serious resumption of hostilities impossible. At the same time, the criminal outcry for instant demobilisation which disgraced still further (if that was possible) our unscrupulous press, hit the corps in France especially hard. No sooner had the battalions been brought again to something like full strength by drafts of conscripted miners, strikers, and professional footballers, who might in time have been knocked into shape, than all these arrivals, who had been only a few months in the Army, were released again—a business which caused very natural discontent among the original rank and file who had done all the fighting and who were still retained.

In the meantime, during the last month of the war, further developments in the composition of the corps had been authorised and carried into effect. The 6th Tank Brigade was formed in October, consisting nominally of the 16th, 18th, and 301st (American) Battalions. The 18th Battalion had just come out from England. This brigade was never in action as a whole. There were now forming at Bovington the 19th, 20th, 21st, 22nd, 23rd, 24th, and 25th Battalions, but none of these would be available before the early spring of 1919. By that date, however, eight tank brigades, with a total strength (if up to establishment) of upwards of 15,000 officers and men and 1000 tanks, should be ready for immediate action. At least two new types of tank, known as the Medium C and Mark IX., were under construction; but the former was not very satisfactory, although fast, and the latter was an infantry-carrying machine; and most of the battalions would be armed with the Mark V. or an improved Whippet. It was hoped, however, provided personnel was available and labour conditions satisfactory, to so expand the battalions as to put a great many more than 1000 machines into the field at once. The dream of the Tank Corps, and one which probably would have materialised if the war had continued, was a vast smashing attack by 4000 or 5000 tanks. With this prospect in view, the organisation of the corps, which threatened to become unwieldy, was also to be expanded, and two days before the Armistice three new formations came into existence, the 1st, 2nd, and 3rd Groups, each consisting of two brigades under a Major-General. Whether this multiplication of large staffs was the best solution of the problem is a matter of opinion. It smacks rather too much of the usual Army method of making any excuse serve for inventing new sinecures, and there was no ambiguity about the manner in which it was rushed through just before the Armistice, so that every staff officer in the Tank Corps got a step in rank (and sometimes two) while yet these pleasant fruits of office were going begging. Bermicourt now began to look like a poppy-field for red hats. At the same time, a more indefensible scheme of centralisation was applied to the technical side, by the formation of what were called Group Inspectorates. This high-sounding title merely concealed the fact that battalions were deprived of their engineer staffs, which were lumped together in itinerant and irresponsible posses, whose business was to supervise all mechanical work in the field. In other words, a fresh set of semi-independent staffs was created.

In the matter of the groups, it is possible of course that it was not intended to increase the number of brigades, but merely to add battalions to them. I have no information about this, but it does not appear very probable. In any case, as the tank fighting unit is still the company, tank battalions being the administrative equivalents of infantry brigades, it would seem that the object aimed at would have been better attained by increasing the strength of battalions and abolishing altogether the intermediate tank brigades. The French system of forming their tank units into regiments of three battalions, on the Continental infantry basis, is yet more practical. All these plans may appear to be but variations of the same theory; but in fact there is a great gulf fixed between the regimental outlook and that of a higher formation, and one of the curses of the British Army is the way in which staffs tend to spring up like mushrooms on the slightest provocation.

This discussion, however, is now become academic. Groups and brigades alike have vanished for the present into the limbo of lost hopes, and what is left of the Tank Corps hangs in a state of suspended animation, conscious of a great past and a very uncertain future. After innumerable tentative schemes for a post-bellum establishment as part of the regular Army, the corps was fixed definitely a few months ago at one brigade of five regular battalions. General Elles remained as Brigadier, and five lieutenant-colonels were selected by seniority from the original group and brigade commanders. Although five battalions was an inadequate force, it appeared as if the war had taught us something, if not overmuch. Remembering what had happened during hostilities, one really had expected to find officers from the Camel Corps or the Life Guards appointed to command tank units in a peace establishment. But when it came to the junior commissioned ranks, the old Adam reappeared with a vengeance. A large number of subalterns temporarily commissioned into the old Tank Corps wished to stay on in the new one, as professional soldiers; and as many of them had one or two years' experience of tank warfare, the retention of the most suitable would seem to be, to a reasonable being, a matter of course, setting aside all arguments of decency or propriety. But this would have been carrying common-sense too far. The War Office, as usual, had a trump up its sleeve. It had granted regular commissions in the infantry and other arms (but never in the Tank Corps itself) on such a prodigal scale during the war that the reduction of the Army left something like 7000 of these officers surplus to establishment. Billets must be found for them, and it occurred to some one that the new Tank Corps would accommodate several hundred. The old tank officers, therefore, having at first been encouraged to apply for regular commissions, were now told that they were not wanted. Sandhurst and the surplus must be considered before suitability.

This was the state of affairs at the end of 1919. What has happened since, or what the end of it will be, I do not know at the time of writing. There was a rumour, just when I was leaving the Army, that everything was to be changed once more, that all tank battalions were to be abolished, and that only a small training and experimental depot was to be maintained at Bovington or Wareham. Every infantry officer, on the other hand, was to pass through a tank course . . . ! Whatever the basis of truth in this circumstantial report (and it has received confirmation in recent newspaper paragraphs), so pernicious a scheme is beyond comment. In the meantime, the new regular brigade has come into being, and so far continues to exist; and since the authorities have discovered the value of tanks during industrial disturbances and in Ireland, they may harden their hearts against the Treasury, and the Tank Corps may tide over this bad hour with the help of Trade Unions and Sinn Fein! It will be the first time that either institution has served a useful purpose.

In the long-run, of course, we shall have to equip ourselves with a large Tank Corps again. Everything depends upon whether we do so before the next war or in the middle of it. Other nations will have tanks, and in large numbers. The French are providing for a corps of 30,000 men, and the Americans (who designed a tank of their own during the war) have also, I believe, taken up the question in earnest. Just as the origins of modern warfare at sea, and of all the scientific methods by which it is carried on, are to be found in the *Gloire* and the little *Monitor* of the early 'sixties, so it is no less certain that future warfare on land will be dominated by the successors of the Mark I. tank which struggled through the mud of the Somme battle-fields. For once this country has taken the lead in military invention; and it has now at its disposal a preponderant body of experience in this new method. It remains to be seen whether the advantage will be maintained, or whether it will be lost by the diversion to political schemes of even the comparatively small annual outlay of money which is essential for adequate experiment.[1]

What form tank development will take is a subject beyond the scope of this book, and one on which I am not competent to speak. We are still on the threshold of the new enterprise, and there seem to be no limits at present to what may be achieved. We have already a tank which will float, and speeds of twenty and twenty-five miles an hour

[1] Since writing the above, a Memorandum has been issued (23rd Feb. 1920) by the Secretary of State for War dealing with the Army Estimates. It contains the following reference to the Tank Corps, which shows that our worst apprehensions are confirmed : " It has been decided that there will be no separate Tank Corps for the present, and that, though non-commissioned officers and men will be posted permanently to tank units as a nucleus, officers will be seconded instead of being transferred to these units for stated periods. The main difficulty which confronts reorganisation is the dearth of regular officers with knowledge of tanks. To some extent this may be overcome by granting regular commissions to temporary officers. Considerable progress has been made with the design of tanks during 1919, a new machine having been produced with a speed of over twenty miles an hour, and which has mechanically a long life. In a trial run of 1000 miles practically no wear has resulted. This type is being further developed. Two other machines have been despatched to India for the purpose of experiment under tropical conditions."

have been attained long ago with experimental machines.
Colonel Fuller, who was G.S.O. 1 Tank Corps in France,
points out in his new book[1] that, in future wars, land will
become "a solid sea, as easily traversable in all directions
as ice is by a skater; the battles in these wars will therefore more and more approximate to naval actions." And
he goes on to remark that "from the present-day tank to
one which can plunge in the Channel at Calais at four in
the morning, land at Dover at six o'clock, and be outside
Buckingham Palace for an early lunch, will not probably
require as many as the fifty-two years which have separated
the *Merrimac* from the *Tiger* or the *Queen Elizabeth*."

V.

When one has written a book of this kind, frankly par-
tisan in character, it is peculiarly gratifying to find one's
arguments supported to the letter by independent testimony
from another and far more authoritative quarter. I have
kept this evidence to the last, in the manner (I believe)
of the practised advocate; but, to be honest, the arrangement is due more to luck than judgment. It was only
when this book was almost finished that I read General
Sir Frederick Maurice's short volume called 'The Last
Four Months: the End of the War in the West.' It is
so complete a confirmation of the case I have attempted
to put forward that I cannot make a better end than by
quoting some of its conclusions.

General Maurice, after discussing the various tactical
expedients adopted by either side in their offensives, and
the ultimate failure of all these methods to achieve the
desired "break-through," describes briefly the invention
and early employment of tanks and the opinion held of
them by the enemy. "It does not appear," he says, "that
Ludendorff was particularly impressed with the value of

[1] 'Tanks in the Great War.' Lieut.-Colonel J. F. C. Fuller. (Murray.)

tanks before the events of 1918 taught him wisdom in this respect." We then come to a consideration of the means the Allies had at their disposal for their counter-offensive in the summer of that year. Speaking of Sir Douglas Haig's plans and resources, General Maurice points out that "in particular the great improvements which had been made in the tanks since their first appearance in battle and the quantities of them available, gave him just the means he needed for carrying through his scheme. Cambrai had proved that tanks could replace the long bombardment and obviate all the slow preparation which it involved."

The action at Hamel is then described: "With this fortunate experiment faith in the tanks spread. The commanders already believed in them, and now that belief in their power to 'make good' spread to the ranks." (Some of the commanders, it must be added, dissembled their belief very successfully until after Hamel!) General Maurice continues. "Tanks made surprise, that greatest weapon of generalship, much easier than it had been: they saved life and economised troops, and, therefore, that quick succession of punches for which Foch was seeking his opportunity became possible. The artist had his materials to hand. Honour to him that he knew how to use them."

Of the great tank attack on 8th August, we read that "the tanks did invaluable service in cutting the German telegraph and telephone communications. . . . The work begun at Hamel was completed, and the moral ascendancy established by tanks, artillery, and infantry, working in combination, affected both private and General in the German Army."

Later in the book General Maurice sums up the influences which together broke down the German *moral*, and again he insists upon the predominant part played by the tanks.

"The tanks had proved their efficacy in the preparations for Armageddon, now they were to take their part in the culmination toward which Foch had been working, and few things helped us more in the decisive struggle than the moral ascendancy which the success of the tanks in the preliminary battles had given us over the Germans. Captured German orders and other documents bear testimony to the dread with which the enemy regarded tanks at this time. . . ." Here follows an extract from one such order, already quoted in an earlier chapter of this book. General Maurice continues: "This is the type of order which is the refuge of authority when caught napping. The German leaders had delayed too long to study the possibilities of tanks and the most effective means of meeting them. The 'counter-measures' presented in this order might have availed against tanks alone. They were useless against tanks, artillery, and infantry working in combination. They were, in fact, worse than useless, they were harmful, for they served to demonstrate to the German soldier, who was already in mortal fear of tanks and prepared to make their appearance an excuse for surrender, that his chiefs were as frightened of them as he was, and that they had no effective reply ready."

And finally, the author makes this definite assertion: "It is certain that neither Foch's skilful preparation for the great battle, nor the valour of the infantry, would have brought us victory if we had had to rely upon bombardment alone in order to batter down the German defences."

These extracts read like a literal, if more sober, repetition of the theses at which I have been hammering, in and out of season, throughout this history; and they are uttered with an authority to which I have no pretence. It would have been difficult to find confirmatory evidence more apt and decisive than chance threw in my way, a fortnight before these lines were written, when I picked up General Maurice's little volume. I would commend it to Sir Arthur Conan Doyle, among other people. The tank, in one sense, needs no advertisement now, any more than the first successful steam-engine or aeroplane needed one: ever since Cambrai, at the latest, all who had adequate acquaintance with the facts realised that it had come, not only to stay, but to predominate. It is one thing, however, to be convinced, and quite another to admit it, even to oneself. In a professional army, which (like any other close corporation) is a body made up of cliques, conservatism, and personal jealousy, held together by interest, no gratitude is felt for innovations once the immediate occasion for their usefulness is past. General officers who called for tanks at all hours in the field, because they could not rely upon their infantry going forward unless tanks were there to lead them, lost all interest in these auxiliaries the moment the Armistice was signed. And further, recognition which cannot be denied to some instrument is often withheld from the hand which directs it. It is for these reasons that unbiassed acknowledgment of the services rendered by the Tank Corps is peculiarly valuable at this time. People talk about tanks, and read more or less worthless books in which these machines figure occasionally as comic and semi-animate monsters moving capriciously here and there without method or principle; but while it is dimly recognised that they influenced powerfully the course of the war, it is hardly suspected that they are governed, like any other military arm, by tactical considerations, that they are not irresponsible units but parts of an organised whole, and that every action they have fought has been planned as carefully as any infantry assault or artillery barrage. Still less attention is paid to the men who fought in them, and whose skill and gallantry, displayed often amid circumstances of horror peculiar even in this conflict, forged in three years, from insignificant and disheartening beginnings, so vast and efficient a weapon as the Tank Corps eventually became. It is these aspects of the case, among others, that I have tried especially to set out in this book.

INDEX.

A5, Turkish post at, 87.
Ablainzevelle, 372, 375, 376, 380-381.
Acheux, 39.
Achiet-le-Grand, 59, 343, 373, 375, 382-384, 429; stockade at, 299.
Achiet-le-Petit, 374, 375, 382-383, 390, 391.
Adinfer Wood, 377.
Admiral's Road, 110, 160.
Admiralty, experiments by, 12.
Agache river, 432, 434, 439.
Aire, 320.
Air Force, Royal, 120-124.
Albert, 258, 308.
Alberta, 132, 179.
Ali Muntar ridge, 73, 76, 78, 79, 82.
Allenby, General Sir E., 82.
Amiens, battle of. See Somme, 3rd battle of.
Anley, General G., 57.
Anthoine, General, 111.
Annequin, 334, 335.
Anneux, 270, 276, 277, 281, 449, 455.
Anti-tank machine-gun, 299-300.
Anti-tank measures, general, 289-300.
Anti-tank rifle, 297.
Approach marches, difficulties of, 140-142, 199-203.
Armin, General von, 110.
"Armour, attack by," 11, 16.
Armour-piercing bullets, 22.
Army, American, 428; 1st, 488.
Army, Belgian, 103, 488.
Army, British—
  1st, 59, 309, 353, 356, 403, 416, 432, 459, 495.
  2nd, 90, 103, 344, 356, 459.
  3rd, 59, 251, 257, 265-268, 315, 342, 372-375, 387, 403, 414, 416, 432, 459, 491, 497.
  4th, 31, 103, 352, 372, 387, 403, 432, 459, 488.
  5th, 31, 59, 61-62, 103, 183-184, 341, 460, 495.

Army, French—
  1st, 103, 351, 352.
  3rd, 352, 366, 459.
  4th, 488.
  5th, 459, 488.
  6th, 304.
  10th, 459, 488.
Army, German—
  2nd, 268, 293.
  4th, 110.
  6th, 319.
  17th, 414.
  18th, 293, 357.
Army Council, trials before, 14.
Arras, battle of, 58-69.
Aubvillers, 351.
Australian Corps, 61-64, 92, 349, 350, 352, 353, 356.
Avesnes-les-Aubert, 497.
Avesnes-les-Bapaume, 393, 401.
Ayette, 372.
Azincourt, 370.

Bacon, Admiral Sir R. H. S., 10, 12.
Baker Carr, Colonel, 54, 59.
Bancourt, 405, 412.
Banteux, 264.
Bantigny, 466.
Bapaume, battle of, 373; capture of, 403.
Barastre, 343.
Bauer, Colonel, 295.
Bazèque Wood, 371.
Beach Post, 86.
Beaucourt-en-Santerre, 363.
Beaucourt-sur-Ancre, 40-41, 375.
Beaumetz-les-Loges, 247-248.
Beaumont Hamel, 40-41.
Beauquesne, 47.
Beaurain, action at, 498-499.
Bécordel, 309.
Beersheba, 73, 82.
Behagnies, 390, 400, 429.
Bellevue, 195, 204.

Bellicourt tunnel, 459.
Below, General von, 414.
Bermicourt, 51, 89, 98.
Bertincourt, 258.
Béthune, 319, 322, 324, 330, 337.
Beugnatre, 403, 405, 406.
Beugny, 342 ; first attack on, 404-413 ; second attack, 417, 420-421 ; third attack, 421-425.
Biefvillers, 390, 392.
Bienvillers-au-Bois, 371, 372.
"Big Willie," 13, 14.
Bihucourt, 389, 396, 429.
Bingham, Major the Hon. J. D. Y., 188.
Bisley, 24, 25.
Blangy-sur-Ternoise, 369.
Blécourt, 466.
Boche Castle, 115, 131, 159.
Bœsinghe, 101, 118, 140.
Bois de Bouvigny, 312.
Bois de l'Abbé, 345.
Bois d'Olhain, 312.
Bois des Neufs, 270.
Bombardment, preliminary, effects of, 6, 16 ; on the Somme, 33 ; at Arras, 59 ; at Ypres, 103, 132-133, 155, 159-160, 217-218.
Bombing, hostile, 120, 135-136, 457.
Bouchoir, 366.
Boundary Road, 160, 200.
Bourlon, 282, 438-439, 449, 452, 456, 457.
Bourlon Wood, 264, 276, 277, 282, 439, 449, 462.
Bouvigny-Boyeffles, 311.
Bovington, 50.
Bradley, Colonel, 24, 28.
Bray, 283, 343.
Briastre, 498.
Bridge Four, 114.
Brielen, 109, 117, 118.
Briquetterie, the, 32.
Broome, Major, 195, 308.
Brough, Colonel, 28.
Bruay coal-fields, defence of, 310.
Brutinel's Brigade, 463, 474.
Buchan, Colonel J., 36, 58, 61, 64, 94, 360, 361, 417.
Bucquoy, 343, 347-348, 371, 372, 375, 383.
Buffs Road, 178, 200.
Bullecourt, 61-64, 69, 265, 278, 431, 454.
Bulkeley Johnson, General, 65.
Bus-les-Artois, 342, 351.
Byng, General Sir J., 251, 265, 278.

Cachy, the Whippets at, 345-346.

Callwell, General, 250.
Cambrai, proposed attack on, 95-97 ; first battle of, 249-284 ; second battle, 432-491.
Cambrin, 334.
Canadian Corps, 60, 312-313, 352, 353, 356, 363, 403, 416, 432, 433, 440, 452-453 (and see Divisions).
Canadian Farm, 110, 132, 155.
Canal de L'Escaut, 264, 274, 433, 459, 491.
Canal du Nord, 264, 403, 432-433, 434-438 ; crossing of, 451.
Capelle, 500.
Capper, General Sir J., 57.
Cars, armoured. See 17th Tank Battalion.
Carter, Colonel, 358.
Cartigny, 342.
Cattenières, 495.
Cavalry, at Monchy-le-Preux, 64-67 ; at Cambrai, 266, 267, 278-279, 283 ; on 8th August, 354, 359-361.
Cavillon, 356.
Cayeux Wood, 361.
Château des Prés, 331-332.
Chaulnes, 352, 366.
Cheddar Villa, 177, 208.
Chipilly, 362, 364, 366.
Choques, 324.
Chuignolles, 359.
Churchill, Winston S., the Right Hon., letter to the War Office, 11-12 ; forms Landship Committee, 13 ; memorandum on "Variants of the Offensive," 14.
Clapham Junction, 91.
Cockcroft, the, 197, 208, 228-229 ; significance of action, 231, 234.
Cojeul river, 68.
Contay, 351.
Courage, Colonel, 54 ; Brigadier-General, 351.
Courcelette, 31, 34.
Courcelles, 375.
Crèvecoeur, 270.
Cricket Redoubt, 86.
Crinchon river, 60.

Débeney, General, 351, 352, 363.
Deir-el-Belah, 73, 74, 81.
Deligny Mill, 453.
"Delta scheme, the," 323.
Delville Wood, 32.
Demuin, 357.
Dessart Wood, 262, 268, 284.
D'Eyncourt, Sir E. T., 13.
Diplock, Mr, 10.
"Ditching," frequency of, 43-45.

INDEX

Divisions, British Infantry—
  Guards, 140, 266, 281, 283, 389, 499, 500.
  1st, 186, 325, 334.
  3rd, 268, 389, 405, 412, 413, 414, 418-419.
  4th, 416, 417.
  5th, 394, 404, 405, 413, 415, 417, 420, 422, 498, 499.
  6th, 268, 270.
  11th, 198, 206, 228.
  12th, 270.
  20th, 270.
  21st, 36-38.
  25th, 500.
  29th, 268, 270, 283.
  36th, 92, 268.
  37th, 375, 380, 383, 389, 392, 491.
  39th, 131.
  40th, 268, 282.
  42nd, 419.
  48th, 198, 206, 230.
  51st, 131, 268, 270, 275, 280, 281.
  52nd, 73, 75, 76-79, 83-87.
  53rd, 73, 76-78.
  54th, 73, 75, 76, 80, 83-87.
  56th, 414.
  62nd, 270, 274, 275-276, 414.
  63rd, 40, 380, 382-383, 393, 401, 443, 493.
  74th, 73.
Divisions, Australian. See Australian Corps.
Divisions, Canadian—
  1st, 416, 439.
  3rd, 456.
  4th, 416, 439.
  5th, 440. And see Canadian Corps.
Divisions, New Zealand, 34, 92, 390, 394, 398, 405, 412, 429, 491.
Doignies, 342.
Doyle, Sir A. Conan, 482-485.
Dranoutre, 91.
Drocourt-Quéant Switch, 63, 68, 416, 417-418.
Duddridge, Sergeant, gallantry of, 413, 475-478.
Dury, 417.

Ecaillon river, 497.
Ecoust, 405, 412, 414.
Ecurie, 59, 500, 502.
El Arish, 71 (note), 73.
El Arish Redoubt, 73, 76-78.
Elles, Colonel H. J., 14, 46, 47-48, 51; Brigadier-General, 89, 108, 251, 271, 272-273, 351, 504; Major-General, 48.
English Trees, 115.

Enguinegatte, 339-340.
Epehy, 258, 342; battle of, 433.
Erin, central stores and workshops at, 51-52.
Ervillers, 390.
Escadœuvres, 494-495.
Essarts, 372, 376.
Esnes, 491.
Estienne, Colonel, 301, 305.
Etaing, 417.

Fanny's Farm, 93.
Favreuil, 393, 401.
Feuchy Chapel, 65, 66.
Fins, 283.
Flammenwerfer, 9.
Flers, 31, 34.
Flesquières, 264, 270, 275, 277, 455.
Fontaine-Notre-Dame, 270, 280, 281.
Forsyth-Major, Major O. A., 76.
Fort Garry Horse, 279.
Forward Cottage, 113, 151, 154.
Fouquières, 322-327.
Foster, Messrs, 14, 25.
Foster tractor, trials by, 12.
Framerville, 358, 363, 366.
Fremicourt, 404, 405, 412.
Frascati Farm, 109, 113, 136, 147-149, 178, 179.
French, General Sir J., 12, 13.
Freyberg, Colonel, 40.
Frezenberg, 111, 182.
Fuller, Colonel J. C. F., 507.

Gas, poison, 9.
Gavrelle, 403.
Gaza, 73; first battle of, 73; second battle of, 74-80; third battle of, 82-88.
Geudecourt, 31, 35, 36-38.
Ghent Cottages, 191, 198.
Gilban, 72.
Gird Trench, 36-38.
Givenchy-les-La-Bassée, 322, 330, 335.
Glasgow, General W., 57.
Glencorse Wood, 236.
Gomiecourt, 389, 429.
Gonnelieu, 265, 283.
Gough, General Sir H., 31, 103, 235.
Gouzeaucourt, 262, 269, 283, 433.
Graincourt, 270, 276, 449, 455.
Grévillers, 390, 392, 393.
Guémappe, 403.
Guilleaucourt, 361, 362.
"Gunpits, The," 207, 218-221.

Haig, Field-Marshal Sir D., 253, 281.
Halfway House, 113, 137, 143-144, 193.
Hamel, action at, 349-350.

2 K

514   INDEX

Hamelincourt, 389.
Hammond's Corner, 150, 200.
Hampshire Farm, 110, 132, 155.
Hangard Wood, 346.
Hankey, Colonel E. B., 149, 208, 268, 308; Brigadier-General, 309.
Hannescamps, 347, 372.
Harbonnières, 358, 361.
Harp, the, 61.
Harpies river, 497.
Hatfield, trials at, 14.
Haussy, 499.
Havrincourt, 270, 273; battle of, 433.
Havrincourt Wood, 264, 268.
Haynecourt, 439, 466.
Heninel, 68, 389.
Herera, 73, 74, 82.
Hersin, 320.
Hervilly Wood, 342.
Hesdigneul, 325, 328, 331.
Hesdin, 370.
Hetherington, Major, 10, 12.
Hendecourt, 63.
Hill 70, 310, 312.
Hill 145, 60.
Hillock Farm, 207, 220, 230.
Hill Top Farm, 149.
Hindenburg Line, 58, 61 63, 251-252, 261, 264-265, 433.
Hindenburg, Marshal von, 295.
Hinges, 324.
Hirondelle river, 298, 434.
Holt tractor, trials of, 12.
Hooge, 111.
Hooglede, 139.
Houthoulst Forest, 90, 111.
Hospital Farm, 113, 125, 138.
Hotblack, Captain, 30, 40.
Hutier, General von, 292, 357.

Imperial Defence, Committee of, 10, 11.
Inchy-en-Artois, 298, 434, 443.
Infantry co-operation, lack of, 29, 70.
Infantry, training with, 6; in Palestine, 84; before Cambrai, 259-261; with Canadians, 320, 339, 340; with Australians, 349; with French, 351.
Iveagh, Lord, 25.

Joint Committee, 13.
Journalists, misrepresentations by, 42, 232, 271.
Joye Farm, 93.

Kemmel, 90, 330.
Kahn Yunus, 73.
Khirbet Sihan, 80.

Kitchener's Wood, 109, 115, 131, 133, 157, 159.
Kressenstein, General von, 73.
Kultur Farm, 131, 157.
Kurd Hill, 76-79.

La Bassée Canal, 330, 335.
La Brique, 109, 114, 116, 178.
La Cauchie, 343.
La Folie Farm, 60.
La Vacquerie, 264, 274.
Lagnicourt, 416.
Landrecies, 500.
Landships Committee, 13, 14.
Langemarck, 107, 115, 194.
Lateau Wood, 274.
Le Quesnel, 361, 363.
Le Quesnoy, 500.
Le Tréport, Tank Corps Depot at, 52, 340.
Les Bœufs, 31, 33.
Les Trois Tours, 132, 138.
Lees Hill, 76-79.
Lens, 311-313.
Lihons, 366.
Lillers, 320.
"Little Willie," 13, 16.
Lloyd, Colonel Hardress, 54.
Logeast Wood, 375, 382, 388.
Longatte, 405, 412, 414-415.
Lone Tree, 115, 157.
Loop, the, 32.
Loos, battle of, 9, 15.
Loupart Wood, 390, 392, 393-395.
Lovie Chateau, 101, 102, 119-120.
Luce river, 363.
Ludendorff, Marshal von, 294-295, 364, 365.
Lulworth, 50.
Lys, the, battle of, 318-319.

Machine Gun Corps, Heavy Section, formation of, 24; departure for France, 27; for Palestine, 71; expansion, 47-57; reconstituted as Tank Corps, 306; original companies—A and B, 26, 27, 53; C and D, 26, 27, 32, 33, 53; E, 27, 50, 53, 71; F, 27, 50, 53, 127.
Maison du Hibou, 197, 207, 208, 229.
Mansura Ridge, 74, 75, 78, 82.
Marcelcave, 357.
Marcoing, 264, 270, 274, 500.
Marengo Causeway, 109, 113, 145-146, 199.
Marquion, 433.
Marquion, Sains-les-, 433, 439, 453.
Martinpuich, 31.
Marwitz, General von der, 268, 292.

INDEX

Masnières, 270, 274.
Maurice, General Sir F., 486, 507-509.
Maxse, General Sir I., 108, 194, 235.
Meaulte, 308-309.
Mechanical Warfare Supply Department, 14, 56.
Merlimont, 52, 368, 369.
Messines, battle of, 90-94.
Meteren, 344.
Middelkerke, proposed landing at, 90, 109, 186-190.
Miraumont, 372.
Mœuvres, 282, 433, 434, 455.
Monash, General Sir J., 357-359, 360-361.
Monchy-le-Preux, capture of, 64-67; abandoned, 316; recaptured, 403.
Montdidier, 366.
Mont St Eloi, 312.
Monument Wood, 401.
Morchies, 342, 416, 418, 430, 431-432.
Moreuil, 352 (note).
Mormal Forest, 500.
"Mother," 13, 16.
Moyenneville, 373, 375, 387.
Munitions, Ministry of, 14.
Murat Farm, 113, 199.

Nelson's History of the War, 94 (note). See also Buchan, Colonel.
Neuve Chapelle, battle of, 9.
Neuville St Vaast, 59.
Neuville Vitasse, 67.
Neuvilly, 497.
Niergnies, Tank v. Tank action at, 492-494.
Noreuil, 418.
Noreuil Switch, the, 405, 413, 414-415.
Notre Dame de Lorette, 312.
Noulette Wood, 320, 368.
Noyelles-sur-l'Escaut, 280.
Nutt, Major, 71, 88.

Oostaverne Line, 90, 93.
Oosthoek Wood, 100-102; tanks detrained at, 104-107; explosion in, 125-126; bombing raids, 135-136.
Orange Hill, 64-67, 316.
Ouderdom, 91, 102.
Outpost Hill, 76, 78-79, 83.

Painlevé, M. Paul, 253.
Palestine Detachment, composition of, 71; suitability of tanks for desert warfare, 74; liaison and training, 84; disbandment, 88.
Passchendaele Ridge, 90, 108, 193, 245.

Peselhoek, 102.
Phillips, Sergeant, 107, 108.
Pierremont, 98.
Pigeons, use of, 54, 167, 222.
Pilgrim's Rest, the, 462.
Pilkem Ridge, 108, 109-111, 115, 131-134, 212, 213.
"Pill-Boxes," 110, 228.
Plateau, 258.
Plumer, General Sir H., 90.
Poelcapelle, 115, 239, 240-242.
Poelcapelle Road, 196, 207, 217.
Poperinghe, 102, 119, 136.
Pozières, 31.
Pronville, 298, 434, 441.
Proven, 120.
Proyart, 359.
Puits No. 12, 338.
Pusieux-au-Mont, 372.

Quadrilateral, the, 33, 35.
Quarry Wood, 438, 452.
Quast, General von, 319.
Quéant, 63, 418.
Queen's Hill, 76, 79.
Quiévy, 497.

Rafa, 73.
Rafa Redoubt, 86.
Raillencourt, 456, 461.
Rawlinson, General Sir H., 31, 103, 488; Special Order to Tank Corps, 365-366.
Regent's Park, 78.
Regina Cross, 131.
Reigersberg Chateau, 113.
Reutelbeek, the, 240.
Rhonelle river, 497.
Ribécourt, 270, 274.
Richardson, Captain, exploit of, 236-238.
Riencourt, 63.
Rivière, 248.
Robecq, 320, 323.
Robertson, Captain, gallantry of, 240.
Roclincourt, 59, 315.
Rœux Chemical Works, 69, 70.
Roisel, 342.
Ronsoy, 460.
Rosel, 351.
Rosières, 362, 366.
Rum Road, 113, 193.
Ruyaulcourt, 258.

Sailly Labourse, 331, 335.
Sallaumines, 313.
Samson's Ridge, 73, 76-78, 82.
Sancourt, 460; action at, 466-480.
Sapignies, 343, 390, 400.

Sarton, 371.
Saulty, 371.
"Savage Rabbit," 317.
Searchlights, mobile, opportunities for, 151-152.
Selle river, 491, 495, 497.
Sensée river, 277, 432, 460.
Seranvillers, 491.
Serre, 40, 343.
Sewell, Lieutenant, gallantry of, 424.
Sheikh Abbas, 74, 75, 82.
Sheikh Ajlin, 76, 82, 83, 87.
Sheikh Hassan, 73, 76, 85-87.
Sheikh Nebhan, 80.
Shellal, 82.
Siegfried Line, 403, 433 (note).
Simencourt, 316.
Soissons, battle of, 304, 350.
Solesmes, 496.
Somme, the, first battle of, 30-41; lessons of, 42, 45-56; second battle of, 341-344; third battle of, 352-367.
Sorel, 258.
Spriet, 242.
Springfield, 180, 238.
St Georges river, 497.
St Jean, 216.
St Julien, 108, 110, 131, 181, 193, 195, 215-216.
St Mihiel, 7, 304, 486.
St Olle, 456, 466.
St Pierre Divion, 40.
St Python, 496, 498.
Steenbeek, the, 108, 110, 131, 207, 215, 223-225.
Stern, Colonel Sir A., 56.
Summers, Major, 32.
Swanage, 51.
Swinton, Colonel E. D., 10, 12, 13, 14, 24; Memorandum on Tactics, 29-30 (note); his removal, 49; suggests use of tanks in Egypt, 71 (note).

Tadpole Copse, 435.
Tanks, British—
 Adverse criticism of, 183-184.
 Early experiments, 12-14.
 Equipment, general, 128; fascines and cribs, 261, 440-441; sponson trolleys, 18-19; trucks, 23; unditching booms, 44, 127-128.
 German opinion of, 285-287, 292-296.
 Marks I-IV, armament, capabilities, design, dimensions, motive power, speed, &c., 15-23; Mark V, 15, 348; Mark V Star, 354; Whippet, 302.
 Moral effect of, 34-35, 183, 233-234.
 Origin of, 8-11.
Tanks, French, 301-303.
Tanks, German, 287-289.
Tank Committee, 14.
Tank Corps, American, 427.
Tank Corps, British (see also Machine-Gun Corps, Heavy Section)—
 Administration, 57, 503-504.
 Antagonism to, 47-50, 185, 352-353.
 Auxiliary branches: Advance Stores, 490; Engineer and Equipment, 53; Central Stores and Workshops, 51-52, 262; Gun-Carrying Tanks, 55; Reconnaissance Branch, 30, 40, 53; Salvage, Signalling, and Supply Companies, 54-56, 490; Workshop Companies, 53.
 Early difficulties of, 29, 45-46.
 Expansion of, 50-54, 234, 306-307, 344, 402, 502-503.
 Official formation of, 306.
 Personnel, 24.
 Training, 24-28, 50.
 Brigades—
  1st, 54, 59, 69, 100, 107, 194, 238, 240, 258, 268, 270, 280, 281, 284, 309, 310, 329, 341, 354, 367, 369, 372, 374, 375, 388, 425, 426, 433, 489, 491, 502.
  2nd, 54, 91, 102, 111, 181, 236, 238, 239, 240, 258, 268, 270, 280, 281, 283, 310, 329, 341, 342, 344, 354, 372, 374, 375, 405, 416, 425.
  3rd, 54, 102, 107, 111, 181, 236, 240, 258, 269, 270, 280, 281, 329, 341, 343, 344, 354, 365, 372, 374, 389, 403, 416, 417, 425, 459, 489, 491.
  4th, 306, 308, 309, 329, 341, 342, 344, 353, 363, 365, 366, 367, 372, 425, 433, 459, 460, 489, 491, 497.
  5th, 306, 329, 341, 344, 349, 350, 353, 363, 365, 366, 372, 425, 433, 459, 489.
  6th, 502.
 Battalions—
  1st (A), 53, 91-94, 182, 239, 269, 274, 283, 342, 345, 354, 363, 489.
  2nd (B), 53, 91-94, 182, 268, 280, 283, 342, 353, 489.
  3rd (C), 53, 59, 60, 64-68, 104, 182, 269, 343, 345, 354, 359-361, 374, 387, 424, 489.

INDEX 517

Tank Corps, British—*continued*.
  Battalions—*continued*.
    4th (D), 53, 61-64, 100, 107, 108, 236, 238, 239, 240, 244, 247, 268, 275, 281, 309, 342, 353, 489.
    5th (E), 238, 239, 244, 247, 268, 275, 309, 342, 353, 489.
    6th (F), 89, 107, 113, 182, 236, 269, 274, 280, 343, 354, 359-362, 374, 390, 416, 489, 500.
    7th (G), 89, 98-99, 100, 104-108, 131, 137-139, 142-180, 181, 193, 195-230, 234, 235, 242-248, 268, 275-276, 281, 282, 308, 311-341, 367, 368-371, 374-403, 404-413, 417, 419-425, 430-453, 456-458, 460-463, 465-494, 494, 495.
    8th (H), 248, 268, 272, 280, 283, 342, 349, 353, 489.
    9th (I), 248, 269, 343, 350, 353, 367, 374, 389, 416, 417, 489, 500.
    10th (J), 343, 347, 353, 366, 374, 376, 387, 389, 393, 489, 500.
    11th (K), 309, 310, 312, 315, 316, 322, 330, 367, 374, 389, 416, 417, 426, 434, 455, 489, 497.
    12th (L), 309, 310, 312, 315, 316, 330, 367, 369, 374, 377, 389, 412, 414-415, 416, 418, 426, 434, 491-493, 495, 497-500.
    13th, 341, 349, 353, 489.
    14th, 353, 374, 416, 418, 489, 500.
    15th, 344, 353, 354, 363, 374, 377, 387, 433, 455, 489.
    16th, 344, 367, 489, 502.
    17th, 344, 354, 357-359, 374, 387, 489.
    18th, 344, 502.
    19th, 20th, 21st, 22nd, 23rd, 24th, 25th, 502.
    301st (American), 426-428, 459-460, 489, 502.
Tank Corps, French, 301-305.
Tank Corps, German, 287.
Tank Groups, 503.
Telegraph Hill, 61, 64, 68.
Ternoise river, 51.
Thetford, training at, 25-27.
Thilloy, Ligny-, 393, 401; German tanks at, 416.
Tilloy, 466, 479.

Tilloy-les-Mofflaines, 61.
Tortoise Hill, 86.
Trescault, 270.
Triangle Farm, 207, 229.
Tritton, Sir W., 13, 14.
Trônes Wood, 32.
Tulloch, Capt. T. J., 10, 12.

Umbrella Hill, 83-85.

Vaire Wood, 349.
Vancouver, 207, 229.
Vanheule Farm, 177, 214.
Vaudricourt, 320.
Vaulx-Vraucourt, 342, 414.
Vauvillers, 358.
Vaux-en-Amienois, 349, 356.
Vendhuile, 265.
Viesly, 497.
Villers-au-Flos, 417, 419-420.
Villers-Bretonneux, German tanks at, 289, 345.
Villers-Guislains, 262, 269.
Villers-Plouich, 284.
Vimy Ridge, 58-60, 310, 315-317, 318.
Vlamertinghe, 101, 132.
Von Werder House, 162, 164, 166.

Wadi el Nukhabir, 75, 79.
Wadi Ghuzze, 74, 75, 76, 79, 82.
Wailly, 52, 98, 245, 248, 263.
Wambeek, the, 93-94.
Wancourt, 68, 403.
Wareham, 51.
Warfusée-Abancourt, 358.
Watson, Major W. H. L., 62.
Westroosebeke, 245.
Wilson, Major W. G., 13.
Wilson's Post, 114-115.
Williams-Ellis, Major C., 14, 183, 190, 240, 297, 300.
Winnipeg, 196, 238.
Wool, 50.
Wormhoudt, 192, 242.
Wrisburg, General von, 293-294.
Wytschaete, 90, 92, 118, 344.

Yperlee, 206.
Ypres Salient, description of, 101-104, 118-119; unfitness for tank warfare, 96, 103-104, 132-133, 161, 183, 193-195, 238-239.
Ytres, 258.
Yvrench, 28.

www.ingramcontent.com/pod-product-compliance
Lightning Source LLC
Chambersburg PA
CBHW052040220426
43663CB00012B/2381